Is Israel One?

Jewish Identities in a Changing World

General Editors
Eliezer Ben-Rafael and Yosef Gorny

VOLUME 5

Is Israel One?
Religion, Nationalism, and Multiculturalism Confounded

by
Eliezer Ben-Rafael
and Yochanan Peres

BRILL
LEIDEN · BOSTON
2005

This book is printed on acid-free paper.

Library of Congress Cataloging-in-Publication Data

Ben Rafael, Eliezer.
    Is Israel one? : religion, nationalism, and multiculturalism confounded / by Eliezer Ben-Rafael and Yochanan Peres.
       p. cm. — (Jewish identities in a changing world ; v. 5)
    Includes bibliographical references (p.) and index.
    ISBN 90-04-14394-7
    1. Israel—Social conditions. 2. Multiculturalism—Israel. 3. Pluralism (Social sciences)—Israel 4. Israel—Ethnic relations. 5. National characteristics, Israeli. 6. Jews—Israel—Identity. I. Peres, Yochanan. II. Title. III. Series.

HN660.A8.B44 2005
305.8'0095694—dc22

2005047036

ISSN 1570-7997
ISBN 90 04 14394 7

PRINTED IN THE NETHERLANDS

CONTENTS

List of Tables vii
List of Figures xi
Foreword xiii

SECTION I
Cleavages and Multiculturalism

CHAPTER ONE
Identity, Nationalism, and Multiculturalism 3

CHAPTER TWO
The Social and Cultural Landscape of Israel 27

SECTION II
Religion and Social (Dis)order

CHAPTER THREE
The Ultra-Orthodox in the City 61

CHAPTER FOUR
Settlers as a Cleavage 87

SECTION III
Sociocultural Divisions

CHAPTER FIVE
Mizrahim and Ashkenazim 107

CHAPTER SIX
Russian Immigrants 129

CHAPTER SEVEN
Ethiopian Jews 151

SECTION IV
Non-Jewish Groups

CHAPTER EIGHT
Arabs and Druze in Israel 167

CHAPTER NINE
Foreign Workers: The Case of the Filipinos 187

SECTION V
Conflictual Multiculturalism

CHAPTER TEN
The Configuration of Multiculturalism 203

CHAPTER ELEVEN
Rules of Multiculturalism 223

CHAPTER TWELVE
Identity and National Politics 245

SECTION VI
Horizons and Uncertainties

CHAPTER THIRTEEN
Cleavages Transformed 265

CHAPTER FOURTEEN
Multiculturalism and the Pursuit of Meanings 283

Bibliography 301
Index 315

LIST OF TABLES

2.1   Strikes in Israel: Duration of One Day or More   45
2.2   Long-Term Indicators of Strike Activity,
      1924–1988   46
2.3   Occupations of Israelis, 1980–1994   46
2.4   Class Distribution of the Ashkenazi/Mizrahi
      Cleavage   47
2.5   Class Distribution of the Jewish/Arab Cleavage   49
2.6   Sample Dates and Methodology   58
3.1   Sociocultural Divisions and Religiosity among Israeli
      Jews   67
3.2   Do You Consider Yourself an Integral Part of Israeli
      Society?   68
3.3   Do You Wish to Live in Israel?   69
3.4   Do You Want Your Children to Live in Israel?   69
3.5   To What Group Do You Feel You First Belong?   70
3.6   How Important is Your Ethnic Allegiance in
      Your Life?   71
3.7   Jewishness and Religiosity   72
3.8   Religiosity over Generations and by Origin   74
3.9   Perceived Tensions in the Context of Religiosity   74
3.10 Perceived Deprivation on Grounds of Religiosity   74
3.11 Religiosity and Personal Experience of
      Discrimination   75
3.12 Social Distance   75
3.13 Willingness to Accept "Intermarriage"   76
3.14 Attitudes toward the Jewish Religious Nature of Israeli
      Culture   77
3.15 Attitudes toward the Western Nature of Israeli
      Culture   77
3.16 Israel as a Democracy versus Israel as a Jewish
      State   78
3.17 Exemption from Military Service   79
3.18 Restrictions on Indecent Advertising   79
3.19 The Necessity of Mutual Concessions among
      Religious Categories   80

3.20 Identity and Identification Variables and Religiosity   83
5.1   Self-Definition of Belongingness, by Demographic
      Origin   114
5.2   First- and Second-Choice Identifies   114
5.3   Aspects of Ethnic Allegiances   116
5.4   Cognitive Distances of Mizrahim and
      Ashkenazim   117
5.5   Amenability to Interethnic Marriage and Tenancy........   118
5.6   Amenability to Interethnic Tenancy—1981
      vs. 2001   118
5.7   Amenability to Interethnic Marriage—1985
      vs. 1999   119
5.8   Feelings of Deprivation, 1988 vs. 2000   120
5.9   Political Behavior   120
5.10 Voting for Shas by Mizrahim   122
6.1   Preferred (First-Choice) Identify, by Origin   135
6.2   Preferred (First-Choice) Identify of Russians, by Length
      of Stay in Israel   136
6.3   Sense of Social Belonging—Russian Immigrants
      vs. Nonimmigrant   137
6.4   Aspirations of Belonging: Russian Immigrants vs.
      Nonimmigrant   138
6.5   Sense of Social Belonging among Russians, by
      Self-Identification   138
6.6   Russians' Attitude toward Nonimmigrants, by Length
      of Stay in Israel   138
6.7   Nonimmigrants' Attitudes toward Immigration, by
      Ethnicity   139
6.8   Attitude of Russians toward Immigration to Israel,
      by Length of Stay   139
6.9   Political Preferences of Russians, by Length of Stay in
      Israel   141
7.1   Ethiopian-Origin Israelis: Aspects of Identity and
      Identification   156
7.2   Ethiopians' Distance form Constituent Groups in Israeli
      Society   158
7.3   Ethnocultural Perspectives of Ethiopian Jews   160
8.1   Distribution of the Samples   171
8.2   Jewish-Arab Contacts: Behavior versus Attitudes I   172
8.3   Jewish-Arab Contacts: Behavior versus Attitudes II   173

8.4 Attitudes toward Jewish-Arab Groups Encounters 174
8.5 Learning from Each Other 175
8.6 War and Peace Expectations: The Impact of the
     Crisis 176
8.7 Amenability to Intergroup Contact: The Impact of the
     Crisis 177
8.8 Perceptions of the Other's Feeling: The Impact of
     the Crisis 177
8.9 Sense of Belonging to Israeli Society 177
8.10 Arabs' Personal Experience of Discrimination 178
8.11 Druze as a Distinct Group in Terms of Cognitive
     Distances 180
8.12 Druze Identity Allegiance 180
8.13 Identities of Druze 181
8.14 Correlations: Druze Identities and Allegiance to Israel 181
9.1 Attitudes of Filipino Foreign Workers toward Israeli
     Society 192
9.2 Cognitive Distance of Filipino Workers from Various
     Categories 192
9.3 Filipino Foreign Workers' Concept of
     Multiculturalism 193
9.4 Filipinos in Regard to Themselves and to Israel 195
9.5 Ethnocentric Attitudes of Filipinos 196
10.1 Cognitive Distances among Groups 209
10.2 Cohesion, Popularity, and Openness to Others 209
10.3 Symmetry/Asymmetry of Social Distance among
     Groups 212
10.4 Group Solidarity 214
10.5 Retention and Use of Language with Spouses 216
10.6 Retention and Use of Languages with Children 217
10.7 Use of First and Second Languages among Jewish
     Respondents—Summary 218
11.1 The Presence of Different Cultures in Israel Enriches
     the Country's Culture 224
11.2 There is No Such Thing as a More- or a Less
     Developed Culture 227
11.3 I Wish all Israelis were More Like Me in Behavior
     and Culture 228
11.4 All Pupils in Israel Should be Taught the Same
     Syllabus 229

11.5	Every Child Should Learn His/Her Language of Origin in School	230
11.6	Appreciation of Groups' Contribution to Israeli Society	231
11.7	Attitudes toward Immigrants' Social Adjustment	232
11.8	Mutual Tolerance	233
11.9	Attitudes about the Authority of the Knesset	235
11.10	Allegiances to the Nationals Library	237
11.11	Israeli Culture and Jewishness	238
11.12	Israeli Culture and "Middle Easternness"	239
11.13	Israeli Culture and Westernization	240
11.14	Would You Prefer Israel to be a Jewish or a Democratic State?	241
12.1	The 2003 Knesset	248
12.2	Israeli Parties and Constituencies	249
12.3	Political Orientation of Ethnocultural Categories	251
12.4	Nonimmigrants' Political Attitudes	252
12.5	Ethnicity, Center/Periphery, and Political Orientations	253
12.6	Political Positions among Russians	254
12.7	Political Positions and Images of Social Distances	255
12.8	Prolonged Right/Left Rule Endangers Israel's Existence as a Democratic State	256
12.9	Politics as a Focus of Tension in Daily Life	257
12.10	Politics as a Focus of Social Tension	257

LIST OF FIGURES

6.1   Summary: Identities of Russian Immigrants   143

14.1   A Heuristic Picture of Israel's Multicultural Setting   286

Jews say much more easily that they "are not religious" than that they "have no religion"

FOREWORD

Ours is definitely the era of pluralism. Many, if not most, contemporary societies are comprised of numerous sociocultural groups—regional, ethnic, religious, national—and experience intercommunity tensions and conflicts of greater or lesser severity. Among other challenges, such societies find themselves in confrontations about rules and perspectives that should be binding on everyone irrespective of the diversity of outlooks and interests. These confrontations transform a pluralistic society into a multicultural setting when its diversity is recognized as a permanent feature of the social reality and as reflected in major areas of activity. This book delves into the case of one society, Israel, in which such conflicts and tensions are legion, relate in one way or another to the religion principle, and are given recognized expression in the social order.

Israel represents the case of a nationalism, articulated by an influential dominant culture, that successfully crystallized and reshaped a large part of a dispersed and highly heterogeneous collective. Although this enterprise has been marked by the emergence of internal cleavages among divergent value systems in a context of powerful globalization, immigrant-society behavior is clearly in evidence and a sharp majority-minority division is a crucial aspect of the sociopolitical reality. Above all, as shown all over these pages, there is the fact that, in addition to the Israeli short but hectic experience, Jewish nationalism draws its vitality from reformulations of the symbols of Judaism and the ancestral link of the Jewish collective (Am Yisrael, in Hebrew), the old faith in a given religion (Torat Yisrael); and an attitude of sanctity to a given land (Eretz Yisrael). The deep relation of Jewish nationalism—not religious included—and Judaism permeates the dynamics of the confrontations of the dominant culture and the numerous parties which, in one way or another and at very diverse but relevant and significant times, contest its exigencies. It is around this common *problématique* that Israel's numerous conflicts come to form one whole made of multiple forces of convergence and divergence.

This kind of approach has rarely been used in the discussion of Israeli society, though during the past five decades, it was the world's most researched society relative to the size of its population (approximately six and a half million souls in 2005). It is from this perspective that this book analyzes the major cleavages of Israeli society both individually and relative to each other as stones in the multicultural mosaic. Due to the sharpness of its contours, the Israeli case may also shed light on several major questions in the sociology of multiculturalism. In this respect, it may even be considered emblematic of the field of multiculturalism at large.

This book is based on comprehensive research carried out in 1999–2001. The two-phase large-scale survey on which the book is based included secular middle-class Jews, mostly of Ashkenazi origin; North African and Middle Eastern Jews; recent immigrants from the former USSR and Ethiopia; members of Ultra-Orthodox (Ashkenazi) communities; national religious settlers in the West Bank; Christian and Muslim Arabs; Druze; and foreign workers. We point to the different models of cleavage that these entities exemplify and note how Israeli society looks when one contemplates them as a whole. Moreover, an enigma that we wish to confront in this context is how and why the universal cleavage of class structure is clearly quite irrelevant in the Israeli case—unlike many other settings—at least when it comes to accounting for the dynamics of society's central sphere.

Our two introductory chapters (Part I) provide a theoretical introduction and a summary of what we knew about Israel's cleavages before our research. Our approach to the notion of collective identity implies that such identity is composed of three representations: of the singularity of the collective, of commitments to the collective, and of the consequent attitude toward "others" who do not belong to the collective. This approach led us to consider, successively, three arenas of debate. First, we discuss (Part II) the issue of the singularity of the collective, which, here, is given strong focus by disputes in which the nonreligious clash with different kinds of observant forces. The second arena (Part III) concerns the nature of commitment to the collective, which leads to the consideration of diverse—although interrelated—ethnic cleavages among Jews. The third arena (Part IV) focuses on "others," i.e., groups that, although not viewed by the majority as belonging to the dominant Jewish category, nevertheless belong to the Israeli society. Part V analyzes how the diverse and numerous factors of pluralism crystallize into the kinds of multiculturalism that this society illustrates. In our conclusions (Part VI), we assess the contribution of our study to knowledge of Israeli society and ask what we may learn from it in terms of the sociology of contemporary multiculturalism and its dilemmas.

We wish to thank the Yitzhak Rabin Center for Israel Studies in Tel Aviv, which financed the research on which this study is based. We are particularly grateful in this respect to Ms. Irit Keynan, who directed the center at the time of our field work. We also thank our students, from whom we learned a great deal. Sabina Lissista, our Ph.D. student, conducted her own research about FSU immigrants in coordination with ours. Avital Fishler did research on Middle Eastern Jews in the context of this study. Nisim Leon produced an outstanding Ph.D. dissertation about Middle Eastern Ultra-Orthodox communities. Lior Ben-Chaim Rafael studied in great depth the impact of higher learning on ultra-Orthodox, national religious and nonreligious Jewish women. Ronen Friedman and Noga Gilad investigated recent developments in the national religious sector. All these former students of ours helped us greatly in completing our investigation by enriching our own efforts.

At Brill, we want to thank cordially Mr. Joed Eilich for his encouragements and Mr. Michael J. Mozina for his most helpful and effective involvement in this publication. I also want to thank Ms. Joyce Fongers and Ms. Katherine Lou for their efficient assistance and kindness. Thank you also to Wiebke M. Light for the comprehensive index which she has composed for this book.

SECTION I

CLEAVAGES AND MULTICULTURALISM

CHAPTER ONE

IDENTITY, NATIONALISM, AND MULTICULTURALISM

IDENTITY AND IDENTIFICATION

Social cleavages exist in a wide variety of forms. One need only contemplate Athens, Rome, and Alexandria, or very different examples such the Indian caste system and the Jewish or Christian millets of Muslim societies (Elias, 1998). In all these cases, however, cleavages were imposed by central authorities or established traditions that were umbilically linked to the nature of social life. In modern settings, in contrast, meritocratic and individualistic civilizations have become dominant and nation-states have emerged as primary focal points of the identification of "citizens." In such settings, many politicians and scholars expected divisive allegiances to become outdated and to disappear (Shils, 1956; Parsons, 1975).

Sociocultural cleavages, though, are neither less numerous nor less blatant today than in the past. They may materialize in highly diverse processes, such as national integration that aspires to an outcome of *e pluribus unum* (not always with much success), regional groups that have languages and cultures of their own, the social absorption of immigrants, or the hardly preventable cross-border expansion of religious movements and congregations (Connor, 1994; Featherstone, 1995). By the first decades of the twentieth century, Max Weber (1958; 1978) called attention to the persistence of religious, historical, linguistic, and racial collectives and considered them integral parts of the contemporaneous social reality. Since the 1960s and the political awakening of the African-Americans, we have observed the growing salience, permanence, and importance of the debate about ethnicity on the American public agenda.

Scholars have responded by proposing diverse theoretical perspectives. Some speak of "imagined" or "invented" communities and tend to attribute the proliferation of such communities to conjectural circumstances (Anderson, 1984, 1991; Hobsbawm and Ranger, 1983). Others speak of "authentic" or primordial bonds (Geertz, 1963; 1973). All agree that the notion of ethnicity may respond to different syndromes but that, as a whole, ethnic or sociocultural groups may become powerful factors of social change. Whenever they find appropriate opportunities, such groups tend, as a rule, to raise demands and evolve into active conflict groups. These demands may pertain to deep-seated interests or express wishes that surface in conjunction with a sense of power. The groups may protest against discrimination in the labor market or put in claims for cult facilities or educational resources. Be this as it may, a group united by common symbols and strong "we-feelings" may find a way to convert its solidarity into achievements. This is especially true in democracies, where groups of all kinds easily enter the political arena in which parties and leaders vie for support and votes.

The notion of pluralism refers to this kind of existence or coexistence of diverse sociocultural groups (Kuper, 1965). Pluralism cannot be characterized *a priori* as having any definite, clear-cut, and rigid configuration. Cleavages are anything but stable and immutable. They delineate spaces of forces in which a wide range of circumstances intervene—the rules of the political game; the assets of each side; the cohesion, specific interests, and cultural orientations of the groups; and the like. Pluralism becomes multiculturalism when sociocultural groups become recognized as permanent and legitimate actors and their specific interests become embedded in the legal organization of the social order. Then, among other things, leaders may act and speak out on behalf of their constituencies, and the groups' share in national politics is cemented in normative and institutional arrangements (Willett, 1998). In a nutshell, multiculturalism denotes "recognized pluralism."

Such a development has numerous social and cultural implications. Meyer (2000), for instance, indicates that in multiculturalism taste is no longer the monopoly of the privileged. In addition to what has long been meant by the notion of "refinement," a concept of taste that is indicative of "authenticity" now exists, that grants particular cultures the right to influence what is "nice" and "good." These notions, in turn, now respond to multiple criteria that may be incoherent and contradictory, often resulting in confusion about the "taste of the public." A multiculturalism that includes reference to lifestyle differences, allows new values to emerge and establishes alternative sources of meaning and moral authority. The confusion is further aggravated by the fact that no one can rank cultures by standards grounded in intrinsic values. No "objective" criterion for the grading of cultures may be devised and the attractiveness of any culture always depends on the evaluator's own values. Within a multicultural society, this is often itself the cause of frictions among contestants over the relative status of their respective legacies. Multiculturalism, by being "multi" and by offering competing answers to the same moral issues, favors the growth of postmodern outlooks that emphasize the relativism of values and truths and, by extension, of any form of cultural assessment (Denzin, 1991).

The concerns of a social researcher interested in empirical investigation and, on this basis, in comparative analyses in a context of a multiplicity of cultures (among societies as well as within a society) can be answered by the multiple-modernities theory (Eisenstadt, 2001; Arnason, 2002). This approach challenges the conventional wisdom in sociology during the 1960s and 1970s, which expected all societies to converge toward one model of "modern society." That wisdom defined modernity mainly in terms of civilizational components such as industrialization, liberal democracy, and the development of higher education and science—components that, to a large extent, effectively characterize many settings that considers themselves—or are considered—"modern." Contemporary scholars, however, suggest that each setting creates its own relationship between the desiderata of modernity and its legacies and cultural particularism. Thus, while societies develop communication opportunities and features that make them familiar to each other because they all participate in modern civilization in one way or another, in essential aspects they continue to present very different characteristics that reflect and determine the effects of specific historical and cultural paths.

By applying this perspective to multiculturalism in individual societies, we create a prism through which we may contemplate different cultures that achieve recognition in society. One may, indeed, regard the different sociocultural groups that evolve in one setting as particularisms that interact in a diversity of forms with the version of modernity that is dominant in society. Each of these groups' cultures confronts—and is influenced by—a center that, as such, upholds the ideal national "spirit" on the "turf" of a culture of its own. We designate here this culture as the "dominant culture" which itself is but another example of the hyphenation of given legacies and modern elements. It is from this angle that analysts may regard the various cultures that evolve in a specific multicultural setting from a comparative perspective the criteria of which could be their proximity

to the specific dominant culture, the principles of modernity that
they adopt, and the kind of attachment to their own original particularism that they demonstrate. Champions of this approach explain
that multiculturalism denotes not only the recognized copresence of
diverse sociocultural groups but also a sociocultural reality made of
unending cultural innovation, change, and transformation at varied
junctions (Ben Chaim, 2003).

Such developments influence fashions in thinking, of course, and
a multiculturalism that is mostly brought about by political games,
when driven by leaders, politicians, and intellectuals, tends to be
understood as responding to ideological exigencies. It is then invested
with positive value judgments and moral meanings, and seen as
responsive to socially desirable goals and as offering "right" ways of
regulating relations among social groups. Above all, a multiculturalist ideology may then define the areas that remain within the
sole responsibility of each sociocultural group and the rules that
should apply to every individual member of the society unrelatedly
to his or her group affiliation.

Interestingly enough, the development of multiculturalism in this
respect is diametrically opposed to what happened in regard to
another, very different ideology, socialism. Socialism was elaborated
by nineteenth-century intellectuals as an ideology that proposed coherent utopias; only later did it denote—in sociological, economic, and
especially political terms—noncapitalistic (social-democratic or totali-
tarian) forms of modern governance. Multiculturalism, in contrast,
has emerged from the bottom up, i.e., within groups that have pro-
gressively attained, within the nation-state, the right to assert their
particularism and related interests. It is in this context that multicultural ideologies have sprouted, either in support of or in opposition to this new reality, and have made multiculturalism the object
of intellectual debates.

As an object of analysis, however, multiculturalism seeks concepts
that can capture its essentials. Prime among these concepts, in terms
of contemporary importance and impact, is collective identity.

COLLECTIVE IDENTITY

A collective identity refers, in general terms, to the ways individuals
perceive themselves a part of what they delineate as a particular

group (De Levita, 1965; Liebkind, 1989). Hence, it may pertain
to a social category within a specific society or to an entity that
spans several societies (Ben-Rafael, 2002a; Abrams & Hogg, 1990).
In the context of the contemporary proliferation of sociocultural
groups, this notion of collective identity has become one of the most
discussed concepts in sociology (Giddens, 1991; Hutchinson and
Smith, 1996).

Although the definitions are numerous, all generally emphasize the
subjective nature of the notion (Barth, 1997). This implies that a
collective identity consists primarily of individuals' perceptions and
convictions and that it may be retained as well as forgotten, remain
unchanged, or undergo transformation, depending directly on individual attitudes. On the other hand, nothing precludes people who
see themselves members of a same group to formulate or construe
this identity differently (Hall, 1994; 1996; 2000). A collective identity is thus not necessarily consensual among all individuals who refer
to it as theirs. It may be the object of formulations that are divergent diachronically (in different periods of time) and synchronically
(among different constituencies, social circles, and individuals). If one
particular version of a collective identity becomes prevalent in a
group, it may receive symbolic confirmation—on an official calendar of events, in public ceremonies, or at sanctified sites—and then
appear as an "objective reality." This "objectivization," in turn, may
become a source of unity among members and strengthen their allegiance to common values and rites. Even then, however, the phenomenon described by the concept of collective identity remains
essentially subjective, i.e., it focuses on how individuals see themselves as members of a given collective. When individuals cease to
see themselves this way, they doom the collective to oblivion and
render its identity and ritual expressions meaningless.

As for the contents of a collective identity—wherever it exists—
we suggest, pursuant to previous formulations (Taylor, 1994a;
Wittgenstein in Schatzki, 1996; Ben-Rafael, 2002a), that they necessarily contain three basic facets (see Benoist, 1977). The first concerns the commitment that individuals who share a given collective
identity feel toward people whom they regard as members of their
group and toward the group itself. This facet corresponds to the
Wittgensteinian assessment about the tendency of men and women
to "hang together." The second facet concerns the perceptions—
diversely shared—of individuals who consider themselves members

of this group, of what they understand as the "unique" or "singular" values, norms or symbols that distinguish this group from its environment and from other groups. The third facet concerns, in relation to the former facets, the way members position themselves vis-à-vis those whom they view as "others," i.e., outsiders, those on the "they" side of the we/they divide.

These definitions of facets also facilitate systematic comparison of different versions of a same collective identity. Indeed, these definitions raise several questions: (1) How far and in what respect do individuals commit themselves to the welfare of their group and its members? (2) What perceptions do individuals share about their group's singularity and what meanings do they attach to it and its symbols? (3) In what terms and with what intensity do they exclude "others" from the limits of their group (See also Eriksen, 1993)? The different manners of answering these questions with respect to a same identity point out to the latter's various particular version. All versions, however, are by definition anchored in individuals' perceptions that are irreducible to structural features or "objective" collective interests standing outside individuals' (self-understandings).

This essentially subjective texture of the collective identity also means that, behind confident assertions, it firstly involves dilemmas which show how differently the various available formulations of one identity may respond to the three facet-questions. From this point of view, one may definitely construe the different versions of the identity as belonging to an "identity space." We mean by an identity space this notion of the set of different meanings attached to a same collective identity.

The question that arises then, however, is how one may determine that a given version of an identity is part of an identity space that it shares with other versions or represents a splitting of identities that no longer belong to a same space. In view of the definitions presented above, the answer is that a particular version of an identity belongs to a given identity space if (1) those who share it still feel committed to the same individuals as group members, irrespective of the specific version of the identity that they endorse; (2) this version of the identity, like all the others, draws many of its symbols, values, and norms from the same stock of cultural resources that makes it singular even when it emphasizes different elements; (3) it relegates the same people, more or less, to the category of non members—even if this exclusion is differentially rigid or if the contours of the category are outlined somewhat differently. Since, however, this formulation includes three conditions and not one, it follows that it should not exclude in-between cases that populate a "gray area" on the fringes of the identity space.

IDENTIFICATION

To be sure, the tenets of a collective identity influence the extent to which the identity may become a vehicle of social mobilization among members of a group, on the latter's behalf we think here of the readiness to accept sacrifices, to participate in a range of, more or less, ritualistic activities, or to feel intense solidarity vis-à-vis people of the group. Hence, all other aspects being equal, a demanding religious identity has greater mobilization potential than a geographical-origin identity. However, such tenets cannot by themselves account for the fact that under given circumstances or in different periods, one identity may have different degrees of appeal to group members. This dimension of individuals' attitudes toward the collective identity refers to what is best described as "identification." It asks not about "who," "why," and "who-not" but about "how far" or "how much" the collective identity—in whatever version—inspires individuals to become involved in the collective and accept self-sacrifice on its behalf. The literature that discusses this aspect suggests that many factors may influence people's attitudes toward the tenets of their identity (see Lewin, 1948, for an early and classic illustration; Banton, 1994), e.g., feelings of discrimination, availability of organizational resources, and the size and sociopolitical conjuncture of the group. In all, the major factors that have been noted as especially determinant in inducing members to identify or dis-identify with their collective-identity group are: the attitude of the dominant culture vis-à-vis the group and the group's own orientation toward the society, as influenced, to a large extent, by both the tenets of the members' collective identity and their stratificational positioning in the setting.

As far as the notion of dominant culture is concerned, as noted above, we use this term to denote the symbols, norms, and values that are embodied by the political center and sustained in the setting by—and identified mainly with—the strongest party: the "dominant class," the "elite," or the "hegemonic milieus." Abercrombie and Turner (1983: 411) maintain here that "The chief impact of the dominant beliefs is on the dominant, not the dominated, classes . . . securing [their] coherence." On the other hand, as Sankoff (1989: 157) states, the dominant culture (he uses the more restrictive notion of "dominant ideology") "is not merely an epiphenomenon. . . . It plays a crucial role in the justification of the existing social order." In a nutshell, the dominant culture is nothing but the presentation of the version of collective identity that is prevalent at the center and that refers to society as a whole.

Following our definition of collective identity, we may state that this notion, too, is marked by three facets. The first concerns—in a manner that is not necessarily consistent or devoid of intrinsic contradictions—the definition of obligations attendant to membership in the society at large (Ben-Rafael, 1982; Ben-Rafael and Sharot, 1991). The second facet, the "singularity-of-culture" dimension, refers to perceptions of values and symbols that represent an interpretation of the national legacy. As for the third facet, the attitude toward "others," the matter of specific interest in our context is the dominant culture's attitude toward groups that evolve within the setting and that, in various respects, exhibit traits that diverge from its representation of society's historical-cultural personality (Lipset, 1967; Eisenstadt, 1966). When it comes to subsequent attitudes of the dominant culture toward groups evolving in the society, the literature (see for a review: Arnason, 2003) widely follows sociolinguistic models of language policies (see Grillo, 1989) and distinguishes two major types:

(a) A *homogenizing dominant culture* defines the setting as the embodiment of a cultural and historical legacy that aspires to minimize heterogeneity and tends to exclude groups that cultivate their "differences." Such a culture accepts new members who are "different" provided that they are willing to conform or, at the most, confine their particularism to the private domain. It does not accept, *a priori*, the legitimacy of communities that decide to retain their singularity in the public domain (see Schnapper, 1991, concerning the case of France) and rather expects new groups to integrate into society on its own terms.

(b) A *pluralistic dominant culture* recognizes social, cultural, and linguistic differences that set groups apart. Permissive of differences, it institutionalizes differential patterns of "living in the same society."

In brief, it encourages the coexistence of different sociocultural groups (see Hollinger, 1995, with respect to the United State's salad-bowl model, and Brubacker, 1992).

These models are by no means mutually exclusive (Ben-Rafael, 2002a; Cohen, ed., 1996; Cohen & Layton-Henry, ed., 1997). One dominant culture may insist that some groups assimilate but may take a decidedly pluralistic approach toward other groups, depending on its cultural proximity to, or alienation from, the groups involved. These attitudes may be influenced by instrumental political or economic considerations and, insofar as laws and policies orient the behavior of members of groups, the dominant culture that stands behind these laws and policies induces members to assimilate into society, to maintain distinctiveness, or to remain outsiders.

Alongside the dominant culture, the group itself plays a role in its social insertion and evolution. A sociocultural group forms wherever individuals develop a sense of collective identity and a boundary demarcated by a given set of symbols. The strength of identification, however, may change over time in the context of circumstances— including the encounter with the dominant culture. Another factor to keep in mind here is the group's own self-image at the onset of the encounter. Arguably, the more members of a group aspire *ab initio* to become indistinguishable from the rest of society, the less tempted they will be to maintain their particularism in their present situation. The contrary is no less plausible. However, once members of a group somehow identify with their collective and distinguish between the loyalty that they owe it and that owed to society, they necessarily face the question of priority and preference, thereby running the risk of experiencing political, social, and cultural tensions. This occurs especially where the group and the dominant culture differ in their perspectives, i.e., where a dominant culture encourages assimilation but the group members wish to remain distinct within society, or vice-versa, where the dominant culture is pluralistic but the group is determined to assimilate.

Class reality, moreover, is another major factor of the tendency of a group to assimilate to society or to stick to particular forms. This factor has long attracted scholars' attention as a crucial aspect of social reality in general. This interest has gradually lost much of its currency as modern societies have become less polarized and more characterized by a large middle class (Robinson and Kelley, 1979).

While class or origin still often correlates with the trajectory of individual careers, contemporary social stratification, as scholars insisted in the 1980s, more closely resembles a *glissando* of individual positions than a set of sharp discontinuities among groups (Manlin et al., 1981). In recent years, as immigrant populations and ethnicities have gained salience as aspects of social inequality, either-or divisions have definitely become obsolete. As Parkin insisted years ago, dominance relations are explained in advanced societies not only by the bourgeoisie-versus-proletariat dichotomy but also, and mainly, by sociocultural cleavages—Protestants versus Catholics, whites versus blacks, veteran residents versus immigrants, and many other antagonisms (Parkin, 1974; 1979). Accordingly, discriminatory practices that a group faces at the hands of stronger elements account for how well it is able to claim its share of social resources. In turn, it may be led to use its own strategies of closure against other groups that aspire to usurp the assets that it still controls. This is not to gainsay that a group's location on the stratification scale is also, and perhaps principally, determined by members' control of human capital—education, vocational training, cultural predispositions to social mobility—that do much to dictate the extent of their ability to exploit social opportunities.

Irrespective of the precise context, however, it may be assumed, everything else being equal, that whenever a sociocultural group masses on the side of the relatively deprived, feelings of exploitation will inspire its members to resent the social environment and become aware of conflictual interests vis-à-vis the rest of society, which should strengthen members' identification with their collective. In contrast, and again only if all other circumstances are equal, the more a group manages to insert itself into society in a way that allows it to climb the stratification ladder, the less it should develop antagonistic feelings toward its surroundings and the less encouraged it should be, in this respect, to emphasize its particularistic allegiance. In an in-between situation, it is conceivable that some group members will remain attached to underprivileged strata while others will experience social mobility and pull away from them in terms of social status.

Obviously, socially mobile elements that experience more contact with privileged milieus than their counterparts that continue to wear the badge of social inferiority become more acculturated to the dominant culture (Smith, 1981). Thus, they should be more likely to evince a weakening of collective identification (Burgess, 1978; Lal, 1983). Mobility, however, may also provide a group with professionals, intellectuals, or businesspeople that control cultural and material resources and may constitute a powerful and efficient leadership—provided that they remain interested in the welfare of their original community. Where, on the contrary, such individuals prefer to exploit their personal success to disengage from their group and assimilate into the surroundings at large, they will contribute to sense of deprivation among the group's remaining members—despite the reality of social mobility. This will leave the group headship in the hands of individuals, such as religious or low-class figures, who will reflect the social marginality of those who remain in the group, even when they eventually achieve notoriety by exploiting political opportunities to enter the national scene.

Whether the group's mobile elements tend to assimilate into the "outside" or remain a part of their original collective, it may be suggested, is largely determined by the two factors considered above. We mean the group's self-image and the extent that it requests from its members to demonstrate loyalty to its retention, on the one hand, and, on the other, the dominant culture's attitude toward the group and whether or not it favors, from its own side, the assimilation of the group.

Social Boundaries

None of the foregoing rules out the possibility that further developments within the group, and the dynamics of interaction between the group and the dominant culture and other groups, may draw and redraw the group's boundaries. Milroy (1989), Dorian (1981), and Haugen (1989) have shown, through sociolinguistic analyses, that such boundaries are neither static nor unchanging. It is our general contention here that the dominant culture and the group's orientations and stratification location do have a "say" in the degree of identification that group members display. We may then speak of "levels of acculturation" to denote the degree to which a sociocultural entity tends to forfeit aspects of its prior collective personality—to become increasingly less different culturally from the milieus that best exemplify the dominant culture. We also speak of assimilation in reference to an acculturation that includes replacement of the particularistic identity with unmitigated allegiance to the identity of the society and renunciation of social distinction (Orans, 1971; Olzak, 1983; Doubnow, 1916; 1970). Acculturation and assimilation are the central aspects of the notion of collective identification and the formation of collective boundaries (Rubin, 1995).

Such boundaries, where they exist, are not of uniform "thickness" in all cases; they may be clear-cut and impenetrable or vague and permeable. They are less precise where the group undergoes general social mobility that disperses members at all levels of social hierarchies. Even then, however, at least symbolically, social openness on either side may still be limited, resulting in twilight zones in which acculturation combined with social mobility does not always imply assimilation. The availability of the assimilation option also depends on the dominant culture's attitude toward the group, but even where it is offered it remains bound to the attitudes of the group and its own prior orientations toward itself and its environment.

The underlying circumstances of assimilation and acculturation affect the kind of collective identity that members adopt, of course. Thus, individuals who experience a situation that brings them into close contact with "others" will probably tend to greater flexibility in their identification with their sociocultural community and will define their collective identity in more flexible terms than individuals who remain confined in a sociocultural niche. It is in this sense that identity and identification are influenced by the same circumstances and interact in the formation of the group's social boundaries. Stronger identification places the contours of the group in sharper relief by encouraging the adoption of more exclusionist definitions of collective identity. Thus, by means of their influence on identification, we may regard the dominant culture, and the group's original orientations and actual stratification as parameters of a group's tendencies to retain its distinctiveness or to assimilate. To phrase this general conclusion more precisely—albeit still very schematically—we may express several propositions about the range of processes that may take shape.

It may be suggested that if the group is concentrated in the lower class, it has little contact with privileged milieus and remains relatively isolated because it is not attractive to outsiders. Under these conditions, the group tends to retain numerous particularistic symbols and models and to cultivate its sociocultural identity. Even then, however, it may be assumed that some group members who are

particularly skilled or encounter especially favorable circumstances experience social mobility. These people, by virtue of their social experience,
acculturate more than others to the dominant culture. Just the same,
they probably stay with their community if neither the dominant
culture nor the group's prevailing orientations encourage assimilation, although some may still be tempted to "cross over" and try to
"disappear" into the mainstream. If the group is assimilationist despite
the dominant culture's exclusionism, mobile elements may be encouraged to leave the community even though they lack easy access to
the mainstream. In such a case, they may form a new and possibly
volatile in-between entity. If the opposite is the case—the dominant
culture is assimilationist but the norm in the group aspires to retain
the collective allegiance—mobile elements may split over the issue
of assimilation. It is when both the dominant culture and the group's
prevailing orientations encourage assimilation that mobile elements
probably tend to join the middle class with the greatest determination, leaving their community of origin marked by social inferiority
despite the reality of social mobility.

In cases of general social mobility, acculturation will also be the
general rule in the group, and the main question is whether or not
anti-assimilationist retentionism may still have an influence. If both
the dominant culture and the group's prevailing orientations oppose
assimilation, one may expect retentionism to be alive in the group,
even though the general acculturation of the group should prevent
abrupt identification with the community and some individuals may
well be tempted to exit the community and assimilate. The combination of an assimilationist dominant culture and a retention-minded
group elicits clashing tendencies. Some members of the group may
take opportunities to join the mainstream and dissociate from the
community while others who remain loyal to the collective display
retentionism. To be sure, the issue of assimilation versus retention
will be a topic of debate within the group. If the dominant culture
exhibits exclusionism vis-à-vis an assimilationist group, group members may scatter and attempt to gain access to the mainstream of
society one way or another, despite the difficulty. The extreme case
is where both the dominant culture and the prevailing attitude in
the group emphasize assimilation. Then the pressure to assimilate—
amidst general social mobility—will be overwhelming, and group
members will probably show a general tendency to "privatize" collective
attributes and reduce them to features of family biography—even if,

in practice, they still meet no few obstacles in their social interactions (Early, ed., 1994).

This approach illustrates the difference between multiculturalism and the mere coexistence of different sociocultural entities. It depicts multiculturalism as a set of different patterns, syndromes, or models of cleavage that create a variety of tensions, claims, and pressures. Its practices respond to coherent principles but are not necessarily coordinated. Complex to begin with, this context has become even more intricate in recent years with the advancement of globalization and the proliferation of transnational interests, new developments that have come to play crucial roles in the formation and conveyance of collective identities.

TRANSNATIONAL DIASPORAS AND GLOBALIZATION

Globalization is defined by scholars (Bauman, 1996; 1998; Albrow, 1996; Beck, 2000) as a worldwide interconnectedness of individuals, organizations, collectives, and societies that transcends the guidance of any central body (Robertson, 1992). Much of the world was included in common borders in other eras, e.g., the Macedonian conquests, the Roman Empire, and the Western colonial expansion. Never before, however, has the globe itself been the theater of innumerable and multifaceted links among actors that outstrip the control of any single authority (for thorough discussion, see Baubock, 1998).

This reality may be analyzed from diverse and contradictory angles. Meyer (Meyer et al., 1997; Meyer, 2000), adopting a Weberian vision, regards globalization as a world-spanning cultural change expressed in the enactment of shared models that circumvent resource and culture disparities among nations. Niklas Luhmann (1990) even ventures to describe the emergence of a global system comprised of a new and unitary "world society." Globalization, however, he emphasizes, may exhibit varying intensities and strengths in different places or groups. Appadurai (1990; 1996) speaks of "global flows" that involve financial resources, population movements, ideas and ideals, media, and technological knowledge. These flows may produce random configurations by disjunctive effects and take on different contours in different spaces, depending on the perspectives of the actors—nation-states, social movements, corporations, or individuals.

Jonathan Friedman (1997) describes a world of rising fragmentation, after a phase of stable relations between hegemonic centers and weak peripheries, due to the emergence of new smaller centers that surmount and "de-hegemonize" the older ones. In a different kind of conflict analysis, Fröbel et al. (2000) illustrate an additional aspect of globalization: an international division of labor that brings about new forms of exploitation of the poor by the rich (Guarnizo and Smith, 1998).

Contemporary reality confirms these approaches in various ways (Hannerz, 1996). One of them—seemingly one of the most important ones—is that the West is becoming an ever-stronger object of reference for underprivileged populations that seek a new destiny, resulting in a permanent flow of legal and illegal immigrants. Moreover, in this epoch direct communication from country to country is easily maintained, travel from one extreme to another has become available to the many, and people can readily keep informed about what takes place in their homeland even when they live at its antipode. Thus, globalization has become a major factor in Western sociodemographic development, which scholars address by coining the term "transnational diaspora" (Soysal, 1994; 2000). This notion denotes the ability of contemporary immigrants to integrate into a new society without emotional, cultural, or even social disengagement from their societies of origin. Indeed, immigrants may from the outset maintain direct contact with families in the homeland and with friends and relatives elsewhere. By so doing, they create a space of exchange—including regular visits to and from the homeland and elsewhere—where the retention of languages and symbols of origin remains pertinent.

The Western societies that most of these population flows choose as their destinations are welfare states and democracies, and these features account for some of the principal outcomes of these flows. In such settings, immigrant groups are entitled to both social and political rights long before they acquire local nationality. These privileges invite immigrants to acquire the skills—including the rudiments of language and culture—that they will need to participate in the public domain of their society of choice. This does not prevent newcomers, under present-day conditions, from retaining allegiance to original cultural symbols and languages—that is, to what they "used to be."

The paradox here is that while the current era is marked at the global level by a tendency to cultural uniformity under the far-reaching influence of the West (Bauman, 1998), Western societies now share a growing internal diversity. The new transnational-diaspora communities, which have become parts of the human landscape in Western societies, have easy access to cross-border and cross-continental networks. On the other hand, their willingness to integrate brings them to learn the language and customs of their new society and adopt them at varying degrees. An experience that is nothing less than a cultural transformation which, in turn, contributes to the cultural heterogenization of the transnational diaspora. As a whole, this twofold process thus implements a dual diversification of our "world society."

Over time, this process may also impact on older groups that evinced other syndromes until recently. The American Irish, for example, are increasingly concerned with, and involved in, the problems of their homeland of origin, Ireland. This transnationalization has probably been influenced by the American Jews, who for decades have been a most overt instance of a transnational diaspora economically and politically mobilized on behalf of Israel. Another case is Québec, where inhabitants exhibit a growing sense of responsibility—at least culturally and linguistically—for Francophone communities all over Canada and even in the United States (such as the Cajuns of southern Louisiana).

All in all, transnational diasporas may illustrate a variety of cultural experiences that are best grasped by following sociolinguists who distinguish between subtractive and additive bilingualism (Beebe and Giles, 1984; Romaine, 1989). Hence, one may speak—in analogy with those notions—of subtractive and additive biculturalism. Thus, subtractive biculturalism denotes the tendency of groups to leave their original culture behind as they acquire the culture prevailing in their new environment, and additive biculturalism denotes the opposite—i.e., the acquisition of the dominant culture without abandoning one's particularistic legacies. In different kinds of transnational diasporas, one might find different kinds of biculturalism according to individuals' feelings about their original homeland versus their new society. In this era of globalization, this dilemma may be manifested in ways other than extreme either-or attitudes. Individuals and groups are more able today than in the past to fine-tune their commitment to their country of origin and their aspiration to attain membership in their new society and, thus, to retain their "old" culture and languages and to acquire "new" ones.

THE POLITICS OF MULTICULTURALISM

An additional and no less critical aspect to be emphasized in this overall discussion of pluralism and multiculturalism transcends the question of how society influences sociocultural groups by asking the no-less-crucial question of how sociocultural groups influence society. A question that, above all, concerns the structure of political opportunities. This dimension of the social reality is especially important in democratic settings, where groups of all kinds may easily access the center and the public domain to press for specific claims. Religious communities, ethnic minorities, regional sectors, and transnational diasporas may, depending on the political circumstances, establish their own parties or lobbies and form political blocs by associating with other actors (Horowitz, 1985). Sociocultural groups may enter this arena if they can mobilize members' support, even if the elite disapproves of their actions. Even then, leaders who speak to and on behalf of sociocultural constituencies may gain power and recognition thanks to the working of democratic rules and the characteristic rivalries that oppose incumbents and opposition parties for the enlisting of supports throughout society. This aspect shifts the focus of the study of multiculturalism from the scene of social dynamics to the polity where actual or potential coalitions and alliances compete over influence on, and access to, central power. Here, large and easily mobilized groups have a clear advantage over amorphous categories, and by accumulating influence and power, they may become major agents of changes: by raising claims and obtaining at least partial satisfaction, they actually create a situation where their action gets recognition, and together with it, the kind of identity politics that it represents. This, in itself, implements a multicultural reality that is from now on an aspect of the social order which may be understood as irreversible and as an opening to new forces and to new possibilities of social change.

This complex reality expresses how sociocultural groups contribute to the evolution and transformation of society at the same time that society molds their development. Multiculturalism is a notion that describes this reality by emphasizing the diversity of forces in presence.

Different from notions like "feudalism," "capitalism," or "socialism," multiculturalism does not represent a concrete formula with definite features as its contours are a function, in each particular cases of conjectural circumstances as well as the nature of its principal actors.

NATIONALISM AND RELIGION: TWO MULTICULTURALISMS

The issue of the substantial aspects of multiculturalism refocuses attention on the contents and formation of the perspectives exhibited by protagonists. The dominant culture, we have said, draws out a historical-cultural "personality" of the society when viewed as a whole and as a process of development. It presents this "personality" as a focus of reference for all members and, as such, elaborates what is meant by the concept of "nation" in terms that carry primordial significance. This practice lies at the core of the universal—but primarily Western—nation-building process and represents a parting of ways, on behalf of modernity, with traditional society and its own forms of primordialism. Indeed, many scholars consider nationalism a modern phenomenon generated by post-Enlightenment culture (Stille, 2003). Vujacica (2002) defines nationalism as a by-product of industrialization, i.e., a secular ideology that overcomes the resistance of traditions and gives meaning to necessary sacrifices. For Gellner (1983), nationalism consists of the emergence of a culture that invents the nation. Hobsbawm and Ranger (1983) see in the nation practices that inculcate new values. The nation-state with its territory and language is a product of modern "social engineering," replacing kinship and religion as the loci of individual loyalty (Anderson, 1991).

In fact, nation-building does not always constitute a total rupture vis-à-vis past cultures. Where it does, however—we think here, of course, of immigrant societies such as Australia, New Zealand, and the United States—it effectively constitutes a purely modern-era construction that conveys unambiguous nontraditional, if not antitraditional, orientations (Daalder, 1971). The "nation" then represents an elaboration of primordialism that has recent roots and symbols that, in some cases, have not yet been sanctified in people's eyes. Though even then one may speak of processes building up a kind of civil religion that substantiates the primordialism that is assumed to be the cement of the nation (Bellah, 1967; see also Calhoun, 1993 and 1997). A nationalist ideology may then help to substantiate its contents and fortify its appeal. However, when nationalism confronts other forms of primordialism that are attached to particular identities and allegiances stemming from local or historical-cultural experiences of given groups, such confrontations of divergent primordialisms may exert pressure to weaken the coherence of the setting as a social entity in its own right. What may then retain social coherence and cohesion is the capability of the dominant culture to compromise with fragmented interests and group demands for autonomy. In such a case, multiculturalization denotes a tendency to liberalization in which the area directly controlled by central institutions shrinks and specific groups acquire greater autonomy in given areas of activity.

In another perspective on nation-building that does not necessarily denote divorce from the past, many contemporary scholars share a view that corresponds closely to the multiple-modernities perspective (Arnason, 2003; Eisenstadt, 2003, vols., 1–2; Brubaker 1992; 1996). This outlook bases nationalism on modern civic values, defines the community of citizens as a voluntary fraternity and sustains the idea of an organic collective—the nation—that is united by a culture rooted in traditions (Guibernau, 1996).

From this perspective, one discovers the role of religion as a founding element of nationalism. Sahlins (1989) shows that religious strife in Europe of the sixteenth and seventeenth centuries was an early phase in the development of nineteenth-century nationalism. Colley (1992) emphasizes that nationalism often started with the demonizing of a religious "other" and the description of one's own camp as a "holy nation" (see also Marx, 2003). Shafer (1972) describes the nationalization of religions and churches in England and Sweden—not to mention the Russian and Greek Orthodox churches—in relation to the development of nationalism. In one more example, a religious war engendered the Netherlands and was the very first case of a national liberation war. In all these cases, religion was the ally of nationalism, and upon the ascendancy of the latter it left strong imprints on its further evolution. Last but not least, religion itself may undergo politicization and play a role of its own within the polity—sanctifying the nation-state through "messianic politics," for instance. Moreover, nationalism may also tend to become a "political religion."

In sum, nationalisms draw on the religious background of the population even if nationalists eschew this background at the personal level. Nationalism, says Anthony Smith (1991; 1998), rests on religious foundations and is infused with religious motives, even though nationalism in each society may create a different blend of sacred and worldly notions with different consequences. Nationalism raises new concepts of collective identity that transform traditions and religion but rarely turns its back on them altogether. It draws symbols from the "warehouse" of traditional symbols, alters their meanings, but still uses them to indicate an allegiance to a past that is both idealized and criticized—idealized because it asserts a collective "historical destiny" and criticized on behalf of new civic values (Schama, 1989; Tamir, 1993). Be this as it may, a dominant culture may be impregnated with primordialism deeply rooted in time, and this may be of critical importance for the development of multiculturalism.

Indeed, groups that evolve in a pluralistic or multicultural setting in which the dominant culture carries a collective identity based on far-reaching historical narratives face very particular conditions. When they are totally alien to those narratives, they may find it difficult to intergrate themselves into the setting indiscriminately without disowning their most elementary identity markers. This, in itself, implies a potential of conflict with the very definition of the general societal "personality" and suggests the possibility of unbridgeable differences of perspective that will brew into momentous divisive threats. In contrast, groups that feel involved in the nationalism-religion nexus that the dominant culture conveys find themselves bound by this culture even if they do not accept some aspects of the formulation of the societal identity that it propagates. Here, nationalism serves as a cement for unity even if it is formulated in divergent if not contradictory ways by the different parties. The other side of the coin, however, is a multiculturalism where sociocultural groups aspire not only to the satisfaction of their specific claims but also to be of impact on the societal identity. Under such circumstances, conflict among groups and between groups and the dominant culture may become permanent features of the social reality; they focus on achieving influence in the center over what each protagonist perceives as commanding for all.

Hence, we may discern two basically different multiculturalisms. We call the first "liberal multiculturalism" because it responds to a situation in which each group tends to strengthen its autonomy while respecting a domain of common norms and institutions. We may, in this vein, think of the multiculturalism illustrated by White ethnics or Afro-Americans in the United States. We may also add here the United Kingdom, with its sociogeographical and ethnic groups which enjoy a degree of autonomy at the level of the community that does not preclude their individual members from full and direct participation, as citizens, in areas of common public life. The difficulties that may arise from the coexistence of these two areas should mainly concern the span of their respective spaces.

We call the second kind of multiculturalism "conflictual multiculturalism" because in this situation each group takes its solidarity with the whole for granted but carries on with its own "truth" that it wishes to impose on the whole. We think here of cases like Canada, where some forces within the Francophone population—and to some extent, also among the English-speaking population—articulate claims which question basic aspects of the existing social order, namely the very federal structure of Canada as a whole. We may also point to Belgium in the 1970s and 1980s which experienced similar circumstances when divergence and drastic demands by ethno-geographical groups were able to bring about the transformation of the country's regime.

These two different kinds of multiculturalism are not independent and unrelated patterns. We may think of conflictual multicultural situations that evolve toward a stable institutionalization of the relations between groups and between them and the center, which would transform a conflictual multiculturalism into a liberal multiculturalism. And vice versa, a stable liberal multiculturalism may undergo crises leading various groups to raise claims that, if implemented, would represent drastic changes of the social order characteristic of conflictual multiculturalism.

Among other factors, the kind of multiculturalism that we tend to encounter in a given society depends primarily we believe, on the nature of the dominant culture and the sociocultural groups that confront each other—whether these relations are bound to the traditional roots of nationalism or they are simply the upshots of modernity.

FAMILY FEUDS AND FAMILY RESEMBLANCE

All in all, the above shows that multiculturalism should be approached from several angles simultaneously. The first angle concerns the components of the collective identity and the formulation of the versions of this identity that circulate among members. The second angle focuses on identification as it crystallizes in the arena of the interaction of the dominant culture and the groups' own prior orientations and class location. The third angle involves eventual external resources, support, and relationships embedded in transnational diasporas. The fourth angle concerns the political order, the formation of coalition, and the development of tensions impending on the shape and evolving of the social order. The fifth angle focuses on the relation of the dominant culture to society's past legacies which it embodies and its connection with the cultural and identity tenets carried by the sociocultural groups which it confronts.

Multiculturalism, be it liberal or conflictual, means the organization of diversity in a reality marked by fragmentation and the proliferation of conflicts that challenge social cohesion. Each type of multiculturalism, from its own perspective and rationale, carries potential structural conditions in which particularisms may find expression concomitant with the retention of a common ground for all. Theoretically, such structural arrangements provide forms of cohabitation and cooperation to actors who are divided by their collective identities. Even then, however, grave tensions may ensue due to the very presence of multiple protagonists who share different if not divergent identities. It is in this context that Touraine (1997) asks about what factually holds these various protagonists within the frame of one setting, without their succumbing to the temptation to "break the rules" and menace what remains of the coherence of the social order.

One appropriate way to answer this fundamental question, we think, is by resorting to Wittgenstein's concept of "family resemblance" (Wittgenstein, 1961). Wittgenstein, who chose this analogy to elaborate on the relationship of language games to language, saw in family resemblance a notion that describes the way a given set of features—height, facial traits, eye or hair color, posture, etc.— are, when considered together, characteristic of one extended family but variously and unevenly distributed among its members. This principle of "heterogeneous resemblance" may apply to the cultural traits unevenly distributed among individuals who belong to different groups but who, in the aggregate, comprise one society. The resemblance does not exclude antagonisms—family feuds are anything but rare, as we know—and must not recognize either attitude, closeness, or antagonism as an overarching "last word." Rather, it points to the existence of common references even as differences fragment the whole.

At the intragroup level, as we have seen, it is the reference to common basic identity questions that structures the space that the diverse identity formulations create and draws the boundaries that distinguish between those who are "in" and those who are "out." At the intergroup level, however, a different mechanism is enacted which is bound to the fact that each group, whatever its particular background, interests, and velleities, confronts in a multicultural setting a same dominant culture and a same set of symbols that pertain to society at large. The very act of establishing a presence in this environment entails the adoption of behaviors and compliance with "rules" that concern all participants—from education and language up to modes of employment and lifestyle. Moreover, insofar as groups mount the political stage, they also learn to adjust to a game that, more often than not, forces them to establish coalitions. Thus, quite unavoidably, groups come to resemble each other, to create connections, and to form a sort of enlarged family, sharing at diverse degree a variety of traits that, as a whole, account for an "air de famille."

This—let us repeat—by no means rules out tensions and conflicts, however. We know how harsh and relentless rivalries may be, especially among siblings—individuals or groups—that share resemblance. It is in this perspective that we may try to point out where lies one possible answer to Touraine's (1997) question about what might hold sociocultural groups together as constituents of a society in an era of multiculturalism. Having come this far, we may argue confidently that each group forges its individuality by culling symbols not only from longstanding legacies that specify its identity but also from the cultural resources to which it is exposed as a part of its environment and, possibly, transnational networks. Each group elaborates an interculture of its own that bears the trademarks of its enterprise as a form of cultural invention that allows original assets and borrowings to mingle. Taken as a whole, diverse sociocultural groups eventually develop a resemblance that accounts for the familiarity that they may come to feel toward each other. By means of this process, the dominant culture may retain some privileges of its former status even as it loses its hegemony. It still serves as an ingredient in the transformation of the cultures that are borne by groups as far as they strive simultaneously to maintain loyalty to some versions of their collective identities and to acquire and adopt new codes and perspectives. This is the kind of adhesive that could restrain those who want to share on a setting which they fragment with their own hands.

It is from this perspective that we turn to the multicultural reality of contemporary Israel.

CHAPTER TWO

THE SOCIAL AND CULTURAL LANDSCAPE OF ISRAEL

NATIONALISM, RELIGION, AND IDENTITY

The Roots of Zionism

The principle of the religion-people unity has always been a primary code in Judaism, and the affinity of Zionism to traditional Jewish values has been noted (Katz, 1960; Buber, 1973; Avineri, 1981; Eisenstadt, 1992). Traditional Judaism is characterized by an emphasis on religious faith and the link of this faith to the Jewish people as its primary element of collective uniqueness. *The Jews*, says Saadia Gaon (quoted in Weinberg, 2002), *are a people only thanks to their Torah (God's teachings)*. Moreover, the religious commandments include allegiance to the Land of Israel as both the past and the destiny of the people, implying an attitude toward non-Jewish "others" as "alien." However, the Jewish faith is also fundamentally monotheistic, and this entails a universalistic perspective that is no less fundamental: the Jews, it is firmly believed, carry the teaching of the universal God. This tension between the particularism of the People of God and the universalism of God is "resolved" by the principle that the Jewish nation, by achieving its own redemption, will redeem the world at large as well. This is the meaning of the portrayal of the Jewish nation as a "Chosen People," charged with redeeming humanity by observing its internal obligations. The resulting type of collective is best described by the notion of caste (Smith, B., 1994; Dumont, 1977).

Like all collective terms, "caste" refers to the many social practices that merge discourse (language, ideas, symbols) with action (specific activities, unique behavioral patterns, environmental and institutional features) (Smith, 1987). In the case of a caste, these practices are given clear religious legitimacy that is anchored in a perception of "purity." Maintaining purity requires a lack of contact—in some cases absolute—with "others," keeping the group separate from everyone else. On the other hand, the term "caste" also relates to the existence of a distinct collective within a larger system. Such a group plays, in its own eyes, a most crucial role in achieving an overall "supreme" purpose for the benefit of all, in-groups as well as out-groups, so that the latter are, whether knowingly or unknowingly, dependent on the former, in this respect. This is, in fact, the essence of Dumont's (1977) definition, which states that a caste is a group with an all-encompassing perception of itself and the organization of its life, but at the same time sees itself as part of a system in which its aspirations are given "transcendental" meaning.[1]

This caste syndrome lost much of its influence over the Jews with the advent of the modern era and emancipation. Many Jews now regarded the basic issues—the "deep structures" of Jewish identity—as questions that could be given new answers. A first question related to the concept of the "Jewish people" and asked whether it could still denote a collective defined primarily as religious or whether Jewry should now be seen as a community in a social, cultural, and political sense. A second question related to the concept of the God and Torah of Israel, i.e., the singularity of the collective in the traditional identity. Growing numbers of Jews began to wonder whether Judaism might not better be seen as a culture, a collection of symbols, and a history rather than a religion. A third question concerned the concept of the Land of Israel, the response of traditional Judaism to the location of a Jewish collective that defines any location outside the Land of Israel as *galut*, i.e., exile. Some Jews wondered now whether this Land was in fact the homeland of the Jews or whether it could be viewed as a metaphor for the quest of a home in which one could live in peace with oneself. As numerous answers were given to these three questions, a plethora of new Judaisms developed (Ben-Rafael, 2002)—from Jewish Enlightenment and Reform Judaism to the Bund and Territorialism. Among them, Zionism, Jewish nationalism, would take the lead over time (Krausz and Tulea, eds., 1998).

---

[1] In these terms, the self-definition of the Jews stands, to be sure, in sharp contrast to their portrayal by their Christian and Moslem neighbors in different eras and places throughout the centuries. The Jews saw themselves as a superior caste, while "others" regarded them as a caste of pariahs. Hence, the Jews and non-Jews remained separate from each other for utterly opposite reasons. By upholding their internal codes, the Jews made it clear that they considered their inferior status in society to be at variance with the "proper" social order. The strict laws of purity and kashrut explicitly prohibited close contact with non-Jews—anything beyond business or practical dealings—and concretized this general caste attitude.

It was in the late nineteenth century that Zionism proposed a national solution to this crisis of orientations. From among the traditional beliefs, it retained the traditional definition of Jewish life outside the Land of Israel as "exile," but instead of pinning its hopes for redemption on the observance of the religious commandments, it called for action—the resettlement of Jews in ancient Israel. In so doing, Zionism borrowed the link of nationhood and territory from the nationalist ideologies of Europe that, in actual fact, corresponded to the emphasis in traditional Judaism on the Jews' bond with the Land of Israel. Thus, Zionism called for the "territorialization" of Judaism, i.e., the conversion of Jewry into a national identity by means of emigration to the very territory that, according to religious exegesis, was both the origin and the destiny of the people (Katz, 1960; Avineri, 1981). This reference to traditional religious values in a mode of modern nationalism explains why Zionism reverberated among the many Jews who searched for a cause that would offer Jewry a collective future. This case of national identity illustrates, in this respect, the transformation of traditional contents, symbols, and axioms that are uncoupled from their conceptual anchorage and invested with new—but related—meanings (Ben-Rafael, 1997). This transformation implies drastic changes in individuals' attitudes but concurrently presents itself as the culmination of a historical collective destiny.

Thus, while Jewish nationalism breaks away from traditional Judaism by demanding redemption independently of religious devotion—by establishing a Jewish nation-state in the Land of Israel—it remains bound by the three basic identity questions of Judaism (see also Arieli, 1986). It offers a secular and political answer to a religious question, whether the Jewish diaspora should be defined not as a demographic fact but as exile. Moreover, Jewish nationalism aspires to lead the people toward the "promised land" and to lift it out of exile. In other words, Zionism exits the caste syndrome but not Judaism. What is more, because of this undeletable link, it also endorses the basic rule of membership in Judaism, namely, that *the Jewish people has only one religion and the Jewish religion has only one people*. A Jew who embraces another faith exits Judaism; a non-Jew who converts to Judaism enters the Jewish people.

From another perspective, however, Zionism is at a disadvantage vis-à-vis traditional Judaism. The caste model links the redemption of the Jews to that of the whole world, whereas Zionism aspires to

Jewish redemption alone, or as it phrases it, the "normalization of
the Jewish people." The price that Zionists pay for this, of course,
is the exposure of Zionism to the criticism of the proponents of the
caste model, who consider it a form of "collective assimilation" into
the non-Jewish world on the basis of the latter's principle. The classic Zionist leaders responded to the critics by claiming that Zionism
endeavored to build an "enlightened society" in the Land of Israel,
where the "chosen people" would be "a light unto the nations." In
their opinion, that was what the "normalization of the Jewish people" meant (Gorny, 1990). By taking up this challenge of combining a modern secular ideology with a uniquely Jewish inspiration
and orientation, the Zionists hoped to present an ideological alternative to the view of the Jewish nation as the carrier of the promise
of messianic redemption. The notion of an "exemplary society" (*hevra
le-mofet*) that this aspiration conveyed included the republican principle of cultural unity (*mizug galuyot*, fusion of exiles) that should direct
the engineering of "the ingathering of the exiles" (*kibbutz galuyot*). The
idea was not only to welcome Jews from all over the world but to
create a new national Israeli culture as well, the exemplary character of which would be determined by its dedication—in a secular
spirit—to the ethics of Judaism.

To these circumstances, one has, of course, to add the impact on
culture and identity of this dramatic event for the Jewish world experience which consisted of the Shoa. Every single Jew who lived in
the 1930s and 1940s either personally experienced or was witness
to this event. For those who survived or watched from a far, the
Shoa has been nothing but the destruction of a world. This tragedy
pertained for long to Israeli Jews' individual awareness only as its
monstrous dimensions accounted for a reluctance to refer to it in
public, as a part of the collective consciousness (Dawidowicz, 1981;
Friesel, 1994). Moreover, it was the Zionists' conviction that this kind
of event is bound to the precarious diaspora condition, which denoted
a kind of disassociation from the Jewish plight outside this country.
Yet, because Zionism, i.e. Jewish nationalism, is unconceivable without Jewishness and solidarity with the world Jewry, the Shoa gradually penetrated the official rituals of the Jewish state (Ben Amos
and Beit El, 1996; Friedman, R., 1997) and unavoidably became a
major aspect of the prevailing perception of the singularity of the
Jewish experience (Gorny, 1998; Bar-On and Sela, 1991).

A New Culture

A crucial element in achieving a new Jewish culture was the revival of Hebrew as the legitimate national tongue (Bachi, 1956). The task of crafting classical Hebrew into a spoken vernacular succeeded essentially because the collective memory of Jews almost everywhere acknowledged Hebrew as the "original Jewish tongue" and the language of the Scriptures. Zionists in Israel called on this knowledge to transform Hebrew into a national language for secular everyday use in the new Jewish society (Chomsky, 1957). The revival of Hebrew is the best example of Zionism's "appropriationist" attitude toward religious and traditional values. Plucking a holy language from the sacred texts and "tossing it into the street" for use in the most prosaic of activities might be considered iconoclastic. It is particularly surprising in view of the fact that those who reinvented Hebrew as a spoken language already had a common tongue—Yiddish, the Eastern European vernacular of many generations. The adoption of Hebrew, more than any other pattern, demonstrated Zionism's basic aspiration to present itself as the heir to the Jews' lengthy history and the potent agent of a secular-national transformation of this people into a culturally unified nation. Thus, Hebrew became the central hallmark of the new society, symbolizing the unique Jewish experience in Israel as an alternative to life in diaspora and implying that this experience was superior to any other Jewish reality (Glinert, 1990). Here lies the source of Zionism as a new form of Jewish identity that draws a distinction between the "Jewish people" in general and the "Jewish nation" in Israel.

The linguistic revolution also served as the basis for the implementation of the national-integration ideology when mass immigration to Israel ensued from numerous countries (Bachi, 1974; Hoffman and Fisherman, 1972). However, the desire for linguistic and cultural unification contributed not only to the unity of the new society but to its further divisions. The same models that sought to produce unity promoted new distinctions. The very call for unification did imply recognition of the special status of those portrayed as the worthiest role models, the "pioneer generation" (Elon, 1971). Furthermore, in Israel, as in any immigrant society where newcomers strive to sink new roots, being "native" became a source of social prestige. It is the children of immigrants who fulfill their parents' lofty ambitions and ensure the success of their endeavors. In the case of Israel, the native-born also carried the bulk of the security burden and the armed struggle that developed with the Arab environment from the earliest stages, reinforcing their image as the "salt of the earth." Additionally, the pioneers' sons and daughters were highly conscious of being the offspring of people who had adopted a new national Jewish identity, and of themselves as representative of a "new type of Jew" who had never known life in "exile." The fact that they were also a minority group for a long time, amidst a population made up largely of immigrants, added to their luster. As an "elite" that prided itself on this status, they created their own symbols, the most conspicuous of which was a typically nonchalant use of Hebrew that could be acquired only by being born "within the language" (Katriel, 1986).

This influence was linked to the Zionists' self-image as the antithesis of a Diaspora Jewry that, in their eyes, carries the markers of dependency. Many sons and daughters of pioneers displayed a similar attitude to the Diaspora Jews who settled in the country, seeing in them people who continued to bear the "stigma of the Diaspora." In contrast, they saw themselves the essence of "Israeliness" that sprouted from the new forms of life in the country.

The Dynamics of Modernity

That Israeli culture, however, underwent profound change over the decades. In the wake of demographic, economic, and political developments, the collectivistic approach that prevailed before independence and in the early years of statehood has been replaced by a much more individualistic model. An *étatist* ideology gained strength in the 1950s and 1960s which stressed the need to move from utopia to nation-building. The concept of "pioneer" was redefined to relate to anyone who "contributed" to the state: not only farmers and settlers as in the past, but also professionals, public functionaries, and businesspeople. A country born in war and severely beset by security concerns now also reserved a place of honor for the armed forces and placed great stock on a military career. Mass immigration, which tripled the population within a few years, brought to the country a broad array of cultural groups that diffused new perspectives and perceptions. Immigration and wars with the surroundings steadily strengthened Israel's relations with the Jewish world, which was now viewed as the country's "natural partner" in contrast to the anti-Diaspora mood that had been in vogue among Zionists in previous years (Rubinstein, 1977; 1980).

Even in this context, however, some signifiers of native culture persist today in patterns of speech, dress, and behavior, even if their sources are now mainly the army, high schools, the university, or pubs. Nevertheless, "nativeness" has inevitably lost much of its appeal as it now characterizes a large sector of the population. This encourages no few individuals who have not internalized the *sabra* (nativist) version of Israeli culture (the meaning of which is quite vague), whether they were born in Israel or elsewhere, to distance themselves from this culture. However, these distinctions seem secondary in comparison with the rampant "middle-classicization" of Israel, a development that can be traced to the cultural impact of the local experience and, above all, of modernity itself (Almog, 1997).

Israel's strides down the path of Western-style modernization—urbanization, higher education, professionalization, and new power centers—are indeed another factor in the transformation of this society. The features of Western consumer society made inroads as the middle class grew. Members of the "1948 generation" (the one that fought the War of Independence) became bureaucrats, politicians, and businesspeople. As this elite came to be defined in terms of achievements, meritocracy adopted a more formal standard language. The original disdain for foreign languages disappeared as international communication gained in importance. English became *de facto* Israel's second language and its importance in the linguistic landscape of the country undoubtedly makes it a "nonforeign" language. Its status is salient at all levels of education and in professional life and business (Rubinstein, 1997). This expresses, concurrently, Israel's severe reliance on its privileged relationship with the United States due to its protracted conflict with its surroundings, its indelible links with world Jewry (most of which resides in Anglophone countries), and the impact of economic, cultural, and political globalization. The role of English also expresses a reality of particularly intense relations with the outside world that clashes with the fact that Hebrew is spoken by one of the smallest national populations in the world and has hardly expanded beyond its national borders. All these factors explain why fluency in English has become an important status symbol. As such, however, it penetrates Israeli society along lines that favor the socially privileged, who use it much more frequently than others both in working life and in cultural consumption and, for this reason, are capable not only of acquiring it but also of retaining it (Ben-Rafael, 1994). In this respect, English serves definitely as a signifier of membership in the privileged class and the elites. At the same time, it imprints itself on spoken Hebrew through borrowings and calques that are legion in the vernaculars of "in" places in Tel Aviv, technocrats' offices, and university classrooms. From this outlook, and considering present-day life circumstances, it is also a basic contention of Liebman (2003) that Jewish youth in Israel (as well as elsewhere) tend to be characterized by a sense of materialistic hedonism, accounting for a weakening of their general identification with collective causes, including Jewishness (see also Furstenberg, 1995).

These developments have not resolved the basic identity dilemmas that lie at the very root of the creation of the Israeli setting but have given them new forms. The original endemic contradictions in Zionism are, indeed, still evident. Even today, Zionist nationalism dichotomizes the notions of Jewish peoplehood and Israeli nationhood, granting Jews who live in Israel a special status vis-à-vis the Diaspora (see also Herman, 1988). However, this dichotomization has lost much of its acuity over the years as the proportion of Jews who live in Israel has risen (more than 40 percent in 2003). On the other hand, Zionism also means an aspiration to integrate into the Middle East and the Arab space. Thus, from its very beginning, Zionism was conscious that it stood in front of two competing categories of "others." Zionism's insistence on connectedness with world Jewry cannot but weaken its urge to integrate into the geopolitical surroundings, and its insistence on the belonging to its surroundings cannot but lessen its emphasis on allegiance to world Jewry. This dilemma is permanent but its forms vary with the Middle Eastern conflict. The higher the tension, the stronger the Israelis' tendency to line up with World Jewry; the lower the tension, the stronger their tendency to emphasize this belongingness to the region.

Revisionist Analyses

One dissident way of tackling these dilemmas, the "Canaanite" ideology, was propagated in the 1930s by radical anti-Zionists who emerged from the leading stratum itself. These intellectuals, taking the Zionists' contradictory attitude toward the Diaspora to its ultimate conclusion, believed that the Jews in Palestine should disengage from the Jewish world and even renounce the very label of "Jew." The leader of the movement, the poet and journalist Yonathan Ratosh, sought to bar all reference to the history and cultures of the Diaspora, to embark on a new era of "normalization" of the Jewish people,[2] and to call the new collective "Hebrews" as opposed to "Jews." The course of history, however, would not encourage the development of this movement. The Holocaust, the establishment of the State of Israel, mass immigration in the 1950s and 1960s, and Israel's recurrent wars with its neighbors strengthened the Israel-Diaspora nexus and relegated the Canaanite movement to the margins of the public scene, where it remains to this day.

However, paradoxically but quite understandably, the Canaanite perspective, a product of extremist Zionism, would eventually find itself linked with left-leaning, pro-Arab, anti-Zionist thought. Boaz Evron (1995), long a sworn Canaanite, advocates a basic redefinition of Israel's national identity on the exclusive basis of the territorial principle. Jews and Arabs in Israel should be totally equal, he believes, and as long as Israel defines itself as a Jewish state its conflict with the Arab world and the Palestinians will continue inexorably. The only way to surmount these difficulties is to define Israel as the state of all its citizens (see also Agassi, et al., 1991). In the long run, Evron also expects Jews to assimilate into non-Jewish populations wherever they are—with the exception of the Ultra-Orthodox, who will cloister themselves in their own communities. Anti-Zionist views such as these are being expressed by no few others who originated in the Zionist Left (see Agassi, 1990; Shapira, 1996). However inconsistent their positions may be (see Lissak, 1996), they have created a new revisionist current in Israeli political thought, "post-Zionism" (for reviews, see Silberstein, 1996, and Ram, 1995), which offers new analyses and conceptions of the history and sociology of the origins of this society and of its conflicts with its environment. Unlike Canaanites, post-Zionists criticize not the Diaspora Jews but those in Israel, who define their state as a Jewish state and not the state of all its citizens. This thinking traces the roots of the Israeli-Palestinian conflict to Israel and Zionism (Shalev, 1996; Orr, 1994).

---

[2] In 1951, he established the Centre of Young Hebrews and began to publish the journal *Alef* as the organ of his movement, which fought for the total separation of Israel from Diaspora Judaism and Jewry.

The overwhelming majority of the Israeli Jews, however, shows no genuine interest in revisionist claims, influenced as they are by the daily vicissitudes of the ongoing hardships of the economic development, the absorption of waves of immigrants, and above all the incessant conflict with the surroundings. For them, the bond of Israel and the Diaspora is still taken for granted (Don-Yehiya, 1991).

Belligerence and Identity

Belligerence with its neighbors has indeed been a focus of tremendous development for Israeli society for three generations now. This reality, to be sure, has had a severe impact on Israeli culture, foremost because it imposes on its youth two or three years of compulsory military service (for girls and boys, respectively). This service is often prolonged by one or two more years for soldiers who wish to advance to the low officer grades; for others who aspire to a military career, the prolongation can span until their forties. Military service, in whatever form, creates a gateway to society by symbolizing the fulfillment of one's national duties. Thus, Arabs who are unwilling to serve because they do not wish to fight their brethren across the border, and the young Ultra-Orthodox who request exemption because they regard the uninterrupted study of the holy writings as their destiny, are *a priori* viewed by others as people who lack a major attribute of citizenship.

For those who do serve, the army is a place of intense socialization. The predominance of a "fighting culture," with its insistence on determination, problem-solving, and survival, accompanies many a former soldier back to civilian life. Women are at a disadvantage in this culture; although many of them serve, they rarely do so in prestigious combat units and are instead often relegated to second-rate services. Women require courage to withstand this cultural pro-male bias and attain equal status. Another aspect, the intensity of the military experience, and more generally the regular encounter with belligerence, imprints the culture of soldiers as well as civilians with a tendency to accept violence as a "regular environment"—to such an extent that many derive from it justification for brutal behavior in daily life. Worse still, these circumstances induce no few individuals to develop attitudes toward Arabs generally, and Israeli Arabs particularly, that are marked by distrust if not hostility.

Some authors (for examples see Ben-Eliezer, 1998; Kimmerling, 2001) infer from their analysis of these aspects that Israeliness is in fact a form of militarism. Without denying the crucial importance of the army and the military institution, this attitude is gainsaid by the way Israelis are actually influenced by, and dependent on, the civilian setting. It is true that the army is a major domain of social mobility in Israeli society (Peri, 1998). Based on mass recruitment and self-selection of officers—up to the highest ranks—it offers a strongly universalistic and egalitarian structure of opportunities that benefits many individuals who have the appropriate human resources. By the same token, since officers leave the army in middle age and turn to the civilian market, the army is also a breeding ground for elite elements who insinuate themselves into diverse areas of activity— politics, national or municipal administration, business, and so on.

In this context, however, the military elite can hardly be depicted as an independent center of political power. Rather, the career pattern creates a dependency relationship between the military elite and the civilian world. Even when former senior officers enter politics or take up public positions, they are bound to need civilian support and they find this an ordeal that quickly distances them from the models and values that were theirs under the flag. These circumstances definitely enjoin Israeli society from responding to the concept of militarism. This, however, does not deny the cultural influence of the military on behaviors, life values, and, more generally, the public atmosphere.

It remains that the gravest issues on the public agenda are subordinated to the state of belligerence and the acuteness of security challenges, which grants strong visibility to the military leadership. On the other hand, these overarching issues are also the cause of the political rift between the leftist (dovish) and rightist (hawkish) forces that dominate the polity, relegating economic and social issues to secondary prominence. Instead of depoliticizing the polity by endowing a prominent role to the military in national decision-making, the protracted conflict of Israel with her neighbors fuels right-left antagonisms revolving principally around security-related issues and strategic war and peace perspectives.

The state of belligerence—with all its cultural, sociological, and cultural consequences—is also related to the identity question that lies at the core of the basic premises of this society, i.e., the definition of Israel as a Jewish state in the midst of the Arab-Islamic world. This Arab-Islamic arena is itself in nationalistic-religious turmoil and views Israel not as the outcome of the Jews' tragic history in Europe and elsewhere but as a manifestation of territorial expansion by the West. As far as Israel is concerned, however, the belligerence represents the continuation, under new circumstances, of a very long history of exclusion that is not yet close to its end.

It is in this context, far from revisionist analyses of the origins of Israeli society, that questions such as "In what sense is Israeli society Jewish?" "How Jewish is it?" and "How Jewish should it be?" remain central items on the public agenda. They set Israeli Jews apart and expose the fact that one may still speak of several Jewish Israeli identities rather than of one. The difficulty of clearly distinguishing between religion and peoplehood in the context of a Jewish state and of the role of religion in the formation of Jewish nationalism is the major reason that a clear formula has not yet been accepted by all, fifty years after the creation of Israel. Indeed, any attempt to work out a definitive *modus vivendi* reawakens unavoidable confrontations.

The essence of these ramified debates, resulting from that special relationship of religion and nationhood, clearly appear, even in a schematic characterization of this society's principal cleavages, with respect to those three facets of its collective identity, as formulated by the dominant culture (Oron, 1993).

THE SINGULARITY OF THE COLLECTIVE: RELIGIOUS CHALLENGES

Israel's Declaration of Independence defines the country as a democracy that bestows equality and liberty on all, irrespective of religion, origin, sex, or race. The same declaration, however, also defines Israel as a Jewish state, i.e., the patrimony of Jews worldwide. This implies an ineradicable link between Jewish peoplehood and Jewish religion (Ben-Rafael, 2002b; Abramov, 1976). Since most Israeli Jews—like most Jews everywhere these days—are not religious, the definitions of Judaism and Jewishness are endlessly debated in the Israeli public arena. These debates revolve mainly around the role that religion should play in defining the singularity of the collective, and the disputants—representatives of the dominant secular culture and of various religious groups—often escalate their disagreements into political crises (Liebman, 1997a). In this country, indeed, which is a defined as a Jewish state, these debates directly impact on politically significant legal stipulations regarding procedures of naturalization, the role and modes, formally recognized, of conversion to Judaism, and institutional support for immigrants. In this respect, the dominant culture is confronted by forces that represent very different claims: the Ashkenazi Ultra-Orthodox, the National Religious, and the Shas Mizrahi (Middle Eastern) movement. As seen further on, the latter case, however, is intimately bound to the scene of ethnicity and will thus be discussed in the following section.

The Ashkenazi Ultra-Orthodox (Heb.: Haredim, i.e., "the fearful" or "the concerned")—whose overwhelming majority consist of Jews of Eastern-European origin—constitutes but a small portion of the Ashkenazi public as a whole. They are primarily interested in advancing particularistic interests. For instance, they aspire to achieve official endorsement of children's *de facto* exemption from military service so that they may pursue religious studies without interruption. In a similar vein, they request special treatment in housing policies on the ground of their typically large families. However, the Ultra-Orthodox also consider themselves mobilized for an all-Jewish religious cause, i.e., the strengthening of religious law in the Israeli constitutional order.

The National Religious—mostly of middle-class background—also have their own practical concerns (support of National Religious schools or funding of youth-movement activities). An issue of much greater significance to them, however, is the alignment of Israel's policies in favor of the annexation and Jewish settlement of the Palestinian territories, which they consider an article of faith that emphasizes the sanctity of the Land and its exclusive connection with the Jewish people. The Ashkenazi Ultra-Orthodox constituency resides mainly in specific quarters in Jerusalem, the Tel Aviv suburb of Bene Beraq, Safed in Galilee, and additional scattered localities. The National Religious constituency is heavily represented in settlements in the West Bank and the Gaza Strip.

The ensuing tensions between these cleavages and the dominant culture should not be considered temporary (Liebman, 1997b). They are fueled by the inability of the dominant culture to respond efficiently to both constituencies' claims. This inability is grounded not only in the crucial role of the religious forces in the political arena, where they account for a quarter of the electorate. It is also explained, in large part, by the fact that, as seen above, Zionism draws its very symbols and themes from the religious tradition (Cohen and Zusser, 1998). These intricate relations are but one example of the difficulty of defining a genuinely secular ("laïc" as would be translated in French) Judaism (Ellenson, 1989; Fackenheim, 1992). In the case of a Jewish nationalism that has become a dominant culture in a state defined by it as Jewish, this difficulty explains that complete separation of religion and state in Israel is difficult to consider, in spite of the fact that the religious parties have always been a minority in the polity. This, in turn, accounts for the fact that confrontations between religious forces and the secular public are a permanent feature of Israeli politics.

COLLECTIVE COMMITMENT: MIZRAHI, RUSSIAN, AND ETHIOPIAN CHALLENGES

Another category of social cleavages relates primarily to the commitment of individuals to the national collective and the extent to which it is influenced, if not buffered, by other collective allegiances. Several examples illustrate the variety of models that Israeli society exhibits in this respect. Scholars have subjected three of them—Mizrahim, Russian Jews, and Ethiopian Jews—to particular scrutiny.

Most of today's Mizrahim (or their forebears, as explained below) arrived in Israel during the first decade and a half of independence. Their traditionalism contrasted with the dominant culture, which often treated them with alienation. This factor, coupled with the limited human capital of many members of these groups, often consigned Mizrahim to the underprivileged class and neighborhoods. Russians, as we called them and who include here the immigrants from all former Soviet territories (more than 1,000,000 people in 2003), arrived much later—some in the early 1970s but most in the 1990s. Their distinctive characteristics are strong human capital and weak Jewish culture. This group also contains a relatively large contingent of non-Jews—about 25 percent—even though many of them assimilate into the Jewish environment. Ethiopian Jews, a much smaller group (about 100,000 in 2003), insinuate a new element into the human landscape of Israeli Jewish society—black African Jews—who were absorbed into Jewish society after harsh polemics about whether they were "really" Jewish.

Each of these cases, against its own background, formulates claims that justify the retention of particularism and challenges the dominant culture's aim of bringing all Israeli Jews under one cultural umbrella. Mizrahim, from the very start, construed the establishment of the State of Israel as the fulfillment of the Biblical promise of redemption. Hence, they found it difficult to abandon, in the Land of the Jews, practices that they had maintained for centuries in "foreign" lands and that, in their opinion, had brought them up to this era of *at'halta di-ge'ula* ("beginning of redemption"). This difficulty is especially voiced by the Shas movement, an Ultra-Orthodox Mizrahi movement, ever since it appeared in the 1980s, on behalf of a project of imposing Sephardic Judaism[3] as Israel's dominant culture. Russian Jews who had lost nearly all contact with Jewish legacies and drew their principal cultural perspectives from the Russian language and symbols now aspired to become Israeli Jews without renouncing their control of cultural resources of which they were proud. Ethiopian Jews regarded their legacies as forms of Jewishness that justified their self-assertion as Jews, which is not easily conceded by many rabbis.

To pursue further, upon arrival, Mizrahim were hesitant to accept unquestionably the way nationalism secularizes the symbols that it drew from ancestral legacies. For the Russians, the question was, on the contrary, how to reconcile a secular attitude toward culture and the emphasis on their own resources with the Jewish identity that they found in Israel, which is oriented much more than theirs to traditional symbols. For the Ethiopians, the question was how to reinterpret particular religious legacies in a way that would allow them to meet their fundamental aspiraton in regard to inclusion in Judaism.

What all these groups share is that their development is bound to the way they respond to the dominant culture's grafting of modern secular nationalism onto the scion of religious tradition. Thus, these cases reflect their belonging and commitment to a whole that binds them and the dominant culture together. Concurrently, however,

---

[3] As discussed later on, Sephardic Judaism refers to the legacy of medieval Spanish Judaism which was diffused in numerous Jewish communities around the Mediterranean sea, including Palestine, where it was for centuries the dominant brand of Judaism taught in religious academies (yeshivot).

they illustrate potential focal points of dissent against the dominant culture that may, under given circumstances, become triggers of active confrontation.

"Others": Arabs, Druze, and Foreign Workers

Furthermore, because Israel is defined as a Jewish state by a nationalism that finds its roots in religious traditions, people who belong to different religions in Israel fall into the category of "others" in one way or another—from the viewpoint of both religion and peoplehood. However, because Israel also professes to be a democracy, they belong to the "we" as well, at least to some extent. Here we examine three groups that come under this heading and reflect the complexity of this contradictory configuration.

The most important, demographically, is composed of Muslim and Christian Arabs or, as they often call themselves (especially, the Muslims), "Palestinians living in Israel." At first glance, Israeli Palestinians have largely stayed within a closed ethnocultural niche, using their own language and remaining loyal to their particular background (see for an early investigation: Rosenfeld, 1978). However, they are citizens of Israel and in their wide majority work outside their communities, albeit mostly in working-class jobs. As a consequence of this relation with the Jewish environment, a silent revolution is transforming their culture in terms of new modes of behavior and life values. Still, every new spike in the intensity of the Israeli-Palestinian conflict strengthens Israeli Palestinians' urge to identify with Palestinians across the Green Line,[4] with whom they share a national allegiance.

Close to them but still distinct by their particular religious allegiance are the Druze, who, unlike Muslim and Christian Arabs, have aligned themselves solemnly with the Jewish state and serve in the military. The Druze, however, are a self-contained group that tries to maintain its community exclusivity and to avoid unrestricted intermingling with non-druze. Acknowledging that they belong, after all, to the Arab nation, they have strong claims against Israel for not always showing them the gratitude they expect for the loyalty.

---

[4] Israel's 1967 borders, before Palestinian territories were conquered by the Israelis following the Six-Day War.

The third category is made up of foreign workers, a quarter of a million people from Asia, Africa, South America, Eastern Europe, and the Balkans. Although theoretically a transient population, they have gradually integrated into the human landscape of Israeli society as living witnesses of globalization. Even though governmental policies try to limit the size of this population and to take care of a turnover of people among them, an ever larger percentage remains here for years, establishing families and raising children. Each group of foreign workers conveys its own religious faith, languages, and orientation toward the host society, and is also widely differentiated here by its working sectors—Thais in agriculture, Filipinos in health care, Romanians in construction, etc.

While Arabs and Druze represent the non-Jewish Israelis and foreign workers fill the slot of non-Jewish non-Israelis, all three categories belong to "others." They present Jewish Israeli society with its greatest domestic challenges. Non-Jewish inhabitants of a democratic state cannot but aspire to obtain and realize rights of citizenship or, at least, of residency. For Jews who attach importance to the Jewish character of Israel, such rights mean that they must maintain demographic supremacy in order to sustain their commitment to the democratic character of the state. Only when Arabs, druze, and foreign workers constitute clear and irrefutable minorities—not only singly but also collectively—can Israel be a democratic Jewish state.

Thus, this *problématique*, too, is related to the unbreakable link between Jewish nationalism and its roots in religious tradition. It is only this link that explains why individuals who profess a non-Jewish religion cannot be viewed as candidates for assimilation among Jews even in a secular state such as Israel. Hence, once proclaimed a "Jewish state," Israel will inevitably find democracy hard to implement as soon as non-Jews become a majority. In these respects, Israel is much different from France, where anyone who is willing to embrace the French culture is welcome to assimilate into the French nation irrespective of his or her religious allegiance, which, in any event, is viewed as a strictly private matter. In this sense, Israel is much closer to Britain, where even though Anglicanism is a state religion (with the supreme national authority, the Queen, being the emblematic head of the Church), millions of nationals belong to other faiths.[5]

---

[5] In Great Britain, non-Anglicans are protected by a profusion of legal dispositions

The Secondary Importance of Class Conflicts

An additional outcome of the importance of the intimate relation between religion and nationalism in the Jewish case is the very relative—and mainly indirect—political importance of the socioeconomic cleavage in this society.

For a strong contingent of Marxist scholars, the roots of social conflicts should be firstly sought in the economic structure of society, i.e., in reference to means of production, market rules, the distribution of the labor force (Wright, 1985) or occupational status (Blau and Duncan, 1967; Treiman, 1977). At first glance, this approach should be relevant to the analysis of Israeli society, since inequality in Israeli is becoming increasingly blatant and severe in recent years. Hence, in the 1950s, one could still speak of Israeli society as a reflection of egalitarian orientations, at least as far as wages were concerned. In 1955, Israelis in the lowest income decile received 3.2 percent of the total national wage income and those in the uppermost decile received 20 percent. By 1974, the lowest decile's share in national income had fallen to 2.6 percent and that of the uppermost decile had climbed to 24 percent (Ben-Porat, 2001). By 2001, the respective shares were 2.4 percent and 28.5 percent (ICBS, 2002). The Gini index of inequality[6] rested at 0.26 in 1954, fluctuated inconsistently between 0.26 and 0.30 between then and 1970, and marched steadily upward thereafter, to 0.38 in 2001. Israel's official statistics, moreover, omit guest workers and commuting Palestinian workers from the territories under the control of the Palestinian Authority; otherwise, the inequality data would be even more extreme. In brief, inequality in Israel is definitely severe and compares with countries such as the United States and the United Kingdom (see Ben-Porat, 2001).

---

minimizing the costs of nonmembership in the predominant group—which may serve as a model for the Israeli case.

[6] In the Gini index, a score of 0 denotes perfect equality and 1.0 denotes extreme inequality.

Table 2.1. Strikes in Israel: Duration of One Day or More

Year	Number of strikers	Average duration (days)	Strikes per 100,000 salaried workers
1956	155	9.76	20
1966	234	2.89	33
1976	1,019	3.01	12
1986	1,126	3.26	9

Source: Ran Chermesh, *A State within a State: Industrial Relations in Israel, 1965–1987*, Greenwood, 1993: 93.

Interestingly enough, Table 2.1 shows that strikes were longer when Israeli society was more egalitarian, in the 1950s and 1960s. Since Israel became more differentiated in its structure, its strikes have tended to be shorter and to diminish. Hence, one can hardly find a correlation between increasing social inequality and the worsening of labor relations. Additional measurements (Table 2.2) point to the same tendency: wider involvement of workers in strikes but shorter strikes, i.e., less labor-dispute intensity.

The class stratification of Israeli society acquired quite stable features in the 1980s and 1990s, as the ranks of the lower-middle and upper classes expanded and the blue-collar working class contracted (Table 2.3). These findings, however, should be treated cautiously because they pertain to citizens only and exclude Palestinian commuters (up to 100,000 in times of calm) and guest workers (approximately 250,000 in the early 2000s), most of whom held unskilled jobs. Be this as it may, however, these data underline that a growing majority of Israel citizens belongs to the "nonproletarian" classes.

This does not mean that Israeli society is becoming more egalitarian even in respect to citizens only. An index such as control of capital and property suffices to refute that premise. Reliable data about this dimension are hardly available, but a survey by a major Israeli bank shows that half a percent of the bank's customers own about half of the bank's financial sources and that 65 percent own 10 percent. Such findings are not exceptional in the context of developed countries.

Table 2.2. Long-Term Indicators of Strike Activity, 1924–1988

	1924–1925[1]	1926–1947[1]	1948–1959[1]	1960–1973[1]	1975–1988
Worker involvements[2]	218	39	23	80	218
Average duration[3]	13.8	11.4	7.7	2.5	2.1

Source: Michael Shalev, *Labour and the Political Economy in Israel*, Oxford: Oxford University Press, 1992: 62.

1. The period averages are expressed as geometric means in order to reduce the impact of unrepresentative years of hyperactivity.
2. "Worker involvements" are the number of persons involved in strikes and lockouts per thousand workers; the latter is calculated on the basis of total employment (and, before 1948, the total Jewish labor force in Palestine, since the strike data used pertained only to the Jewish sector).
3. "Average duration" is the number of working days on strike per worker involved.

These findings call attention to the fact that much of Israel's economy is effectively controlled by a few powerful corporations. The process gathered speed in the 1980s and the 1990s, when the government privatized public capital and actions of similar intent were taken by the once-powerful Histadrut (General Federation of Labor in Israel, a national federation of trade unions, recently renamed the New Federation or Ha-Histadrut Ha-Khadasha), which had maintained large holdings in a variety of domains.

Table 2.3. Occupations of Israelis, 1980–1994 (Percent)

Occupation	Class	1980	1994
Academics, liberal professions, managerial	Upper	26	31
White-collar, salespersons	Middle	26	25
Service workers	Lower-middle	11	14
Agricultural, skilled, and unskilled workers	Lower	37	30
Total		100	100

Source: Yaar, E., and Shavit, Z. (eds.), *Trends in Israeli Society*, Tel-Aviv: The Open University of Israel, 2001: 558.

In addition, we also know that since the late 1980s, the number of households under the poverty line has been revolving around one-third (34 percent in 1994), inducing the government to augment social budgets in order to halve the proportion (e.g., to 18 percent in 1994, after transfer payments) (Ben-Porat, 1989). Although these data suffice to show that Israeli society has a well-differentiated class structure, this structure, it turns out, is anything but polarized. Indeed, data show that less than a third of the Israeli population belongs to the blue-collar working class (Table 2.3). On the other hand, a crucial aspect of this class structure is its partial overlap with ethnic cleavages. Table 2.4 shows the Mizrahi/Ashkenazi class divide but also stresses that this divide is by no means rigid.

Table 2.4. Class Distribution of the Ashkenazi/Mizrahi Cleavage (Percent)

Classes	1961		1972		1983	
	Miz	Ashk+[1]	Miz	Ashk+[1]	Miz	Ashk+[1]
Capitalists	0.4	2.2	1.4	2.1	1.3	2.4
Less wealthy bourgeoisie	15.0	26.2	16.7	21.4	12.6	11.7
Semi-self-employed	14.0	20.0	23.0	26.5	32.6	28.9
Executive, academic, white-collar	6.6	17.8	8.7	27.9	16.7	32.9
Blue-collar	64.0	33.8	50.2	22.1	36.8	24.1
Total	100.0	100.0	100.0	100.0	100.0	100.0

Source: Ben-Porat (1989: 69).

1. The Ashkenazi+ category includes Ashkenazim and Israel-born persons of other origins.

Table 2.4 should be treated cautiously because the "Ashkenazim+" category includes second-generation Mizrahim, due to the difficulty of separating them from Ashkenazim in the available statistics. Thus, it provides but an approximate portrayal. Polarization should be more severe if second-generation Mizrahim were excluded, as they probably hold an in-between position. On the other hand, the picture would be less dichotomous if second-generation Mizrahim were added to first-generation Mizrahim and counterposed to Ashkenazim of both generations.

Be this as it may, Table 2.4 evinces that the class dimension of the ethnic cleavage has become less salient over the years even as general social inequality has worsened. It is in fact the Jewish/Arab cleavage, much more than the Ashkenazi/Mizrahi cleavage, that is strongly underlined in regard to class distribution: Table 2.5 shows that while the share of Jews in blue-collar occupations is trending down, that of Arabs has remained stable with a slight uptrend. Concurrently, the "less wealthy bourgeoisie" has contracted severely over the years while the modern middle class has grown.

It is actually the strong correspondence of sociocultural parameters with class structure that accounts for the fact that class conflicts *per se* play a secondary role in Israel. While Israel is known for severe social tension, and while politicians and trade-union leaders indulge liberally in social demagogy, labor disputes rarely spill into other fields. Even when the Histadrut declares a general strike—a frequent occurrence—one can hardly speak of confrontations that have a direct and visible political impact.

In fact, population groups tend to hang their social plight on their ethnocultural features rather than on the structure of the socio-economic regime. Arabs, as a rule, tend to interpret their overrepresentation in the lower class, relative to Jews, as an outcome of Jewish–Arab antagonism. Furthermore, no few Mizrahim, a group overrepresented in the lower classes relative to Ashkenazim, picture their collective social situation in terms of ethnic deprivation rather than class oppression (Ben-Rafael and Sharot, 1991). For another example in the same vein, class differentiation merely adds "color" to group like the Ashkenazi Ultra-Orthodox that is essentially viewed as a religious category. A large number of Ultra-Orthodox are, indeed, among the economically underprivileged, since men in this group are often lifetime religious students who receive paltry incomes from their institutions and the state and, in addition, have numerous children. However, since dedication to religion is their prime imperative, they do not regard the consequent hardships of life as related to class. Recent Russian immigrants display a similar pattern; they usually interpret their presence in the lower classes as related to the very experience of immigration.

These considerations suffice to sustain the claim that Israel is a society of salient and worsening inequality that, however, plays a subordinate role in the formation and dynamics of tensions in the national-political arena. The direct expression of this state of affairs is evident in the politics of labor disputes. Most trade unions are affiliated with the Histadrut and, for this reason, wield considerable power in social and economic affairs. The federation leadership is chosen in general elections in which nationwide parties interrelate in various coalitions. The strife that the Histadrut leads or sponsors,

Table 2.5. Class Distribution of the Jewish/Arab Cleavage (Percent)

Classes	1961		1972		1983	
	Arabs	Jews	Arabs	Jews	Arabs	Jews
Capitalists	—	1.7	1.2	1.9	0.8	2.0
Bourgeoisie	36.0	21.3	24.0	19.1	10.3	12.2
Semi-self- employed	4.0	19.2	11.7	25.3	13.5	32.3
Academics, white-collar	3.2	16.2	6.4	20.7	14.3	27.3
Blue-collar	56.8	41.0	56.7	33.0	61.1	26.2
Total	100.0	100.0	100.0	100.0	100.0	100.0

Source: Ben-Porat (1989: 69).

however, is never political; it concerns labor issues only. The most powerful groups in the Histadrut are workers' organizations in large corporations and public administrations such as the Israel Electric Corp., the Airports Authority, defense industries, or Teachers' Trade-Unions.

In the 1990s, the leading faction in the Histadrut split from the Labor Party, which had been the federation's mentor until then. It then managed to piece together a broad coalition, from left-wing parties (including Arab parties and, in the Jewish sector, left-wing Meretz) to the right-of-center Likud. This coalition became possible only due to a pragmatic program that addressed workers' demands and nothing else. By the same token, when important leaders of the Histadrut—scions of the Labor Party—ran for the Knesset (the national parliament) on their own ticket, they routinely obtained no more than 3–4 percent of ballots cast. This outcome, in the long run, induced them to reunite with the Labor Party in 2004. Thus, this cleavage can hardly be depicted as "polar;" it is plainly of secondary significance to the major religious, ethnocultural, and national cleavages of which Israel's multiculturalism is composed.

In conclusion, the class cleavage cannot be viewed here as an active cleavage in its own right on the central political scene. This too, may be attributed to the essence of Israel's dominant culture, which evinces a nationalism stemming from religious traditions. It is this type of collective identity that awakes in this society the major cleavages that it experiences, and that, thereby, overshadows the significance of socioeconomic antagonisms per se.

CONFLICTUAL MULTICULTURALISM AND THE RIGHT/LEFT CLEAVAGE

Following our discussion of Israel's religious, ethnic, and national-cleavages and our assessment of the irrelevance of class conflict regarding this society's major controversies, we may turn to the question of the kind of multiculturalism it might illustrate. This requires delving into the incoherence of the forces in presence and the many directions in which they push and pull the social order, and it might well yield the impression that Israel is an atomized society that defies all consistent order. Such an endeavor, however, should also acknowledge that the groups involved are not always discrete entities that challenge each other head-to-head. Individuals of the National Religious persuasion, for instance, may be Mizrahim or Russians and may have diverse and diversified interests. Furthermore, the disruptive significance of each cleavage may be eventually buffered by in-between categories. Many individuals, for instance, may be reluctant to alienate themselves from traditional symbols even when they do not see themselves as "believers;" they might thus stand between the religious and the nonreligious. In the same vein, offspring of marriages between Ashkenazim and Mizrahim may tend to blur the divisive line between these categories. Druze and Bedouin, moreover, are positioned between Jews and other Arabs, and, among the latter, Christians are closer to models exhibited by the Jewish population than Muslims.

Last but not least, each entity interfaces with the same dominant culture and, while asserting its contrastive particularism vis-à-vis this culture, is exposed to its influence in various ways. All groups, for instance, have acquired the legitimate language even though each might give Hebrew a specific "coloration"—accents, borrowings, calques, etc.—that originates in vernaculars such as Yiddish, Judeo-Arabic, Russian, Arabic, and Ladino and in the context of different cultures. The groups may also invest Hebrew with different meanings—a national signifier for the nonethnic middle-class, a vulgar vernacular for the Ultra-Orthodox, a vehicle of traditional Judaism for Mizrahim, the language of the target society for Russian immigrants, and a second but dominant language for Arabs and druze. Nevertheless, the generalized use of Hebrew means a reference to a common set of symbols and, thus, the possibility of meaningful communication. Moreover, we have also mentioned the spread of English through

Israeli society which cuts through all groups and might encourage rapprochement among their socially mobile elements.

These convergence-divergence dynamics impact on the rule of national politics. This is best illustrated by the left/right cleavage, which Israelis have often come to consider as their major divide since the late 1970s when the country's two leading parties, the right-of-center Likud and the left-of-center Labor Party, found themselves as genuine alternative ruling elites. It is, indeed, in 1977, that the Likud succeeded to win the general elections for the first time, interrupting the Labor Party's quasi-monopolistic rule for tens of years. Ever since, no party is assured of its supremacy and both the Likud and the Labor invest their best to evince the differences that oppose them, especially regarding their approaches toward the conflict with the Palestinians, the Likud leaning toward hawkish positions (though its leaders may show varying degrees of flexibility) and Labor taking a dovish tack (though again with diverse degrees of toughness among leaders).

Sociologically, however, the differences transcend political views. Many scholars (see Yaar and Peres, 2000) have found that the core of the left is composed mainly of the predominantly Ashkenazi and nonreligious middle class, *a fortiori* when one moves from Labor to the more leftist Yahad (the recently founded successor to Meretz). Farther to the left, one finds Arab—Communist and nationalist—parties. The core of the right, in contrast, has a large proportion of Mizrahi, Russian, and Orthodox Jews. More specifically, Ashkenazi Ultra-Orthodox parties are natural allies of the Likud, the asserted nationalism of which is closer to their own emphasis on traditional symbols than the liberal and social-democrat left. The National Religious, in turn, are more strongly represented in far-right parties that view West Bank and Gaza settlers as their reference group.

In a nutshell, Israel's multiculturalism is reflected and articulated on a national political scene where left-right perspectives create a framework in which sociocultural cleavages are expressed. Israel's particularisms do not eradicate concern about national interests but combine with them in coalitions where ideological and purely political preoccupations and primordial claims intermingle. Protagonists appear here not only to strive to wrest power and autonomy from the political center but also, through coalitions and aggregates, to influence the center in order to leave their imprint on the social setting at large—each in its own way. It is in this respect that the essence of primordialism, as expressed by the kind of dominant culture prevailing in this setting and the related dilemmas that it forces the various social cleavages to confront, again seem to evince the effects of a nationalism that was engendered by the conjunction of the goal of building a modern national society and an inspiration derived from religious traditions.

THE RESEARCH QUESTIONS

Translating these considerations into research questions, it is by viewing Israeli society as an entity that, like its components, implies a collective identity—what we termed "dominant culture"—that we classify its cleavages in terms of the facets of this identity that they challenge most particularly by articulating their own identity perspectives and aspirations. We do this in order to capture the essentials of the interactions of these cleavages with the dominant culture and with each other and to gauge the effects of these interactions in society. In the aftermath of our theoretical discussion and overview of major lines of development of the Israeli society, we can now express this aspiration more precisely by asking specific guiding questions that refer to individual cleavages, on the one hand, and to the whole of which they are comprised, on the other.

In regard to the *singularity of the collective*, as defined by the dominant culture, we see the principal dilemmas in the relations of religious sectors with the nonreligious:

(1) The attitude of the *Ashkenazi Ultra-Orthodox* toward the predominantly nonreligious society at large is fundamentally alienated, even though the Ultra-Orthodox cannot avoid viewing themselves as a part of it. Our guiding question here concerns the relative strength of these two contradictory forces and if and how they give shape to new tendencies and long-term trends. Are the tendencies leaning toward divergence and secession or toward symbiosis and weakening of boundaries? If so, in what sense—a rapprochement between the Ashkenazi Ultra-Orthodox and the secular, or the other way around?

(2) The *National Religious*, as we know, are challenging the social order on the basis of their understanding of a quasi-messianic Zionism. In conflict today with much of society, this sector, and especially West

Bank settlers, faces the dilemma of whether to adopt a strategy of irredentism or to do the opposite, i.e., to reformulate its objectives in order to steer away from extremism. Our inquiry will look for signs that point toward the outcome and the extent that this inner tension jeopardizes the very cohesion of this most active—and activist— segment of society.

As for cleavages that challenge *collective commitments* on behalf of particularistic allegiances:

(3) We have learned that the *Mizrahim*, especially those in lower social strata, are widely marked by underprivilege, ethnic allegiance, and traditionalism. Our question asks, first, why is this population more attracted by hawkish nationalism and a Mizrahi strain of Ultra-Orthodoxy than by working-class politics or plain ethnic protest?

(4) We acknowledge that *Russians* wish to become an integral part of Israeli society without renouncing their cultural and linguistic resources as signifiers of their community. Our question concerning them is how far one may speak of potential limits to ethnic expression. When Russians aspire to retain elements of their original culture, do they also wish to retain their original models of Jewish identity? Do these versions of Jewish identity, composed more of allegiances than of contents, account for a basic alienation from the rest of the Jewish population? If so, how do Russians interpret the notion of "Israeliness"?

(5) As seen above, *Ethiopians*, although a small group, are special because they are marked not only by ethnic allegiances and strong reverence for particular religious traditions but also by racial features. The question here is whether such a group is inevitably doomed to ghettoization within Israeli society or whether the Jewishness that is theirs warrants progressive access to the mainstream.

As for cleavages that challenge relations with "others:"

(6) *Israeli Arabs* are torn between Palestinian nationalism and Israeli citizenship and culture. We wish to determine the extent to which this dilemma remains open or is tending to wind down in some definite direction. Does cultural socialization in the context of an Israeli society that, in many respects, encourages the Palestinians'

"Israelization" fade in view of their particularistic collective identity? What is implied by the fact that the issue concerns groups that have different religious faiths? Regarding the *Druze*, who for centuries have had a tradition of being a niche-type, ethnoreligious minority, we may ask whether this model remains sustainable in a society that is widely modern and secular. And what is the impact, in this respect, of the fact that Israel is defined as a Jewish state?

(7) *Foreign workers* are an obvious case of outsiders who are expected to comprise a transient population with permanent turnover, even though many of these guests remain in Israel for a long time if not forever. Our question here is how far one may go in speaking of cultural "Israelization" in this case and whether, over time, new and less alienated relationships with some groups in Israeli society may be observed. Moreover, how are they affected by their confrontation with a dominant Israeli culture that links nationalism to allegiance to a specific religious faith that excludes them?

Pursuant to this discussion of individual cleavages, we probe the nature and dynamics of the reality that they create when viewed as a whole. We ask about the configuration of Israel's multiculturalism, the rules of the multicultural game, and the strategic goals and identity politics of the actors involved. In other words, and according to our conceptualization, we ask if the country is in fact tending toward "liberal" or rather "conflictual" multiculturalism:

(8) When we speak of the configuration of Israel's multiculturalism, we mean the ways in which the various collectives position themselves vis-à-vis each other and, together, structure the multicultural space as groups and as clusters of groups. Our research question in this respect concerns the extent to which one may speak of central versus peripheral groups and of rivaling coalitions that circumscribe major forces of divergence. More generally, we wish to know whether some issues—the religiosity principle, ethnic issues, and attitudes toward "others"—intermingle to crystallize central coherent forces or, on the contrary, remain focused on different dimensions of the social order.

(9) We also wish to explore the groups' understanding of the multicultural game and to identify rules that the groups are willing to accept in their interrelations. This question is close to the issue of legitimacy that people grant to others' actions and behaviors. Do the

various groups express respect for each other or do they share disparaging images of, and conflicting attitudes toward, each other?

(10) The third step in our investigation of Israel's multiculturalism concerns the groups' strategic goals and identity politics, which may presage the future of this emblematic example of multiculturalism. May one speak of Israeli multiculturalism as a model of cooperation that allows each participant to attain the goals that are important to it, or the opposite, as a model of conflict in which each participant "knows" what is good for all and seeks to impose it on them?

These aspects of the investigation of Israel's multiculturalism should reveal the particular features of a setting that conveys a national identity drawn from given religious traditions and confronted by inner and outer perspectives alike. The analyses of these confrontations should bring us closer to the possibility of assessing the extent that the dominant culture still retains its dominance and, in turn, its hegemony.

THE RESEARCH PROJECT

Our research project was conducted on the basis of surveys in 1999–2000. Our major research tool was a questionnaire that we applied to all groups investigated, *mutatis mutandis*. In the sample, we included a large number of groups, including Ethiopian Jews, druze, and foreign workers who represent relatively small percentages of the population at large.

The surveys were conducted in several phases (Table 2.6). Survery 1 (May 1999) focused on the major Jewish groups; Survey 2 (January 2000) centered on the coexistence and tensions between these groups and Muslim and Christian Arabs; Survey 3 (August 2000) added Ethiopians, Druze, and Filipinos; Survey 4 (October 2000) focused again on Jewish-Arab relations following a violent crisis that took place in the aftermath of the outbreak of the Intifada in the Palestinian territories. The questionnaire itself comprised of several categories of items. The first category, as is usual in sociological questionnaires, dealt with issues of context—age, religion and religiosity, origin, and socioeconomic status. The second category of items asked about group commitments and the importance of allegiances in respondents' lives. The third delved into perceptions of, and attitudes toward, the singularity of the subjects' allegiances. The fourth focused on feelings of closeness to, and distance from, a variety of social categories. The fifth group concerned respondents' political attitudes and behavior.

The successive surveys allowed us to address complex issues that focused on the willingness of the groups and communities that make up Israel's mosaic to accept certain rules and norms as universally applicable, to treat these rules as the basis of their common endeavor, and to consider them distinct from the areas in which each group wishes to retain its particularism. Here, as noted above, we also turned our attention to groups that, although small, are quite apposite in Israel's human landscape. The relatively recent Ethiopian-Jewish immigrants, whose Jewishness was not easily recognized by religious authorities, have raised to the front page the issue of race relations in this society. The druze are the main segment of the Arabic population that mainstream society considers fully Israeli because they officially assert their loyalty to the country and serve in its military. The third group is composed of Filipino foreign workers, whom we chose as representatives of foreign workers at large—inhabitants who are neither Israelis nor Jews—because they are the longest-tenured group among them.

The survey questionnaire also helped us to probe the left/right cleavage, a crucial element in the debate over the political dimension of Israel's multiculturalism. At this phase our focus on multiculturalism prompted us to examine four basic aspects: (1) respondents' identification with their groups as opposed to the national collective; (2) respondents' propensity to display tolerance toward the cultures and behavior patterns of others in their surroundings; (3) the "rules of the game" that respondents would like to prevail in the divided setting; and (4) the actual and desired positions of the various constituents in Israel's multicultural mosaic.

More specifically, items about respondents' allegiance to their group in comparison with the national collective, and about their retention of culture and language, belong to the first category. The second category included items about respondents' attitudes toward other groups or categories, their subjective distances from them, and their tolerance of "different" cultures and languages. Items in the third category solicited respondents' views about the limits of freedom of speech, the concept of civism, the obligations of all citizens to the national collective, universal social and political entitlements, and respondents' assessment of the areas of activity that should be placed at the top of the national priorities. Items in the fourth category asked respondents to assess various categories of national welfare, the meanings of multiculturalism in Israel, and the groups' role in the formation of the Israeli culture.

The questionnaire items—were formulated in ways that made them suitable for any group. This assured the integrity of our tools and the comparability of the responses. However, we did formulate the same questions in different ways for different groups when sensitivity to particular situations so required.

The sample populations are presented in Table 2.6. For most groups (Ashkenazim, Mizrahim, Russians etc.), we obtained a satisfactory number of respondents by random sampling; for the three smaller groups (Ethiopians, Druze, and Filipinos), we made do with an explorative investigation and samples. The interviews were conducted by telephone and the responses were generally given willingly. Respondents had to be aged eighteen or older. Among nonimmigrants, we defined as Ashkenazim respondents who were born in Europe or in America, or whose fathers or grandfathers were born there. We classified as Mizrahim respondents of Asian or African extraction, or whose fathers or grandfathers were similarly defined. First-generation Ashkenazi or Mizrahi respondents are those who were born abroad. Those born in Israel to foreign-born parents were defined as second generation. Third-generation respondents were those born in Israel to Israel-born fathers.

To make the data easier to compare and evaluate, we subjected them, where appropriate, to a linear transformation that re-expressed them on a scale of 0–100. Thus, if an item had five possible answers— 1 = completely agree; 2 = agree; 3 = have no idea; 4 = disagree; 5 = completely disagree—we subtracted 1 from each answer and obtained a 0–4 scale, divided the number obtained by the answer by 4, and multiplied the result by 100. This allowed us to present all possible data on a simple 0–100 scale. Since fewer than 5 percent of respondents answered "don't know" to most items, we were able to exclude this category from the calculations. Our statistical analyses made do with standard statistical tests—means, χ^2, t-test, and bidirectional variance analyses. We made several attempts to perform regression analyses but did not obtain convincing results for inherent reasons. Thus, where functional we used the answer tree technique to determine the influences of given variables on the situations that we investigated. In the following analyses, we make of the various surveys interchangeably in accordance with the items that appeared in the questionnaires.

Table 2.6. Samples Dates and Methodology[1]

Groups	Survey 1 May 1999	Survey 2 January 2000	Survey 3 August 2000	Survey 4 October 2000
Ashkenazim	400	382	505	87
Mizrahim	4000	317	429	108
3rd generation Israelis[2]	–	50	69	51
Nonreligious	200	397	517	164
Traditional	200	236	337	84
Religious	200	74	99	31
Ultra-Orthodox	200	42	50	25
Total Jewish old-timers	800	749	1003	246
Russian*	400	–	408	57
Ethiopans	–	–	50	–
Arabs**	–	410	300	302
Druzes**	–	–	150	–
Filipinos***			50	
Grand total	1200	1159	1961	605

[1] The surveys were conducted by telephone with a Hebrew questionnaire, except where indicated below.
[2] Third generation Israelis were left out in this survey.
* Questionnaire in Russian
** Questionnaire in Arabic
*** Face-to-face interview with English questionnaire

We departed from this methodology in one case: the West Bank and Gaza settlers. In view of difficulties in accessing settlements during the research years due to the Intifada, we made do with a content analysis of the settlement movement's principal organ, the journal *Nekuda*, and interviews with selected informants.

SECTION II

RELIGION AND SOCIAL (DIS)ORDER

CHAPTER THREE

THE ULTRA-ORTHODOX IN THE CITY

ULTRA-ORTHODOX ASHKENAZIM

The principal confrontations experienced by the Israeli public about the singularity of the collective involve, we have said, groups that define themselves in terms of religiosity. The Ashkenazi Ultra-Orthodox are here the major protagonist standing in opposition to the secularism of the mainstream.

Long before the establishment of the State of Israel, Ultra-Orthodox[1] viewed the national enterprise as a betrayal of the essence of Judaism, which, they say, requires Jews to work toward messianic redemption by dedicating themselves to the strict observance of the religious commandments. For them, modern nationalism is alien to Judaism and Jewish peoplehood hinges solely on religious faith. The collective identity of the Ultra-Orthodox remains loyal to the traditional version of Jewishness that entails dedication to the notion of *Am Yisrael*, the People Israel; *Elohei/Torat Yisrael*, the God/Teaching of Israel; and *Eretz Yisrael*, the Land of Israel. Among these three principles, they emphasize the second above all, since it establishes the religious principle as the unique and deep-seated singularity of Jewishness and the *raison d'être* of the other two principles. Hence, Ultra-Orthodox Jews reject modernity as a totalistic worldview and strive to control its inroads in their lives. It is in this light that they generate a profusion of markers that they evince in their daily lives in the modern city—black suits, fur hats (in some communities) and characteristic beards among men, and long dresses, dark socks, and wigs among women. Linguistic markers are the wide use of Yiddish, a symbol of Jewishness for centuries, in the community and Loyshen Koydesh, or Biblical Hebrew, for prayer and study in the yeshiva (religious academy). These markers do not, however, imply the rejection

---

[1] We use the notion of Ultra-Orthodox in the sense of Ashkenazi Ultra-Orthodox, unless differently specified (such as "Mizrahi Ultra-Orthodox").

of modernity *en bloc*. Among other examples, Ultra-Orthodox use regular and mobile phones, exploit the advantages of satellite communication, and organize in political parties.

Due to their parochial living patterns, large families, and strong affinity for lifelong religious study, few Ultra-Orthodox Jews are wealthy—although some are successful businessmen or professionals—and most tend to concentrate in the economically underprivileged strata. Because of the strength of their religious practice, however, their poverty is not reflected in a poverty culture. Yet, the dominant culture has always been hostile to this form of Judaism, which, due to its estrangement from Zionism, was never included in the national project of "ingathering the exiles." Hence, according to our parameters of collective identification, the Ultra-Orthodox represent an extreme case of "retentionism," i.e., strong unwillingness to abandon their particularism. If their strong definitions of collective identity were not enough, the underprivileged social condition of the Ultra-Orthodox, the dominant culture's disapproval of them, and their own tendency to emphasize their distinctiveness account for their unambiguous determination to avoid any form of assimilation into their surroundings. It is in this context that anthropological studies have for long insisted on the "cloistered" character of Ultra-Orthodox communities (see Friedman, 1986).

Just the same, Israeli Ultra-Orthodox have not managed to remain indifferent to Israeli society at large. Since this society is Jewish, the Ultra-Orthodox, who consider themselves the custodians of authentic Judaism, cannot but feel religious responsibility for the Jews around them. Indeed, it is by dint of the spiritual fervor of the Jewish people as a whole, they believe, that the Jews and the world will merit redemption (Ben-Rafael, 2002). In this, they see themselves as a sort of "vanguard" of the Jewish people and are convinced that their mission is to spread their version of Judaism among Jews. For these very reasons, they are prompted by their own faith, willingly or unwillingly, to involve themselves in every matter of public interest on the general Israeli scene on behalf of the values and laws of the Torah. Hence, Ultra-Orthodox (with the exception of a handful of hard-liner groups) participate in Israeli elections and try to attain political power despite their scanty demographic clout.[2] This enables

---

[2] We estimate the Ultra-Orthodox at 8 percent of the Israeli Jewish population; see below.

them to obtain concessions on behalf of their material interests and, from time to time, to promote religion-inspired national legislation.

By keeping the public at large under constant pressure, Ultra-Orthodox have deeply antagonized much of nonreligious society but, for the very same reasons, increasingly regard themselves as an intrinsic part of this society. This ever-stronger social rootedness is best reflected in language. By no means have Ultra-Orthodox renounced their diglossia—Yiddish as the vernacular and rabbinical Hebrew, spoken in an Ashkenazi inflection, for religious activity. The major fact here, however, is that in addition to and often instead of these languages, Ultra-Orthodox turn more and more to modern Hebrew, which, despite their initial resistance to what they once saw as the "Zionist disrespect for the holy tongue," has practically become their main vernacular. This Hebrew, it is true, is often characterized by "yeshivish" enunciation, heavy use of religious phrasings, rampant borrowing from Yiddish, and code-switching. Although it is a marked Hebrew, it is nevertheless Israeli Hebrew in its major intonations and vocabulary. It is on this basis that the Ultra-Orthodox are expanding their relations with society at large and, especially, with the other religious sectors closest to them outside their neighborhoods.

This relative narrowing of the gap between Ultra-Orthodox and the rest of Jewry in Israel distinguishes them from other Ultra-Orthodox communities in the world which remain, in their countries, much less involved in nonreligious public affairs (Jewish and non-Jewish). In spite of this difference, Ultra-Orthodox in Israel maintain strong ties with their counterparts all over the world—in England, Belgium, the United States, Russia, or Australia. Everywhere, one finds Ultra-Orthodox enclaves with yeshivas and related services. The strong transnational-diaspora relations among these communities are reflected in periodic world congresses, exchanges of scholars and students, and—and this is especially important here—arranged marriages among families. Paradoxically enough, for communities that have always been reticent toward, if not frankly hostile to, Zionism, Israel has come to play the role of a world center, since it is here that Ultra-Orthodox have developed the widest proliferation of devotional institutions and well-established settings of political-religious leadership. Thus, ironically, it is in Jerusalem, the capital of the State of Israel, that the Ultra-Orthodox transnational community holds its world congresses.

The President of Israel, it is true, regularly avoids these congresses in the awareness that an Ultra-Orthodox assembly would not rise to its feet for any dignitary of a nonreligious Jewish state—irrespective of protocol. It remains that one cannot describe today's Ultra-Orthodox, with the exception of small radical groups such as Naturei Karta (Guardians of the City), as anti-Zionist. Their presence in the Israeli public scene—for cooperation or for confrontation—has long made them a part of this setting for all practical purposes. Consequently, the *Moetset Gedolei ha-Torah* (the Council of Torah Sages, a panel of leading rabbinical figures that represents the supreme leadership of the Ashkenazi Ultra-Orthodox) has become a well-known institution in Israeli society at large.

   In this context, and with the purpose of shedding light on long-term developments, our research will ask Ultra-Orthodox respondents in Israel about the extent to which their attitude toward society at large still effectively reflects basic alienation—even though they rub shoulders with secular people in many spheres of activity.

RELIGIOSITY AS A GLISSANDO

Actually, a major feature of the Jewish-Israeli human landscape is that one cannot speak in terms of polarization in respect to religion, at least regarding practical behavior. When Israeli Jews in general define their attitude toward religion, they render the religious-nonreligious dichotomy wholly unsatisfactory. Many Israelis, and presumably Jews in other countries, find it difficult to answer such a question in binary yes/no terms and tend to place themselves in one of at least four categories: nonreligious, traditional, Orthodox, and Ultra-Orthodox. We strongly hesitate to call even the nonreligious "completely secular," since very few Israeli Jews defy all norms that mark the Jewish legacy. Nearly all Jewish parents, for instance, have their male babies circumcised, and no one in Israel has ever proposed transferring the day of rest from Saturday (Shabbat) to Sunday, as is the rule in the Western world. Thus, we prefer to speak of the "nonreligious" rather than of the "completely secular" or, to use the French term, *laïque*. We may define nonreligious people as those who do not observe any tradition in a religious spirit, i.e., if they do observe some traditions, they do so more in a national spirit or in deference to community norms. Beyond this category, Israel also has a large group of individuals who are reluctant to call themselves either "nonreligious" or "religious." They tend to view themselves as "observant of some traditions," such as lighting Hanukka candles, having a festive family dinner on Friday evening, attending synagogue on major festivals (especially Rosh Hashana and Yom Kippur), observing some Jewish dietary laws (kashrut) (such as refraining from eating pork), and so on. These people feel at ease with the label "traditional," which expresses the importance they attach to cultural continuity in community and family. The next category is comprised of those who define themselves as "religious," i.e., committed to the imperatives of the faith—nay even, mostly, to the Halakha, the Talmudic Law—but still fully immersed in modernity with respect to occupational life, consumption styles and educational philosophy. At the end of the continuum are the Ultra-Orthodox (Haredim)—and we mix here Ashkenzi and Mizrahi Ultra-Orthodox in one category—who pledge their lives to the observance of the commandments, foremost in the sense of religious study, and who usually belong to one of the Ultra-Orthodox denominations. In brief, we have here a glissando of sorts, in which a majority belong to the nonreligious and traditional categories and minorities to the religious and the Ultra-Orthodox.

Our data, which focus on the sociocultural background of religiosity and the variety of identity attitudes, confirm this depiction. We found that 51 percent of Israeli Jews define themselves as nonreligious, 32 percent as traditional, 11 percent as religious, and 6 percent as Ultra-Orthodox.[3] Apart from the predominance of the nonreligious (half of the population) and the traditional (another third), Table 3.1 illustrates the complex ethnocultural contours of the distribution of religiosity in Israeli society when one distinguishes Ashkenazim from Mizrahim by first (born abroad) and second (born in the country but fathers born abroad) generations but does not define third-generation (or more) Israeli Jews in terms of ethnic origin. In all, 37 percent of respondents were born abroad, 40 percent are second-generation Israelis, and 23 percent are third-generation Israelis. The Ultra-Orthodox are predominantly Ashkenazi and this widely includes most probably the one-third who are third-generation

---

[3] This finding is consistent with many other surveys, but the real percentage of Ultra-Orthodox is probably higher in view of their natural reticence to answer researchers' questions and thus not to appear in survey samples. Thus, we estimate the share of Ultra-Orthodox at around 8 percent.

Israelis.[4] Among the religious, Mizrahim and Ashkenazim are more or less equally represented—from 40 percent to one-third—while third-generation Israelis are one quarter. Among the traditional, however, Mizrahim hold the lead at nearly 60 percent while Ashkenazim are but one-fourth, slightly less than third-generation Israelis. Ashkenazim also prevail among the nonreligious: half of the nonreligious respondents were Ashkenazim while the others were evenly divided between Mizrahim and third-generation Israelis. Thus, the Ultra-Orthodox are mainly Ashkenazi, the religious are an integrative category, the traditional are overwhelmingly Mizrahi, and the nonreligious are primarily Ashkenazi.

From the perspective of origin groups, blatant differences separate Mizrahim and Ashkenazim: Ashkenazim belong mostly to the nonreligious category, even though a small minority of Ashkenazim suffices to constitute a majority of the Ultra-Orthodox. Mizrahim concentrate among the traditional, while the religious are the most mixed category. Overall, religiosity correlates with origin but does not create a polarization effect. There are Ashkenazi majorities at both ends of the continuum and, of the two in-between categories, one is mixed and another has a Mizrahi majority. Thus, in this respect, the boundaries between categories are somewhat vague. Moreover and interestingly enough, third-generation Israelis, a minority of less than one-fourth, share the in-between distributions and, thereby, help to make the general picture even less dichotomous.

Turning to the generation effect, we find that second-generation Israelis tend to be less religious than their parents among both Mizrahim and Ashkenazim but especially among Mizrahim. The distribution of Israel-born Mizrahim by religiosity strongly resembles that of foreign-born Ashkenazim in this respect. In other words, the differentiation by religiosity between Ashkenazim and Mizrahim is tending to narrow. This clashes with the impression one may gain by focusing on the current Israeli scene, in which religiosity is a banner around which much political energy is mobilized.

The glissando perspective is still reinforced when we relate religiosity to aspects of collective identity such as subjects' identification

---

[4] The Jewish population of the 1920s and 1930s, in the country, were overwhelmingly Ashkenazi (more than 90 percent).

Table 3.1. Sociocultural Divisions and Religiosity among Israeli Jews

Categories	Mizrahim		Total	Ashkenazim		Total	3rd gen.	Total
	1st gen	2nd gen		1st gen.	2nd gen.			
Ultra-Orthodox (N = 49)	4	5	5	5	8	6	8	6
Religious (N = 87)	17	11	13	9	10	10	10	11
Traditional (N = 255)	51	45	47	26	15	21	29	32
Nonreligious (N = 408)	28	39	35	60	67	63	53	51
Total	100	100	100	100	100	100	100	100
Total N	90	183	273	203	152	323	183	799

** Cramer's V = .17**. Source: Survey 3.

with the country, as measured by their wishes to live in Israel and have their children live in Israel. An overwhelmingly large majority (nearly 90 percent) wants to live in Israel, with little variance among the categories. Thus, 83 percent of the nonreligious, 86 percent of the traditional, and 97 percent of the religious and the Ultra-Orthodox see Israel as their home. Religiosity plainly adds an edge to respondents' attachment to the country (Israel has always been the "holy land" in their eyes),[5] but this attitude is also strong among nonreligious Israelis.

Much more significant differences were found, however, in parents' wish that their children live in Israel, even though the same trend is evident. When we add the positive and the strongly positive attitudes, we obtain mean scores from 87 to 97 in all four categories. However, when we isolate the strongly positive from all other attitudes, we find 55 percent of the nonreligious, 77 percent of the traditional, 85 percent of the Ultra-Orthodox, and 91 percent of the religious. The steepest drop-off occurs among the nonreligious.[6] This may be explained by citing the relatively greater willingness of the nonreligious to leave decisions to their children and to value other cultures and societies. Another explanation is that the nonreligious

---

[5] Cramer's V = 0.13**.
[6] Kendall's tau-c = .19**.

are more aloof than the other categories to the ethnocentric emphasis that one finds in the Jewish faith and symbols. Be this as it may,
the findings indicate that the differences may be real and may point
to genuine cleavages.

RELIGIOSITY, NATIONAL IDENTITIES, AND ETHNICITY

Indeed, additional data show that religiosity may set population
groups against each other. Although Table 3.2 indicates that, generally
speaking, a large majority of Israelis consider themselves integral
members of society, it also brings out differences that are incompatible
with the simple notion of a religious-to-nonreligious continuum.

The Ultra-Orthodox, who fully identify with Israel in the sense
noted above, are also the ones who feel *least* involved in society. We
may interpret the discrepancy by suggesting that religiosity, with its
emphasis on the holiness of Eretz Yisrael, accounts for their attachment to the country while the predominantly nonreligious character
of Israeli society explains their low level of identification with it.
Interestingly, the nonreligious are not the category that most closely
identifies with society; in fact, the traditional and the religious exhibit
stronger degrees of identification. To interpret these findings, we suggest that once individuals do identify with a society due to their
national orientation, the fact that they also share an adhesion to traditional norms and religious values strengthens their nationalism
even more.

Table 3.2. Do You Consider Yourself an Integral
Part of Israeli Society? (Percent)*

	Not at all	To some extent	Yes/ much so	Total
Ultra-Orthodox (N = 48)	21	17	62	100
Religious (N = 87)	1	7	92	100
Traditional (N = 255)	3	11	86	100
Nonreligious (N = 408)	4	20	76	100
Total	4	16	80	100
N	36	125	632	793

* Cramer's V = .18**, Kendall's tau c = −.11**. Source: Survey 3.

Table 3.3. Do You Wish to Live in Israel?*

If you had a choice, in which country would you choose to live?

Respondents (N = 798)	Israel	Other than Israel	Total
Ultra-Orthodox (N = 48)	96	4	100
Religious (N = 87)	97	3	100
Traditional (N = 255)	83	17	100
Nonreligious (N = 408)	86	14	100

* Cramer's V = .13**, Kendall's tau c = .05*. Source: Survey 3.

Table 3.4. Do You Want Your Children to Live in Israel?*

Categories (N = 800)	Very much	Yes	Not much	No	Total
Ultra-Orthodox (N = 48)	86	10	4	0	100
Religious (N = 88)	91	7	1	1	100
Traditional (N = 256)	77	18	3	2	100
Nonreligious (N = 408)	56	32	8	4	100

* Cramer's V = .18**; Kendall's tau c = .19**. Source: Survey 3.

We also found a correspondence between religiosity and a strong wish to live in Israel for oneself as well as for one's children: Ultra-Orthodox and religious respondents are followed, in this respect, by the traditional and the nonreligious, with the last-mentioned clearly at the least "pro-Israeli" end of the continuum. This means, in contrast to sociological common sense, that identification with the nation and its major symbol does not necessarily correlate directly and positively with aspirations to be a part of the nation's society and to have one's children be so. These aspirations relate as well—and, seemingly, with greater strength—to individuals' attitudes toward religion and the meanings they give to the country and to living there.

Having observed the correlation between religion and origin, we also wanted at this point to ask respondents about their attitudes toward ethnic allegiances. Again we found a glissando among the categories: the less religious the respondents are, the less ethnic they tend to feel. For the nonreligious, the importance of ethnic allegiances is close to nil, the religious and the traditional stand in the middle, and the Ultra-Orthodox show a clear tendency to emphasize their ethnicity. Adding to these data the fact that the gradation of ethnic allegiances does not follow the differentiation found in regard to involvement in Israeli society, we are definitely invited to conclude that the findings point to the existence of different models and not just to a glissando effect.

Table 3.5 reinforces this conclusion. The table focuses on the collective identity that respondents value most—Israeli, Jewish, or ethnocultural—commensurate with their degree of religiosity. This question yielded an interesting picture: the Ultra-Orthodox, understandably, feel Jewish above all, although an important cohort among them, which takes Jewishness for granted when everyone in the society at issue is Jewish, emphasizes "Ashkenaziness" or—though much less—"Mizrahiness." The religious also display a strong commitment to Jewishness, but they rank "Israeliness," and not ethnicity, second. The traditional also rate Jewishness highest and feel more Israeli than ethnic. Among the nonreligious, Israeliness leads by far in this respect.

Table 3.5. To What Group Do You Feel You First Belong? (Percent)*

	Ashk.	Mizr.	Total ethnic	Israeli	Jewish	Total national	Total
Ultra-Orthodox (N = 48)	21	8	29	6	65	71	100
Religious (N = 88)	5	5	10	17	73	90	100
Tradition (N = 256)	6	9	15	40	45	85	100
Nonreligious (N = 408)	18	4	22	65	12	77	100

* Cramer's V = .33**. Source: Survey 3.

Table 3.6 shows that the Ultra-Orthodox are the most ethnic-oriented (ethnicity plays a significant role in the lives of about 60 percent of them) and that the nonreligious have the weakest ethnic feelings (only 15 percent consider ethnicity of at least "some importance" in their lives). The religious and the traditional stand in the middle of the continuum (nearly 40 percent in each category). This confirms that the large nonreligious strata, which are predominantly Ashkenazi in origin, tend to see themselves as non ethnic *and* are estranged from religiosity.

When we add the generation effect shown in Table 3.1, which points to declining religiosity from parents to offspring, we can only conclude that the ethnic cleavage as well is seemingly on the decline, from this perspective. Overall, a clearly different pattern of relating to society and community appears in each category of religiosity.

Table 3.6. How Important Is Your Ethnic Allegiance in Your Life?*

	Not	Slightly	Somewhat	Very	Total
Ultra-Orthodox	25	17	19	39	100
Religious	45	16	22	17	100
Tradition	45	17	24	14	100
Nonreligious	66	19	11	4	100
N	434	140	134	85	793

* Cramer's V = .20**; Kendall's tau c = .22**; Source: Survey 3.

* Jewishness in conjunction with ethnicity among the Ultra-Orthodox;
* Jewishness as nationhood among the religious;
* Nationalism coupled with primordialism among the traditional;
* Heightened nationalism among the nonreligious.

These differences, to be sure, fuel religious—or more accurately, religiosity—conflicts.

MEANINGS OF RELIGIOSITY AND CONFLICT

Table 3.7 shows that Jewishness—as such, and not necessarily Jewish religiosity—is an important constituent of the identity of Israeli Jews in all categories of religiosity. It also shows, however, that the non-religious attach relatively less importance to this aspect. This means that the religious camps are more committed—under their own formulations—to a collective identity that is shared by all or, at least, by a large majority. On the other hand, it also appears that the nonreligious and the traditional are by no means hesitant or undetermined in their attitude toward their nonreligiosity or traditionalism, respectively.

We did not present this question to Orthodox and Ultra-Orthodox respondents, because it would have expressed mistrust about their declared self-definitions. Be this as it may, we find camps that view themselves as effectively contrasting with each other. The contrast is most acute at the extremes, i.e., the nonreligious and the Ultra-Orthodox. Nearly half of the respondents in both of these categories perceive themselves as having stronger attitudes in their orientations—which are opposed and divergent—than their parents. The religious,

Table 3.7. Jewishness and Religiosity

Issues	Scale	Nonrelig	Trad	Relig	Ultra-O
Importance of Jewishness in your life	Yes	67	94	97	100
Is your attitude to religion a matter of belief?	Yes	74	74	n.a.*	n.a.*
Do you have a stronger approach to religion than your parents?	Yes	42	22	26	47
	Same	51	29	60	46
	Less	7	48	14	7
N		408	255	87	49

* n.a. stands for "not asked." Source: Survey 3.

in contrast, were more likely to assess their approach as the continuation of their parents'. Moreover, Table 3.8, in a finding that reinforces what we have already seen, shows that nearly half of the traditional (twice the percentage as in the opposite case) say that they are less traditional than their parents, which in this case means that parents were generally more religious than they are. In view of the importance of traditional people in the Israeli public, it appears again that one may speak of a trend—not very strong but still real—of disengagement from religiosity over generations.

Table 3.9, moreover, shows that the overall picture carries a high potential for conflict. While the traditional and the religious, are quite close to each other, the Ultra-Orthodox and the nonreligious, tend to frankly oppose each other. Nonreligious people feel involved in a state of active conflict with the Ultra-Orthodox, who reciprocate although with less acrimony. The Ultra-Orthodox seem to be convinced that they are acting in the best interests of the nonreligious; the nonreligious definitely do not feel that they behave the same way toward the Ultra-Orthodox. The nonreligious seem to feel more threatened by the Ultra-Orthodox than the other way around, even though the conflict is by no means one-sided. On the other hand, the traditional and the religious do not overemphasize such tensions as may characterize their relationship.

Turning to perceptions of power relations (Table 3.10), we find paradoxically that the nonreligious—who, more often than the traditional, the religious and, above all, the Ultra-Orthodox, are well-to-do—feel the most deprived. Among members of other categories, the strongest perception is that no side is particularly deprived.

Interestingly, traditional-minded respondents who tend to feel some-what less powerful than the religious do not have this feeling vis-à-vis the nonreligious. This corroborates that religion in Israeli society effectively constitutes as a factor of power—or at least is perceived this way by many.

Few people in any category feel that they faced discrimination due to their religiosity (Table 3.10). Only among the Ultra-Orthodox does a large minority have complaints on this score. However, both religiosity and nonreligiosity are strong factors in self-segregation; the nonreligious are the most self-segregated, followed by the Ultra-Orthodox and, at some distance, by the religious (Table 3.11). Again we see that the traditional category holds a middle-of-the-road position.

In the same vein, Table 3.12 shows that the Ultra-Orthodox are inclined to be closest to people of their own persuasion but are rel-atively open to the traditional and the religious as well. At the other end of the spectrum, the nonreligious are less blatantly alienated from the Ultra-Orthodox than the other way around. The tradi-tional and the religious also seem much more reticent toward the Ultra-Orthodox than toward the nonreligious. Things are somewhat different when it comes to marriage, the ultimate level of socializing (Table 3.13). Ultra-Orthodox are definitely the least open, followed by the religious. The most open are the traditional, followed at a short distance by the nonreligious. It also appears that the nonreli-gious are the least desirable group for the Ultra-Orthodox and the religious and that the Ultra-Orthodox consider even the traditional undesirable, an assessment that the traditional do not reciprocate. Concurrently, Ultra-Orthodox are unanimously the least desirable category for the traditional and the nonreligious. However, while the nonreligious largely consider the religious undesirable, the religious extend the range of undesirability to the traditional, despite the lat-ter's affinity for them.

Table 3.8. Religiosity over Generations and by Origin*

Are you more or less religious than your parents?		Less	Same	More	Total
Ultra-Orthodox (N = 49)	Mizrahi	5	35	60	100
	Ashkenazi	5	63	33	100
	M+A	6	47	47	100
Religious (N = 87)	Mizrahi	21	52	28	100
	Ashkenazi	12	55	33	100
	M+A	15	60	26	100
Traditional (N = 255)	Mizrahim	53	33	14	100
	Ashkenazi	45	39	16	100
	M+A	48	30	22	100
Nonreligious (N = 411)	Mizrahi	60	32	8	100
	Ashkenazi	46	45	9	100
	M+A	42	51	7	100

* Mizrahim: Cramer's V = .35**; Kendall's tau c = .46**; Ashkenazim: Cramer's V = .26**; Kendall's tau c = .32**; Ashkenazim+Mizrahim: Cramer's V = .24**; Kendall's tau c = .17**. Source: Survey 3.

Table 3.9. Perceived Tensions in the Context of Religiosity (Percent)

To what extent is there tension between:	Respondents	Severe tension	Some tension	No tension	Total
Traditional and religious	Traditional	23	31	46	100
	Religious	2	18	80	100
Nonreligious and Ultra-Orthodox	Nonreligious	69	19	12	100
	Ultra-Orthodox	47	22	31	100

Source: Survey 3.

Table 3.10. Perceived Deprivation on Grounds of Religiosity (Percent)

Who is more deprived?		My group	The same	The other
Traditional vs. religious	Traditional	37	49	10
Traditional vs. nonreligious	Traditional	15	69	12
Religious vs. nonreligious	Religious	26	67	4
Nonrel vs. Ultra-Orthodox	Nonreligious	61	23	9
Tradit vs. Ultra-Orthodox	Ultra-Orthodox	39	56	3

Source: Survey 3.

Table 3.11. Religiosity and Personal Experience of Discrimination (Percent)

Issues	Scale	Nonrelig (N = 411)	Traditional (N = 252)	Religious (N = 87)	Ultra-Orth (N = 48)
Have you personally experienced discrimination due to your kind of religiosity?	Yes, negative	23	7	21	40
	Never	74	91	70	57
	Yes, positive	2	1	8	3
Total (N = 798)		100	99	99	100

Source: Survey 3.

Interestingly, the religious and the traditional—the groups in the middle of the spectrum—differ from each other in their relative distance from the extremes of the continuum; the religious are closer to the Ultra-Orthodox and the traditional to the nonreligious.

Table 3.12. Social Distance*

Do your close friends belong to your group? religiosity	All or nearly all	Half and half	Nearly none/ none	Index of closure*	Total
Ultra-Orthodox (N = 49)	58	37	5	5.4	100
Religious (N = 87)	22	61	17	0.7	100
Traditional (N = 255)	89	11	0	1.7	100
Nonreligious (N = 411)	63	30	6		100
Respondents (N = 802)	73	25	2	13.0	100

* The ratio of expected responses to observed responses. Cramer's V = .38**; Kendall's tau c = .35**. Source: Survey 3.

Table 3.13. Willingness to Accept "Intermarriage" (Percent)*

Would you agree to see your daughter marry a Jew who is:		Non-religious	Traditional	Religious	Ultra-Orthodox
Ultra-Orthodox	Certainly/yes	n.a.	29	0	0
(N = 48)	No/by no means	47	0	0	
Religious	Certainly/yes	39	n.a.	47	19
(N = 87)	No/by no means	18		16	33
Traditional	Certainly/yes	23	79	n.a.	81
(N = 255)	No/by no means	52	4		2
Nonreligious	Certainly/yes	13	37	62	n.a.
(N = 411)	No/by no means	72	20	4	

* n.a. = not asked; Cramer's V = .23**. Source: Survey 3.

DIFFERENT CULTURES

Beyond different degrees of religiosity, these categories illustrate different perspectives on the collective, society, and the world. Thus, Table 3.14 shows first that there is a genuine tendency to polarization when it comes to the Jewish-religious nature of Israeli culture. The Ultra-Orthodox strongly favor a greater emphasis on this aspect than exists today, and the nonreligious, on the contrary—but more mildly—favor a weaker emphasis. The religious are much less militant in this respect than the Ultra-Orthodox but are still closer to them than to the nonreligious, while the traditional are more attracted by the secular pole.

Concurrently, as Table 3.15 indicates, the Ultra-Orthodox are by no means—and in contradiction to widely held prejudices—hostile to Western culture. In this respect, they are close to the religious, who actually seem less tolerant. The traditional are again in the middle and the nonreligious are the staunchest champions of Western culture. All four categories regard the present situation favorably in this respect.

When it comes to the democratic nature of the State of Israel and its concomitant ambition to be a Jewish state, however, we again find a clear tendency to polarization. Table 3.16 points out a very wide gap between the Jewish orientation of the Ultra-Orthodox and the democratic orientation of the nonreligious, again with both the religious and the traditional in the middle—closer to the Ultra-Orthodox and closer to the nonreligious, respectively.

Table 3.14. Attitudes toward the Jewish Religious
Nature of Israeli Culture (Percent)*

In comparison with the current situation, Israeli culture should be . . .	Ultra-Orth	Religious	Traditional	Nonreligion	Total
Much less Jewish	0	3	5	24	14
Slightly less Jewish	2	0	15	29	20
As it is	10	29	45	38	38
Slightly more Jewish	10	31	24	7	16
More Jewish	78	37	11	2	13
Total	100	100	100	100	101
N	50	96	322	471	939

* Cramer's V = .39; **Kendall's tau c = −.44**. Source: Survey 3.

Table 3.15. Attitudes toward the Western Nature of Israeli Culture*

In comparison with the current situation, Israeli culture should be . . .	Ultra-Orth	Religious	Traditional	Nonreligion	Total
Much less Western	11	10	7	1	4
Slightly less Western	16	23	10	9	11
As it is	42	46	57	46	50
Slightly more Western	26	13	15	22	19
More Western	5	8	11	22	16
Total	100	100	100	100	100
N	19	48	169	218	454

* Cramer's V = .15; **Kendall's tau c = .13**. Source: Survey 3.

Each group thus has its own perspective on the desirable "contents" or values of Israeli society as a whole. For the Ultra-Orthodox, Israel should be a Jewish state first and a democracy second. For the non-religious, the priorities are reversed. The religious lean strongly toward the Ultra-Orthodox stance; the traditional tend toward that of the nonreligious. While these findings tend to blur the distinction between the Ultra-Orthodox and the religious and between the nonreligious and the traditional, things are different when one addresses a specific issue such as exemption from military service, a matter that relates to the basic attitude of the Ultra-Orthodox toward Israeli society. The Ultra-Orthodox, who see Judaism mainly as a religion, demand that Jews who wish to pledge themselves to religious studies should be exempt from the military. It is important to bear in mind that the Ultra-Orthodox themselves came to Israel as an expression of their religious devotion and emphatically not by virtue of any political or nationalist project. Thus, for them, defending Israel from external threats is less important than complying with the imperatives of the faith, for faith alone will lead the Jewish people to salvation—and, until then, will also protect the Jewish people from its enemies.

Table 3.16. Israel as a Democracy versus Israel as a Jewish State (Percent)*

Which would you prefer: Israel as a democracy or Israel as a Jewish state?	Ultra- Orthodox	Religious	Traditional	Nonreligion	Total
Jewish state	84	59	32	9	26
Both equally important	10	30	34	29	30
Democratic state	6	10	34	63	45
Total	100	99	100	101	101
N	50	96	332	493	971

* Cramer's V = .37**; **Kendall's tau c = .41**. Source: Survey 3.

As we have seen, the modern Orthodox—mainly the National Religious—illustrate a contrary tendency: to endorse Jewish nationalism and the building of a Jewish state in Israel as a holy task in itself. Hence, they have developed a staunch nationalist outlook that emphasizes the acceptance of national duties—above all, military service. In this respect, they and the Ultra-Orthodox are unbridgeably divorced. Table 3.17 reflects this well; it shows that the religious are much closer to the traditional and the nonreligious than to the Ultra-Orthodox even though they may display more understanding for the difficulties of the Ultra-Orthodox (not for themselves, of course) than the other two categories.

Another point where this divorce is apparent is the item discussed in Table 3.18—the question of restricting "indecent" advertising. This issue, which comes up from time to time, concerns advertisements for women's swimsuits or revealing garments. The Ultra-Orthodox often organize mass rallies to protest against public posters or billboards in their neighborhoods. This attitude indicates how determined the Ultra-Orthodox are to reject given aspects of contemporary lifestyles. In this respect, however, we see again that the attitudes of the religious and the traditional are far from those of Ultra-Orthodox and converge with those of the nonreligious.

Table 3.17. Exemption from Military Service (Percent)*

The military service is important but religious women, Ultra-Orthodox men, Arabs, and pacifist should be exempt	Ultra-Orthodox	Religious	Traditional	Nonreligious	Total
Oppose	27	56	74	78	72
Compromise	23	24	13	14	15
Agree	50	20	13	9	13
Total	100	100	100	101	100
N	48	95	334	494	971

* Cramer's V = .19**; Kendall's tau c = .16**. Source: Survey 3.

Table 3.18. Restrictions on Indecent Advertising (Percent)*

Indecent advertising should be forbidden.	Ultra-Orthodox	Religious	Traditional	Non-religious	Total
Opposed	13	58	76	90	78
Neutral	13	2	6	3	5
Agree	74	40	18	7	17
Total	100	100	100	100	100
N	23	50	175	239	487

* Cramer's V = .27**; Kendall's tau c = .26**. Source: Survey 3.

Table 3.19. The Necessity of Mutual Concessions among Religious Categories (Percent)*

Who should make concessions in religious–non-religious relations?	Nonrelig only	Chiefly nonrelig	Both sides	Chiefly religious	Relig only	Total	N
Ultra-Orthodox	11	11	75	2	0	100	44
Religious	2	8	89	1	0	100	83
Traditional	0	13	75	10	2	100	247
Nonreligious	1	1	60	29	9	100	391
Total	2	6	69	18	5	100	765

* Cramer's V = .26**; Kendall's tau c = −.25**. Source: Survey 3.

Respondents in all categories agree, however, that "both sides" should make concessions to ease social tensions. Remarkably, the nonreligious are the least eager to endorse this position.

CONCLUSION

This chapter focused on the Ultra-Orthodox in the context of the more general question about the role of religion in defining Israeli Jews' collective identity. We chose this strategy after observing that religiosity among Jews—including Israeli Jews—is a matter of degree and definitely not an either-or dichotomy, even among those who declare themselves "nonreligious." At its extreme, Judaism is the religion of which even the most "antireligious" think when they define themselves as "not religious." In other words, Jews find it much easier to say that they are not religious than to profess "no religion." For an overwhelming majority of Jews, to think in terms of another religion—even in the sense of *not* professing it—means positioning oneself outside the bounds of Jewishness. Hence, the Israeli nonreligious can hardly embark on radical "antireligious" militantism without exposing themselves to the charge of being "anti-Jewish." The religious principle, whether or not endorsed at the level of personal beliefs, simply constitutes, in one way or another, a component of individuals' perception of the singularity of the collective. This principle pertains to all phrasings of individuals' Jewish collective identity—be they religious or nonreligious, which is actually confirmed by national and comprehensive surveys (Katz, 1997; Levy, 1996).

This statement is also confirmed by the fact that the nonreligious are truly antagonistic to the religious only in regard to extreme religiosity, that of the Ultra-Orthodox, who actually seem to be a genuine focal point of hostile feelings. Even so, Ultra-Orthodox do not reciprocate this antagonism with the same virulence. Ultra-Orthodox seem more inclined than the nonreligious to understate their antagonism. This is congruent with the assumption we emit that Ultra-Orthodox aspire to influence society and not just to struggle against it, as also illustrated by their adoption of modern Hebrew and their rapprochement with the national scene over the years.

This, however, does not gainsay the reality of conflicts. Israelis' attitudes toward religion vary among respondent and individuals in the various groups do not identify with the collective identity with equal emphasis. In the context of the longstanding link between Judaism and peoplehood, the religious' belief that Judaism conveys a "truth" unattainable by nonbelievers explains why they feel not only that their versions of collective identity draw on revered traditions but also that they draw out the *authentic* collective identity. For these very reasons, the religious—and *a fortiori* the Ultra-Orthodox that firmly regard their dedication as the sole path to the messianic era—are convinced that they have an edge over the nonreligious, in spite of the fact that they never were a dominant group in Israeli society. Yet, it remains that many traditional and nonreligious Jews perceive themselves as less observant than their parents, indicating a clear tendency to declining religiosity in the Jewish population over the generations—even though religiosity *per se* remains an important source of conflict. Thus, many respondents on both the nonreligious and the Ultra-Orthodox sides describe themselves as more determined in their *divergent* attitudes toward religion than their parents. This conflictual characteristic of the field takes on a peculiar form when it is emphasized more strongly by the less-religious than the more-religious.

This undoubtedly shows that the less-religious feel more threatened by the more-religious—specifically by Ultra-Orthodox—than vice-versa. The more-religious, especially the Ultra-Orthodox, seem convinced that they are acting in the best interests of the less-religious. The nonreligious and the traditional have no such conviction vis-à-vis the religious in general and the Ultra-Orthodox in particular. Again, the only way to account for this is by stressing the singular role of religion, however phrased, in Jews' collective identity. This question of legitimacy may well explain why the nonreligious, who have always been the leading force in Israeli society, feel vulnerable to the Ultra-Orthodox, a relatively small minority composed largely of impoverished and very large families in which husbands often spend their lives at religious study that provides hardly any remuneration.

It is in the same context that Ultra-Orthodox feel more than the nonreligious that they are victims of personal discrimination, but they feel less so than them—the nonreligious, are more likely to be well-off—that they are victims of collective deprivation. An additional indicator of this antagonism, the nonreligious and Ultra-Orthodox also come across as self-segregative, leaving the religious and the traditional to be much more open to each other and to both the nonreligious and the Ultra-Orthodox. Other data substantiate this picture (see Table 3.20 for a condensed presentation.) The nonreligious, as we have shown, distance themselves from all other groups more than the other groups distance themselves from them. Since the nonreligious are the strongest stratum in Israeli society, this also signifies and explains why they are a major focal point of social conflict and tension. All in all, the main conflict that divides Israeli Jews with respect to religiosity is the one that opposes Ultra-Orthodox and the nonreligious.

In this conflict, Ultra-Orthodox may rely on the religious and, sometimes, on the traditional for support of exigencies related to their sectorial interests or the imposition of general rulings compatible with rabbinical law. At day's end, however, they and they alone are the core group in the struggle against the nonreligious for the expansion of the role of religion in Israel.

Although the nonreligious widely surpass the Ultra-Orthodox in numbers and resources, our data show that the latter are by no means at a total disadvantage in this struggle. The Ultra-Orthodox are by far the most cohesive category, which grants it power that is still multiplied by the legitimacy they enjoy as self-appointed "guardians" of symbols and traditions that are honored by the many. Our data, indeed, do not point to any transformative change in the Ultra-Orthodox collective identity. Today's Ultra-Orthodox, like those of decades ago (Ben-Rafael, 2003), still seem to endorse fully a conception of Jewish singularity that is conditioned by their attachment to the ancestral Jewish faith and commandments.

Their commitment to Jews in general, and to fellow Ultra-Orthodox Jews in particular, is grounded in the understanding of their own role as the dedicated standard-bearers of the faith that, in their view, singularizes the Jewish people up to now. Last but not least, their profound attachment to Judaism over Israeliness explains why they continue clearly to represent the case of a transnational diaspora that is attached both to the Jewish world at large—especially the Ultra-Orthodox world—and the Jewish society in which they live, and which they wish to influence.

This loyalty to the Ultra-Orthodox collective identity as formulated several generations ago, cannot, however, prevent exposure to the influence of the Jewish society amidst which they live. Thus, Ultra-Orthodox are showing signs of convergence with Israeli culture, possibly more so than the Ultra-Orthodox in America, England, and Belgium are converging with the American, English, and Belgian cultures. These aspects, we believe, relate to our original research question about Ultra-Orthodox's identification. In this respect, our

Table 3.20. Identity and Identification Variables and Religiosity

Religiosity—from more to less	Kendall's Tau c	Cramer's V
Identification with (Jewish/Israeli) collective	—	**33.
Close friends in other religiosity groups[2]	**35.	**38.
Belongingness to Israeli society[1]	**11.	**18.
Wish to live in Israel[1]	*0.5	**13.
Wish for children to live in Israel[1]	**19.–	**18.
Intergenerational difference[3]	**17.	**24.
Religiosity-based feelings of discrimination[2]	—	**17.
The Jewish religious character of Israeli culture[1]	**44.–	**39.
Israel as a Jewish state and/or a democratic state[1]	**41.	**37.
Exempting the Ultra-Orthodox from military service[1]	**16.	**19.
Controlling advertisements for immodest clothing[1]	**26.	**27.
Mutual concessions by religious and nonreligious[1]	**25.–	**26.

[1] The more religious one is, the more one tends to define oneself as Jewish, the more one aspires to a more Jewish culture in Israel, the more one feels that a Jewish state is more important than a democratic one, the more one feels attached to Israeli society, the more one wishes to live in Israel (including one's children), the more agreeable one is to the exemption of Ultra-Orthodox or other groups from military service, the more one opposes immodest advertisements, and the more one tends to demand concessions by the secular.

[2] The socially closest categories are those at the two extremes, the secular and the Ultra-Orthodox. The more socially open categories are the two in-between categories, the traditional and the religious. The two extremes also feel a stronger sense of discrimination due to religiosity than to the two in-between categories.

[3] The Ultra-Orthodox are tending to identify more strongly with the religious category; the secular and the traditional are leaning toward secularization; and the religious tend to continuity.

findings in no way show that the Ultra-Orthodox are profoundly alienated from contemporary Israeli society. The Ultra-Orthodox category appears to be relatively close to much of this society. What is more, we found in no few respects that the Ultra-Orthodox, contrary to expectations, exhibit a sense of vacillation and lack of self-assertiveness vis-à-vis their environment. These findings, we think, bring out an aspect of the Israeli Ultra-Orthodox condition that previous works rarely stressed: the chronic crisis that the Ultra-Orthodox have been experiencing ever since Judaism entered modernity, a condition that the circumstances of this society have modified and, possibly, aggravated in some respects. The Ultra-Orthodox, as we have seen, are committed to the retention of their calling despite all the distractions that hedonistic modernity offers. The purpose of their numerous signifiers is to protect them and to signal that they are "not like others." In Israel, however, the Ultra-Orthodox are committed, by their own faith and imperatives, to try not only to protect themselves but also to enter the contest for influence and to expose

themselves more than anywhere else to modern realities. Their task
is undoubtedly more difficult in Israel than abroad, where they live
among Gentiles: in Israel they must make a greater effort to retain
their identification with their ambitious collective goals.

It is in this context that the Ultra-Orthodox have probably been
losing some of their cohesion over the years. One indicator concerns
political behavior. This group, we know, has—by religious conviction—the highest birth rate of all groups in Israel, while the number of Ultra-Orthodox delegates to the Knesset Israeli has been stable
at five or six out of 120 (4–5 percent) over the decades, even though
the population group is believed to have grown to 7–8 percent of
the population. Ostensibly, part of the answer is that some children
in this sector have moved to less religious categories. This, however,
cannot be the entire answer, since even if two or three children out
of ten leave the community, enough remain to allow for demographic
increase. Thus, one cannot but consider the possibility that many
Ultra-Orthodox vote for parties other than their own,[7] following their
personal political preferences and in disregard of the explicit direc-
tives of their rabbis. Moreover, no few youngsters and young adults
have committed themselves to the political game of the Zionists, got-
ten close to the National Religious—especially the more radical
ones—and formed a new brand of Ultra-Orthodoxy, namely "national-
ultra-orthodoxy," "Hardal," which eventually joined the settlers on
the West Bank (Horowitz, 1996).

In a change of similar conceptual nature, as recent research has
shown (Ben-Chaim, 2003), many Ultra-Orthodox women today take
part in programs of academic education (with the support of Ultra-
Orthodox institutions) to obtain diplomas that will help them to
become not only breadwinners for husbands who dedicate themselves to religious study but also breadwinners with careers, in which
they will be susceptible to new horizons and interests. This mode is
bound to damage the cohesion of the community by creating new
foci of reference among women that are external to their milieu. As
another example, we also know of tens of young Haredim who enroll
in the army (in units especially conceived for them: "nakhal haredi"),

---

[7] Agudath Israel and Degel Hatora are the two Ashkenazi Ultra-Orthodox parties that ran for elections in Parliament; they represent different configurations of
the major Ultra-Orthodox groups and in most cases make up a united front.

and this time against the explicit exhortation of rabbis who, in this case, are unable to inflict any sanction.

In other words, one can no longer describe the Israeli Ultra-Orthodox community as an enclave. While the tenets of their collective identity still hold, the nature of their identification has changed and is tending to weaken the ramparts that separate them from the rest of Israeli Jewry.

CHAPTER FOUR

SETTLERS AS A CLEAVAGE

The Challenge of the National Religious

Chapter 3 showed that the main source of friction in Israel's religious diversity is the cleavage of the Ultra-Orthodox versus the nonreligious. Additional religiosity-related tensions pertain mainly to the religious category in which the Ultra-Orthodox are not included, that is, the National Religious. Chapter 3 found that the National Religious (hereinafter, for brevity's sake, the "religious") are often closer to the nonreligious than to the Ultra-Orthodox and that the nonreligious, in turn, are not overly estranged from the religious. In terms of religiosity per se, the religious certainly constitute a weaker focal point of pressure than the Ultra-Orthodox.

Our study thus far, however, also noted that the religious are committed to a political undertaking that, in certain respects, places them, too, at the far end of a spectrum. The project at issue, of course, is the "Greater Israel" enterprise, which is no less radical in significance than the project of the Ultra-Orthodox. Our survey did not take up this aspect because it belongs less to the issue of religiosity than to a field in which religiosity is interconnected with national, political, and ideological aspirations, i.e., security policies and strategies in regard to the territories that Israel has occupied since the 1967 Six-Day War. In this sphere, the religious face opponents (from left-of-center to far-left) and make alliances (from right-of-center to far-right) that slice across the categories of religiosity. Here the religious do not appear to be protagonists vis-à-vis the nonreligious, who themselves are divided between left/doves and right/hawks. In fact, as we showed above, the religious occupy the middle of the spectrum of religiosity-bound allegiances and mitigate, rather than aggravate, the tensions that pit the nonreligious and the Ultra-Orthodox against each other. By positioning themselves this way, they express their sensitivity to the attitudes that characterize the majority of Israeli Jews.

Those who belong to the category of the religious are Orthodox Jews. As such, they are as attached to traditional Judaism as the

Ultra-Orthodox. As Zionists, however, they define the second and third facets of the identity structure differently. Like the Ultra-Orthodox they affirm their commitment to the People of Israel as a religious duty, but they also regard their dedication to the God of Israel and His teachings as broadly compatible with participation in modernity, a stance that the Ultra-Orthodox hesitate to endorse. Moreover, they understand the attitude toward "others" from strongly phrased territorial perspectives, i.e., in terms of the project of building Eretz Yisrael (the Land of Israel), which steers many of them to a Greater Israel posture that opposes any territorial concessions to the Palestinians.

By defining itself as Orthodox-and-modern, the constituency at issue defects *ab initio* from the Ultra-Orthodox sphere and justifies, in its own eyes, the wish to insinuate itself into general society—a wish that the dominant culture does not reject. This integrationist aspiration, however, encounters three major difficulties. First, as Orthodox Jews who are committed to rabbinical law—observance of kosher restrictions, the Sabbath, public worship in synagogue, etc.—the religious are dependent on appropriate community services and structures and feel more comfortable living among themselves. This explains why they wish to manifest their social integration by establishing settings of their own that replicate, in religious forms, structures instituted by the nonreligious, such as kibbutzim (collective villages), moshavim (cooperative villages), and a university (Bar-Ilan University in Ramat Gan).

The second impediment to total social integration is the fact that, as religious people, the National Religious recognize the authority of renowned rabbis who "know the Torah," resulting in an infatuation with authoritative rabbis in the Ultra-Orthodox camp. Thus, in nearly all disputes between the nonreligious establishment and the Ultra-Orthodox leadership, they tend to side with the latter, although unenthusiastically at times. This surely drives a wedge of distrust between them and the nonreligious.

The third difficulty is that religion, in the eyes of religious Jews of all persuasions, is the very essence of Judaism and always implies faith not only in God and His teachings but also in the religious calling of Jewish peoplehood. Hence the National Religious, by being religious and nationalist concurrently, face the dilemma that the juxtaposition of their codes—Zionism (nationalism) and Judaism (religion)—embodies. Originally, Zionism meant something quite simple to them: the aspiration, as religious Jews, to be a part of the Zionist enterprise and the new national society, i.e., to be religious and Zionist. However, since, as a brand of religious Judaism, they define Jewish peoplehood in religious terms, religious Jewish nationalism easily relates the religious principle to Zionism by demanding a religious reinterpretation of Zionism. This, in turn, impels the religious who accept this outlook to fight for influence over, and impact on, the very significance of Zionism (see Yanovitzky, 1996). Their rival in this struggle is the very society that nonreligious Zionists created. Not all Israelis in the religious category are willing to carry this thinking to its logical end; they seek an interpretation of Judaism that does not preclude a secular outlook on Zionism. Those who are willing to go "all the way," however, tend to link Judaism and Zionism in a way that invests Zionism with new meanings and Judaism with new emphases (Don-Yehiya, 1993). These National Religious—like the Ultra-Orthodox but in their own different way— are then convinced that they constitute a "vanguard" that possesses the only "true" formulation of Zionism and Judaism and that, for this reason, is entitled to leadership over the Jewish people at large. In a nutshell, while the first model—religion *and* Zionism—limits the political role of the religious to lobbying society at large for the right to be one of its constituents, the second model—Zionism *accounted for* by religion—bases Israel on a religious narrative that is linked to the Biblical calling of Judaism. Zionism, the ideology of return to the Holy Land, is then termed as a religious imperative, and so are the national policies that this camp believes appropriate.

This model began to prevail among the religious in the aftermath of the 1967 war, when the retention of the newly conquered territories in the West Bank and the Gaza Strip became a major issue on the country's political agenda. A strong faction among the religious censured any territorial concession of "ancestral" soil that would "betray" Israel's commitment to the "Promised Land." This camp among the religious now preached the revival of pioneer values and social mobilization for the task of populating the new areas. This development, which added a drastically dramatized dimension to the state's national and international challenges (see Liebman and Don-Yehiya, 1984), could not but cause tensions even among those religious who still aspired to insinuate themselves into the larger Israeli setting as nothing more than one of its components. The ensuing internal strife prompted a faction of the National Religious to secede from the National Religious Party (the main political vehicle of this population group) and establish the Meimad Party, which adopted centrist policies on territorial, religious, and social issues.

These two models of national religiosity remain congruent mainly in the linguistic field, as both encourage the use of Hebrew as a link between the contemporary experience of this society and its national and religious past on the very same soil. By means of linguistic activity, individuals of both leanings can emphasize the special contribution of the religious to society. This contribution is manifested in their closeness to the cultural and spiritual wellsprings of historical Judaism, practical affirmation of special signifiers such as avoidance of vulgar speech, and frequent use of religious interjections that assert the religious roots of the collective identity (Ben-Rafael, 1994).

Like secular Zionists—if not more so—and unlike the Ultra-Orthodox, the religious see in the attachment to the Land of Israel the primary facet of Jews' collective identity. Hence, they too dichotomize Jewry into national (Israeli) Jews and Diaspora Jews. By stressing the role of religion in the Jews' territorialization in their "ancestral" land, they give priority to that segment of Jewry that happens to be living—or that has chosen to live—in Israel. In Israel itself, they give the same priority to those who are religious and, among the religious, to those who adopt the role of pioneers and settle in Judea-Samaria, the heart of Biblical Israel, thereby asserting the religious-territorial essence of Jewish nationhood.

Matters are different when it comes to identification. Most of the religious belong to the privileged middle class and are viewed by the dominant culture as an integral part of the national society. Followers of the Zionism-*and*-religion model definitely consider themselves one of the several constituents of society, even when for convenience's sake they tend to establish surroundings of their own. Naturally, this group exhibits a rather weak degree of particularistic identification. Adherents of the Zionism-*accounted-for-by*-religion model view the matter differently. Predicating their claims on their own religious creed, they insist that they play a crucially distinctive role in society. This approach inspires much stronger identification among its followers than supporters of the first model display toward theirs. The main factor that sustains this identification is the relocation of tens of thousands who subscribe to this trend of thought to scores of settlements of their own that have been established in the West Bank and Gaza Strip during the past three decades.

That the settlers live among themselves in a state of permanent mobilization is certainly an additional factor in determining their collective identification and consolidating themselves as a distinctive sociocultural entity. It is as such that they belong to Israel's multiculturalism.

"YESHA"

In 2001,[1] there were about 208,300 Jewish inhabitants in Judea, Samaria, and the Gaza District—the West Bank and the Gaza Strip—areas that are commonly abbreviated in Hebrew as *Yesha* (Yehuda-Shomron-ʿAza, which, uttered as a word, denotes deliverance or salvation). Most of this population lives in towns close to Central Israel or urban neighborhoods around Jerusalem. Others (25–30 percent) live in semi-rural settlements dispersed throughout the territories. Many of these localities are close to the Green Line (the 1949 armistice line that separates the West Bank from pre-1967 Israel). Some more distant towns and villages have developed their own economic infrastructures such as workshops, high-tech enterprises, and farms.

Most Jews who settled in Yesha did so for practical reasons such as inexpensive housing and high quality of life. Thousands of immigrants have gravitated to Jewish towns and villages in the West Bank. Many towns, urban neighborhoods, and settlements on the Yesha side of the Green Line were established under government policies (prompted by strategic considerations such as strengthening Israeli control of the surroundings of Jerusalem or widening the country's narrow central coastal area), but dozens of settlements—generally the smallest—were set up against the government's wishes and at the initiative of militants. These settlements, most often found deep in Palestinian-populated territory, make up the "hard core" of the colonizing movement that emerged after the 1967 war among supporters of the Zionism-*accounted-for-by*-religion model.

The direct historical context was particularly appropriate for such a development because, in the aftermath of their stunning military victory in the Six-Day War, Israelis found themselves in possession

---

[1] Israel Central Bureau of Statistics (2003) website.

of all of the holiest places in Biblical Judaism—in Judea, Samaria, and, above all, Old Jerusalem. Zionist religiosity suddenly became a full-blown political program, on the basis of which the Gush Emunim ("Bloc of the Faithful") movement emerged (Aran, 1987).[2] The founders of Gush Emunim could not but interpret the present time as the very beginning of the messianic era of Jewish redemption (Liebman, 1992), a perspective that, to its adherents, justified the call for the immediate and thorough annexation and colonization of the newly occupied territories as a part of the Holy Land. To renounce this portion of the Promised Land, it was contended, was tantamount to repudiating an extraordinary opportunity to bring about the salvation of which the Prophets had spoken (Alpher, 1994; Shafir, 1984). Referring to the old image of the Zionist pioneer, they saw in themselves a new version of it (Segal, 1987, 31).

Gush Emunim soon established a set of institutions and settings that would flank the *mitnahalim*, a term that hearkens to the Israelite settlers of Eretz Yisrael under Biblical Joshua. From the founding days of their new sector, these militants established a grip on the leadership of the entire Jewish population of Yesha and tightened it as the years passed, even though the majority of the Yesha population—immigrants and nonimmigrants alike—had settled there for instrumental reasons. The Gush Emunim people were strong enough in their convictions and cohesive enough as a movement to maintain leadership of the settler population at large. Their political influence in their areas of residence transcends their numbers and plays a crucial role in the regional councils under which the small localities are governed. They have done much the same in the leading body in the territories, the Yesha Council, an umbrella organization that represents Jewish communities in Judea, Samaria, and Gaza.[3] Their activism was not only inward-facing—toward the

---

[2] The Gush Emunim theology was instilled by Rabbi Abraham I. Kook, Chief Rabbi of Palestine until his death in 1935, and was later rewritten as a political ideology by his son, Rabbi Zvi Yehuda Kook (1891–1982). Its principles are taught in Yeshivat Mercaz Harav, which the elder Rabbi Kook established, and in other academies that subscribe to it (Ravitzky, 1993).

[3] The Yesha Council is a chartered voluntary nonprofit organization, directed by the heads of the local and regional councils and several highly respected public figures. Accordingly, its role surpasses that of an ordinary municipal umbrella organization. Its main function is to spearhead political action on behalf of the communities and inhabitants of Yesha. The council and all of its department heads engage in leading the battle to keep all parts of these territories under Israeli control.

sector that it was now building—but also outward-facing, toward the central political scene, where it was manifested at both the extra-parliamentary and the parliamentary levels (Sprinzak, 1989).

In the wake of Gush Emunim, an organization called *Amana* (in Hebrew: covenant) was established as a department of the Yesha Council for the purpose of direct settlement activity meant explicitly to settle the territories as widely as possible.[4] However, Amana is not responsible for settlement in the urban centers that have evolved in the territories; these are controlled by public authorities and most of their inhabitants do not necessarily share an idealistic calling. Most settlements founded by Amana are inhabited by nationalist religious settlers and a small minority of nonreligious ones (Goldberg, 1993; Goldberg and Ben-Zadok, 1983). These localities comprise up to 200 families (Horowitz, 1990; Appelbaum and Newman, 1990).

The Discourse of Confusion

Literature shows that the ideological settlers have established a new discourse that attempts symbolically to appropriate the territories (Feige, 1999). This discourse glorifies the Biblical past, speaks of imminent redemption, and downplays the obstacles of the present. Settlers perceive the contemporary Israeli left, in its willingness, to make territorial concessions to the Palestinians in return for peace, as the "defeatist" aisle of the Israeli society.

In fact, one does find very extremist elements among settlers (Sprinzak, 1998). Back in the mid-1980s, a Jewish underground initiated several attacks against Palestinians, including mayors of West Bank cities. In 1994, a Jewish kamikaze killed tens of Palestinians in the holy shrine of the Cave of the Patriarchs in Hebron. In 1995, Yitzhak Rabin, the Prime Minister of Israel who concluded the Oslo accords, was murdered by yet another fanatic who identified with the settlers' cause—although he did not live among them. This fringe of Jewish extremism was fueled by a messianic fundamentalism that in a variety of ways relates to messianic Zionism.

In fact, the leaders of Gush Emunim chose from the very outset to use extra legal means to induce the creation of new settlements as *faits accomplis* without waiting for the authorities' permission

---

[4] "Yesha Council Diary" (1995–1996).

(Friedman, 1990). Drawing their inner legitimacy from their belief in the paramount theological significance of the present stage in Israel's history, these leaders exploited the government's reluctance to wage an implacable struggle against its own citizens at a point in time when such a confrontation seemed to be only to the Palestinians' advantage. However, this attitude fueled not only Palestinians' resent of what they perceived as Jewish expansionism but also a sense among many Israelis that the government was being manipulated by a minority (Goldberg and Ben-Zadok, 1983). In this respect, the confrontation with Yesha is conducive to nothing less than the formation of a geopolitical cleavage delimited by the Green Line.

It is in this context that the 1993 Oslo agreement would bear crucial implications (Alpher, 1994; Hirschfeld, 2000). It was the first official agreement between Israelis and Palestinians and the first setting in which Israel and the Palestinians recognized each other and concluded on the necessity to reach a negotiated peace settlement. One direct consequence of the new peace process, once formally accepted domestically and internationally, was to render the Greater Israel discourse obsolete. From now on, it was clear that Jews would have to make "painful" concessions in the framework of a peace agreement with the Palestinians.

This turnabout caused a deep crisis in Yesha, where people now had to explain to themselves a new reality that was in complete dissonance with the redemption theology and the belief in the divine imperative to retain every inch of Eretz Yisrael. Many did not hesitate to demonize the Oslo process as a "national disaster" and a "crime against the Holy Land." Others found somewhat more moderate definitions of the move toward peace with the Palestinians, but the settler population as a whole became a major factor of opposition to the agreement (Friedman, 1990).

In contrast, the Israeli public at large accepted the accord and, by so doing, declared its divorce from Yesha. Thus, media now often depicted settlers as "anti-peace troublemakers" (Wolfsfeld, 1997a). Despite their messianic convictions, however, as Feige (1999) insists, the bulk of Yesha activists are determined people also able of pragmatism. Yesha leaders now orchestrated a campaign against the increasingly fashionable description of Yesha as "foreign" land, depicting the settlers as victims and emphasizing that the fundamental purpose of their struggle for Yesha was to adhere to basic national motives. The goal now, it was contended, was concurrently to fight the Palestinian Authority's unjustified ambitions and the Israeli Government, which was too weak to meet a crucial national challenge. The campaign was largely ineffectual. All public opinion surveys—especially the monthly Peace Index, a regularly recurrent opinion survey of the Tami Steinmetz Center for Peace Studies at Tel-Aviv University (Yaar and Hermann, 2000–2004)—show invariably that a majority of Jews remain willing to make territorial concessions in return for peace with the Palestinians.

Things changed with the outbreak of the latest Palestinian uprising in 2000 and its attendant campaign of terrorism against Israel's civilian population. Many Israelis now adopted "harder" attitudes toward the Palestinian cause, but only to advocate unilateral disengagement from the Palestinian population—including, where necessary, the dismantling of settlements. The construction of a defensive fence to impede terrorist infiltration from Judea-Samaria was contemplated with rising seriousness as the number of civilian victims of attacks against Israeli targets climbed into the hundreds. Construction of the fence began in 2003 and after much hesitation, the government chose a path that would, for the most part, approximate the Green Line. Concurrently, and in the same spirit, Israeli leaders also began to plan a unilateral disengagement from the Gaza Strip and the dismantling of Jewish settlements there.

It is clear that unilateral disengagement will jeopardize many Yesha settlements that were established in the heart of Palestinian-populated territory, far inland from the route of the fence. Another major difficulty is that while these measures are presented as purely tactical tools against terrorism—i.e., devoid of political significance—they inescapably allude to an Israeli disengagement from large parts of the territories before the conflict with the Palestinians reaches an agreed termination. This will leave Israel with few bargaining chips in its permanent-status negotiations, if and when they take place. These considerations fuel the opposition to the unilateral steps.

Be this as it may, it is obvious that years of unrest in Israel originating in the territories—the conduct known by its Arabic term, *intifada*—has not reinstated confidence in the Greater Israel project outside of Yesha. Now more than ever, the settlers face the problem of defining their perspective vis-à-vis society, the state, and their own community. This situation still worsened, in the settlers' eyes, with the government's one-sided steps to disengage from the Palestinians in the Gaza Strip and Northern Samaria (summer 2005), and the installment of a Palestinian government, after Arafat's death, decided to compromise with the Israelis.

INDIVIDUAL FEELINGS IN YESHA

To what extent, however, do the "macro" problems of Yesha affect settlers' awareness? How do these problems influence the way they see themselves, understand their position, and define and formulate their collective identity? These questions belong to this study of Israel's multiculturalism as the settlers have become a constituency in their own right.

We did not study this group on the basis of our standard questionnaire, believing that it would be difficult to obtain straightforward answers from people who are severely preoccupied about their future. Thus, we base our discussion here on face-to-face and in-depth interviews conducted by Noga Gilad (forthcoming), who in 2000–2001 met with twenty settlers who belong to Yesha's hard core and completed her study with a content analysis of the settlers' organ, *Nekuda*. We bring here the general picture that comes out from the findings.

Gilad's work shows that both the 1993 Oslo agreement and the outbreak of the second intifada in 2000 sowed great confusion among settlers and subjected them to an acute sense of threat to their endeavor in Yesha. These feelings, however, by no means add up to dislocation. Instead, we find willingness to close ranks and strengthen the commitment to the collective. Settlers are free to leave whenever they wish, and, as a matter of fact, the weaker or more hesitant easily find a way out, leaving the more resolute behind. Due to this ongoing selection process, the more acute the crisis, the stronger the hard-line stream gets among the settlers.

Obviously, indeed, many Yesha inhabitants who moved to these territories for instrumental, and not ideological, motives contemplate with less reluctance the eventuality of leaving Yesha. For them, there is also the consideration of their entitlement to financial compensations if obliged to relocate for political reasons. However, the very logic of these expectations and of the bargaining that will probably take

place between them and the Israeli authorities invites them to subscribe provisionally to the radical line by making their eventual withdrawal as dramatic as possible. At this time of crisis, be it for mere
tactical purposes or to press a genuine ideological case, the radicalization
of the settlers' commitment is finding expression in demonstrations
against officials and institutions, unrelenting attempts to establish new
settlements, and extenuating protests against police and soldiers who
are sent to dismantle illegally established colonization outposts.

The intrinsic legitimacy of all these actions traces to the religious-
nationalist mystique which is symbolized by numerous collective
markers—pilgrim-like clothing and simplicity, large white yarmulkes
for men and head-kerchiefs and long dresses for women. Staunch in
their belief in their interpretation of Judaism, they also invest much
time in religious study with heavy emphasis on the teachings of Rabbi
A.I. Kook.

It is on this basis that the concept of "others" points to two distinct spheres of reference in the case at hand: "other" Israelis and
Palestinian neighbors. Due to their elitist self-image, settlers do
consider themselves "different" and replicate to some extent, in
their relation with other Israelis, the Zionist dichotomization of
Israeli and Diaspora Jews, using "Eretz Yisrael" to denote *only* Yesha
inhabitants in contrast to "Israel." Aware of the fact that the Israeli
authorities and many Israelis, individually, often view them dimly,
settlers speak of "us" in Yesha and "them" in Israel. Their "extrater-
ritorial" endeavor is so central to their lives and identities that they
often tend to subordinate their "Israeliness" to their "Yesha-ness."
The principal meaning of this distinction is that settlers consider
themselves an elite, if not *the* elite, of Israel, the only category of
Israelis who devote their lives to the "genuine salvation" of their
people.

It is subsequently that settlers view Palestinians who inhabit and
claim the territories as implacable enemies who will never truly accept
any form of accommodation with the Jews. At best, this Palestinian
population, in settlers' eyes, might be subjugated and colonized if
it is to remain there—which is not a necessity, since it is conceivable, in their eyes, that material incentives might induce Palestinians
to leave.

In brief, settlers define their collective identity in a way that gives
preeminence to allegiance to the land through a notion of collective

uniqueness that is elaborated by a very specific version of the Jewish faith. Their formulation embodies, by implication, sharp conflictual assertions about "others" that one may, in its more extreme manifestations, describe as fundamentalism.[5]

SETTLER'S IDENTITY

We know that some towns and settlements in Yesha are hardly attractive to adherents of strong religious orientations and are tenanted due to purely instrumental motives. Here applies that inhabitants may be ready to relocate in the event of agreements with the Palestinians or unilateral disengagement, although, for the sake of negotiating over the terms of their evacuation, they might have an interest in taking a radical stance. Hence, instrumental-minded settlers may find it worthwhile to accept the leadership of militants. This probably explains why the voices that challenge the prevailing discourse of the radicals have been feeble thus far.

Viewed from the perspective of Israel's multiple cleavages, the settlers—especially those of the militant persuasion—represent the development of the National Religious cleavage. This is not only because they have established themselves in geographical areas that set them apart from the rest of the society but also because they inhabit the very land that lies at the crux of Israel's relations with its neighbors. Hence, the settlers have actually elevated the National Religious cleavage to a plane that has unhinged it from its point of departure. Actually, no few settlers even distance themselves now from the National Religious Party to join factions that speak directly on behalf of the far right.

Thus, the settlers embody tensions of their own vis-à-vis the rest of the society that are not necessarily shared by the National Religious sector at large. Hence, for instance, in the context of the economic and security difficulties that have buffeted Israel since the outbreak of the intifada in September 2000, inimical forces single out investments

---

[5] By "fundamentalism," we mean adherence to an ideology and a program that aspires to bring to the fore given interpretations of religious legacies by means of extremist political action (Eisenstadt, 1999).

made in Yesha as detrimental to other more needy sectors, such as peripheral towns in Israel proper. The settlers also attract criticism from the Ultra-Orthodox, who view them as rivals for the allegiance of their own youth. Indeed, no few Ultra-Orthodox youngsters who wish to involve themselves in Israeli society find in the settlers' movement an outlet that does not alienate them from Ultra-Orthodox religiosity and ethnocentrism. As already mentioned, the attractiveness of Yesha to young Ultra-Orthodox has contributed to create the phenomenon described as *Hardal*. This label denotes both Ultra-Orthodox Jews who join the ranks of settlers and adopt some behaviors of the national-religious, and National Religious individuals who aspire to a stronger religious definition and take up some Haredi behaviors.

In sum, settlers are definitely a part of contemporary Israeli society that is characterized by cultural, religious, and political features of its own. Above all, they have worked out their own version of the notion of collective identity, which makes them yet another—and most active—actor in the complex game of recognition and politics in Israel.

IDENTIFICATION: LONG-TERM CHANGES

From the viewpoint of identification processes, the settlers represent quite a special situation. On the one hand, they belong to the socially privileged classes; they own residences in surroundings that evoke jealousy over quality of life. Moreover, whenever the Israeli Government is dominated by right-wing parties—as it has been for most of the time since 1977—the Authorities, if not a large majority of the population, have considered the settlers a fully legitimate sector and an integral member of the overall setting. Settlers themselves aspire to be universally recognized as such.

However, since the Oslo agreement and more so since the outbreak of the 2000 intifada, many Israelis, including no few right-wing politicians—and not the least powerful among them—have come to view the settlers as an obstacle to the national security and a "reasonable" peace agreement with the Palestinians. One way or another, the very survival of the settlers as a particular entity has come into question, since a large majority of Israelis favor arrangements—either unilateral or concluded with the Palestinian Authority—

that will restrict the scope of Jewish colonization in the Palestinian territories.

In this situation where settlers, involuntarily and pursuant to political developments, are in confrontation with such broad segments of society, one may speak of a genuine crisis of legitimacy among the settlers themselves. Unsurprisingly, they are dealing with this crisis by hardening their positions. A behavior that one may interpret both as a posture meant to create a convenient opening position for bargaining, and expression of concealed profound despair. Be this as it may, settlers are show strong identification with their movement's original aims.

It is in this context that we also note changes of a completely different type that have been taking place over the past decade and a half among settlers and the National Religious at large—changes in the very essence of their religiosity. Hence, in a study of the National Religious, Friedman (2004) focuses on the cultural and ideological reflections of people in their twenties and thirties. The context of his research was the profound crisis of self-legitimacy that has been shaking this sector ever since the Oslo agreement and with greater intensity since the eruption of the intifada in 2000.

More specifically, studying a corpus of projects by national religious students of cinema, including many young people from Yesha, Friedman found several recurrent themes that were quite unexpected. One of them was the world of the settlers, which the films portray in terms of ideological and existential uncertainty if not of cultural decline. These works give the impression that cinema students of national-religious allegiance and from the settler population have abandoned the notion of the sanctity of Eretz Yisrael and are driven, instead, by ecological, spiritual, or individualistic interests—with emphasis on the last-mentioned. Thus, it would appear that young people are moving away from their parents' world of collective symbols. Even though the collective continues to play a significant role in their lives, the young aspire to master them on their own terms. The young filmmakers also show a strong interest in ideas that are current in the world at large, i.e., a refusal to eschew the secular universe, while displaying an urge to create syntheses between the religious and the nonreligious worlds.

Friedman elaborates on the attempt by these religious filmmakers to develop a genre of "Jewish cinema." The activities of the recently established Maale School of Television, Film, and the Arts, which draws its students from the national religious education system, are strongly indicative of this development. They tend to create a nexus of Judaism and cinema which relates to religious revivalism and may be seen as a step to bring the national religious public closer to secular culture and art.

Friedman also delves into the national religious feminist movement, another quite new phenomenon in this population, focusing on the Kolekh ("Your voice") Forum, gathering strength among the national religious, including in Yesha. Kolekh demands a broader role for women in religious congregational practice, the dissemination of new attitudes toward women's status in the curricula of religious schools, and protection of women against abuse by husbands, officials, and rabbis. Kolekh places special emphasis on feminist religious awareness, women's participation in the religious culture, and assistance to women in distress. It stands up against rabbis as self-appointed decisors in lifestyle issues.

Under the impact of such changes, a genuine transformation in national religious education is coming into sight. Young educators and parents are creating educational settings that offer alternatives to the religious education disseminated by nonprogressive rabbis. Changes in subjects and methods of teaching that often clash bluntly with the programs of established yeshivas are being proposed and implemented.

Friedman's review of trends of change also includes patterns of leisure and recreation of religious youngsters. He reveals, among other phenomena, that the pub has become an accepted form of entertainment. Visiting the Bar Da'at pub in Tel-Aviv, Friedman found an attempt to combine the secular pub culture with religiosity. Friedman also discovered receptiveness among members of this generation to influences of New Age culture and Eastern religions, as young people, following the lead of tens of thousands of secular Israeli youth, now take part in New Age festivals in Israel and lengthy trips to India or other parts of the world where Israeli youngsters are eager to spend numerous months before getting back to "normal" life. Evenings of music by candlelight in the religious café, a New Age festival, or meditation in an ashram in India provide religious experiences that are now understood as legitimate. Tangentially, Friedman also reports changes in patterns of dress, acceptance of "piercing culture," and drug use and abuse.

In all, young Orthodox Israelis—like youngsters in other categories and other societies (see Champion and Hervieu-Léger, 1990)—seem to be expressing a quest for creative endeavor, apparently integrating

into the global trends of what the literature calls "postmodern religiosity." By diversifying their religious interests, the national religious
of this persuasion are creating a genuinely pluralistic market of
lifestyles that often takes secularization for granted, and may even
abandon typically religious lifestyles, including yeshiva studies. The
quest for authentic and direct religious experiences is praised both
in community rituals and "outside" the community.

The penetration of postmodern thinking in Israel's Orthodox world
prompts Friedman to propose—pursuant to discussions of postmodern religiosity (Hervieu-Léger, 1998; see also Inglehart, 1997)—
a concept of *postmodern Orthodoxy* to describe the tendency among
some believers to soft-pedal the principle of holiness and to view
religion mainly as a set of practices aiming at the traditional out-
ward-looking Jewish principle of *tiqun ʿolam* ("repairing the world")
and sustaining a personal quest for truth and confidence.

Conclusion

The above provides elements of answers to the basic research question that we asked in the conclusion of Chapter 2 with respect to
the national religious.

We have seen that the national religious experience two basic
options in their relation toward society that are dictated by two
different formulations of their collective identity, especially regarding
the singularity of their calling. We called one option Zionism *and*
religion, and the second, Zionism accounted *for* by religion. The first
option minimizes the saliency of the national-religious vis-à-vis the
rest of society; the second option amplifies its saliency, especially in an
epoch when related political questions—the future of the West Bank
and the Gaza Strip and the peace process—are at the heart of
national debates. This option has led to the formation of a new constituent of Israel's multiculturalism, Yesha, which comprises both ideological and instrumental settlers who as a rule align themselves along
the line advocated by the leaders of the former. In this way is set
down the ground for making this cleavage the most arduous of this
society during a time of aggravated conflict with the Palestinians
over space and rights. In these circumstances, the radical religious
understanding of Zionism by much of the national religious sector

is challenging society's ability to confront its difficulties. This in itself constitutes a major problem for the stability of the social order.

Another major difficulty implied by this cleavage resides in the fact that it is spoken of a sector of the population, the settlers, who have cemented their distinctiveness from the rest of the population and the strength of their collective identification by locating themselves in a particular geographical space where they often constitute the only Jewish population. This geographical dimension, with all its political significance, implies that, on both sides—the national religious and other Israelis—there exists a degree of estrangement, alienation and hostility. It is only when the question of the Palestinian territories is settled in a peace agreement, we may assume, that settlers—whether or not their settlements are dismantled—will cease to constitute a focus of conflict and that the fact that they mostly belong to Israel's middle class will strongly encourage their assimilation in the mainstream of the society, from where they originally stemmed for the most parts.

Gilad's research, moreover, shows that the irredentism of the settlers should not always be taken at face value and may, for no few settlers, be a tactic ahead of negotiating compensation. On the other hand, Friedman's work shows that profound processes among the second generation in Yesha, and among national religious youngsters at large, make a strategy of irredentism quite inconceivable for many individuals in the long run and actually tend to favor a reformulation of objectives that might provide a path away from extremism (see also Sheleg, 2000).

Such a development, of course, still hinges on political circumstances that are by no means controlled exclusively by actors on the Israeli side. However, the more the trends analyzed above are given a chance to gain in importance among the national religious and second-generation settlers, the more one may expect identification with the sector as a collective political imperative to weaken in favor of cultural preoccupations.

Still another cleavage, however, is fomented by religious forces which emerge from a completely different sociocultural horizon.

SECTION III

SOCIOCULTURAL DIVISIONS

CHAPTER FIVE

MIZRAHIM AND ASHKENAZIM

Introduction

The preceding chapters dealt with the role of religiosity in domestic debates about Israel's social order. We focused first on the Ashkenazi Ultra-Orthodox and the nature of their relations with the nonreligious; later we turned to the national religious and Yesha perspectives. Still to consider is the sphere of the Mizrahi Ultra-Orthodox who stand close to the large Mizrahi public that more often defines itself as "traditional." We have said little about this latter category thus far because the traditional represent a middle-of-the-road position that, at first glance, does not have radical claims to make. This category stands between the religious and the nonreligious in most respects, and while it demonstrates a lack of cohesion and unity, it also seems quite distant from the Ultra-Orthodox.

Viewed from a contrary perspective, however, the traditional may be considered a "periphery" of the religious sector, which might be able to enlist it under given circumstances. It may also be a mistake to underestimate the potential ability of this population to form organizations and generate leaders of its own. Of Mizrahi origin, this public also belongs to the scene of ethnicity. The other religious cleavages, it is true, also share ethnic features—the Ashkenazi Ultra-Orthodox, for instance, clearly convey ethnocultural markers, while many national religious individuals stem also from Ashkenazi milieus. Yet, it would be unjustified to liken them to the Mizrahi traditional public, as these factions never present demands that may categorize them as ethnic actors, as do the movements that aspire to enlist traditional-minded Mizrahim. Moreover, ever since the early 1980s, a political party, Shas, that presents itself as both Mizrahi and Ultra-Orthodox, has become the major force of social mobilization of this public, on behalf of both its traditionalism and ethnicity. It is as such that Mizrahi traditionalism and Ultra-Orthodoxy merit to be discussed under the heading of sociocultural divisions, though they also belong to this society's religious cleavages, and, as we will see further, are by no means alien either to the particular link that exists in Israel's dominant culture between religion and nationalism.

A COMPLEX BACKGROUND

In 1948, shortly before the State of Israel was established, 85 percent of the country's Jewish population was of Eastern and Central European origin. The share of Middle Eastern and North African Jews climbed in the 1950s and 1960s, peaked at 43–45 percent in the 1980s, and receded to 40–42 percent in the 1990s due to mass immigration from the former Soviet Union (Ben-Rafael and Sharot, 1991; ICBS, 1999). Unlike most Ashkenazi groups, Mizrahi communities have always tended to perpetuate their ethnic identity and culture by retaining traditional patterns and forms of religious observance (Ben-Rafael and Sharot, 1991; Weingrod, 1990; Shokeid, 1985). Like the Ultra-Orthodox and the national religious, Mizrahim adhere to the three principles of the Jewish traditional identity—'Am Yisrael (commitment to the notion of the "People Israel"), Elohei/Torat Yisrael (the perception of Jewish singularity in terms of dedication to the God of Israel and His teachings), and Eretz Yisrael (the belief that any Jewish condition outside the Land of Israel is a state of exile). Among the nonelite, religiosity is more strongly embodied in the retention of folk customs than in theological conviction. This was also the case in the Diaspora, especially in collectives that skirted modernization processes, i.e., rural and provincial communities and urban quarters populated by the lower classes (Cohen 1983).

In Israel, most of the more modern—and, generally, the more secular—Mizrahi Jews underwent rapid social individualization as they acquired human and material assets that ushered them into the middle class. By behaving this way, they followed the pattern of groups that preceded them. By the same token, Mizrahim of rural or of urban lower-class origin, who also happened to share traditional outlooks, tended to concentrate at the bottom of the social ladder due to the weakness of their predisposition to enter a modern economy. Moreover, another important factor here consists of the undeniable discriminatory practices by the establishment—manned predominantly by Eastern Europeans—that oversaw their absorption and shared but little empathy for their cultures. While the establishment's attitude did not always apply to the poorly educated only,

better educated and more affluent Mizrahim surmounted the prejudices by tackling the exigencies of social mobility head-on.

Mizrahim who found themselves in Israel's lower strata and shared
strong allegiances to their traditional models, reestablished communities—Yemenite, Moroccan, or Kurdish—around synagogues and
extended family networks. Still in the diaspora, many of them had
construed the very creation of the State of Israel as the onset of the
promised redemption that would reward the Jews for their longstanding dedication to their covenant with God (Ben-Rafael, 1982).
Thus, now and here, they were loath to abandon in the Land of
the Jews the ways that they had always observed among the gentiles as customs and symbols of Judaism itself. Manifestations of this
allegiance to the "old ways" included a proliferation of ethnically
marked synagogues and the observance of ancestral folk customs,
such as pilgrimages to tombs of saints, ethnic festivals, or old models
of wedding ceremony. None of this, however, could overcome the
powerful influence of the new Israeli environment, particularly the
school system, military service, new occupations, or incentives of a
consumer society that caused these groups to undergo a genuine
cultural transformation.

Over time, moreover, many of these Mizrahim—or their children—experienced social mobility by going into business or pursu-
ing educational or professional careers. These mobile elements, more
exposed than the rest of their communities to the dominant culture,
tended as a rule to abandon the practice of community traditions
and joined the middle class. Thus, by the early 2000s about 60 percent of Mizrahim belonged to the middle class, in which they often
marry spouses of Ashkenazi origin and raise children who are hardly
aware of any ethnic allegiance. These processes correspond with the
patterns of the broadly non ethnic "all-Israeli" spirit that prevails in
Israel's middle class secular milieus. In this respect, the Zionist ideological concept of *mizug galuyot* ("ingathering of exiles") has succeeded,
albeit among the privileged only.

This assimilative tendency of mobile Mizrahim is firstly sustained
by the fact that their communities of origin tolerate if not encourage it. Indeed, they can hardly brand assimilationists as "traitors"
since the predominantly Ashkenazi middle class into which they integrate is, after all, composed of other Jews who belong to the same
peoplehood. In these communities, allegiance to "Moroccanness,"
"Yemeniteness," or even "Mizrahiness" is unmistakably secondary to

Jewishness and refers to nothing more than modes of Jewishness. It is in this sense that Mizrahim and others describe the Mizrahi origin groups as *edot ha-mizrah*. *Mizrah* denotes "East"; *eda* (plural: *edot*) is a concept that combines meanings of "community," i.e., a solidaristic collective, and membership in a larger whole, as in a tribe or a clan.

The Biblical notion of eda was adopted by Jerusalemites of Sephardic origin who called themselves, in the 1930s, the *eda sepharadit* (the Judeo-Spanish community). Their aim was to express inalienable membership in the Jewish people on the basis of their own long-standing heritage (Ben-Rafael, 1982). At roughly the same time, an extremist Ashkenazi Ultra-Orthodox group in Jerusalem adopted the term eda to name itself the *eda haredit* and, thereby, to also designate itself as a distinct segment among Jews. In contemporary Israel, the concept of eda, generally speaking, applies to any Jewish group that crystallizes as a community that is differentiated by its own Jewish customs and perspectives and based on an *ab initio* sense of belongingness to the larger Jewish collective. Obviously, due to its anchorage in a relationship with heritages and ancestral symbols, the notion of eda is more appropriate as a description of a group of shared traditional background than for more secular groups that have largely jettisoned the ethnocultural community link.

As shown in previous pages, the concept of eda is hardly a relevant way to describe the predominantly Ashkenazi secular middle class, which partly originates from the first waves of Jewish immigrants—the "founders"[1]—and their offspring, and is the stratum closest to the dominant culture. This stratum cannot legitimately object to the social acceptance of individuals of Middle Eastern origin once their occupational achievements entitle them to membership and, *a fortiori*, if mobility results in greater exposure to the dominant culture and rapprochement to secular patterns of life.

---

[1] The main reference is to immigrants who arrived in 1904–1922. Known for their strong ideological motivation, they played a primordial role in the creation of the institutional framework that served as a backbone for the new society—the kibbutz, the moshav, the Histadrut (the General Federation of Jewish Labor), major political parties, etc. They also accounted for the switch to Hebrew as the vernacular of this society.

The outcome of the intersection of the openness of the predominantly Ashkenazi middle class and the Mizrahi communities's tolerance of its abandonment by mobile elements is that, *ipso facto*, these communities continue be characterized by lower-class features—despite the reality of significant mobility of individual Mizrahim. By the same token, the predominantly Ashkenazi middle class is becoming increasingly heterogeneous by origin but hardly so by culture.

In view of this partial "fusion of exiles," many members of the lower-class ethnic communities resent the salient correspondence in Israeli society between Mizrahiness and inequality and deprivation. The fact that this is so prompts Mizrahi communities to stress their particularism, as reflected in a profusion of symbolic and linguistic markers. To take an example from the area of linguistic activity, Mizrahim, aware that modern Hebrew is a descendant of the language of the Bible, enthusiastically embraced it as the national language from the earliest stage of their resettlement. This, however, is not to say that they immediately abandoned their original Judeo-Arabic vernaculars. Thus, many second-generation Mizrahim still master elements of their original vernaculars which they use with their parents. Moreover, many individuals of the second or third generations like to retain, in Hebrew, a characteristic accent and lexical elements to mark their distinctive origins (Hoffman and Fisherman, 1972).

In parallel, there is also widespread resentment, at least among the religious leadership, about why they perceive as "morally depraved" the secular culture that prevails in Israeli society. This view induces no few individuals to enter the "world of the Torah," i.e., the yeshiva; to immerse themselves in religious study; and thence to pledge themselves to the restoration of the "lost luster" of Judaism. Those who return to their ethnic communities do so in the traditional public-leadership roles of rabbis and Torah students. The tendency of secular mobile elements to leave the community for predominantly Ashkenazi neighborhoods, as we have seen, makes their task easier. Over time, these religious leaders become a political elite that, by adopting an attitude of protest against the dominant secular culture, eventually constitutes a counter-elite.

It was this relatively recent group that established the Shas party in the 1980s, at a time of national political conjuncture where right and left found themselves in the sharpest competition over ballots and the peace process in the area was polarizing the political map as never before.[2] This new political reality gave Mizrahim, who had been relatively passive in political life, extraordinary bargaining power, since their votes were now decisive for the outcome of general elections. These circumstances impelled the leaders of nearly every party to elevate politicians of Mizrahi origin to prominent positions in order to mobilize Mizrahi support. At the same time and for the same reasons, there was a general political awakening among Mizrahim, manifested among other things in the establishment of Shas. This ethnic Ultra-Orthodox party, under the tutelage of a former Sephardi Chief Rabbi of Israel, Ovadia Yossef (an Ultra-Orthodox authority in his own right), recruited the Mizrahi rabbinical elite that had emerged during the past decades. Within a few years, Shas became one of Israel's major political forces.

The role that Mizrahim play in the political arena today, either through their bargaining power in non-ethnic parties or through the power of Shas, is reflected primarily in the opening of many paths of political mobility. Dozens of Mizrahim serve in the Knesset, quite a few obtained cabinet portfolios at the highest levels of responsibility, many leading positions in trade unions, and two prominent figures have been presidents of the state. From the political arena, Mizrahim have expanded their achievements to the media, the world of entertainment, and the army. By the same token, underprivileged Mizrahi communities are also primary targets of the social policies of successive governments.

In brief, we may undeniably speak of a new era in Mizrahi-Ashkenazi relations in Israeli society. This raises many questions that have not yet been answered. Above all, we do not know how far these changes have strengthened the resolve of Mizrahim to identify with their ethnic identity because ethnicity has proved to be beneficial

---

[2] This conjuncture had been generally caused by Mizrahi voters who over the last decades turned from the left—the ruling wing—to the right, which had been in opposition ever since the creation of the state—in order to express their alienation from the establishment that had absorbed them in the 1950s and 1960s, and which was held responsible for the achievements and, mainly, for the shortcomings of their absorption. It is also their ethnic culture that explains why they felt closer to nationalist rhetoric than to social-democratic outlooks. This culture allowed them to express these preferences more freely over time as they learned how Israeli democracy works.

or, on the contrary, to feel more straightforward belongingness to general Israeli Jewishness due to the ebbing of their erstwhile deprivation. Surveys 1 and 2 (Table 2.6) were intended to answer these questions.

ETHNIC VERSUS NATIONAL IDENTIFICATION

The respondents were first asked to assert their identification with both their ethnic identity (Ashkenazi or Mizrahi) and national identity (Jewish or Israeli). They had to limit themselves to first and second choices in order to yield a sharper and more apposite picture than a wider range of choices would have elicited. Table 5.1 divides the respondents into five groups by distinguishing among broad ethnic categories and generations (foreign-born versus Israel-born).

As the table shows, a large majority in all groups define themselves primarily in terms of broader-than-ethnic identities (Israeli or Jewish). First-generation Mizrahim, it appears, are equally divided among those who define their first allegiance as Jewishness or as Israeliness; their offspring tend more clearly to rank Israeliness in first place. Among Ashkenazim, both generations prefer Israeliness, but the first generation is more prone to emphasize Jewishness. Overall, the differences between the two categories tend to zero in the second generation. Interestingly enough, however, the third generation—in which Ashkenazim and Mizrahim are not differentiated—shows equilibrium between Jewishness and Israeliness.

Furthermore, the minority of respondents in the first generation who expressed their primary identification in ethnic terms was substantially smaller among Mizrahim than among Ashkenazim—and the difference in this respect tended to be sustained in the second generation. These findings seem to tell us that Ashkenazim are "more ethnic" than Mizrahim. This contradicts earlier research that compared Ashkenazim and Mizrahim (Ben-Rafael and Sharot, 1991) and found that Mizrahim of both generations are more ethnic than Ashkenazim. In the earlier study, however, respondents were asked to state the degree of their identification with four relevant identities—Jewish, Israeli, broad-ethnic (Mizrahi versus Ashkenazi), and narrow-ethnic (country of origin). Thus, the findings are hardly comparable. Moreover, our surveys may reflect the outcome of the changes in recent years in the power of Mizrahim, as described above.

This may sustain the proposition that Mizrahim today tend to identify more with broader collective identities and that Ashkenazim may
feel more ethnic than in the past. Table 5.2 shows that while
Ashkenazim seem more ethnic and that the differences narrow when
the first and second choices are added, the all-collective identities
are by far the more emphasized on both sides, even though Mizrahim
are somewhat "more Jewish" than Ashkenazim.

Table 5.1. Self-Definition of Belongingness, by Demographic Origin*

Self-asserted "belongingness"—as first choice out of two

Demographic origin	Ashk	Miz	Jewish	Israeli	Other	Total	N (597)
Asian/African	—	10.2	43.2	43.2	3.4	100	88
Israel, Asian/Afr father	0.6	11.6	28.3	59.5	—	100	173
European/American	22.1	2.5	28.8	45.4	1.2	100	163
Israel, Eur./Am. Father	13.5	2.1	17.7	66.0	0.7	100	141
Israel, Israeli father	19.8	3.7	37.4	39.0	—	100	67

* Chi-square: 114.6**; Cramer's v =.25**. Source: Survey 3.

Table 5.2. First- and Second-Choice Identities*

Self-defined belongingness	First choice (percent)			Second choice (percent)		
	Miz	Ashk	Israel	Miz	Ashk	Israel
Ashkenazi	0.4	18.0	19.8	0.8	31.0	1.2
Mizrahi	11.1	2.3	3.7	26.5	3.2	11.1
Israeli	54.0	54.8	39.0	26.5	24.9	36.4
Jewish	33.3	23.6	37.4	44.1	37.7	51.2
Other	1.1	1.8	—	2.1	3.2	—
Total	100	100	100	100	100	100

* Cramer's v = .17**; Kramer's v = .25**. Source: Survey 3.

Table 5.3, moreover, shows that the ostensibly stronger ethnic allegiance of Ashkenazim should not be taken at face value. People may
understand ethnic allegiances as classificatory concepts within the
broader collective without attaching great importance to them. Be
this as it may, when asked, "Does your ethnic allegiance play an
important role in your life?" respondents throughout the sample
tended generally to reply "not at all" or "somewhat." Hence, ethnicity as such is definitely not a strong identity reference. More
specifically, Table 5.3a shows that even respondents who stated

ethnic allegiance as their first choice do not necessarily consider it important at all. In this respect, the order of the categories is reversed: no less than three-quarter of Ashkenazim who placed ethnic identity first do not consider this identity at all important in their social lives, as opposed to fewer than one-third of Mizrahim in the equivalent identity category who gave this response. On the other hand, fewer than 20 percent of Ashkenazim in the same category defined ethnicity as important in their lives, while the corresponding figure among Mizrahim was nearly two-thirds. If so, the findings oppose Ashkenazim and Mizrahim on incongruent terms: Ashkenazim attach much less importance to their ethnicity than Mizrahim do. The findings as a whole, however, show that ethnicity among both groups is declining in importance over generations and that, as Table 5.3a shows, third-generation Israelis are the least ethnic of all.

Importantly, however, the sense of Jewishness does not necessarily obliterate ethnic allegiances. Mizrahim who feel more Jewish than Ashkenazim do also assert their ethnicity more vigorously. This evidently relates to the fact that Mizrahi ethnicity, as explained above, is grounded in a traditionalism that, for many, represents the meaning of singularity when it comes to Jewishness itself.

Considering the relationship between ethnic origin and ethnic allegiance (Table 5.3b), we find that the differences discussed above correspond to the fact that more Mizrahim than Ashkenazim—although still a minority—define ethnicity as important in their lives. These differences are again consistent with the data about generational phenomena (Table 5.3c). Thus, second-generation respondents, both Mizrahi and Ashkenazi, are much less ethnic than first-generation respondents. By the same token, Ashkenazim are much less ethnic than Mizrahim at both counts.

Table 5.3d also shows that religious and traditional people tend to be much more ethnic than the nonreligious. This reinforces our aforementioned belief that Jewishness and ethnicity are not necessarily mutually exclusive. The basic reason, we contend, has to do with the nature of ethnicity in the case at hand, anchored in the perception of particularistic versions of Judaism. In this vein, a lessening of religiosity—in the sense of heritage and traditions—may serve as evidence of "de-ethnicization."

Table 5.3e, which probes ethnic allegiance in the context of education, confirms this proposition to some extent. Making do with a

Table 5.3. Aspects of Ethnic Allegiances

Does your ethnic allegiance play a role in your life?	Not at all	Somewhat	Quite	A lot	Total	N
a. Among those who defined ethnic allegiance as their "first allegiance"						
Ashkenazim	69.9	5.4	16.1	8.6	100.0	93
Mizrahim	22.0	12.2	43.9	22.0	100.0	41
Israeli	66.0	20.3	8.7	5.0	100.0	379
Jewish	42.5	19.7	25.4	12.3	100.0	228
Total	56.7	17.7	16.8	8.8	100.0	741
b. By ethnic origin (Cramer's v = .18**)						
Ashkenazi	60.4	17.8	13.5	8.3	100.0	302
Mizrahi	45.1	21.6	17.6	15.7	100.0	255
Israeli	66.5	12.2	20.7	0.5	100.0	188
Total	56.7	17.7	16.8	8.8	100.0	746
c. By ethnic origin and generation (Cramer's v = .17**)						
For-b Ash	58.3	13.5	17.2	11.0	100.0	163
Isr-b Ash	62.9	22.9	9.3	5.0	100.0	140
For-b Miz	39.5	16.3	23.3	20.9	100.0	86
Isr-b Miz	47.3	24.3	15.4	13.0	100.0	188
3r gen (A & M)	66.5	12.2	20.7	0.5	100.0	188
Total	56.6	17.7	16.9	8.8	100.0	746
d. By categories of religiosity (excl. Ultra-Orthodox) (Cramer's v = .20**)						
Religious	44.8	16.1	21.8	17.2	100.0	87
Traditional	44.8	17.1	24.2	13.9	100.0	252
Nonreligious	66.5	18.5	11.1	3.0	100.0	406
Total	56.6	17.7	16.8	8.9	100.0	745
e. By education (Cramer's v = .12**)						
Non academic	56.4	15.8	18.9	8.8	100.0	512
Academic	54.6	23.5	11.5	10.4	100.0	183
Total	56.0	17.8	17.0	9.2	100.0	685

Source: Survey 3.

rough differentiation between those who have an academic background and those who lack it, we find a moderate but significant differentiation between less-ethnic academics and more-ethnic non academics. Since much of the Mizrahi population tend to be traditional and lower-class while most Ashkenazim belong to the less religious and more educated segments of the population, our observations on the class-and-ethnicity nexus are confirmed. Thus, Israel has non-ethnic (or less-ethnic) middle and upper classes, in which people of Ashkenazi origin are predominant but that also include numerous socially mobile Mizrahim, as opposed to a more ethnic Mizrahi population in which the traditional, the religious, and the less educated are more numerous.

SOCIAL DISTANCES

In respect of social distances, Ashkenazim and Mizrahim are symmetrical in their attitudes toward each other and toward themselves; each side prefers itself to the other in similar and moderate terms and regards itself as similarly distant from the other (Table 5.4). Attitudes toward ethnic exogamy ("intermarriage") reinforce the point (Table 5.5).

Table 5.4. Cognitive Distances of Mizrahim and Ashkenazim*

Cognitive distance	Miz (254) Means	Ashk (301) Means	3^{d}g. Isr (187) Means	F
From Ash	44.5	26.4	31.8	38.6**
From Miz	27.9	42.7	38.1	31.4**

* The answers started with "very close" (1) and ended with "very far" (5). This continuum was transformed into a 1–100 linear scale. Source: Survey 3.

Neither the Mizrahi group nor the Ashkenazi group oppose ethnic exogamy. Ashkenazim are less amenable to interethnic marriage than Mizrahim but not radically so. This openness also applies to the sharing of apartment buildings. These scores should not be surprising when one considers the relatively high proportion of interethnic marriages and the absence of ecological ethnic segregation in Israel.

Table 5.5. Amenability to Interethnic Marriage and Tenancy

	Miz* (N=258)	Ashk* (N=296)	3dg* (N=67)	F
Would you agree: to see your daughter marry a man of the other ethnicity?	8.6	9.5	8.5	0.4
to live in a building were most tenants are of the other ethnicity?	11.3	14.3	8.3	6.9**

* Calculated on the basis of a 1–5 scale, where 1 = completely agree and 5 = by no means.
Source: Survey 3.

Table 5.6. Amenability to Interethnic Tenancy—1981 vs. 2001

Attitudes	Groups	Halevy (1981)	Our study (2001)
Amenable to living in proximity[1]	Mizrahi	57.4	88.6
	Ashkenazi	89.1	94.0
	N	(230)	(712)
Not amenable to living in proximity[1]	Mizrahi	22.5	11.4
	Ashkenazi	3.9	6.0
	N	(40)	(70)

Source: Survey 3.
[1] Halevy (1981) asked about neighborhoods; Ben-Rafael and Peres asked about buildings.

By comparing our findings with earlier studies, we find important change. The findings of a study by Halevy (1981), that asked questions very similar to ours about twenty years earlier compare with our data significantly. The comparison (Table 5.6) confirms that both the Ashkenazi and the Mizrahi sides are more amenable to interaction today. We find the same trend, with strong saliency, in regard to marriage when we compare our findings with those of Peres from the mid-1980s (Table 5.7). By comparing our findings with those of Tsfati (1999), we find a similar tendency in regard to the feelings of Mizrahim about social deprivation, a charge that has been at the center of Mizrahi–Ashkenazi controversy ever since the earliest manifestations of ethnic tension in Israel.

Foremost among these manifestations are the 1960 riots in Wadi Salib, a Haifa slum inhabited by Jews of Moroccan origin; the 1970

Black Panthers movement, which unleashed an unprecedented spate of ethnic unrest in Jerusalem; and subsequent protest demonstrations and public debates initiated by various self-appointed speakers for the Mizrahi communities—from the Ultra-Orthodox Shas to the Mizrahi Democratic Rainbow, a radical club of middle-class Mizrahim. The principal message of all these has always been the presumed deprivation of Mizrahim at the hands of Ashkenazim.

Table 5.7. Amenability to Interethnic Marriage—1985 vs. 1999

Amenability to interethnic marriage by one's daughter	Mizrahim		Ashkenazim	
	1985[1]	1999	1985[1]	1999
Totally amenable	29.0	74.0	13.0	60.7
Amenable	50.0	22.4	24.0	30.3
Prefer my group	15.0	2.3	38.0	4.9
Not amenable	2.0	0.8	20.0	2.1
Absolutely not amenable		0.5		2.0
N		195	362	143	426

Source: Survey 3.
[1] Source: Peres 1976.

Our findings point to drastic changes in attitudes over time (Table 5.8). As late as 1988, a slight majority of Mizrahim and a large minority of Ashkenazim were still convinced that Mizrahim are socially deprived. Our research, on the other hand, found comfortable majorities who believed, "Mizrahim are discriminated against to a small extent, if at all." Although this majority is larger among Ashkenazim than among Mizrahim, it is nevertheless also substantial among the latter.

When it comes to personal experiences of discrimination, the change is even more abrupt. In 1988, a majority of Mizrahim indicated that they had experienced discrimination personally (to a large extent or to some extent); in 2001, nearly 90 percent graded this kind of personal experience as "to a small extent, if at all." The new clout of Mizrahim in Israeli society—including and mainly the lower class traditional communities—does seem to affect feelings and perceptions in the direction of a more equitable perception of ethnic relations.

120 CHAPTER FIVE

Table 5.8. Feelings of Deprivation, 1988 vs. 2000*

To what extent do Mizrahim face ethnic discrimination?	1988 (percent)[1]		1999 (percent)	
	Mizr	Ashk	Miz (357)	Ashk (416)
To a large extent	21.1	11.9	12.7	1.9
To some extent	30.0	26.6	28.2	5.7
To a small extent, if at all	48.9	61.5	59.2	92.3
Total	100.0	100.0	100.0	100.0

Have you personally experienced discriminated due to your origin?	Mizrahim (1988) (percent)	Mizrahim (2000) (percent)
Often	13.5	4.8
Sometimes	40.7	9.0
Rarely if ever	45.7	86.2
Total	100.0	100.0

* The data here include the Ultra-Orthodox in order to assure comparability. Source: Survey 2.
[1] Source: Tsfati, 1999.

POLITICAL BEHAVIOR AND THE ROLE OF SHAS

Beyond these lines of convergence, divergence is still evident in one domain: political behavior. Here, in contrast to everything noted above, we do find a wide gap between Mizrahim and Ashkenazim (Table 5.9).

Table 5.9. Political Behavior*

Origin	Rightist voting	Leftist voting	Total
Mizrahim	62.5	37.5	100.0
Ashkenazim	22.7	77.3	100.0
Total	40.5	59.5	100.0
N	(227)	(334)	(561)

* Tau b = 0.40**; based on respondents' reports about their voting in the 1999 general elections for the premiership—Benjamin Netanyahu (right) versus Ehud Barak (left). (Barak won the elections by an overwhelming majority). Source: Survey 1.

Table 5.9 shows the contrasting patterns of electoral behavior among Mizrahim and Ashkenazim. Although the latter are more determined than the former (a larger percentage of the Ashkenazi group votes in accordance with its orientation), one may still speak of two divergent political constituencies. We should mitigate this conclusion, however, by noting that not only are Mizrahim a less cohesive constituency than Ashkenazim but also many Mizrahim have preferred in the past decade and a half to vote Shas, a party that defies clear positioning on the political spectrum. Shas has never ruled out participation in a left-of-center coalition even though it prefers a rightist coalition. Although it has hawkish leanings on issues related to the Israeli-Palestinian conflict, it officially favors concessions to the Palestinians within the framework of a peace agreement. In its social policies, Shas sees itself as the first defender of the underprivileged. Thus, the political option created by the growth of Shas has made Israel's political arena less rigid. Rather than right or left, it is to the Ashkenazi Ultra-Orthodox that Shas feels the closest.

Indeed, Shas, whose leadership waves the banner of ethnic recognition to mobilize support from a public widely traditional rather than deeply religious, is now by far the strongest force in the religious camp. In the 2003 general elections, for instance, it earned eleven seats in the Knesset (parliament) as against five for the National Religious Party and six for the Ultra-Orthodox. Moreover, because most of the Shas constituency is traditional, in contrast to its Ultra-Orthodox leadership, this party is also the only force that represents for the religious camp a major potential of outside followers.

It is in this context that Table 5.10 sheds light on the characteristics of Shas supporters (in 2001). Shas supporters tend more than others to view ethnic allegiance as their first-choice allegiance and, thus, to seem *a priori* more ethnicity-oriented than supporters of other parties (Table 5.10a). Among Mizrahim in general, Shas supporters tend to be more religious than those who do not support Shas—a finding that is congruent with the character of the Shas party, of course (Table 5.10b). This point is underscored by the fact that the most fervent stronghold in Shas is composed of the relatively small public of Mizrahi Ultra-Orthodox, while traditional Mizrahim provide the party with a rather broad basis of support (Table 5.10c). Last but not least, less education—which also means a greater likelihood of belonging to the lower socioeconomic strata—correlates positively with support for Shas.

These findings confirm that Shas is a party that derives its power from outside the narrow confines of the direct constituency of its leadership—Mizrahi rabbis and religious scholars. Its hinterland is composed of Mizrahim who consider themselves bound by religion and traditions and who make up much of Israel's lower class. This target population is broad enough to allow Shas to depict itself as Israel's leading Ultra-Orthodox party, since the Ashkenazi Ultra-Orthodox parties may hope to mobilize only the support of their own public.

Table 5.10. Voting for Shas by Mizrahim

	Voting		Total	N
	against Mizrahim	for Mizrahim		
a. First collective allegiance				
Mizrahi	67.9	32.1	100.0	28
Israeli	97.2	2.8	100.0	141
Jewish	86.2	13.8	100.0	87
Total (Chi-square: 25.977**)	90.4	9.6	100.0	260
b. Religiosity, not including Ultra-Orthodox				
Religious	82.9	17.1	100.0	35
Traditional	86.8	13.2	100.0	129
Nonreligious	97.9	2.1	100.0	96
Total (Chi-square: 10.433**)	90.4	9.6	100.0	260
c. Religiosity, including Ultra-Orthodox				
Ultra-Orthodox	38.5	61.5	100.0	13
Religious	82.9	17.1	100.0	35
Traditional	86.8	13.2	100.0	129
Nonreligious	97.9	2.1	100.0	96
Total (Chi-square: 10.433**)	87.9	12.1	100.0	273
d. Education				
Non academic	88.7	11.3	100.0	212
Academic	95.5	4.5	100.0	44
Total (Chi-square: 1.833)	89.8	10.2	100.0	256

Source: Survey 1.

Thus, Shas is able to play on two "fields" simultaneously—the ethnic-cleavage field and the religious field—and to use each field to enhance its power on the other. These findings also confirm, however, that ethnicity as a political cause is strongly dependent on three variables that, in the Israeli society, often coincide but may also be dissociated: ethnic origin, religiosity, and lower status. It is the combination of the three that delineates the potential constituency of Shas supporters. This constellation has no counterpart among middle class nonreligious Ashkenazim, for whom, as we have seen, ethnicity plays a limited role if any. What is also evident from our data, however, is that while the development of Shas marks a sharpening of public articulation of the Mizrahi–Ashkenazi cleavage, the attitudes and perspectives that stand behind this sharpening indicate the opposite: a general tendency of mitigation of ethnic differences.

Rapprochement

In sum, the Ashkenazi-Mizrahi ethnic cleavage is diminishing in importance. The dominant identification in the sample of nonimmigrant Jewish Israelis is national rather than ethnic and the decline of the ethnic allegiance does not seem important to the majority, although this is more the case among Ashkenazim than among Mizrahim. Data collected over the past thirty years indicate that this diminishing of the ethnic cleavage is a long-term trend that is also marked by the narrowing of cognitive and social distances between the categories and the deintensification of ethnic-deprivation charges by Mizrahim. Substantial differences do remain in voting and political behavior, although they do not seem as blunt from up close as they do at first sight. These developments, we suggest, correlate with the shift in Mizrahi power in the political arena and among elites that influence the feelings and perceptions of Mizrahim about their social station.

In part, these achievements trace to growing left-right polarization in the national political scene, which has vastly enhanced the political bargaining power of the Mizrahi public. These circumstances also explain why former taboos against autonomous ethnic parties (on the grounds of the divisiveness among Jews that they would supposedly cause) have lost their inhibitive power, allowing a party like Shas to emerge and become a major political actor—a development that, in turn, made the Mizrahim even more powerful in the polity at large.

The kind of ethnicity illustrated by Mizrahim does much to account for these developments. The Mizrahi collective identity centers on basically positive orientations toward heritages. Like all Jewish traditional identities, it is grounded in the three principles of *'Am Yisrael, Elohei/Torat Yisrael,* and *Eretz Yisrael.* Even though concurrently they are open to their environment and to cultural transformation, this explains why many Mizrahim are reluctant to renounce in the Land of the Jews the markers of their Judaism which were theirs when they lived among Gentile attitudes. This interested individuals to turn to the "world of the Torah" and gradually form a new religious-political elite. The existence of this kind of collective identity is confirmed by the relationship of ethnic allegiance and religiosity evinced by Mizrahim. In this sense, Mizrahim contrast with Ashkenazim (excluding the Ultra-Orthodox), who, by embracing secular Jewish nationalism, are willing to de-emphasize the importance of their ethnicity. In contrast, among Mizrahim, ethnic allegiances—especially in lower-class communities—represent tributes to customs reflecting religious legacies that imply a notion of nationhood. What the dominant culture would favor here is that ethnic allegiances, reference to traditions, and religious faith shrink at the benefit of direct and unbuffered loyalty to nationhood, in a secular-nationhood spirit that gives new meanings to old-symbolic resources and religious principles. This is the context of Mizrahim's ethnicity and its undeletable link to religion, as apparent in our data which show that Mizrahi ethnic allegiances fluctuate with religiosity, education, and social status. At the same time, these data also show that this syndrome is losing ground over time and in socially mobile milieus, and all in all, one may speak of a rapprochement of Mizrahim and Ashkenazim.

Mizrahi Ultra-Orthodoxy

To discuss the Mizrahim in these first years of the twenty-first century requires a consideration of the emergence and development of Shas as such a focus on one of the most intriguing paradoxes in this area, namely that Mizrahim who are mostly "traditional" find a channel for the expression of their feelings by supporting Shas, even though few of them follow the movement's Ultra-Orthodox calling.

This paradox was the object of previous study (see Ben-Rafael and Leon, 2005) which firstly evoked cultural codes—reverence for traditions and spiritual leaders—that existed in Mizrahi communities and were never shattered by an inner cultural revolution com-

parable to the one that swept the Jewish communities of Eastern
Europe during the nineteenth century (Deshen, 1999). These codes
were strong enough to bring some youngsters—probably among the
more talented and promising—to go to yeshivas (of Sephardic as
well as Ashkenazi styles) and become rabbis. Thus, ever since the
1970s and early 1980s, a generation of rabbinical scholars emerged
and could be found in numerous rabbinical positions in Mizrahi
communities as well as at the head of a whole network of schools
and yeshivas.

On the other hand, these codes of respect for the world of the
Torah were not strong enough to withstand the long-term challenge
of many Mizrahi young people who, like nonreligious Ashkenazim,
are increasingly inclined to place "Israeliness" before "Jewishness"
and tend to weaken their commitment to religious Judaism. This
development, to be sure, is an indication of the fact that the Mizrahi-
Ashkenazi cleavage has lost much of its acuity. At the same time, it
is an alarm for the new Mizrahi religious elite that the loyalty to past
legacies and to the ancestral faith is going through a far-reaching
crisis. It is in this context, we may suggest here, that one observes
during these years the formation of a new brand of Mizrahi religiosity that, in various respects, duplicates the generation of Ashkenazi
Ultra-Orthodoxy in the late 1800s. At this epoch in Central and
Eastern Europe, also, modernity and secularism were making progress
together with the emancipation of Jews who were easier to distance
themselves from traditional beliefs and customs. Religious leaders
were often ousted from central leadership while the status and authority of community institutions were declining dramatically. It is in this
context that Eastern European rabbis joined the initiative of the creation of Agudat Yisrael, in view of fighting back, among Jews, the
desertion of what they saw as the only legitimate Judaism (Bacon,
1996; Mittleman, 1996). They created thereby a new pattern of
Jewish behavior marked by zealous investment in Jewish commands,
enrollment in the fight for the survival of Judaism, and a multiplication of markers symbolizing their mission among Jews. These principles came to distinguish what was to be called by the individuals
involved "haredim" (the "anxious") and was translated as Ultra-
Orthodox by outsiders.

The difference of circumstances notwithstanding, it is the same
kind of situation that the new Mizrahi religious elite encountered in
the 1970s and 1980s: the strength of secularism in a Jewish sovereignty

where to loosen the ties to the faith and to legacies does not mean
ceasing to be Jewish. This latter trait only made things worse in the
eyes of the religious, as it still amplified the removal of Jews from
the only "true" way that warranted collective salvation. It is against
this background that many of the new Mizrahi religious elite drew
inspiration from their Ashkenazi predecessors and adopted the three
principles of Ultra-Orthodoxy—exhibiting zealous loyalty to Jewish
commands, enrolling themselves in every task perceived as forward-
ing the survival of their concept of Judaism, and multiplying their
distinctive markers (actually borrowing many of them from Lithuanian
Judaism). Last but not least, like their Ashkenazi counterparts, these
Mizrahi Ultra-Orthodox also created their party, Shas, which was
not only to be an electoral engine but also a community of dedicated individuals—scholars, rabbis and students—attached to the
commands of Haredi Judaism. In this respect, Shas constitutes a tool
for struggle over the religious "soul" of the Mizrahim.

On the other hand, Shas was also able to obtain political suc-
cesses, exploiting the respect for the learned and the rabbi in the
Mizrahi community, and the consequent frequent feeling of veneration, on the side of many a traditional—nay even a nonobservant—
Mizrahi for the leaders and spokesmen of Shas. What fueled this
support was also, of course, the emphasis of Shas on its acting at
the benefit of underprivileged Mizrahi communities. Hence, Shas
played on no less than three boards: the religious, the ethnic, and
the social. For Shas itself, it is the religious issue that is principally
at stake, but for Shas as a party, the social and the ethnic constitute in their conjunction the best cement of a new force which shares
strong political ambitions.

If, as asked at the onset of this part of our investigation, Mizrahim—
especially those who are marked by underprivileged status, ethnic
allegiance, and traditionalism—are relatively numerous to sustain
Ultra-Orthodox Mizrahi rabbis, this is not necessarily accounted for
by the project for which these rabbis stand for, or because their condition has worsened unbearably and they look for "responsible" leadership. The reason rather lies in the fact that Shas, headed by spiritual
and rabbinical authorities, reinforces their sense of dignity as members of a Jewish society respectful of traditions.

These developments, let us add, may even impact on some socially
mobile individuals of Mizrahi origin in spite of their quasi disap-
pearance in the non ethnic predominantly Ashkenazi middle class.

In the atmosphere created by the strengthening of the Mizrahi collective in the polity, Mizrahi origin now represents a capital asset for use in social advancement—initially under politicians' control and eventually by its own dynamics. This may be primarily—as an additional asset—to the advantage of those who are already socially mobile, even though, according to their own testimonies, such people rarely encounter discrimination. The interesting interaction revealed here shows that the strengthening of non mobile Mizrahim, as a disputed constituency for all parties and as a basis for the emergence of an important ethnoreligious party, has widened the space of social opportunities available to mobile Mizrahim, many of whom have actually seceded from their ethnic community.

Of course, Mizrahim are not the only group that has contributed to the confusion that besets Israel's ethnic landscape: recent immigrants are another.

CHAPTER SIX

RUSSIAN IMMIGRANTS

Introduction

We use the term "Russian Jews" or "Russians" to denote the immigrants who have been arriving *en masse* from all parts of the Soviet Union and the former Soviet Union (FSU) since late 1989. Russian Jewry, as we may recall, was one of the largest and most active Jewish communities in the world before the Bolshevik ascension in 1917. It was in Imperial Russia that Zionism and Jewish Socialism were born, that Hebrew theater and Yiddish literature flourished, and that new forms of Judaism emerged. It is also from Russia that Jews emigrated to Palestine and created the structures of a new society, and that others—much more numerous—emigrated to America to establish new powerful diasporas. Starting in 1917, however, three generations of Russian Jews experienced massive pressure and repression of public and free expression of their Jewishness (Gold, 1995; Leshem and Sicron, 1998). After more than seventy years of Marxist-Leninist rule, Jews were dispossessed of their singular culture and left with only vague notions of Judaism.

What remained, for the most part, was Jewish identification (Gittleman, 1994; 2003). Soviet Jews knew that they were Jews, empathized with fellow Jews and, later, with the State of Israel, and resented the plight that was theirs in the Soviet Union, confined as they were to a vulnerable economic, social, and political situation vis-à-vis the non-Jewish population and the establishment alike. Although officially defined as one of the Soviet nationalities, they were denied an institutional, territorial, and even cultural setting of their own. The "autonomous territory" of Birobidjan in Siberia, "allotted" to Jews in the 1930s but settled by few, was by no means a satisfactory solution. The Soviet authorities themselves changed their minds about this territorialization of the Jews, and after World War II, ceased to regard Birobidjan as a solution to the "Jewish problem." Although antisemitism was officially condemned in vehement terms, anti-Zionism was loudly and actively articulated in the media and in trials of prominent Jews. Under these conditions, no few Soviet Jews immersed themselves in mainstream Russian culture and eventually became ambivalent about their Jewish identity. Still, in the last phases of Soviet rule a reawakening of Jewish national consciousness occurred (Rothenberg, 2000). Many Jews seized the opportunity of the crumbling of Communism to emigrate to safer shores—the U.S., Germany, and, principally, Israel (Troen and Bade, 1991; Groman, 1999; Aptekman, 1993).

Since the mid-1990s, Israel has been the largest center of Russian-speaking Jewry (Khanin, 2003).[1] According to the Israel Ministry of Immigrant Absorption and the Jewish Agency, approximately 1,100,000 Israel citizens had immigrated from the USSR/FSU by 1999, including the immigrants of the early 1970s[2] and those who came after 1980.[3] These immigrants tend as a rule to remain distinct vis-à-vis the absorbing society and to form speech communities of their own (Kagansky, 1999). This also seems to be the rule for Russian-Jewish immigrants in Western diasporas such as the United States (Markowitz, 1993; Gold, 1995) and Germany (Zilberg, 1998).

---

[1] The FSU remains the second-largest center of Russian-speaking Jews, with a population estimated at 600,000–1,000,000 despite mass emigration and depopulation. More than half a million Russian Jews and members of their families live in North America, Jewish immigrants from the FSU constitute about one-third of the 80,000 registered members of the Jewish community in Germany, and no fewer than one-fourth of the 100,000 Russians in Australia are émigré Jews (Kupovetsky, 2000: 134). The recent Jewish migrations from the USSR/FSU have also led to the establishment or strengthening of Russian-speaking Jewish communities in other countries. In all, over the past thirteen years about 1.6 million people (some sources number them at about 2 million) have taken advantage of the "Jewish channel" to leave the USSR/FSU—about a million Jews, 400,000 ethnic Russians, and more than 100,000 Ukrainians (Groman, 1999: 3–4). As a result, according to some data, "Russian-Jewish communities" now exist in fifty-two countries on five continents (Slutsky, 1999: 16).

[2] Interview by Zeev Khanin with Dr. Marina Solodkin, then Israel Deputy Minister of Immigrant Absorption, Herzliya, Israel, November 1999. According to available data, about 100,000 of these people subsequently repatriated to the FSU or emigrated to the U.S., Canada, or other countries (see Khanin, 2003).

[3] According to official Jewish Agency data, 790,475 people moved from the USSR/FSU to Israel between 1989 and May 1999. Of them, 240,402 (30.4 percent) came from the Russian Federation 249,103 (31.5 percent) from Ukraine, 127,927 (16 percent) from other European post-Soviet republics; and 154,465 (19.5 percent) from republics of Central Asia and the Caucasus. See "Mid-Year Summary of the Jewish Agency Activities in the FSU, January–May 1999," submitted to the Jewish Agency Board of Governors, Jerusalem, June 1999, p. 13. About 50,000 more came between May 1999 and May 2000 (*MIGNews*, No. 2 [May 10, 2000], p. 5).

The Israeli case, however, is special because mass immigration from the FSU soon accounted for a large percentage of both the population of origin (around 40 percent of FSU Jews now live in Israel) and of the target population (nearly 20 percent of Israeli Jews and 17 percent of the total Israeli population). Before their immigration, many of these Jews had belonged to the middle class—doctors, engineers, teachers, scientists, writers, and artists (Solodkina, 1995). The percent of persons with higher schooling was four times higher among FSU immigrants than the Soviet average (ibid.). Some 55 percent had at least twelve years of schooling as against 28 percent among the Jewish population of Israel in 1989, the year preceding the onset of mass immigration (Sicron, 1990). Upon their arrival, the immigrants shared the feeling and the awareness that they were coming from a country that had been one of the world's two superpowers for decades. The international status of Russian culture also gave them a sense of value (Horowitz, 1989). At the time of their immigration, however, their country of origin was undergoing a severe social, political, and economic crisis (Brym, 1997). They were aware of this, if only due to the antisemitic nationalist movements that they had to confront (Gudkov, 2000; Solodkina, 1995). Their difficult relations with non-Jewish populations in the FSU were among the major push factors in their immigration (Horowitz and Leshem, 1998; Leshem and Sicron, 1998). Pull factors were at work as well, including expectations of Israel that were encouraged by Israeli, Zionist, and American Jewish organizations (Solodkina, 1995). These organizations stressed the right of Jews anywhere to immigrate to Israel, as embodied in the Law of Return, a statute that entitles Jewish immigrants to citizenship and economic support as soon as they take their first steps in the country. These dispositions themselves nourish expectations that are often dashed by the practical hardships of adaptation. Indeed, the absorption of so many immigrants within so few years presented Israeli society and its physical, occupational, educational, and cultural structures with a severe challenge (Zilberg and Leshem, 1999).

Some circumstances, however, helped the FSU immigrants to form a rather coherent population group, thereby justifying their description as "Russians." Throughout the Soviet empire, not only in Russia, Jews generally belonged to the most educated milieus. People in these milieus, even in areas where different languages prevailed, knew Russian, used it as their principal language, and were immersed in mainstream Russian culture.

On the other hand, it is also estimated that in 2003, 25 percent of the FSU immigrants did not meet the religious criteria of Jewishness (Jewish matrimonial descent or religious conversion). However, an estimated one-third of these individuals had a Jewish parent, grandparent, or spouse. Another third were socially assimilated among Jews; and the last third simply pretended to be Jews in order to leave their country of origin and be allowed in Israel. Here, most of these people have joined Russian-Jewish communities, assimilating easily because many Russian Jews themselves lack Jewish education and willingly allow the non-Jews to settle among them. Few (less than 7 percent) of these non-Jews, as defined above, revert to their original religious identity after their settlement in Israel and establish or join Christian congregations.[4]

Even among Russian immigrants who are Jewish, however, hundreds of thousands were motivated to immigrate more by instrumental than by nationalist considerations. In Israel, they, like immigrants everywhere, aspired to find work and reestablish their homes in the most profound sense of the term. Although they now learned about Jewishness and adjusted to their new Israeli identity, they were unwilling to abandon their cultural and linguistic resources. Today, in fact, they do their best to retain Russian as the family and community vernacular and continue to appreciate Russian and its culture more than Hebrew and Israeli culture. This, however, does not prevent them from considering it important to acquire Hebrew in order to ease their acculturation and "feel Israeli." In a nutshell, Russian Jews feel committed to their fellow ethnics in one way or another and also, to a lesser degree, feel that they belong to the Jewish people at large and the Jews of Israel in particular.

The Russian Jews' continued identification with their ethnic group, however, varies in accordance with their personal paths. After their arrival, many initially find themselves in low-status jobs but their high incidence of above-average schooling, professional experience, and status self-image betray their middle-class ambitions (Ben-Rafael, et al., 1997). These traits, to be sure, weaken their ethnocultural identification. By the same token, the Israeli establishment in charge

---

[4] Vladimir Khanin, "Russian Jews in Israel," lecture at the New Israeli Elites Seminar, Tel Aviv University, April 20, 2003.

of their absorption is by no means aggressive and no longer feels obliged to implement the *mizug galuyot* ("fusion of exiles") ideology with zeal. This is a direct consequence not only of the Russians' own wishes but also of the rising strength of the Mizrahi public which earned recognition for its own particularism ever since the 1980s. The ascendancy of Mizrahi strength encourages Russian Jews, too, to pursue an ethnocultural orientation and to find ways of fulfilling it in community, cultural, social, and political activities where the Russian language plays a major part.

Moreover, Russian Jews also maintain strong relations with their country of origin and with kindred communities elsewhere (like Germany and the United States). These relations, under today's conditions of globalization, have transformed Russian Jewry into a "transnational community" (Soysal, 1994; Baubok, 1994). This is evidenced by frequent visits among friends and relatives who live in diverse parts of the world, tours in Israel of artists from Russia, and daily watching of Russian television, to name only a few. These phenomena do not gainsay that no few middle-class Russian Jews are tempted to assimilate into Israel's predominant non ethnic middle class; in fact, the process is already under way. However, for the time being, many also wish to identify with their community and affirm their Russian culture and language. These people are contributing to the emergence of an Israeli-Russian ("Hebrush") that borrowing numerous Hebrew tokens and forms of speech up to forming a kind of interlanguage indicating Israeli-Russian Jewishness.

It is in this context that we phrased the research questions that guided us in this part of our research project. We thought it especially important to focus on this issue, that is, how strongly ethnicization affects Russians, and to what extent they tend, in parallel, to "Israelize." In a related context, we asked how confidently we may expect the "ethnicization" of the Russians to remain a one-generation phenomenon or to tend to replicate itself in time.

The Encounter with Israel

A body of research works about Russian Jews in Israel (Adler, ed. 1999) shows that many of the Russian immigrants' characteristics take on new significance in their encounter with Israeli society. Coming from a world power, they often perceive Israel as a small, isolated, and culturally provincial country that has not yet solved its problems of defense, borders, and governance (Leshem and Sicron, 1998). On the other hand, this group, in which doctors, scientists, artists, and other professionals are overrepresented, is often marked by feelings of failure due to their difficulties in finding appropriate fields of activity in Israel.

Immigrants who do not always acknowledge the value of the local culture also fail to meet the absorbing society's expectations (Solodkina, 1995; Leshem, 1993). The most negative response to such immigrants comes from nonimmigrants—of North African and Middle Eastern origins—who happen to live in the neighborhoods where they settle and who most often themselves belong to underprivileged strata and are especially distant from Russians' culture (Lewin-Epstein, et al., 1993; Lissak, 1995; Damian and Rosenbaum-Tamari, 1993). The acculturation benefits that government institutions give newcomers do not soften the attitude of this population toward them, and the immigrants' small families, higher schooling, and occupational experience that ease their access to social opportunities often generate envy and resentment. Yet while other categories of nonimmigrants are not always eager to make heavy sacrifices to assure the successful absorption of recent immigrants, some still regard FSU immigrants as potential allies in their confrontation with other segments of the population. Indeed, quite a few nonreligious Israeli Jews expect these immigrants to reinforce their own resistance to pressures exerted by religious factions.

These circumstances illustrate an insertion process fraught with difficulties that leads to divergences within the immigrant population itself. Quite a few tend to segregate themselves, expressing no interest in dialoguing with other Israelis; some orient themselves toward Western culture exclusively (Zilberg, 1998). Nudelman (1997) describes a "separatist" group of immigrants who resent the loss of status that their immigration has caused. In brief, and according to Zilberg and Leshem (1999), FSU immigrants go about their socialization in Israel in three ways: assimilation tendencies, partial insertion, and self-segregation. All in all, they do experience a downgrading of their human resources as a result of immigration, and many now find themselves in lower-status strata, but no few invest in their best in adjusting to the reality they find here and enter channels of social mobility—quite a few with impressive success in professional areas and business (Raday and Bunk, 1993).

It is in this context that our research expected to find a complex identity among Russian respondents. This is generally typical of migrants who switch cultures, but it should especially be the case of FSU immigrants in Israel, because members of this group were notably ambivalent about nationality and ethnicity in their country of origin as well. In the USSR, as we recall, being Jewish cast a pall over one's Russianness (Farago, 1989; Rothenberg, 2000; Gittelman, 1994, Ritterband, 1997). Immigration to Israel redefined the relationship between these identities: Jewishness was now the prevailing identity in the national society; the Russian identity metamorphosed into an ethnic token (Nudelman, 1997). Concurrently, the immigrants developed a third identity, the Israeli one. Hence, our research questions asked about the extent and the ways in which acculturation in Israel transformed the immigrants' identities.

COLLECTIVE IDENTITIES

The first question asked how effectively Russians adopted Israeliness as an identity and how they related it to Jewishness and to Russianness. FSU immigrants still seem to emphasize their Russian and Jewish identities (more or less equally) more than they do their Israeli identity (Table 6.1). To set these findings in perspective, they were compared with those of nonimmigrants, whom we divided here according to broad ethnocultural divisions and who, as a rule, emphasize Israeliness much more. Concomitantly, preference of the ethnic identity is much stronger among FSU immigrants than among both nonimmigrant categories.

Table 6.1. Preferred (First-Choice) Identity, by Origin (Percent)*

First-choice identity	Respondents by Origin			
	Ashkenazim	Mizrahim	Russians	Total
Ethnic (Ashk, Miz, Rus)	19	11	47	28
Jewish	40	40	45	41
Israeli	41	49	8	31
Total (Chi-square: 203,8**)	100	100	100	100
N	300	300	397	997

* Cramer's v = 0.32**. Source: Survey 1.

Immigrants, to be sure, emphasize ethnicity much more than Mizrahim and Ashkenazim, though they seem to find a common language with them when it comes to Jewishness. However, when we bear in mind the contrasting backgrounds of the groups, we realize that the respective categories reflect very different notions of Jewishness. For Russians, as we know, Jewishness denotes mainly the awareness of belonging to a particular historical-cultural collective, and this kind of approach differs from the legacy-allegiance and the Jewish-nationalism brands especially characteristic (respectively) of Mizrahim and Ashkenazim (see Chapter 5). The contrast, actually, is particularly striking with respect to the weakness of "Israeliness" as a first-choice collective identity, in comparison with nonimmigrants.

Identity preferences, moreover, are clearly affected by length of stay in Israel: the longer this stay, the more immigrants prefer the Jewish identity over the Russian one. This may reflect gradual social adjustment and the importance that Israeli society attributes to Jewish identity. However, it may also be assumed that the various waves of Russian immigrants differ from each other in their motivations and perspectives. Thus, those who opened the path of emigration to Israel from the FSU may well have been those with the strongest Jewish-Zionist awareness, while those who followed might have been more motivated by instrumental reasons (like the fear of deteriorating economic conditions). In any case, both explanations help to account for the gap between earlier and later immigrants.

Table 6.2. Preferred (First-Choice) Identity of Russians,
by Length of Stay in Israel (Percent)*

First-choice identity	Immigrated			Total
	1989–1992	1993–1996	1997+	
Ethnic (Russian)	37	59	63	47
Jewish	52	36	33	45
Israeli	11	6	4	8
Total (Chi-square: 20,5**)	100	100	100	100
N	226	123	48	397

* Cramer's v = 0.16**. Source: Survey 1.

It comes out in Table 6.2 that even among first-wave immigrants, a relatively small percentage—though larger than in the other two categories—selected Israeliness as their first-choice identity. This seems to indicate that the tendency among Russian Jews in Israel to "go ethnic" is not transient and is corroborated by the fact that while many immigrants (42 percent) consider Israeliness an important component of their identity, fewer (11 percent) speak of it as their first identity while a majority (58 percent) define "Russian Jewishness" or "Jewish Russianness" as their primary identification.

These findings do not indicate that immigrants refrain from developing any sense of solidarity with their new society. However, they reveal a gap between immigrants and nonimmigrants (Tables 6.3 and 6.4). We approached this issue from two different perspectives— sense of belonging ("To what extent do you feel an integral part of Israeli society?") and aspirations for children's future in Israel ("Would you like your children to live in Israel?"). We found substantial differences in the responses to both questions. A complementary question on this topic showed that more than two-thirds of the immigrants wish to live in Israel, 9 percent would rather live in their country of origin, and 18 percent prefer some other third country. The proportion of respondents who would like their children to live in Israel is somewhat lower among immigrants (70 percent) than among nonimmigrants. However, if we bear in mind that immigrants' sense of social belonging is much lower than nonimmigrants', we see that we encounter here a complex attitude that combines a degree of alienation from Israeli society with an unequivocal sense of patriotism. Unsurprisingly, it was also among immigrants who emphasize their Russian identity as their preferred identity that we found the highest rate of alienation from Israeli society (Table 6.5).

Table 6.3: Sense of Social Belonging—Russian Immigrants vs. Nonimmigrants (Percent)*

To what extent do you feel an integral part of society?	Mean
Nonimmigrants (N = 594)	82
Russians (N = 386)	48
Total (N = 980)	68

* t = 19.7**; scale 0–100: 0 = not at all; 100 = very much. Source: Survey 1.

Table 6.4. Aspirations of Belonging: Russian Immigrants vs.
Nonimmigrants (Percent)

Do you want your children to live in Israel?	Immigrants (N = 400)	Longtimers (N = 800)
Not at all	18	4
Indifferent	11	5
Want very much	71	91
Mean (0–100 scale)*	70	91
Total	100	100

* Diff: 21; t = 15**; P < .05*; P < .01**. Source: Survey 1.

Table 6.5. Sense of Social Belonging among Russians,
by Self-Identification

To what extent do you feel an integral part of society? First identity of respondents:	Mean
Russian (N = 183)	37
Jewish (N = 90)	57
Israeli (N = 24)	63
Total (N = 386)	48

F = 27**. Source: Survey 1.

SENSE OF DISTANCE

The next item asked about how distant Russian immigrants and non-immigrants feel from each other. Overall, Russians feel quite close to Ashkenazi nonimmigrants and much less so to Mizrahim (Table 6.6).

Table 6.6. Russians' Attitude toward Nonimmigrants,
by Length of Stay in Israel (Percent)

How distant do you feel from . . .	Year of immigration	N	Mean
Ashkenazim	1989–1992	224	22
	1993–1996	120	30
	1997+	47	34
	Total (F = 7.4**)	391	26
Mizrahim	1989–92	220	63
	1993–96	120	63
	1997+	47	65
	Total (F: not significant)	387	63

Source: Survey 1.

As time passes, Russians feel closer to Ashkenazim but remain as distant from Mizrahim. Thus, Russians are by no means a "neutral" element in Israel's ethnocultural landscape. The underlying attitude of nonimmigrants toward immigrants is also of interest. Here, we phrased our question differently in order to avoid a conflict with social desirability. Instead of asking about feelings of closeness to immigrants, we inquired about willingness to shoulder the burden of immigration. As a general rule, immigrants are quite welcome, although this attitude varies strongly according to ethnic categories (Table 6.7).

Nonimmigrants are favorably disposed to immigration even when this entails sacrifices. Clearly, however, Ashkenazim are more positive about immigration than Mizrahim. Thus, Ashkenazim reciprocate the Russians' positive feelings about them and Mizrahim reflect less-positive feelings—seemingly due to Russians' human capital which threatens their own relative status in society.

Table 6.7. Nonimmigrants' Attitudes toward Immigration,
by Ethnicity (Percent)*

Should immigration be sustained even at the cost of a decline in standard of living of people like yourself?	Ashk	Miz	Total
Yes, definitely	34	21	27
Yes	33	19	26
Indifferent	7	26	22
No	10	16	13
Not at all	6	18	12
Total	100	100	100
N	290	298	588
Mean	30.3	47.9	39.2

* Cramer's v = 0.24**; t = 6.66**. Source: Survey 1.

Table 6.8. Attitudes of Russians toward Immigration to Israel,
by Length of Stay

Would you urge your friends in Russia to immigrate to Israel?	%
Strongly	23
So-so	74
No	3
Total (no statistical difference)	100
N	397

Source: Survey 1.

Be this as it may, it is also obvious that immigrants do not affirm the principle of immigration to Israel as an unmitigated blessing (Table 6.8). Their willingness to urge friends who stayed in Russia to immigrate to Israel, an indicator of their appreciation of the society that they found and of their own experience, is hesitant. This attitude, widely held among Russians, does not correlate with any major background factor such as length of stay in the country, education, or income.

Irrespective of any other aspect investigated, a large majority of immigrants take a moderate stance toward the reality that they have found in Israel: they neither idealize their situation nor treat it with excessive pessimism. When asked about their expectations in the near future (three years), 55 percent of immigrants are optimistic, 30 percent expect no changes, and only 10 percent are pessimistic.[5] Notably, the older the immigrants, the less optimistic they are,[6] but on the other hand, the longer immigrants stay in the country, the more optimistic they become.[7]

THE POLITICAL DIMENSION

The crucial question that we ask at this juncture concerns the extent to which Russians are inclined to become politically active in order to press their particularistic claims efficiently and to participate in shaping the general social order.

According to Khanin (2003), very favorable conditions for the establishment of a Russian-Jewish political community are taking shape in Israel. This is so for several reasons, foremost demography. As of 2003, FSU immigrants accounted for about 14 percent of the Israeli electorate, the equivalent of 17–18 seats in the 120-seat Knesset (Israel Parliament). Even more important—and following the political success of the Mizrahim—is the ongoing ascendancy in Israeli public consciousness of the idea of multiculturalism and social heterogeneity as a natural phase in the development of this society. It is in this context that the institutional, social, and economic infra-

---

[5] The average optimism score was 65 on a scale of 0–100, with 0 as utter pessimism and 100 as total optimism.
[6] Correlation coefficient: –38**.
[7] Correlation coefficient: 0.20**.

structure of the Russian-Israeli community developed rapidly in the 1990s. This development drew on two kinds of initiatives—those of Israeli authorities, meant to facilitate the immigrants' insertion, and those of the immigrants themselves in social, political, economic, and cultural fields. From this point of departure, leading immigrant personalities advanced to the next phase, the establishment of political movements of their own while others, however, advocated making do with strong Russian caucuses in mainstream parties. The debate resulted in the formation of both Russian lobbyist groups in national parties (Labor, Likud, National Religious Party, Shinui, and even Shas) and independent "Russian" parties, such as the right-of-center Yisrael Ba'aliya (Israel in Immigration), the far-right Yisrael Beiteinu (Israel, Our Home), and the leftist Ha-behira ha-Democratit (Democratic Choice) (Khanin, 2003). In 2002, however, the modest achievements of these parties brought leaders back to the alternative strategy, i.e., to form ethnic caucuses within national parties.

Be this as it may, nearly one-third of our respondents tend to abstain or remain aloof from the political scene, 50 percent profess allegiance to Russian parties, and fewer than 20 percent pledge political allegiance to national parties. We found no systematic correlation between sociological factors, like education or income, and willingness to support overt ethnic politics.

Table 6.9. Political Preferences of Russians,
by Length of Stay in Israel (Percent)*

If elections were held today, how would you vote?	Arrived 1989–1992	Arrived 1993–1996	Arrived 1997+	Total Immigrants
Likud	11	3	6	8
Labor	6	7	15	7
Meretz	3	4	4	4
Yisrael Ba'aliya	40	41	25	39
Yisrael Beiteinu	10	12	10	11
Other/no opinion	30	33	40	31
Total	100	100	100	100
N	226	123	48	397

* Cramer's v (length of stay in Israel × voting pattern) = .14. Source: Survey 3.

Table 6.9 shows that the most recently arrived are also the most aloof politically, with 40 percent expressing "other" or "no opinion" as against 30 percent among those of the longest length of stay.

Furthermore, in comparison to the more recently arrived, the two other categories illustrate a quite strong ethnic political allegiance, with 50 percent supporting the two main Russian parties as opposed to 35 percent of the most recently arrived. Overall, severe aloofness from the political scene is quite characteristic of a large part of this new population group, while more veteran individuals seem to exhibit stronger political interests and to favor ethnic parties.

The solidity of this support for Russian parties, however, should not be overestimated. The sharp decline in the power of these parties in 2002 is probably explained by general dissatisfaction among their constituencies with leaders who, according to many critics, are more eager to bolster their personal stature than to serve Russian Jews' specific interests. It is in this manner that many interpret the manifest gliding to the rightist wing of the political spectrum of most Russian public figures elected to the Knesset by ethnic ballots, in the context of the right-of-center Likud's political dominance since the mid-1990s.

A Transnational Diaspora

An additional point that deserves emphasis is the gradual development of Israel's Russian-Jewish community into a transnational diaspora. This type of development, which we monitored from a source other than our own research (Liciczia, forthcoming), is marked by various aspects and actions such as the establishment of transnational professional networks and organizations that hold conferences, issue publications, perform research, and, above all, engage in educational activities. Literary activity is one of many examples: scores of Russian writers who live and write in Israel have their manuscripts printed in Russia, where the cost is lower, and distribute their books in Russia, Israel, and other Russian-speaking communities around the world.

We also know of Russian Jewish financial "tycoons" who develop their businesses in Russia and Israel concurrently and, eventually, in the U.S and other countries. This is expressed, among other things, in the development of global Russian-speaking television channels, a highly relevant type of activity since Russian-speaking media are largely watched throughout the Russian diaspora. Thus, it is no wonder that television broadcasts from Moscow carry advertisements

Figure 6.1. Summary: Identities of Russian Immigrants

Aspects of Israeli Identity of Russians

---

1. Only a small percentage selected Israeli identity as their first choice; this is a much smaller percentage than among nonimmigrants

2. A much larger percentage use selected Israeli identity as their second choice

3. The longer Russian immigrants stay in Israel, the more they tend to adopt an Israeli identity

4. A clear majority would like their children to live in Israel, but less than nonimmigrants

5. Respondents whose identity is Israeli are more likely to feel an integral part of Israeli society than those who maintain their Russian identity

6. Russian respondents are not eager to persuade others to follow in their footsteps

---

for products sold in Tel Aviv, since Tel Aviv is part of the market of Moscow television. This extensive transnational activity is augmented by numerous visits to Israel by Russian artists—singers, dance troupes, orchestras, etc. At a more personal level, tourism between Russian-speaking communities in Israel and elsewhere is progressing. Last but not least, during 2000 and 2002, a new organization has appeared, the "World Congress of Russian-Speaking Jews" that has opened offices in Jerusalem, Berlin, New York, and other places of the world, not to mention Moscow and other cities in the FSU. This framework encourages conferences and cultural activities, and cultivates political interests within the Jewish world as well as vis-à-vis national and international organs and institutions. All these signify the retention of cross-border connections and the presence of multiple agents that embody the very concept of a transnational diaspora.

It is true, of course, that Russian Jews are not the only transnational diaspora in Israel. Jews have always been paragons of transnational diasporic behavior in world history. Moreover, that the Russian Jewish transnational diaspora involves one specific group of Jews and not Jews at large is also illustrated by the Ultra-Orthodox, who also maintain strong worldwide relations with communities of their kind, and, to some extent, Sephardics, who tend to establish global umbrella organizations of their own. Even so, however, the case of Russian Jews is singular because it concerns individuals who identify with Jewishness but "ethnicize" on non-Jewish cultural and linguistic grounds.

ETHNICITY AND ISRAELINESS

The findings of this study do not convey an unequivocal message about the state and direction of the absorption of Russian Jews in Israel. Few FSU immigrants in the 1990s considered Israel the old-new homeland with which they wished to bond after generations of yearning. Neither, however, did they think of it as a mere way station. Niznick (2003) seconds our conclusions by describing the process of "shopping" for a new identity that she perceives among immigrants.[8] This wave of emigration to Israel, she reminds, is neither Zionist nor traditionally Jewish. Since immigrants had been strongly exposed to Russian culture before leaving the USSR/FSU, they have continued to assert their original cultural identity in Israel (Ritterband, 1997). The establishment of numerous Russian-language newspapers, community centers, theaters, and even schools is cited as evidence (Spolsky and Shohamy, 1999).

Ben-Rafael, et al., (1997) also believe that Russian Jews are attached to their original culture and identity and show that there is a high probability that they will become a new sociocultural entity of their own. Other studies reach similar conclusions (Rosenbaum-Tamari and Demiam, 1996). Accordingly, immigrants seem eager to acquire Hebrew mostly for utilitarian reasons and report a strong commitment to the Russian language and culture. Donitsa-Schmidt (1999), however, shows that positive attitudes toward the maintenance of Russian culture and language have not deterred the young, in the main, from undergoing a process of language shift.

Interestingly enough in regard to these conclusions, in 1992, a study among 100 FSU adolescents attending basic Hebrew courses (Kraemer, et al., 1995) revealed a highly positive attitude toward Hebrew, even though the respondents defined their identity as Russian first, Israeli second, and Jewish third. Immersed in Hebrew, almost from the moment of their arrival, in all walks of life outside the home, immigrants gradually relinquish their language of origin—even though they regard their Russian roots very favorably and con-

---

[8] Nonimmigrant Israelis disapprove of the newcomers' seeming lack of enthusiasm about the idea of becoming "real Israelis," and most recent Russian immigrants are disturbed by nonimmigrants' refusal to admit that they might benefit from newcomers' unique cultural experience.

sider their cultural origin an immense advantage (see also Donitsa-Schmidt (1999).

It is at this point that we can answer the research questions that guided our investigation of this group. Russian Jews in Israel are definitely undergoing "ethnicization" but their "Israelization" is undeniably progressing—especially where the younger generation is concerned. Where as well the older generation insists more on Jewish Russianness, the young are more likely to speak of Russianness and Israeliness.

Russian Jews, it is worthwhile to note at this point, share several similarities with another European group, the German Jews who arrived in the country in the 1930s fleeing Nazism. Most of the German-Jewish immigrants, like today's Russian Jews, were both secular and estranged from Jewish nationalism if not from Judaism itself. They identified with the German language and culture much as Russian Jews identify with the Russian language and culture. Moreover, the German Jews, like today's Russian immigrants, were strong in human capital and climbed rapidly from the bottom of the social scale to the core of the middle class. They made immense efforts to remain a distinct speech community, using German among themselves, with their offspring, and in cultural consumption. Their efforts would probably have left stronger imprints on Israel's culture and society than they did had the Holocaust not stripped everything German in Israel of its prestige and had triumphant Zionism, at this epoch, not won over the allegiance of German-Jewish youth.

Zionism is much less vigorous today than it was in the 1930s and Israel's relations with the former USSR are not overshadowed by anything resembling the memory of the Holocaust. These differences may well give Soviet Jews an opportunity to develop cultural and social life within Israeli society without encountering the same hardships as German Jews. Moreover, Russian Jews arrived for the most part after Shas had imposed by political means the recognition of Mizrahi ethno religious particularism, which, as such, paved the way to a wide recognition of the legitimacy of pluralism. Russian Jews thus benefited from the openness of the political center to multiculturalism and have been able to establish the community structures considered in the above. As a potentially mobile group, Soviet Jews may actually become Israel's first secular middle-class ethnic group of (mostly) European origin. Even if no few socially mobile Russian Jews will probably succumb to the temptation to assimilate due to social mobility, as far as the rest of the group is concerned, the very fact of social mobility may then serve as an asset for ethnic politics.

This analysis would not be complete without reference to the non-Ashkenazi Jews who have been immigrating from the southern tier of the FSU (mainly from predominantly Christian Georgia and the Muslim republics). Although they account for less than 10 percent of Russian Jews as we have defined them, they play an interesting role. Even today, very little is known about them and their acculturation in Israel. However, if we recall the experience of other groups of non-Ashkenazi Jews in Georgia, Bukhara, or Uzbekistan who immigrated in earlier years, we may assume that more than three generations of Sovietization have made the recently arrived non-Ashkenazi groups feel more a part of the Russian immigration than of the Mizrahi population. Though it is also to note that they generally exhibit stronger allegiance to a Jewish heritage that, in the Diaspora, was kept alive with relatively more success than in other parts of the USSR.

In sum, FSU Jews in Israel are building a collective identity that blends elements of three distinct identities. They are primarily Jewish—a Jewishness that is expressed more in commitment than in contents and that conveys weak notions of collective boundaries. They are, of course, also Russian—or, more accurately, "Russian Jews"—, which refers mainly to Russian cultural contents and linguistic resources, as well as an orientation toward a transnational diaspora. Last but not least, in Israel they are also becoming Israelis. This clearly visible token of their identity represents a new allegiance embodied in the acquisition of new symbols and a new language. In terms of identity, ethnicization in this case denotes a process of different criteria that clash, supersede each other, and respond to different codes. What is clear about FSU Jews is that the ambiguity of their identity allows different versions and emphases to surface.

One important underlying factor in this lack of clarity is the varying degrees of identification that one encounters among FSU Jews in Israel. In this respect, we have already emphasized that the dominant culture, which has long tended to favor the social uniformization of immigrants, has become much more tolerant of group differences. The group itself, in turn, values its symbols and language and widely rejects total assimilation as a goal. On the other hand, the tendency of this group to scatter across social classes with an important segment rapidly reaching the middle class influences in the sense of a mitigation of ethnic velleities. All in all, it seems that the likely outcome of the process will be partial assimilation and partial retentionism. FSU immigrants are so numerous that even if many assimilate enough may remain to perpetuate a "symbolic ethnicity" (Gans, 1979).

WHEN RELIGION IS MISSING

Russians, as shown by the above, certainly constitute a major component of contemporary Israeli multiculturalism. Yet, this is by no means a "regular" case of cleavage, by Israeli standards of multiculturalism. We, indeed, assumed at the onset of this work that a major characteristic of multiculturalism in this country is the link between religion and nationalism embodied by the dominant culture. This link, we assumed, impacts on the dominant culture's confrontation with diverging versions of the all-societal identity stemming from particular groups, which they too refer, in their own ways, to the religious principle in connection with their understanding of this identity.

When it comes to Russian Jews, however, it seems that things stand differently. Russian Jews, we have seen and emphasized, carry weak convictions and knowledge about Judaism, and for many of them, one may even speak of ignorance. One example that comes to mind is that for no few Russians—as the authors know from their personal dealings with students—there is nothing in the belief in Jesus that could be seen as contradictory to a Jewish identity. Testimonies confirm that in Russia itself, no few Jews attended Christian-Orthodox services. Moreover, the halakic regulations concerning "who is a Jew" were often completely disregarded even where they were of public knowledge among Jews. Here in Israel, it is hard for many a Russian Jew to cease seeing the child of a Jewish father and a non-Jewish mother as a non-Jew, while such a person was always considered Jewish in Russia itself, provided he or she felt Jewish. For him or for her, that this people has only one God and that this God has only one people, so to speak, was not really assimilated, and if it was, not as an identity imperative.

For both many halakic and non-halakic Jews who immigrated to
Israel, the embedment of religious dispositions, references, and symbols in the secular dominant culture came as a shock and often created a feeling of estrangement. A feeling of distance and an incapacity
to recognize oneself in the definitions and symbols offered by the
dominant culture to immigrants as a basis of sociocultural insertion.
In this, Russian Jews are certainly affected by the link of religion
and nationhood in the dominant culture, at least in a negative sense,
that is, as a factor of remoteness.

Yet, at the same time, as far as one can observe in the middle
of the first decade of this century, it also comes out that Russian
Jews do not appeal straightforwardly against the premises of the
dominant culture according to which an undeletable link ties up the
Jewish religion and Jewish nationhood. Actually, what one observes
is that spokesmen and women for the Russian Jews emphasize by a
variety of behaviors and discourses that Russian Jews do belong to
the Jewish nationhood to no lesser degree than anyone else. Hence,
one may interpret in this manner the rightism of the wide majority
of Russian-Jewish political forces. While it is public knowledge that
about 25% or 30% of the group are not halakic Jews, by no means
can one observe that Russian Jewish elites act in favor of a constitutional change of legal dispositions—for the need of civil registra-
tion—concerning "who is a Jew" and personal status. In brief, Russian
Jews do not belong, in Israel, to the ongoing debate of separating
or, at least, redefining, in a liberal sense, the religion-state relations.
In contrast, Russian Jewish political elites are at the forefront of the
fight over the retention of the West Bank and the Gaza Strip in the
frame of the Israeli sovereignty, a posture that corresponds both to
the power-oriented political culture that Russian Jews brought with
them from the USSR/FSU and to the elite's aspiration to insert
itself in the all-Israeli leading stratum. In brief, Russian Jews aspire
to advance their particular interests within the frame of existing
rules of the political-cultural all-national game despite the fact that
they are quite estranged from the premises that stand behind these
dispositions.

One may suggest here that this position reflects the fact that one
finds here a dominant culture that draws its legitimacy—even though,
selectively and not *en bloc*—from primordial legacies sanctified by
religion and history. It is this dominant culture that is confronted,

through the Russian Jewish group, with ethnic contents and symbols borrowed from non-Jewish cultural and linguistic resources. In a society like Israel, moved as it is by the kind of nationalism described here, this ethnicity can hardly stand the comparison—in terms of commitments and obligations as well as of relative weight and value in the eyes of the many—with that nationalism. Hence, the distance from religiosity of Russian Jews comes out not only as an axis of intellectual autonomy that contributes to creativity and capacity of criticism. It is also and mainly a source of weakness vis-à-vis the dominant culture when things come to confrontations and velleities to carry substantial changes in the definition of the all-national identity. This weakness, we think, should explain that, despite their numerical importance and the weight they might achieve in the polity, Russian Jews are reduced to a defensive, adaptive and pragmatic position over the multiple specific interests that singularize their plight in the Israeli society, from the viewpoint of constitutional dispositions—the problems of non-halakic Jews, marriage and conversion, the status of children of mixed marriages etc.

An additional—and crucial—aspect of this weakness, is precisely this very distance of Russian Jewish immigrants of recent decades from substantive definitions of Judaism, which also explains that many nonimmigrants reciprocate their feeling of estrangement. This is particularly paradoxical with respect to the offspring of veteran immigrants who came from Russia, Ukraine, and other former territories of the USSR. These daughters and sons of immigrants who belonged to the founding fathers of this society and had transferred to their new Hebrew culture many Russian cultural and linguistic elements could have found easily, at least in principle, a common language with the new Russian immigrants. But, the veterans actually came here not only with a rich Russian culture but also with a strong Jewish culture and a deep sensitivity for everything Jewish. To the extent that this sensitivity was transferred to the younger generations, directly or via the educational system that they created and inspired, these generations could not easily find a bridge of communication with the "new" Russians who had gone through about seventy years of Marxist-Leninist repression of Jewish culture and identity.

The historical, cultural, and social gap between these two branches of Russian Jewry that was widened over years and generations, cannot, today, be filled rapidly, and this signifies, that the new brand of Russian Jewishness will develop as its own aspect of the Israeli society for many years to come. This brand, moreover, in contrast to the other cleavages overviewed in previous chapters, is not in a position to challenge the basics of the all-national identity, largely due to the nature of its collective identity. For this reason, among others, it mainly aspires to warrant a flexibility of the dominant culture that could enable it to insert itself in the society, and accede to full membership in the national society without conceding its aspiration to continue to belong, in parallel, to the Russian culture and the Russian-speaking transnational diaspora. It is, indeed, by reference to this culture that, up to now, it draws pride from its historical experience.

Russian Jews thus represent here a force of liberal multiculturalism sustaining the autonomy of its constituents within the national society, rather than conflictual multiculturalism where groups primarily compete over the very definition of the national collective.

CHAPTER SEVEN

ETHIOPIAN JEWS

BACKGROUND

Within the Jewish world, Ethiopian Jews represent a group that could not be more different from Russian Jews. *Beta Israel* (the House of Israel), as the group was called, consists of a centuries-old ethno-religious minority in this country. Its Jewish origins are grounded in a form of religiosity culled from the Bible, several books in the Apocrypha, and other post-Biblical writings. The members of Beta Israel lived in provinces surrounding, and north of, Lake Tana. They were known until recently as Falashas, a term that they regard as derogatory and contemptuous (*Encyclopedia Judaica*, 2002).

Beta Israel traces its origins to inhabitants of Jerusalem who settled in Ethiopia with Menelik, son of King Solomon, and the Queen of Sheba. Historians and anthropologists take issue with this traditional belief defining Beta Israel as one of the Agau tribes that populated Ethiopia before the arrival of invaders from southern Arabia, including Jews who diffused Judaism among them. Be this as it may, Judaism in Ethiopia predates the formation of a Christian kingdom there (fourth century CE). Later, Jews who retreated from the coastal area of Ethiopia established an independent state in the Lake Tana region. In the sixth century, Jews also settled in the Semyen region by order of King Kaleb. In the thirteenth and fourteenth centuries, Beta Israel lost its independence and many Jews were forced to convert to Christianity. When Christian Ethiopians and Arab Muslims went to war in the sixteenth century, Beta Israel joined both camps depending on the circumstances. Accounts of these wars reached Jewish scholars in Safed (Galilee), who mentioned them in their writings. After the Ethiopian kings defeated the Muslims for good, Beta Israel became subjects of the crown and lost much of their freedom of action. In the early twentieth century, Jacob Faitlovitch, a French Jew, visited Ethiopia (first in 1904) and approached King Menelik II (1889–1913) on behalf of Beta Israel. The "Pro-Falasha Committees" that he established set up mobile schools and a boarding school in

Addis Ababa. Eventually scholarships for youngsters to study in Europe and Palestine were made available.

Most of Beta Israel lived in the north of Ethiopia, between the Takkaze River to the north, Lake Tana to the east, the Blue Nile to the south, and the border of Sudan to the west. They inhabited villages of their own, the most important and best known of which were near the town of Gondar. A Beta Israel village was a cluster of straw-thatched huts, one of which was the place of prayer (the *mesgid*, a cognate of mosque). They practiced agriculture and crafts.

Beta Israel observed the Pentateuchal laws; they washed their hands before partaking food, and recited grace before and after meals. Beta Israel was monogamous. Sons, as in any branch of Judaism, and daughters, as in Africa generally, were circumcised on the eighth day after birth. The holy scriptures and liturgy of Beta Israel are in Geez, the holy language of the Ethiopian Orthodox Church and the precursor of Amharic, the modern vernacular and official language of Ethiopia. A minority of Beta Israel in Tigre and Eritrea spoke Tigrinya. Beta Israel observed the Sabbath rigorously (as set forth in the Pentateuch but not as prescribed in the Talmud, which was unknown in the community). In recent times, there was some knowledge of Hebrew among Beta Israel because the Jewish Agency sent emissaries to Ethiopia to diffuse its teaching of the language. Beta Israel also had monks and nuns who lived in monasteries or in seclusion. Beta Israel's calendar, which differs from the Ethiopian and resembles the Jewish, was the basis on which the Jewish festivals of the Pentateuch were celebrated. Devoted to the God of Israel, Beta Israel considered itself the Chosen People awaiting the Messiah, who would bring them back to the Holy Land.

The guiding question in our investigation was the extent to which such a group, marked by ethnicity, religiosity, traditionalism, and particular racial features, is doomed to form a ghetto in Israeli society or, for the very reason of its Jewishness, is posed to insert itself in the mainstream.

Beta Israel in Israel

In Israel, the immigration of tens of thousands of Beta Israel starting in the 1970s provoked discussions among rabbis about their Jewishness. Ovadia Yossef, then the Sephardi Chief Rabbi, referred to them as descendants of the Tribe of Dan, a view based on the ninth-century writings of the Jewish traveler Eldad ha-Dani. In a decision by a 1975 interministerial committee, Israel recognized the entitlement of Ethiopian Jews to automatic citizenship and full benefits under the 1950 Law of Return. Ashkenazi Chief Rabbi Shlomo Goren initially disapproved of the ruling but changed his mind in 1978 and greeted a group of newly landed from Ethiopia by saying, "You are our brothers; you are our blood and our flesh. You are true Jews. . . . You have returned to your homeland." Just the same, Rabbis Yossef and Goren asked them to take part in a ceremony that, as opposed to a conversion or a period of compulsory study, was a symbolic act of "renewing the covenant with the Jewish people," Rabbi Yossef explained (*The Jerusalem Post*, August 1977).

To this day, many Ethiopian Jews feel insulted by the ceremony in view of the sufferings they endured to preserve their Jewishness. Still, they generally agree to participate in it in order to settle their Jewish status once and for all. More importantly, Ethiopian Jews in Israel also demonstrate on behalf of relatives who remained behind, accusing the authorities of ignoring their plight and refusing to make the effort to bring them here. Pursuant to the demonstrations, Israel's governments set out to facilitate the immigration of the remainder of Beta Israel.

Most of those who came before 1984 were from northern Ethiopia; they made their way in small groups through Sudan and were settled throughout Israel. In 1984, over 10,000 Jews from the Gondar region crossed into Sudan and were flown to Israel after a spell in refugee camps. Deteriorating conditions soon necessitated a more dramatic approach. In a period of less than two months starting in mid-November 1984, more than 6,500 Beta Israel were airlifted to Israel in what would be known as Operation Moses. Premature publicity impelled the Ethiopian authorities to halt the operation, but n March 1985 650 Jews were rescued in Operation Joshua. The resumption of diplomatic relations between Israel and Ethiopia paved the way for legal emigration on the basis of family reunification. By the summer of 1990, over 20,000 Ethiopian Jews had moved from the countryside to Addis Ababa, the Ethiopian capital, in the hope of being taken to Israel. During a thirty-six-hour period on May 24–25, 1991, as rebel troops threatened to overrun the city, 14,000 Beta Israel were airlifted to Israel in Operation Solomon. Several thousand joined them during the next year and a half. Thus, by the end of 1992 more than 45,000 Ethiopian immigrants had arrived and only a handful of Beta Israel remained in Ethiopia. By the early 2000s, the total population of Ethiopian Jews in Israel, including the Israel-born, had climbed to approximately 80,000, 30 percent of them under the age of twenty. Although most had been villagers in Ethiopia, the large majority of Ethiopian-origin immigrants to Israel settled in a small number of cities and towns in the central and southern parts of the country.

Nonimmigrants have not always given Ethiopian Jews the warmest of welcomes. Naim et al. (1997) show that where Ethiopians are especially numerous in a neighborhood, their neighbors tend to describe them as "noisy," "dirty," and "inconsiderate." In some cities, however, Ethiopians and other residents have established positive relations. The most difficult relations are between Ethiopians and Russian Jews, two contrasting groups that share in common the label of "new immigrant."

A study on Ethiopian young adults—in their twenties and early thirties—who reached Israel as children shows that in most cases their parents enrolled them in state religious schools instead of state secular schools (Weil, 1997). Moreover, most pupils attended boarding schools, which alleviated the burden on parents but may have caused some emotional deprivation. About one of seven earned a matriculation certificate at the end of high school, as against one in three among Israelis at large. Respondents did not mention any special difficulty during their studies but expressed regret that the curriculum paid no attention whatsoever to the Ethiopian-Jewish culture. Furthermore, girls of Ethiopian origin apply for an exemption from military service due to their religious or traditional background; boys, in contrast, all enlist in the army willingly and report strong satisfaction with their service. Now that many of them are married and have children, one third of Weil's respondents report that they are unemployed and most of the others indicate that they hold blue-collar jobs. At the time of that research, many Ethiopians lived in neighborhoods where they were numerous and where life was strongly imprinted with respect for the Jewish faith and Ethiopian-Jewish traditions.

Ethiopian Jews also reported about another category of people in Ethiopia, the *Falashmura*, that numbers tens of thousands, if not more, and consists of Christians of Beta Israel descent. These people, it is contended, are, in reality, Jews in disguise who converted for practical reasons. Always suspected as Jews, they live in Ethiopia under precarious conditions. Many of them have relatives among the Beta Israel in Israel who are urging the government to allow them, too, to immigrate. This demand has become a major cause of discord between Beta Israel and the Israeli establishment. For several years, small groups of Falashmura have been flown to Israel every month on an experimental basis that is meant to lead to a final decision about the whole population. The major question for the Israeli authorities is whether or not the Falashmura will agree to re-embrace Judaism once they arrive and, thereby, justify the benefits they will have received under the Law of Return.

Concurrently, however, the resettlement in Israel of the large majority of Beta Israel remains far from satisfactory. Many aspects of their absorption are still fraught with difficulties. Most parents who immigrated were illiterate; most children had rudimentary literacy skills. This is the major reason why most Ethiopians, even today, find jobs only in low-status industries, agriculture and construction. In their communities in Israel, they exhibit a strain of religious traditionalism that couples allegiance to ancestral customs with willingness to adopt major symbols and norms that they observe among traditional and religious nonimmigrant Israelis—Torah scrolls in Hebrew, study of Talmud, or new liturgical texts. Many students and soldiers of Ethiopian origin, however, identify with an Israeliness that is less traditional and religious than that of their parents (Lipschitz and Noam, 1996; Shabtai, 1995).

Since the Ethiopian-origin group is an anomaly in the Israeli sociocultural landscape, we were eager to include it in our investigation despite its relatively small size. For this very reason, however, and in view of our limited research resources, we had to make do with a sample of fifty subjects—obviously not enough to provide us with an exhaustive picture. At least, we thought, we might be able to sketch the contours of the Ethiopian Jews' absorption into the multicultural scenery of this society and consider here too the impact of the link articulated by the dominant culture between religion and nationalism.

IDENTITY AND IDENTIFICATION

Our questionnaire focused mainly on identity, identification, and social attitudes. The answers we obtained from our Ethiopian respondents elicit an ambiguous picture (Table 7.1). To sharpen the significance of our data, we compare Ethiopians with both non immigrants and Russians:

Table 7.1. Ethiopian-Origin Israelis: Aspects of Identity and Identification

Items	Attitudes	Percent	Mean (Standard Deviation)		
			Ethiopian	Russian	Nonimmigr
1. Do you	Very/strongly	58			
feel an	Not too much	26	64	52	81
integral	No/not at all	16	(32)	(29)	(25)
part of	Total (N)	100	(50)	(402)	(996)
Israeli					
society?					
				t Ethiopian-Russian = 2.6**	
2. Do you	Very/strongly	60			
want your	Not too much	28	76	71	87
children	No/not at all	12	(30)	(25)	(24)
to live in	Total (N)	100	(49)	(391)	(489)
Israel?					
				t Ethiopian-Russian = −.82	
3. When	Strongly/yes	66			
someone	Not too much	10	69	76	79
accuses	No/not at all	24	(33)	(25)	(27)
Israel of	Total (N)	100	(50)	(405)	(489)
something,					
you feel					
insulted.					
				t Ethiopian-Russian = 1.5	

Source: Survey 3.

(a) A majority of Ethiopians of our small sample feel that they are part of Israeli society, but it is a relatively slender majority of fewer than 60 percent. Thus, 40 percent do not feel well integrated. This suffices for us to conclude that many Ethiopians sense the existence of an "Ethiopian problem" in Israeli society.

(b) More often than not, Ethiopians express a sense of being part of Israel with greater conviction when it comes to wanting their children to live in Israel. Here again, however, their response to this question does not reflect overwhelming enthusiasm and the data elicit a measure of alienation.

(c) When it comes to collective identity, however, most of our respondents emphasize tokens of society at large (Israeli/Jewish). This shows that, irrespective of their degree of alienation from the setting or the establishment, they do feel that they are an integral component of the national collective—at least as far as our small sample is concerned.

(d) No less interesting, Ethiopians, like other communities in Israel, emphasize Jewishness as their primordial token and rank Israeliness second. Thus, Ethiopians, like the Moroccan or Polish Jews who arrived long before them, as well as the Russian Jews of which the more recent influx is composed, tend to construe their immigration to Israel as related to their *ab initio* allegiance to the Jewish collective.

(e) Despite their affinity for "Jewish Israeliness," Ethiopian Jews are also strongly motivated by a sense of internal solidarity. Nearly all our respondents asserted their personal allegiance to the group in rather strong terms ("I am one of them") and only 6 percent stated that they feel "more or less" or "not at all" a part of the Ethiopian ethnic group. The respondents' attitudes toward the continuation of Ethiopian immigration give further evidence of the sense of solidarity: three-quarters want Ethiopian immigration to continue even at the cost of a decline of general standards of living.

ATTITUDE TOWARD "OTHERS"

The picture is no less interesting when we consider Ethiopians' perceptions of closeness to or distance from specific constituents of Israeli society (Table 7.2):

(a) Ethiopians feel that they are a part of what is called "traditional people." As such, they are not seriously distant from the non-religious and the religious. Interestingly, however, despite their traditional affinities, they are subjectively closer to the nonreligious than to the religious.

(b) Ethiopians feel very alienated from the Ultra-Orthodox, probably because they realize that the most rigorous group in matters of religion, is the least enthusiastic about accepting them as full-fledged Jews.

Table 7.2. Ethiopians' Distance from Constituent Groups in
Israeli Society (Percent)

How far do you feel from:	Attitudes	Percent	Mean distance* (Standard Deviation)
The traditional (N = 48)	One of them	82	
	So-so	16	17
	Far from them	2	(19)
The nonreligious (N = 49)	One of them	58	
	So-so	28	27
	Far from them	14	(27)
The religious (N = 48)	One of them	50	
	So-so	36	30
	Far from them	14	(24)
Mizrahim (N = 50)	One of them	38	
	So-so	40	46
	Far from them	22	(26)
Ashkenazim (N = 48)	One of them	18	
	So-so	42	63
	Far from them	40	(27)
Arabs (N = 48)	One of them	16	
	So-so	32	66
	Far from them	52	(29)
Druze (N = 45)	One of them	8	
	So-so	44	68
	Far from them	55	(28)
Russians (N = 47)	One of them	16	
	So-so	28	71
	Far from them	56	(31)
The Ultra-Orthodox (N = 50)	One of them	12	
	So-so	30	73
	Far from them	58	(18)
Guest workers (N = 44)	One of them	6	
	So-so	20	87
	Far from them	74	(25)

* The lower the score, the less the distance. Source: Survey 3.

(c) As for ethnic categories, Ethiopians feel relatively close to the Mizrahim, who, as we know, account for the largest segment of the traditional category, to which they feel they belong. Hence, Ethiopians feel more aloof from Ashkenazim.

(d) The Ethiopians' aloofness from Ashkenazim, however, does not begin to approach the animosity they feel toward the Russians. This may stem from their impression that Russians enjoy more immigrant privileges than they do even though both groups immigrated approximately at the same time. An additional source of animosity may be the Russians' reluctance to socialize with them due to their "cultured" self-image.

(e) Ethiopian Jews who aspire to emphasize their Jewishness feel as estranged from non-Jewish Israeli minorities (Arabs and Druze) as from the Ultra-Orthodox and the Russians.

(f) The highest level of estrangement is felt vis-à-vis non-Israeli non-Jews, i.e., guest workers. Here the Ethiopians are seemingly willing to stress their own membership in Israeli society and to express their displeasure about being confused with people who are often quite close to them in terms of social class. The sizable presence of Africans among the guest workers, a circumstance that may increase the confusion, may be an additional factor that explains the Ethiopians' wish to "draw the line."

In brief, Ethiopian Jews feel relatively isolated from major components of society and relatively close to others. The overall balance is one of marginality. However, they do not respond by drawing closer to other isolated groups. Despite their own social hardships, Ethiopians are not willing to renounce their sense of social belonging. In practical terms, they position themselves somewhere near, but clearly not as part of, the Mizrahi category.

ETHNOCULTURAL PERSPECTIVES

Table 7.3a yields more precision regarding Ethiopians' ethnocultural perspective. First, Ethiopians are not ethnic-oriented in their politics; they state with emphasis that politicians should deal with national issues first.

They also favor interethnic tolerance and are open-minded about cultural and linguistic heterogeneity. However, they do not consider all cultures equal; they assign different values to the various cultures that they find in Israel but also insist that Judaism should be the primary source of Israeli culture. This, we suggest, may be influenced by the longstanding debate among rabbis about their status as Jews.

The Ethiopians' assertive affinity for Jewishness may be their way of defending their claim to full Jewishness and expressing their total commitment to this identity. This, however, does not stop them from appreciating "Americanness" and—to a lesser extent—"Westernness" as well. This evidence of high regard for what Ethiopians construe as modernity is consistent with their differential assessments of the

Table 7.3. Ethnocultural Perspectives of Ethiopian Jews

a. Items	N	Attitudes	%	Means (S.D.)
Leaders should look after their own constituency first.	48	Disagree. So-so. Agree.	62 18 20	33.8 (32.8)
You are sitting in a bus; two people near you speak in a language that is not yours. Does this bother you?	50	Yes. A little. No.	16 26 58	71.0 (37.9)
All cultures are equal; none is superior	48	Disagree. So-so. Agree.	64 14 22	44.8 (30.0)
Israel's culture should be more Middle Eastern.	45	Less. As it is. More.	30 34 36	53.9 (38.4)
Israel's culture should be more Western.	45	Less. As it is. More.	16 40 44	64.4 (35.1)
Israel's culture should be more American.	47	Less. As it is. More.	12 32 56	70.2 (30.1)
Israel's culture should be more Jewish-religious.	50	Less. As it is. More.	12 18 70	77.0 (33.4)
Ashkenazim have made no positive contribution to Israeli culture.	50	Disagree. So-so. Agree.	84 8 8	17.0 (27.9)
Mizrahim have made no positive contribution to Israeli culture.	50	Disagree. So-so. Agree.	82 10 8	20.5 (26.1)
Arabs have made no positive contribution to Israeli culture.	49	Disagree. So-so. Agree.	48 18 34	44.9 (33.1)
Druze have made no positive contribution to Israeli culture.	47	Disagree. So-so. Agree.	62 18 20	26.6 (26.3)
The Ultra-Orthodox have made no positive contribution to Israeli culture.	50	Disagree. So-so. Agree.	16 26 58	30.5 (33.6)

b. Ethiopians' attitudes toward their heritage				
Children should learn their language of origin in school.	50	Disagree. So-so. Agree.	16 10 74	75.0 (32.3)
I would like other Israelis to be more like me in their culture and behavior.	50	Disagree. So-so. Agree.	34 26 40	47.5 (35.1)

Source: Survey 3.

contributions to Israeli society of its constituent groups. Ethiopians appreciate the contribution of Ashkenazim and Mizrahim, less of druze, and even less of Arabs. Most saliently, they dismiss whatever contribution the Ultra-Orthodox may have made, thereby again revealing their resentment of a population group that has always shown reticence for their absorption among Jews.

In brief, as far as the Ethiopian respondents of our limited sample are concerned, they do not regard cultural influences from diverse sources as mutually exclusive but differentiate among them in terms of their relative importance. They emphasize Jewish religious values above all, rank modernity second, and leave Middle Eastern cultural values behind. Ethiopians are firmly pluralistic about themselves and favor having their children learn their language of origin in school (Table 7.3b). Since they do not really expect other Israelis to be attracted to their culture, they advocate a situation that gives cultural differences room for expression and retention.

IDENTITY, IDENTIFICATION, AND RELIGIOSITY

Our data should be considered but as an explorative work intended to draw out some very basic features. As far as we rely on our data, they bring a complex identity picture to light. In terms of the three dimensions of this concept of identity, we obtain the following:

(a) *In their commitment to the collective,* Ethiopians demonstrate strong feelings of group solidarity and an aspiration to see Ethiopian immigration in Israel continue. Ethiopians feel that they are part of Israel, hope that their children will feel the same way, and fully identify with Israeli Jewishness. This feeling, however, is not unreserved. Ethiopians know they are vulnerable and are convinced that they face special difficulties in Israeli society.

(b) *In regard to the perception of "singularity,"* Ethiopians, like members of other immigrant communities in Israel, emphasize Jewishness more than Israeliness. They tend to construe their immigration to Israel—and their Israeliness—as bound primarily to their allegiance to Jewishness. Our data also confirm that Ethiopians aspire to stay distinctive on the basis of respect for their own heritage.

(c) *In respect to self-location vis-à-vis "others,"* Ethiopians seem to be a rather isolated group even though they share a pluralistic and tolerant perspective toward society. They consider themselves part of

the traditional category and, as such, do not feel far from other categories even though they definitely dislike the Ultra-Orthodox. In
practice, however, they feel that they are hardly connected to other
players in the Israeli scene, from Ashkenazim to guest workers,
although they do sense a relative proximity to Mizrahim.

As for identification, Ethiopian Jews present a profile of disadvantage. They seem to have scanty chances of social mobility because
so many members of the community are poorly predisposed to achieving it. This impedes their social positioning vis-à-vis other groups
and is bound to strengthen their sociocultural retentionism. Moreover,
the hesitancy of the dominant culture to express an unequivocal
demand for social and cultural homogenization may influence the
group not to abandon rapidly the patterns and norms that denote
its particularism. Last but not least, the Ethiopians' orientation steers
them toward a moderate outlook; due to their very distinct heritage,
they attach great importance to their insertion into the Jewish national
collective.

In a nutshell, the Ethiopians, a new and small group in the Israeli
setting, constitute a saliently special case in Israel's multiculturalism.
Amidst this diversity, they are concurrently very distinct in heritage
but very moderate in retentionist demands.

It will take much more research to answer thoroughly our research
question about the likelihood of their eventual confinement in a
"racial ghetto," an isolated niche where racial features become the
principal barriers to intergroup relations. However, our limited data
may provide some elements of an interim answer. For the time being,
our data do not indicate that the racial question *per se* is a major
issue. The Ethiopians' hardships in Israel generally trace to matters
related to human capital and predispositions to adjust to a setting
such as Israel's. Moreover, the particularism of the Ethiopian Jewish
heritage seems to have been an impediment to communication with
many other groups. These factors suffice to explain the Ethiopians'
relative social isolation. Yet, the Ethiopians' answers to our questionnaire show that they do not feel relegated to a niche, at least
for the time being. They situate themselves in the large traditional
category, close to the Mizrahim, and exhibit a collective identity that
relates them, and leads them, to identify with Jewish Israeli society.
In other words, their Jewishness, insofar as one can tell on the basis
of the current data, favors some form of insertion into the social
mainstream.

This is not to say that the racial question will not become crucial in the future. Ethiopian Jews are the only black Africans among Israeli Jews and the largest group of dark-skinned people of whatever confession. Their only "rivals" in this sense are the Cochin Jews, a very small group from India, the non-Jewish Black Hebrews, a group of American origin that is no larger, and West African guest workers who are neither Jewish nor Israeli. It remains that some testimonies indicate occasional manifestations of racism among non-immigrants vis-à-vis Ethiopians. Shmuel Yalma, an Israeli of Ethiopian origin, remarks in his book *The Way to Jerusalem* (1980), "The color of [our] skin was strange to them and they liked calling us 'little Negro'; they saw us as strange objects; they were afraid to mix with us." Yalma suggests that blackness was imposed on him and his fellow ethnics as a more important identity feature than Jewishness. These feelings receive confirmations, from time to time, as racial incidents take place in the army, at school or in night clubs. Still, one cannot assert that, up to now, racism has been a salient trait in the relations of Ethiopians with non-Ethiopians. Our data do not elicit this impression; they trace the hardships of Ethiopians in Israel more to the vicissitudes of adjustment to the surroundings. Only after more and more Ethiopians climb the social ladder will they put society to test on this most crucial matter.

When looking at the significance of our data and the material cited in this chapter as a whole, we may indeed conclude that, for the time being, racism has not become a major issue—or at least *the* major issue—regarding the insertion of Ethiopians in the society. Instead, of much more weight is the question of the recognition of Ethiopians as Jews in view of their rites and customs: while they were in possession of a part of the Bible in the Guez language and practiced many a pattern of traditional Judaism, they ignored the role of Hebrew as the Jews' ancestral code and had not knowledge of the existence of the Talmud—neither the Babylonian nor Jerusalemite. These aspects were crucial given the role of religion in the definition of Jewishness and Jewish nationhood as defined by the secular dominant culture itself.

It is accordingly that Ethiopians in Israel have been pressured to invest their best in adapting to Judaism as it prevails in this country, and effectively, most Ethiopians have come to adopt skullcaps, keep kosher homes, and observe practices that did not belong to their customs in Ethiopia. In their synagogues, for instance, it is the

Hebrew Holy Scrolls that have been adopted, though the Guez texts are still available. All in all, Ethiopian Jews who have by no means abandoned their customs with their insertion in a secular society, have changed their lifestyles as many have remained religious and express it in a mixture of former and new patterns.

Ethiopians, to be sure, do resent their condition and do articulate claims—they call for bringing in their relatives of the Falashmura and they demonstrate for their rights as new immigrants in face of what they see as privileges enjoyed by Russians. Yet, they by no means develop as a conflict group appealing against the dominant culture and its linking religion and nationhood. They protest against the power of rabbis who are not always—to say the least—sympathetic to their plight, but they do not call for a detachment of religion from the state.

In brief, the fact that religion plays here a major role in the definition of the national collective brings an underprivileged group like Ethiopians to firstly emphasize their very participation to the—so understood—primordialism of the national collective and collective identity.

SECTION IV

NON-JEWISH GROUPS

CHAPTER EIGHT

ARABS AND DRUZE IN ISRAEL

Introduction

From the standpoint of the Jewish Israeli collective, Israeli Arabs, Druze, and guest workers are "others." They are components of the Israeli setting but stand outside the Jewish Israeli nation referred to in the Declaration of Independence. These groups may enjoy democratic rights, social privileges, and status, but as minorities they are not supposed to determine the prevailing identity of the state (Abu Nimr, 1993). Thus from the Israeli Jews' point of view they constitute "others." This chapter deals with Arabs and Druze who are non-Jewish Israelis; the next chapter takes up the guest workers who are non-Jewish non-Israelis.

Arabs have been a part of Israel ever since its creation. For them, however, the founding of the state represented a collective tragedy: it transformed their community from a large majority of the population to a minority of 156,000 souls as against approximately 650,000 Jews. In the 1948 war, Israeli troops did not always treat hostile Arab inhabitants with the greatest of consideration; in some places, officers even undertook to evacuate residents by force (Morris, 1987). The Arab leadership itself encouraged inhabitants of what was to become Israel to move out of the territory in view of a victorious return. Those who remained behind were detached from their elites, which had withdrawn with the Arab armies amidst Jewish resistance and counterattacks. The Israeli victory was a disaster for Arabs generally and Palestinians particularly, who recall it as "the Catastrophe" (*a-Naqba*). In Israel itself, all that remained was principally a population of villagers—with the exception of the city of Nazareth and neighborhoods in several cities with a large Jewish majority like Haifa, Acre, or Jaffa. For seventeen years, until 1966, this Arab population was set under military rule that restricted their movements and required them to obtain special permits to move about the country. These rules were eased over time until they were abolished altogether. What remained was an aliened and resentful

Arab national minority in a state defined as Jewish (Al-Haj, 1997; Ruhanna, 1999).

Many Arab citizens expressed their resentment by voting for the Communist Party, which was actually an Arab nationalist party in disguise (Rekhess, 1996). Others, however, adjusted to the situation by cooperating in a patrimonial vein with the establishment in the frame of Arab parties allied with the social-democrat dominant party, Mapai (the predecessor of Labor). The young generation, however, refused to remain silent about what it perceived as anti-Arab discrimination by the Jewish majority. Organizations, clubs, and public-opinion movements began to demand with rising vehemence egalitarian treatment in education, public services, and jobs. Consequently, the Arab question became increasingly visible in the polity (Landau, 1969; 1993; Smooha, 1976).

The Israeli conquest of the West Bank and the Gaza Strip in 1967 marked a dramatic escalation in this respect. Israel's Arabs were now suddenly reconnected with the Arab world and, above all, with the major part of the Palestinian population. Conscious of being part of Israel, this population group was unwilling to disavow its citizenship altogether, but many sympathized with—and even sustained—the Palestinians in their conflict within Israel. A body of leadership representing the Israeli Arab sector began to evolve in the 1970s; in 1974, a convention of mayors of all Arab cities, towns, and villages a Supreme Committee of Arab Localities was established. In 1982, these leaders of major communities formed a Supreme Steering Committee, which gradually earned countrywide recognition in matters pertaining to the Arab sector at large.

The 1993 and 1995 agreements between Israel and the Palestine Liberation Organization, which instigated a peace process were, however, received by Israel's Arab citizens with mixed feelings. While hoping that genuine peace would be given a chance, Israeli Arabs were afraid that they would be left outside the Oslo loop and forced to cope with their difficulties alone. It was also then that they showed the strongest tendency to recognize that they were part of the Israeli setting (Smooha, 1992; Amara, 1997). In 1995, about 70 percent declared that they were closer to the Israeli Jews in their ways of life than to Palestinians in the West Bank or the Gaza Strip; in 1985, only 56 percent gave such a response. However, when the peace process ran aground and erupted into crisis in September 2000 with the outbreak of an "intifada," major Israeli Arab political factions hardened their attitude toward the Jewish state.

In 2003, Israel's Arab minority (not including Druze) numbered approximately 1,100,000 souls, approximately 18 percent of the population of Israel (ICBS, 2003)—86 percent Muslim, 14 percent Christian. As a national minority, this group demands that Israel as a democracy safeguards its liberties and rights challenging the fact that it draws its national identity from an entity, the Palestinian people outside Israel, that is in bitter conflict with the State. The problem is further intensified by economic, educational, and political gaps that place Israeli Jews and Israeli Arabs in contrasting class conditions due, among other factors, to gaping disparities in human capital.[1] Furthermore, in view of their numerous and dramatic challenges (immigration, security, economic problems, etc.), the Israeli authorities have not been overly sensitive to the special needs of this minority. These circumstances account for most of the *de facto* discrimination that Israeli Arabs have faced for years. In 1990, for example, expenditure in the state education system was three times higher per Jewish pupil than per Arab pupil and eighteen of twenty-three localities that had unemployment rates in excess of 10 percent were populated by Arabs (Otzki-Lezer, and Ghanem, 1995; Employment Office, 2000). Unavoidably, these circumstances are bound to explain rates of crime and poverty. In the background of all these, moreover, there are the Arabs' hard feelings due to their minority status contrasting with the numerous Arab sovereignties all around them (Lewinson, 1995).

It is in this context that Israel's Arab citizens have become a major focal point of research for Jewish and Arab scholars in recent years. Many researchers (see Kimmerling, 2004) emphasize the Palestinian outlook of the Arab case in Israel. Others insist that beyond and despite the "Palestinization" of Israel's Arabs with respect to emotional identification, one should also speak of their "Israelization," i.e., the ever-stronger feelings among Israeli Arabs that they belong to their surroundings (Smooha, 1992). There is also the progressive adoption by Israel's Arabs of many patterns of life which they learn from Jews—the reduction of the number of children per family, the

---

[1] In 1948, an overwhelming majority of Arab women and more than half of men were still illiterate (Rekhess, 1996).

expansion of higher education in general and for girls in particular, individual employment providing a relative autonomy of nuclear families from the authority of heads of enlarged families, political parties based on individual allegiances, etc. When seen conjunctively, the widely contrasting identity and cultural processes sketch a two-dimensional picture: a divergence of collective identity that places Israeli Jews and Israeli Arabs in opposition, coupled with a cultural convergence of Arabs toward Israeli-Jewish norms and patterns of life (Ganam and Ginat, 1995).

It is against this background that this chapter investigates the Arabs' commitments, self-images of distinctiveness, and perception of their location vis-à-vis "others" in consideration of these contradictory drives. We used the same questionnaire (in Arabic) as with other groups. The survey took place in January 2000 with 410 Arabs and 749 Jews. In the months that followed, a crisis developed due to difficulties in the peace negotiations between Israel and the Palestinian Authority. Thus, we repeated the survey in August 2000 with 300 Israeli Arabs and 1,003 Jews. In a third step—October 2000—we investigated 302 Arabs and 246 Jews—this time with a shorter questionnaire, immediately after the eruption of anti-Israeli violence within Israel that echoed the outbreak of the intifada in the territories controlled by the Palestinian Authority.

IDENTITIES

Using comparison between Arabs and Jews in order to evince the significance of the data, Table 8.1 shows that Arabs are younger, more religious, less educated, and poorer than Jews. Identity questions presented to both Jews and Arabs elicited complex pictures. When asked about their most important collective identity, nearly half of the Jewish respondents (46 percent) answered "Israeli," more than one-third (36 percent) emphasized "Jewish," and fewer than one-fifth (17 percent) opted for an ethnocultural identity. In contrast, almost half (45 percent) of Arab respondents answered the same question by saying "Arab," and about the same proportion—a bit more than a quarter—answered "Israeli citizen" (28 percent) and "Palestinian" (27 percent). Placed in the context of expectations, the contrast between Jews and Arabs seems surprisingly moderate in view of the saliency of the "Palestinian" token in the public discourse of

Table 8.1. Distribution of the Samples (Percent)

		Jews (N=749)	Arabs (N=410)
Gender	Men	47	49
(Cramer's v = .01)	Women	53	51
Age	18–22	10	19
	23–29	19	23
	30–39	19	29
	40–49	20	16
	50–59	15	7
	60+	17	6
Mean age (t = 7.4**)		42	34
Income	Far lower than median	18	39
	Slightly lower	12	28
	Average	36	17
	Slightly higher	16	6
	Far higher	11	4
	No answer	8	7
Education	Up to secondary	13	48
	Complete secondary	35	24
	Post-secondary	17	9
	Partial academic	8	5
	Undergraduate	18	11
	Graduate	8	5
Religiosity	Very religious	6	11
	Religious	10	21
	Traditional	30	63
	Nonreligious	54	5
Religion of non-Jews	Muslim		85
	Christian		15

Source: Survey 2.

Israel's Arab leaders. The relatively high percentage of respondents who identified themselves firstly as "Israeli citizens" was also surprising. Nevertheless, the ethnic-national definition ranks first among Arabs and the national identity is prime among Jews.

As for the social characterization of the various formulations of collective identity among Arabs, we find again that the Palestinian token is more widespread among Muslims (29 percent) than among Christians (15 percent). Christians are more prone than Muslims to see themselves as "Israeli citizens" (40 percent vs. 26 percent). Unsurprisingly, the Palestinian token is also encountered more frequently among younger strata than among older.

Moreover, adding the Arab respondents' first *two* choices, the Israeli component is present in 68 percent of responses, either as the first choice (41 percent) or as the second (26 percent). The Arab component is selected in 72 percent of responses—as the first choice (30 percent) or the second (42 percent). The Palestinian component is present in 45 percent of responses—as the first choice (21 percent) or as the second (23 percent). Thus, "Israeliness" is clearly important in the identities of Israeli Arabs after all, although "Arabness" prevails and "Palestinianness" is by no means negligible.

Cognizant of the extremism that often typifies the Arabs' public rhetoric against the Israeli state, we were again surprised to find a strong attachment to the country in both attitudes and practical contacts (Table 8.2). This shows that despite their minority status, Arabs feel that their place is, or at least should be, in this society. This undoubtedly relates to the fact that they are native and longstanding inhabitants of the country and enjoy relative advantages in comparison with realistic alternatives. This, we contend, expresses the tendency of Israeli Arabs to "Israelize" in the sense of cultural rapprochement with Israeli Jews.

Table 8.2. Jewish-Arab Contacts: Behavior versus Attitudes I (Percent)

Aspects	Positive attitudes			Actual contact		
	Arabs v J (N=410)	Jews v A (N=749)	Cramer's V	Arabs v J (N=410)	Jews v A (N=749)	Cramer's V
Intermarriage	16	19	.01	—	—	—
Colleague at work	—	74	—	45	36	.09**
Residing in same building	54	52	.05	10	5	.11**
Having close friends	77	64	.16**	65	26	.39**

* The scores are calculated on a 0–100 scale, with 100 signifying the most positive response in both cases.
Source: Survey 2.

Social Closeness and Distance

Nevertheless, Arabs feel estranged from Jewish society. An overwhelming majority (about three quarters) of respondents reported social distance from Jews, and no neighborhood contacts with them. The general explanation for this is that about 80 percent of Israeli Arabs live in villages, towns, and urban neighborhoods of their own. However, quite unexpectedly in this context, many do report in response to additional questions that they meet and socialize with Jews. Many Arabs even report friendship and, to a lesser extent, colleagueship with individual Jews.

Much fewer Jews report such relations with Arabs. Some of this is due to the demographic factor, i.e., the fact that Jews outnumber Arabs by more than four to one and, therefore, have much fewer opportunities to meet Arabs than the other way around. Jews are also less willing than Arabs to sustain such relations—although the differences are by no means dramatic (Table 8.3). Thus, although both groups' attitudes toward inter group contacts are more positive than the reality, such contacts do still exist in daily life.

These data, however, should be treated cautiously because they refer primarily to the individual level. When it comes to intergroup attitudes, Arabs and Jews insist on alienation. On a 0–100 scale of intergroup distance (0 = feeling of minimal distance; 100 = maximal distance), Arabs tend to score their distance from Jews in general at the high mean of 83. Their feeling varies when one asks them about specific categories of Jews—72 vis-à-vis Mizrahim and the political

Table 8.3. Jewish-Arab Contacts: Behavior versus Attitudes II (Percent)

Aspects	Arabs vis-à-vis Jews (N=410)		Jews vis-à-vis Arabs (N=749)	
	In actual fact	Positive	In actual fact	Positive
Acceptance into family	—	16	—	19
At work	45	—	36	74
In the same building	10	54	5	52
Close friends	65	77	26	64

Source: Survey 2.

left, 78 vis-à-vis the nonreligious, 80 vis-à-vis the traditional, 83 vis-à-vis Ashkenazim, 84 vis-à-vis the political right, 86 vis-à-vis settlers, 88 vis-à-vis Russians, 89 vis-à-vis the religious, and 93 vis-à-vis the Ultra-Orthodox. The attitude of Jews toward Arabs is not much different; the mean score is 76 and also varies among different Jewish groups: 64 for the nonreligious and the traditional, 65 for Ashkenazim, 76 for Mizrahim, 82 for Russians, and 92 for the Ultra-Orthodox (Spearman's Ro = 60*). Thus, there is a clear discrepancy between predispositions and practical reports about experiences at the individual level, and perceptions of the macro social reality.

In this context we wanted to know whether these high scores of intergroup distance, on both sides, correspond to an aspiration to draw farther apart or to narrow the distances. In this respect, it comes out, one cannot speak of unequivocal rejection of the other by either side; both aspire to more intergroup contacts, although Arabs are more eager than Jews to pursue them (Table 8.4). Does this mean that each side appreciates the other's eventual contribution to the common pool? To answer this question, we asked Jews and Arabs to what extent and in what respect they are willing to learn from each other. The data show that (Table 8.5) Arabs are much more willing to learn from Jews than vice-versa in areas like science, technology, working life, and democracy. Jews, in turn, appreciate Arabs' contributions in working life and land-rootedness and some aspects of their family life—a characteristic that would apply mainly to religious and traditional Jews.

In sum, Arabs are willing to learn from Jews, while Jews consider learning from Arabs much more moderately and in specific domains only.

Table 8.4. Attitudes toward Jewish-Arab Group Encounters (Percent)

Encounters of Jewish and Arab youth[1]	Arabs (N=410)	Jews (N=749)
You would prefer:		
Fewer Jewish-Arab encounters than now	4	16
As many encounters as now	6	25
More encounters than now	90	56
Don't know	—	3
Total	100	100
Means[2] (Cramer's v = .51** t = 18.8**)	92.0	65.1

[1] As initiated by schools, youth organizations and other goodwill movements.
[2] Calculated on a 0–100 scale, 100 = more encounters.
Source: Survey 2.

In a related manner, we asked Arabs and Jews whether they should learn more about the history and customs of the other group in order to understand it better. Here the Arabs' mean score was 73 and that of the Jews was 53. On the whole, this points to a situation of relative openness that is especially valuable under the current conditions that argue against Jewish-Arab rapprochement. However, the Arabs are more open to the Jews than vice-versa.

Table 8.5. Learning from Each Other

To what extent should your group learn from the other group in the following areas:	Arabs from Jews, mean[1]	Jews from Arabs, mean[1]	t
Discipline	39.2	37.1	0.8
Work ethics	65.9	37.6	11.2**
Science and technology	71.5	8.3	34.7**
Affinity to Israel	61.1	42.4	6.9**
Family relations	35.1	41.1	2.2*
Democracy	62.1	7.9	28.2**
Mean[1]	55.8	29.1	

[1] On a 0–100 scale, where 0 signifies minimal willingness to learn from the other and 100 signifies strong willingness.
Source: Survey 2.

THE 2000 CRISIS

The foregoing discussion gives evidence of the difficulties that arise in Jewish-Arab relations in Israel. Apart from the difficulties occasioned by the majority-minority situation *per se*, conflictual events that pit Israel and the Palestinians of the West Bank and the Gaza Strip against each other revolve simultaneously around the question of the creation of a Palestinian state and the recognition of Israel as a Jewish state. This issue has ebbed and flowed ever since the end of the 1967 Six-Day War. Each new wave of hostility and terrorism has a direct impact on the trend in Jewish-Arab relations in Israel proper. The most severe phase in this tragic process—thus far—took place in the autumn of 2000, at the beginning of the intifada in the territories. The incidents prompted tens of thousands of Israeli Arabs to take to the streets in violent demonstrations against the police, whose response left more than ten demonstrators dead. The episode strained Jewish-Arab relations in Israel to an unprecedented degree.

In view of these circumstances, we repeated our survey immediately
after the outburst of violence (in October 2000—Survey 4—about
ten months after our January 2000 survey—Survey 2) in order to
evaluate the effect of the events on Jews' and Arabs' attitudes toward
and perceptions of each other, i.e., to determine whether matters
had spun out of control. The tables below present our major findings.

Table 8.6 shows a lowering of expectations on both sides, especially
in perceptions of the prospects of a solution to the Israeli-Palestinian
conflict. Both Arabs and Jews were much more pessimistic than they
had been before the crisis that had just passed. In January 2000,
most people—both Arabs and Jews—expected peace within ten years
or "couldn't tell." In October 2000, a majority (although not an
overwhelming one) expected another war to break out.

Table 8.7 shows that this pessimism also relates to apprehensions
about relations between Jews and Arabs. At the same time, both
sides appear less amenable to intergroup contacts among adolescents.
However, both—perhaps surprisingly—still favored encounters, although
a higher proportion of Arabs than of Jews did so. Concurrently,
polarization between Jews and Arabs marked their belief about the
other side's perception of them. Although both parties stressed this
polarization, it was stronger among Jews than among Arabs. Thus,
in this respect, too, the crisis sharpened conflictual outlooks of Arabs
toward Jews and Israeli society at large. Yet, this polarization did
not signify a rupture and a total loss of interest in coexistence; nearly
half of the Arabs and one-third of Jews still refrained from depicting
the other's image of them as necessarily negative.

Table 8.6. War and Peace Expectations: The Impact of the Crisis[1]

Do you expect an Israel-Arab war, rather than peace, within the next ten years?		Jan. 2000 (N=410)	Oct. 2000 (N=302)
Arabs	War	25	52
	Can't tell	34	11
	Peace	37	25
	Mean*	53(N=410)	38(N=302)
Jews	War	29	59
	Can't tell	25	17
	Peace	41	19
	Mean*	53(N=749)	34(N=306)

[1] Calculated on a 0–100 (war-peace) scale; F = 32.7**.
Sources: Surveys 2 and 4.

Table 8.7. Amenability to Intergroup Contact: The Impact of the Crisis

Do you favor more encounters of Arab pupils with Jewish pupils?		Jan. 2000	Oct. 2000	F
Arabs	More	90	79	
	Like now	6	5	
	Less	4	16	
	Mean	92(N=410)	80(N=302)	
Jews	More	56	42	
	Like now	25	15	
	Less	16	38	
	Mean	*65(N=749)	*50(N=302)	47.7**
F (Jews-Arabs)			326.7**	

Sources: Surveys 2 and 4.

Table 8.8. Perceptions of the Other's Feelings: The Impact of the Crisis

What is the predominant attitude of Arabs toward Jews as against that of Jews toward Arabs?		Jan. 2000	Oct. 2000	F
Arabs toward	Negative	21	51	
Jews	Mixed	58	40	
	Positive	19	6	
	Means	49*	36*	
	N	410	302	179.8**
Jews toward	Negative	28	64	
Arabs	Mixed	51	28	
	Positive	16	5	
	Means	45*	26*	
	N	749	302	
F (Jews-Arabs)			41.2**	

Sources: Surveys 2 and 4.

Table 8.9. Sense of Belonging to Israeli Society

Issue		Jan. 2000 (N=410)	Oct. 2000 (N=302)
How strongly do you feel that you are an integral part of Israeli society?	Not much	19	39
	Somewhat	46	41
	Much so	34	18
	Mean score	57*	42*

Sources: Surveys 2 and 4.

In this context, Israeli Arabs definitely feel much less a part of Israeli society than they did before the crisis (Table 8.9). Here again, however, more than 60 percent responded in the negative. The growing sense of social alienation is expressed in perceptions of greater suffering from personal discrimination (Table 8.10). Already in January 2000, nine to ten months before the outbreak of the intifada, Israel's Arabs were inclined to report discrimination, but the tendency to do so became much stronger after the intifada began. Thus, the 2000 Jewish-Arab crisis in Israel, in the wake of the intifada, unquestionably made things worse.

Before we conclude this description of the views and feelings of Israel's Arab minority, however, we should first compare the case of the Arabs—at least partially—with that of a smaller but especially important minority, the druze.

Table 8.10. Arabs' Personal Experience of Discrimination[1]

	Answers	Jan. 2000 (N=410)	October 2000 (N=302)
Have you ever personally experienced discrimination?	Yes	55	70
	No	40	28
	On the contrary	4	2
	Mean score[1]	29*	22*

[1] The 0–100 scale runs from 0 = "very often" to 100 = "definitely not."
Sources: Surveys 2 and 4.

THE ISRAELI DRUZE

The Druze, about 10 percent of the Arab population and 1.7 percent of the total Israeli population (90,000–100,000 souls), present another case of a national minority in Israel. Druze should not be confused with other Arabs since, according to their religious beliefs and collective memory, they are a distinct ethno-religious minority in their countries of residence (Lebanon and Syria, principally, in addition to Israel). Their total population throughout the Middle East is about 250,000. In ethnological terms, they are Arabs and belong to the Arab space, culture, and language. However, they consider themselves "different" from other Arabs and are so viewed by them. It is in this sense that our study distinguishes between Druze and Arabs.

The Druze are best described as a sect. This sect is characterized by an eclectic set of doctrines and by a staunch solidarity among members; these aspects have sustained the druze community for nearly a thousand years of turbulent history. What is remarkable about the druze is that they permit neither conversion (in or out) nor intermarriage. Their religious teachings are the monopoly of an elite of initiates and are kept secret not only from the outside world but, in part, even from their own members. These teachings developed out of Ismaelian Islam by merging Jewish, Christian, Gnostic, Neoplatonic, and Iranian elements into a strict monotheism. They originated in Cairo in 1017 as a doctrine asserting the divinity of the sixth caliph (996–1021) of the Fatimid dynasty of Egypt. Druze believe that this caliph (al-Sekim) is a non-mortal who will come back as a messiah. In spite of these sect-like features, druze are active players in the societies where they live and cooperate with the rulers of the country most of the time. They have been conspicuous participants in numerous events in Middle Eastern history, from the Arab war against the Crusaders to the twentieth-century civil wars in Lebanon.

Druze in Israel solemnly recognized the Jewish state as soon as 1948, during the War of Independence. Since then, they have aspired to the status of a distinct recognized minority, which the Israeli authorities have granted them. Ever since, druze men have served in the Israeli army on equal terms with Jews, unlike Muslim and Christian Arabs, who are exempt from military service due to their refusal to side with Israel in its conflict with Arab countries and Palestinians. In view of the difficulties that often arise between non-druze Arabs and Jews, relations between the Druze and the Jews may be instructive of what one may expect in this regard once the Palestinian conflict is terminated. This question, however, is parenthetical to our interest in the druze minority as an aspect of Israel's ethnocultural diversity.

When asked how strongly they regard their own group as an entity in its own right and how far they perceive its distance from other groups (Table 8.11), Druze assert their internal solidarity first, though they also feel close to other Arabs and at the same time feel much farther removed from Jews. When comparing Druze with other Arabs in the same respect, Arabs also appear to feel close to them, although, unlike the Druze, they feel as far from Druze as from Jews. Israeli Arabs definitely do not think of Druze as "belonging" to them. The

Table 8.11. Druze as a Distinct Group in Terms of Cognitive Distances (Percent)[1]

How distant, in your opinion, is your group from:	Druze	Arabs	Jews
Jews (N = 749)	64	71	—
Arabs (N = 410)	56	7	57
Druze (150)	3	15	53

[1] The rates refer to a 0–100 scale in which 0 = no distance at all and 100 = maximal distance.
Source: Survey 2.

Table 8.12. Druze Identity Allegiance (percent; N = 150)

Identity allegiances	Agree
Everyone should look out for members of their own group first.	68
Leaders should look out for those who elected them first.	49
When a member of my group is accused of something, I feel that I am accused, too	53

Source: Survey 2.

Jews, as for them, also feel distant from both Arabs and Druze but less so from the latter. This picture leaves each of these three groups quite isolated from each other. The situation is especially uneasy for the Druze, who are the smallest group and whose feelings of closeness to Arabs are not reciprocated.

Table 8.12 confirms that the druze are a solidaristic if not an ethnocentric entity. Most respondents affirm the legitimacy of ethnic preferential treatment by individuals and leaders and half of them share a vision of politics that champions the group's specific interests.

Regarding their collective identity (Table 8.13), most Druze tend to emphasize "Druzeness"—up to nearly 87 percent as the first (60 percent) or the second (27 percent) component of collective identity. "Arabness" ranks first in 23 percent of the answers and second in 35 percent, 58 percent in all. "Israeliness" is noted first in 17 percent of the responses and second in 38 percent, 55 percent in all. These findings give further indication of the importance of Druzeness for the druze. Of special interest here, however, is that Arabness and Israeliness are valued almost equally.

Table 8.14 shows that these findings are also relevant to the question of allegiance to Israel. Indeed, the more the respondents empha-

Table 8.13. Identities of Druze (Percent)

Druze-Israeli	29
Druze-Arab	31
Druzeness as the first-ranked identity	60
Israeli-Druze	13
Arab-Druze	14
Druzeness as the second-ranked identity	27
Israeli-Arab	4
Arab-Israeli	9
Druzeness-not mentioned	13
Total (N = 150)	100

Source: Survey 2.

Table 8.14. Correlations: Druze Identities and Allegiance to Israel

Interactions	Pearson correlations
Druze identity * feeling an integral part of Israeli society	.23**
Druze identity * when Israel is accused of something, I feel accused, too.	.17*
Druze identity * distance from Jews	−.22**
Druze identity * distance from Arabs	.09

Source: Survey 2.

size Druzeness, the more they feel a solidaristic part of Israeli society and the closer they feel to the Jews. Additional data show, however, that Druze do not differ from Arabs in respect to their relative identification with "Israeliness." Forty-five percent of responses in each group do not mention this token as either the first or the second collective identity. On the other hand, druze do feel much more than Arabs that they are part of Israeli society and are more likely to want their children to live in Israel. Concurrently, Druze, like Arabs, expect their children to follow their lead and retain their particularism. Interestingly, Palestinianness as a token of identity is almost unknown among druze. A substantial minority of Arabs—20 percent—affirm this identity but only 1 percent of Druze wish their children to be Palestinians.

Furthermore, while Arabic is the universal vernacular among Druze and Arabs, three out of four respondents in both groups appear to know Hebrew. This points to a process of linguistic accommodation, if not acculturation, of both Druze and Arabs in Jewish Israeli society.

Moreover Druze and Arabs converge in respect to their tolerance of multiculturalism (78 percent and 73 percent, respectively, state that they "do not mind other people speaking another language in their proximity"). This vision is also essentially democratic; Druze (71 percent), like Arabs (67 percent), believe that rules in regard to human rights should be respected by law in Israel and only minorities of respondents (41 percent and 27 percent, respectively) dispute the Knesset's entitlement to pass legislation that clashes with their leaders' positions.

PERSPECTIVES

In conclusion, and considering first the case of Israel's Arab minority (not including the Druze), it is to be remembered that this group was a large majority in pre-Israel Palestine and became a marginal and isolated minority with the creation of the State of Israel. Yet, while retaining this linguistic and cultural distinctiveness as a non-Jewish group, Arabs were directly exposed to Israel's version of modernity (see for a broad perspective, Bowen, 1993). They learned Hebrew and integrated into the national economy; youngsters enrolled in universities and gradually created a new stratum of professionals. In 1967, as a direct outcome of the Six-Day War, they reconnected with the Arab world and the Palestinian inhabitants in the West Bank and the Gaza Strip. This allowed them to reconstruct and reassert their Palestinian identity, notwithstanding their concomitant cultural convergence toward Israel's modernity. These contradictory and somewhat incongruent parameters of Israeli Arabs' perceptions of their distinctiveness became even sharper as the Israel-Palestine confrontation spiked in periodic crises until it peaked with the *intifada* that broke out in 2000. The resulting reinforcement and solidification of the Palestinian identity of Israel's Arabs only exacerbated the animosity that opposed Arabs to Jews in this country.

Even so, as it comes out in our data, neither Israeli Jews nor Israeli Arabs have adopted attitudes of outright schism. Both sides tend to believe that rapprochement is still on the agenda. Thus, Israeli Arabs tend to emphasize their Palestinianness as their way to be Arabs without gainsaying the fact that they are citizens of Israel. However complex this identity structure is, the data also show clearly that it implies, concurrently, cultural Israelization.

The commitment dimension of Palestininanness, or more accurately, of Israeli Palestininanness causes Arabs to turn, primarily, to themselves and to Palestinians outside Israel. The contents of this identity include allegiances to heritages that bind them to the Arab world, to symbols and aspirations culled from Palestinian nationalism, and to a familiarity with, and a willing attraction to, Israel's version of modernity. As for their position vis-à-vis "others," Israel's Arab citizens emphasize that they are Arabs and not Jews, that they are Palestinians and not only Arabs, and that they are also, in some ways, Israelis and not just Middle Easterners. In all, they encounter difficulties in defining clear-cut concepts of identity and boundary. These conceptual difficulties are paradoxically evinced by Israeli Arabs who live in a heavily Arab-populated area situated within Israel but nearby the territory controlled by the Palestinian Authority. When asked whether they would prefer to remain in Israel or to join—along with their land and houses—a Palestinian state when one comes into being, they firmly assert (at more than 90 percent) that they resolutely oppose any attempt to exclude them from the Israeli state (Yaar and Herman, 2002).

This paradox by no means signifies that Israeli Arabs are characterized by weak collective identification. In fact, all conditions for strong collective identification are present. Many Arabs are characterized by underprivileged class conditions, a fact that alone should lead to relatively weak exposure to the dominant culture and slow acculturation. The dominant culture asserts the Jewish character of the state, which, again, discourages the assimilation of Arabs even when they acculturate to the prevailing norms of behavior. It is against this background that socially mobile Arabs are by no means encouraged by the dominant culture to envisage mingling up with middle-class Jews. On the other hand, the group's own unwillingness to relinquish its identity also pressures its socially mobile elements to remain in their communities. Remaining, therefore, a part of "their people," they have good chances to join the leading stratum of Israel's Arab-Palestinian population (see also Yaniv, 1998).

When considering this case of minority from a broader perspective, one must agree that an ultimate assessment of the plight of a non-Jewish minority in a state defined as the state of the Jew is obscured and overshadowed by the conjectural hostile relations that oppose this state and Arab countries and the Palestinians of the West Bank and the Gaza Strip. What can be pointed out to without hesitation is the fact that Israel's Arabs, even more than Russian Jews and the Ultra-Orthodox, provide a straightforward illustration of a transnational diaspora. Although they are not a group of immigrants to which the concept usually applies, they formulate their collective identity by referring to a major Palestinian center outside their own setting—the West Bank and the Gaza Strip—and, in one way or another, maintain various relationships with Palestinian communities in various Middle Eastern countries (Lebanon, Syria, Iraq, and, above all, Jordan). It is a transnational diaspora that is certainly among the most diversified in the world, as it consists of refugees in several countries, immigrant communities in others, an occupied population in the West Bank and Gaza Strip, and, last but not least, a national minority in Israel.

The Israeli Palestinians, more specifically, if we may revert to the terms of our research question concerning them, are torn between Palestinian nationhood and Israeli citizenship. This dilemma seems basically unresolved and pendulates in accordance with the pendulations of the Israeli-Palestinian conflict. As for the group's ultimate inclinations, however, we find that the strategic choice of Arabs in Israel—for the time being—is to be a part of the country, even if Palestinians establish their own state and Israel retains a dominant Jewish majority.

Druze are also a transnational diaspora. They live in several Middle Eastern countries and in each of them they have a special relationship with the state, varying with circumstances, that has little effect on the continuity and stability of their interconnectedness. For this very reason, the fact of dispersion plays a minimal role in the attitude of the druze minority toward the holders of political power in each society, and it is in this context that their case takes on all its importance—both as an Israeli case on its own right and as an example of relations between Jews and a non-Jewish ethnically Arab minority.

Our data show that even though Druze have formally sided with the Jews, they definitely do not wish to be confused with them and are determined to retain their particularism. This factor, along with the Jews' adherence to their own primordial distinctiveness, easily explains why Druze continue to hold a special position in Israel's sociocultural spectrum. In the background, there is the fact that ever since the establishment of the Jewish–druze alliance in 1948, patrimonial and patronizing relations have prevailed between the druze traditional leadership and the Israeli Jewish political elite that receive recurrent ritual expression on Druze festivals and national commemorations the year round.

Thus far at least, these relations have remained viable because Druze themselves have been undergoing modernization under the influence of their Israeli environment and their exposure to this version of modernity. Yet, be this as it may, Druze show that modernization does not rule out the retention of particularism in a modern and secular society. Actually, this importance of primordialism in minority cultures is compatible with—and probably fueled by—the dominant culture's own emphasis on a national collective identity that also evinces primordial commitments that exclude the minorities from the mainstream.

In fact, it is our contention here that, again, the religion-nationhood link implied by the dominant culture sets Druze and Muslim and Christian Arabs, in Israel, in a definitive position of minorities vis-à-vis the main stream of society, as these groups represent different religious faiths that cannot be reconcilable with membership in Jewry. From this *a priori* follow, we think, the main features of the Jewish–non-Jewish relationship in a setting that grants Jews the status of mainstream. It defines boundaries that can hardly be transgressed from either side and sets down a dynamic further nourished by additional aspects—such as the Israeli-Palestinian conflict and the under-privileged condition of many members of the minorities (Ben-Rafael and Brosh, 1995).

It can be also expected that an easing of the protracted violent external conflict and circumstances providing the members of the minorities with better possibilities to improve their socioeconomic conditions should contribute to a context where legal stipulations—along with the example of a country like Britain—would diminish the cost—in terms of civil rights and privileges—of nonmembership in the mainstream of society.

CHAPTER NINE

FOREIGN WORKERS: THE CASE OF THE FILIPINOS

INTRODUCTION

This chapter analyzes a case of residents who are neither Jewish nor Israeli. The literature shows that since the 1950s, labor migration has been a major vehicle of immigration "to the West from the rest," i.e., from low-income countries on all continents including Eastern and Southern Europe. This immigration may be legal, regulated by official documents, or illegal, effected by cross-border infiltration. These forms of labor migration tend to become permanent features of wealthy societies, resulting in the emergence of new minorities. This broadens cultural diversity in the target countries and weakens state control over the population. Many countries enact policies to stanch immigration at times of economic recession but the efficiency of these initiatives is generally less than perfect. As a rule, temporary workers have been quite successful in their encroachments, becoming *de facto* permanent residents (Brubaker, 1989, 1992; Castles, 2000; Jenkins and Sofos, 1996).

Foreign workers also bring new problems to their new societies. They are generally employed in the worst-paying jobs and create new cycles of poverty. Far from affluent neighborhoods, they form communities of their own that amount to new urban ghettos that bespeak social exclusion. They send much of the money that they can spare "home," where it is crucial for families that remain behind and live in misery.

Scholars emphasize that from the macrosociological standpoint this labor migration brings about an uneven distribution of membership in Western democracies (Walzer, 1981). Martiniello (1994) elaborates on this issue by coining a triangular structure of membership comprising citizens, denizens, and margizens. Citizenship denotes full access to social, economic, and political rights; denizenship consists of partial access to entitlements insofar as they apply to legal immigrants; and margizenship describes a new category of people who are denied membership and are unrecognized in established legal, social, cultural, and political settings. Illegal foreign workers fall into the last-mentioned category.

Over time, however, democracies cannot remain indifferent to the plight of marginal groups which, in one way or another, find ways to form institutions of their own—religious, social, cultural, and even political (Miller, 1989). While this process is hardly discernable at times (Chaney, 1981; Walzer, 1981; Soysal, 1994), migrants are often quick to establish associations that penetrate the public sphere and lobby on behalf of their interests—including protesting against exploitation and paternalism (Goulbourne, 1991). Such associations are politically significant to illegal migrants who, individually, are powerless vis-à-vis state agencies (Kemp et al., 2000, Ong, 1996). These organizations may also eventually serve both as facilitators of incoming migrants' adjustment to the host society and as a link with the home country by means of networking and transnational communication. Most importantly, they present the local and national public spheres with demands (Soysal, 1994).

By creating such self-help organizations, foreign workers develop tools of collective empowerment that may serve as levers of social mobilization. From there it is a short distance to the fringes of the political arena, which in a democracy can never be entirely off-limits to political actors—as illustrated by the cases of the Turks in Germany and North Africans in France (Miller, 1989; Withold de Wenden, 1994). The very context of a democratic culture as it prevails in Western societies is favorable to the politicization of foreign workers (Soysal, 1994; Jacobson, 1996), which, in many cases, has contributed new challenges to the political culture and applied pressure for the redrawing of the contours of multiculturalism.

Historical Background

The case of Israel provides another illustration of these issues. Israel began to admit foreign workers mainly after the 1967 war, when an economic boom set in motion the recruitment of cheap external labor. At first, this manpower came from the newly occupied Palestinian territories; it entered the lowest stratum of the job market and its very presence elevated the entire labor hierarchy by one rung (Semyonov and Lewin-Epstein, 1987). The advantage of Palestinian workers was that they commuted daily and did not settle in the country.

Their numbers quickly increased, from 20,000 in 1970 to 95,000 in 1986, 7 percent of the Israeli labor force (Kemp et al., 2000).

The first Palestinian uprising (*intifada*) against Israeli occupation, which began in 1987 and lasted for about six years, reduced the number of incoming Palestinian workers drastically, by tens of thousands. This unavoidably led to a shortage in low-status labor, especially in agriculture and construction. In response, Israel opened its gates to foreign workers from overseas. From 1993 on, pressure from large corporations induced the government to be increasingly liberal in its policies on the recruitment of foreign workers.

The first contingents were Romanians who were employed in construction. They were soon followed by Thais, who were engaged in agriculture. Filipinos followed suit in personal services (geriatric care, nursing, and housekeeping) (Bartram, 1998; Bar-Zuri, 1996). The number of yearly foreign-labor permits issued by the Ministry of Labor climbed from 2,500 in 1987 to 9,600 in 1993 (Kemp et al., 2000). The biggest leap took place in 1993–1994, when the number of permits jumped to about 30,000. Since then, the sources of this migration have become more diverse; they include African countries, South America, and the Far East. In 1996, the total number of authorized foreign workers was estimated at 103,000 (Bartram, 1998)—72 percent in construction, 16 percent in agriculture, 7 percent in nursing and geriatric care, and 5 percent in light industry, catering, and hotels (Lerer, 1996). The population of illegal workers also increased considerably while foreign workers as a whole became a visible feature of Israeli society—their share in the national labor force climbed to 7–8 percent. By the turn of the century, the Ministry of Labor and Social Affairs estimated a total of 150,000 labor migrants, half documented and half not (Rajman and Kemp, 2002). From the state's point of view, the problems raised by the presence of this new population devolve on municipal authorities (especially those of Tel-Aviv), which, together with relevant NGOs (human rights organizations), are tasked with assuring the foreign workers' civil rights.

From a bureaucratic standpoint, labor permits in Israel are given to employers and not to employees, thereby turning documented labor migrants into a *de facto* captive labor force. Recruitment itself is conducted by manpower agencies and employers. Undocumented workers fall into two categories: those who enter on tourist visas and overstay, and documented workers who leave their employers. A problem that cannot be overlooked and is presented by this new population group has to do with Israel's self-definition as the State of the Jews. With this in mind, the government emphasizes the importance of returning undocumented workers to their countries of origin. The policy on this matter, in effect since 1996, has been implemented with relative success.

Although the state itself tends to minimize its involvement in foreign workers' affairs, the complex issues relating to the human rights of migrant labor have prompted the courts to intervene on their behalf repeatedly. Local authorities (especially the Municipality of Tel-Aviv) and NGOs began to serve this new population and have been increasingly involved in its welfare. Sometimes municipal government and central bodies cooperate in specific areas on behalf of foreign workers. In July 1999, Tel Aviv established a Center for Assistance and Information for the Foreign Community, Mesila, which is linked to social welfare services, information, and education structures. This center locates kindergartens run by foreign workers—in 2001, preschool classes were opened for foreign workers' children, jointly subsidized by the municipality and the Ministry of Education. Mesila also encourages migrants to establish organizations, promotes the emergence of community leaders among the various subgroups, and aspires to create an intermediary body of representatives.

Moreover, several NGOs focus on foreign workers' rights. The leading organization in this respect is the Association for Civil Rights in Israel (ACRI), which, along with other organizations, attempts to influence the authorities and raise public awareness as part of an effort to prevent the migrants' rights infringement by the state and by abusive employers. These groups wish to enhance public consciousness of the plights that befall many foreign workers. One of their principal achievements was the enactment of the Health Insurance for Children of Foreign Workers Law (February 2002).

Although the authorities wish to keep foreign workers on temporary status and deport those who overstay their visas, the migrants are often inclined to marry local spouses, have children, and settle in the country for long periods of time, if not definitively. For these migrants, the actions taken by the Tel Aviv Municipality constitute a development that might finally grant them permanent status. One also observes a proliferation of community activities, in which each group expresses its particularism. Foreign workers from Latin America, for example, have established soccer clubs that arrange competitions among themselves. Africans have created religious services, especially Anglican, that attract thousands to Mass in customary festive dress. Churches organize choirs, made up of foreign workers, which rehearses on a regular basis, provide entertainment on festive occasions and sponsor organized trips around the country on holidays.

In brief, in Israel as in other countries, foreign workers have established new communities despite their marginal status and the domestic population's perception of them as cultural, social, and political outsiders (Schnapper, 1994a; Weiner, 1996). They learned how to organize effectively and raise claims vis-à-vis institutions and political elites. Gradually, they have found their way into the public sphere in order to articulate their demands and requirements. They bring their complaints to the media and NGOs, and even apply to courts for protection (Kemp et al., 2000).

It is against this background that our project investigated foreign workers as an aspect of Israel's multiculturalism. In the context of this work, we confined ourselves to a small sample ($N = 50$) of one group of foreign workers which happens to be the one of the longest-landed and largest groups, the Filipinos, and restricted ourselves to selected issues. We took the liberty of regarding veteran Filipino foreign workers as *somewhat* representative of what one might expect to occur among other more recent groups of migrant labor, and it is in this perspective that we primarily see this part of our work as but an explorative attempt to insert the discussion of foreign workers in the frame of Israel's multiculturalism.

IDENTITY AND IDENTIFICATION

Only a small minority of Filipino workers, in our sample, feel like total strangers in Israel (Table 9.1). This is confirmed when we consider attitudes about the possibility of their settling and raising children in Israel. Although a larger minority rejects this prospect, the majority does not, and more than one-third of respondents express an unambiguous positive inclination. Thus, quite a few would like to consider their presence in Israel permanent.

Interestingly, Filipinos feel quite close to the Israeli Jewish population (Table 9.2). This finding reflects that they are mainly employed by Jews, and the picture is different, when it comes to Israeli Arabs.

Table 9.1. Attitudes of Filipino Foreign Workers toward Israeli Society

To what extent do you feel a part of Israeli society?	Percent
Not at all	12
So-so	45
Very much	43
Total (N = 50)	100
Do you want your children to live in Israel?	
Not at all	43
So-so	19
Very much	38
Total (N = 49)	100

Source: Survey 2.

Table 9.2. Cognitive Distance of Filipino Workers from
Various Categories[1]

Issues	Categories	Percent
Distance from Israeli Jews	Close	73
	Somewhat	21
	Far	6
	Total (N = 51)	100
	Mean	19
Distance from Israeli Arabs	Close	7
	Somewhat	42
	Far	51
	Total (N = 37)	100
	Mean	76
Distance from non-Filipino foreign workers	Close	43
	Somewhat	41
	Far	16
	Total (N = 47)	100
	Mean	40

[1] t (Filipinos-Jews; Filipinos-Arabs) = −15**; t (Filipinos–non-Filipino foreign workers; Filipinos-Arabs) = −5**; t (Filipinos–non-Filipino foreign workers; Filipinos-Jewish Israelis) = 9**. Source: Survey 3.

Table 9.3. Filipino Foreign Workers' Concept of Multiculturalism[1]

Categories	Percent
1. Should children study in their language of origin in school?	
Not at all	4
Somewhat	10
Definitely	86
Total (N = 51)	100
Mean	74
2. Everyone should look after members of his/her group first.	
Not at all	18
Somewhat	33
Definitely	59
Total (N = 51)	100
Mean	60
3. Does it disturb you when someone speaks a language you do not know?	
Not at all	45
Somewhat	49
Definitely	16
Total (N = 51)	100
Mean	65
4. All cultures are equal.	
Not at all	51
Somewhat	12
Definitely	37
Total (N = 51)	100
Mean	48
5. The presence of different cultures means cultural enrichment.	
Not at all	35
Somewhat	26
Definitely	39
Total (N = 47)	100
Mean	52
6. Would you like to see Israelis become more like you?	
Not at all	24
Somewhat	41
Definitely	35
Total (N = 46)	100
Mean	55

[1] $F_{(1-6)} = 852$**. Significant differences were found between the means of the following items (Scheffe Procedure): (1,4)**; (1,5)**; F (1,6)**; (3,4)*. Source: Survey 3.

A large minority does feel what we might call "familiarity" with them but only a small cohort feels close: Filipino workers, seemingly, are aware of the weak status of the Arab minority.

On the other hand, Filipinos feel close to other categories of foreign workers. The common condition of migrant labor, the closeness of residence (many foreign workers in all groups tend to live in the same poor neighborhoods, especially in Tel Aviv), and their confrontation with a society that defines them all as "different" contribute to the gradual crystallization of an aggregate cluster of foreign workers.

Yet, Filipinos have a strongly particularistic attitude about themselves and profess an equally strong multiculturalist attitude toward society (Table 9.3). They think that schools should teach in native languages, meaning that they would like to see in Israel a coexistence of different symbols rather than a monolingual culture. Hence, Filipino foreign workers are tolerant of cultural diversity. As a feeble group in a host society, they probably consider general tolerance the best guarantee of their freedom. Filipinos, as our data show, do not argue that all cultures are equal and do not expect that those in their environment become more like them. Concomitantly, they support the idea that leaders should look after members of their specific constituency first. In other words, Filipinos believe that the public scene should be a direct reflection of the cultural diversity of the society.

The Filipinos' group solidarity is shown by Table 9.4. When added to other relevant aspects, the findings leave no doubt—in our restricted sample, at least—that they constitute a genuine ethnic group in which individuals feel a commitment to fellow ethnics and wish to safeguard their language and culture. However, Filipinos—who, as we have seen, do not rule out the possibility of integrating into Israeli society—are also strongly willing to accept Israel citizenship, at least for their children. This attitude is emphasized more in respect to their own group than to the wider heterogeneous category of foreign workers, although it is anything but negative in regard to the broader group. The data make it quite clear that the Filipinos share a sense that their group is a special entity.

Table 9.5 fine-tunes the picture. Filipinos are amenable to social closeness with other groups that share their marginality and with Israelis. Hence, they do not aspire to any form of self-segregation. In view of their comparative advantage over other groups of foreign

Table 9.4. Filipinos in Regard to Themselves and to Israel[1]

Issues	Percent
1. When Filipinos are accused of something, do you feel accused as well?	
Not at all	6
Somewhat	10
Definitely	84
Total (N = 51)	100
2. Children of Filipinos born in Israel should be Israeli citizens.	
Not at all	25
Somewhat	16
Definitely	59
Total (N = 51)	100
3. Foreign workers should become Israeli citizens after five years in Israel.	
Not at all	25
Somewhat	30
Definitely	45
Total (N = 51)	100

[1] Kendall's Tau b (items 2, 3) = .25*.
Source: Survey 3.

workers—due to the fact that many are employed in the relatively privileged area of personal services—they might have tended to snobbishness toward them. This is definitely not the case. By the same token, they are willing to become more familiar with Israeli culture.

It remains that to the question "I would like to see more foreign workers in Israel" (Table 9.5), about three-quarters of the respondents answer negatively. We seem to have captured here an attitude that did not appear in previous questions. In this respect, Filipinos tend to behave in the very manner described in classic sociological literature (Glazer and Moynihan, 1974), which shows that groups that are about to gain—or that hope to gain—social acceptance often tend to "throw the ladder away" in order to avoid the degradation of status that would occur if they had to share their privileges with others.

DISCUSSION AND CONCLUSION

The intention of our own study of foreign workers in the frame of this investigation of Israel's multiculturalism was to focus on their attitudes toward both themselves as a group evolving in this society,

Table 9.5. Ethnocentric Attitudes of Filipinos

Issues	Attitudes	Percent
1. I would not like to have non-Filipino foreign workers in my neighborhood.	I don't mind	66
	Somewhat	18
	I don't want	16
	Total (N = 49)	100
2. I would not like to have Israelis in my neighborhood.	I don't mind	56
	Somewhat	34
	I don't want	10
	Total (N = 50)	100
3. Everyone who lives in Israel should accustom him/herself to the Israeli culture.	Not at all	16
	Somewhat	24
	Definitely	60
	Total (N = 51)	100
4. The longer a guest worker lives in Israel, the more he or she should look like an Israeli.	Not at all	31
	Somewhat	28
	Definitely	41
	Total (N = 49)	100
5. I myself would like to be more like Israelis.	Not at all	30
	Somewhat	35
	Definitely	35
	Total (N = 49)	100
6. I would like to see more foreign workers in Israel.	Not at all	76
	Somewhat	14
	Definitely	10
	Total (N = 49)	100
7. Israeli culture should be more . . .	Asian	21
	As it is	51
	European	28
	Total (N = 47)	100

Source: Survey 3.

and their perceptions of their environment. Our questions concerned the extent to which they see themselves here as "permanent" and, if so, how important they consider their cultural-linguistic particularism. Furthermore, in accordance with our analytical scheme, we also wanted to know how they perceive "others."

Overall, our data tend to show that Filipinos do not feel like strangers in Israel any more. Few feel totally alienated and many contemplate positively the eventuality of staying on in Israel—for themselves as well as their children. In fact, many feel close to Israeli Jews while they also feel close to non-Filipino foreign workers, with whom they bond in an aggregate of sorts.

Filipinos have strong feelings about themselves—an assertion of solidarity that denotes ethnic commitment—and, on this basis, a strong multiculturalist perspective which is by no means related to specific or ideological claims. While Filipinos feel a connection with other categories of foreign workers, they are also willing to emphasize the special merit of their group in this society and express willingness to become more familiar with Israeli culture. All in all, it seems undeniable that Filipino foreign workers constitute a new ethnic entity in the Israeli social landscape.

These findings also confirm the high level of collective identification that we would expect from our structural parameters when applying to Filipinos. We know that Israel's dominant culture stresses the primordialism of the national identity and is thus quite segregative vis-à-vis residents who are both non-Jewish and non-Israeli. We also know that a group composed of skilled or unskilled workers who have been brought to a new country on the basis of purely instrumental considerations integrates itself *a priori* as a lower-class entity. This should account for relatively narrow exposure to the dominant culture. Our own data showed that Filipinos who display much elasticity in the realm of culture and cultural identity still feel committed to their own symbols. These aspects together account for a rather strong (self-)segregative model and a strong tendency to identify with themselves as an ethnic entity.

Additional research should be needed to confirm that this picture reflects faithfully the general development of the Filipinos in Israel, though our feeling is that a larger survey would not obtain drastically different findings. Actually, we tend to see the development of a kind of Filipino in the Israeli society as a model that should reflect, in its broad lines, the plight of other groups of foreign workers, which over time should illustrate some "hodgepodge" tendencies.

It is, however, important to emphasize at this stage that these new communities of foreign workers are transnational diasporas. For Filipinos, as for other groups, the link to the homeland and to family and friends who remained behind is the very rationale—or at least the original rationale—of their emigration to Israel. Indeed, a study in the Philippines themselves (Semyonov et al., forthcoming) shows the importance of the resources sent to families in the homeland by foreign workers—up to the point that these resources are creating new forms of social stratification. These resources not only allow individuals to attain a new level of consumption but also provide the means to establish new family enterprises.

On the other hand, in contrast to the pressures exerted on foreign workers by relatives who stayed behind and depend on them economically and socially, foreign workers may also be attracted to the possibility of remaining in Israel, as a country that has much more to offer in terms of living conditions—notwithstanding the low and marginal social positions where they are confined. Hence, they may be tempted to prefer Israel to the relative privileges that they would obtain by returning to their homeland after years of work and saving in Israel. Our globalized society actually offers them the opportunity to reconcile these two perspectives, as remaining in Israel should not preclude retaining continuous contact with relatives in the homeland.

These conclusions relate directly to our basic research question about Israel's foreign workers. We asked about the extent to which one may speak of cultural "Israelization" in this case and of a tendency to integrate into the target society. Our findings show that this part of Israel's social multiculturalism tends to look for ways to insert itself into the social reality. It is eager to attenuate, as far as possible, the tensions that this insertion might occasion and to seek compromises between its wish to remain loyal to itself and its willingness to adjust and endorse models that it finds here. At the same time, the neighborhood with other groups of foreign workers cannot remain without impact on their culture, horizons, and social life. From a broader perspective, Filipinos who reached Israel on the wings of globalization are contributing new forms to the country's multiculturalism while they themselves undergo changes of lifestyles and perspectives. In the specific Israeli context, all these also represent change of Israel's multiculturalism by introducing an element that is not only non-Jewish—Arabs and druze already play this role—but also non-Israeli (at this particular moment). This element, we have also found, is tending, at least for the time being, not to join and strengthen the non-Jewish component of this society but rather to settle on the margins of the Jewish population.

Here, too, it may again be contended, the religion-nationhood link implied by the dominant culture plays a crucial role, and differentiates the plight of foreign workers in Israel from their counterparts in countries like Germany or France. This link, in a Jewish state, means that foreign workers are set in a definitive position of minority that cannot hope to belong to the mainstream of society, as these groups represent different religious confessions irreconcilable with membership in Jewry and, thus, in the Jewish nation. As for Arabs, boundaries can hardly be transgressed from either side. Religious conversion is here the only bridge to join society's mainstream—that in itself indicates the practical significance of the religion-nationhood link.

What makes things worse, in this case, is the Israeli government's policy—implemented with energy in the 2000s—which tries to keep control of the contract-bound turnover of foreign workers and to prevent thereby the definitive settling of a new permanent non-Jewish population. This policy that is motivated by the preoccupation to retain the Jewish character of the state, however, carries an economic cost as it brings over individuals who lack any experience of local work conditions and takes out others who have reached high levels of competence. It is this price, for the time being, that Israel's government is ready to pay to meet the challenge represented by foreign workers to the solid Jewish majority of the Israeli population.

SECTION V

CONFLICTUAL MULTICULTURALISM

CHAPTER TEN

THE CONFIGURATION OF MULTICULTURALISM

THE CONCEPT OF MULTICULTURALISM

Israeli society, we have seen, is made of a large variety of sociocultural groups that evolve interactively but by no means uniformly. Tensions oppose the dominant culture and the religious and ethnoreligious groups—over the status of the religious law (Haredim), the relation of the national policy to religion (the National Religious), and the relation of religious-national symbols to particular legacies (Mizrahi Ultra-Orthodox). This scene clearly relates to the link of religion to nationalism embodied in the dominant culture in a manner which is diversely criticized by the various religious forces.

This link stands also behind the ethnocultural cleavages of the setting and makes up a major dimension of the hardships (very different as such) encountered by groups like Russians and Ethiopians. For the Russians, it is their aloofness from Judaism that is the principal factor of distance separating them from the society's mainstream, and for the Ethiopians, the specific kind of closeness to it which they illustrate. Last but not least, it is also this very link that—in one way or another, and under one version or another—is common to all Jewish components of the Israeli setting, that accounts, in large part, for the relative alienation that separates Israeli Jews from non-Jewish Israelis, and from non-Jewish, non-Israelis.

Each of these cleavages represents different challenges and involves different considerations which together amount to the multiplicity of divergences and convergences that makes up Israel's conflictual multiculturalism. It is to the overall and endemic dynamics of this brand of multiculturalism that we now turn asking: what kind of multiculturalism do these cleavages form by means of their juxtaposition, interaction, and interrelation?

Multiculturalism is brought about by social and political confrontations and denotes recognition of the sustainable existence of distinct sociocultural groups (see also Willett, 1998). By extension, multiculturalization is the process through which mere sociocultural heterogeneity, or pluralism, becomes multiculturalism. This process is anchored in the polity and the extent to which it enables factions and pressure groups to force the dominant culture to recognize their "difference" and their specific interests. It implies, in one way or in another, a rephrasing of the dominant culture, legitimizing the new reality in terms of its overall representation of what the society stands for.

The literature addresses multiculturalization in various ways. Castoriadis (1997) considers it the maturation of frictions between capitalism—which embodies rationality and is geared to mastering the environment—and democracy—which leaves room for the manifestation of subjectivity in seeking self-expression and participation. Dahrendorf (1959) elaborates on this tension, noting specifically that it takes place between capitalist economic demands, implying structural inequality, and the democratic demand for political equality, with an open-ended potential for expansion to additional issues. Furet (1981) adds that democracy may even give rise to demands for the wholesale reconstruction of society along radical egalitarian lines. Touraine (1992) summarizes the confrontation between capitalism and democracy in terms of a debate between fundamentally rivaling projects that coexist within Western modernity. In all, commentators agree widely that democracy encourages highly diverse groups to put forth claims and enter the political game. This opportunity inspires sociocultural groups to emphasize their particularism as a basis for social mobilization and to formulate political demands that aim to strengthen their participation in society. This endeavor, if successful, merely whets the motivation of such groups to be present and active in the polity, even though in other respects—lifestyles, mobility aspirations, identification with the dominant culture—members of the same groups may tend to become less and less "different" from nonmembers.

Such developments restrict the center's span of control over the social order as it grants a degree of autonomy to sociocultural constituencies and allows them to use their power as a basis for claims—a configuration that has numerous social and cultural consequences. Once it solidifies and imposes itself, multiculturalism confirms the coexistence of lifestyles and social values and legitimizes alternative sources of meaning and moral authority. Thus, Taylor (1994; 1998) contends that multiculturalism emphasizes the cultural components of justice at the expense of material components. H. D. Meyer (2000)

illustrates Taylor's argument by noting that in a multicultural society taste is no longer the monopoly of the privileged who have always
kept their distance from other classes. A new concept of taste comes
about which insists on "authenticity" rather than refinement.

Not unrelatedly, scholars also stress the conflictual potential of
multiculturalism. Harvey (1989; 2000) points to crises of identity that
lead to racism and ethnic conflict. Pursuant to these reflections,
Kincheloe and Steinberg (1997) include race, gender, and language
under the heading of causes of multicultural conflict. Multiculturalism,
they assert, involves competing definitions of the social order that
are grounded in divergent interests.

In this context, Soysal (2000) mentions a paradox in the evolution of civism in contemporary Western society. She observes that
Western societies inspired by their value system and political ambitions grant rights to new groups irrespective of whether they achieve
social insertion. This contradiction, she contends, weakens the motivation of groups to undergo complete assimilation. We may add that
groups that express multiple claims on the basis of their society's
democratic discourse often embody the nexus of the development of
multiculturalism and the expansion of globalization. Indeed, globalization may be seen as the direct context of the proliferation of
transnational diasporas, which, in turn, are an increasingly important factor in multiculturalism.

Israel, in this respect, is like many other developed countries that
have become a magnet for individuals outside their borders. In this
case, most of these individuals are Diaspora Jews who settle in Israel
for reasons that range from the ideological to the purely instrumental.
However, as the examples of foreign workers and non-Jewish Russian
immigrants show, Israel also attracts non-Jewish immigrants.

The concept of transnational diaspora embraces several interconnected phenomena. It concerns individuals who, in the context of
today's intense global interconnectedness of societies, are quite easily
prompted to emigrate from their (low-income) countries to more for-
tunate ones—as foreign workers, "regular" immigrants, or "illegal"
immigrants. They tend naturally to settle in cities and neighborhoods where they find relatives or people of like origin who facilitate their adjustment to their new environment. They learn the
vernacular and the prevailing habits and customs of their new surroundings, but their very concentration allows them to continue to
use their languages of origin and to retain aspects of their culture.

Advanced communication technologies, the ease of international travel, and access to global mass media are additional factors that allow immigrants to retain ties with relatives everywhere—"back home" and in other diasporas. Diaspora communities in Western societies may remain involved in cross-border and cross-continental networks of varying amplitude without being precluded from striving to integrate into their new societies.

Furthermore, while the combination of democracy and globalization does much to account for the multiculturalization of societies, multiculturalism itself also engages in a two-way relationship with the concept of multiple modernities. By multiple modernities, we mean that in every society that is characterized by a given historical culture and allegiances to given civilizations (Christian, Islamic, or other), the penetration of modernity, its basic approaches to life and society, and its emphases on new values and social projects may follow different paths and form diverse configurations of social patterns, cultural symbols, and ways of acting (Eisenstadt, 2000; Arnason, 2002; Wittrock, 2002). Hence, one cannot expect all modern or modernizing societies to converge toward one model. One may, however, expect diverse modern societies to share features that allow them to communicate meaningfully and, on this basis, to contribute to the global interconnectedness that the concept of "one world" represents. In this world of multiple modernities, individuals everywhere share—although not necessarily equally—several basic notions conveyed by modernization in respect to labor-market participation, economic affairs, and even forms of mass culture, politics, and family life. This diffusion of modernity, in its various forms, creates elements of a common language that crosses national borders.

If multiculturalism denotes the coexistence of diverse sociocultural communities within the boundaries of one society, the multiple-modernities perspective suggests the possibility that these communities will also embrace versions of modernity that differ from each other in various ways. While such communities influence each other as they coexist in a common setting, each one's particular "modernity project" is also—and firstly—shaped by its own ethnocultural, religious, and social orientations. In other words, the multiple-modernities theory, although devised primarily as a tool for the comparative analysis of different societies, is also relevant for the study of the development and dynamics of multicultural settings.

We apply this set of considerations to the investigation of Israeli society as a multicultural setting. To delve into this added dimension of our analytical scheme, we focus on the reality established by the cleavages from a holistic standpoint. We begin this discussion by asking about the configuration of Israeli multiculturalism. This issue—as explained in Chapter 2 ("Research Questions")—refers to the way the various collectives position themselves vis-à-vis each other and structure the multicultural space. Our research question here concerns the extent to which one may speak of a periphery-and-center configuration where different collectives—or aggregates of collectives—compose different circles. This line of inquiry should show us whether the social dynamics are dominated by particular aspects of the social order—the religiosity principle, ethnic issues, or the attitude toward "others." Subsequent chapters will then discuss the rules of the multicultural game and the strategic goals and identity politics of the actors.

Before we analyze the data, we should note that the reference to origin categories in the tables of Chapters 10–12 do not include the "Israeli" category—used up to now to designate third-generation Israelis—as a group in itself, since we do not know the origin of these respondents' grandparents. We do, however, include these respondents in other types of categorizations. Furthermore, when necessary, the tables treat ethnic and religious groups as distinct categories even where they widely overlap, e.g., Ashkenazim and the nonreligious or Mizrahim and the traditional. This allows us to distinguish between religiosity effects and ethnic effects, though the fact of wide overlapping is kept in mind in the interpretations of the findings.

COHESION, OPENNESS, AND ATTRACTION

Tables 10.1 and 10.2 consider how close to and, of course, how far from each other the components of Israel's multiculturalism are. We also wished to determine whether they scatter across the space that they create or tend to form clusters and aggregates. Table 10.1 elaborates on the constellation of the groups and ranks them in three ways, according to (1) individuals' attitudes toward people of shared origin, indicating group formation; (2) the attitudes of members of groups toward other groups, indicating the extent of their association with, or dissociation from, others; and (3) the differential attraction that groups have on members of other groups.

This table shows that Ashkenazim and the nonreligious (among whom the former are dominant), and Mizrahim and the traditional (again among whom the former are dominant), are relatively close to each other and tend to form one cluster. The religious feel not far from these groups—although they do not find the same favor in the eyes of Ashkenazim and the nonreligious—nor from the Ultra-Orthodox. The Ultra-Orthodox do not attract other groups but feel close to Ashkenazim, Mizrahim, the religious, and, to some extent, the nonreligious. Ethiopians appear quite isolated; they feel close only to the traditional and, somewhat, to Mizrahim. Similarly, Russian Jews feel close only to Ashkenazim and the nonreligious—a sentiment that is not fully reciprocated. Last but not least, Arabs feel close to no one and Druze feel close only to Arabs, although the latter do not respond accordingly. Interestingly, foreign workers feel close to Ashkenazim, the nonreligious, and the traditional—probably because they are employed by members of these groups—but this is not reciprocated. Generally speaking, the major focus of attraction crystallizes around Ashkenazim, Mizrahim, and the traditional, while the Ultra-Orthodox, Russian Jews, and Arabs stand at some distance and in relative isolation.

As for internal cohesion, Tables 10.1 and 10.2 show that the nonreligious are the most cohesive—though the Ashkenazim who constitute the largest part of this category are less cohesive, which shows their nonethnic character. The most cohesive groups apart from the nonreligious are the Arabs, the Druze, the Ethiopians, and the Ultra-Orthodox, all of whom are also relatively isolated. The religious, the traditional, and Russians stand somehow in the middle. Overall, the constituents of multiculturalism that are not part of the cluster identified above constitute distinct, isolated, but cohesive entities. The exception to this rule is the foreign workers, who are both socially isolated and weak in cohesion. This is by no means surprising in view of the internal diversity of this category.

Interestingly enough, Ashkenazim and Mizrahim constitute the central focus in this constellation, though the Ashkenazim to some extent the Mizrahim are not among the most cohesive groups. This is an important finding because sociologists often regard them as the principal protagonists in Israel's ethnocultural scene. Moreover, our results also show them to be less assertive than others.

As for openness to others, the positive end of the continuum—which is not far from the middle-ranking category—consists of the

Table 10.1. Cognitive Distances among Groups*

How distant do you feel from people who belong to the following groups?

Rsp	N	Ash	Miz	Russ	Ethi	N-re	Trad	Rel	Ultr	Arab	Druz	Fo.w
Ash	505	23	41	52	64	16	37	53	72	67	60	79
Miz	429	41	23	55	53	22	24	41	58	66	58	78
Russ	408	33	74	17	90	21	48	71	89	90	89	89
Ethi	50	62	46	71	5	38	17	37	73	66	68	87
Ultr	209	18	26	55	63	37	25	13	3	86	79	90
Rel	99	25	22	47	49	29	17	12	39	70	57	76
Trad	337	40	23	54	54	27	17	42	61	69	57	79
N-re	499	30	40	55	64	9	43	60	79	63	59	76
Ara	300	75	68	84	87	71	80	87	88	7	56	82
Druz	150	66	65	83	85	69	77	83	83	15	3	86
Guest	50	35	43	67	70	42	42	51	71	76	71	40

* The values in the table were computed on the basis of the answers to the question; the scores were converted into a scale from 0 (very close) to 100 (very distant).
Source: Survey 3.

Table 10.2. Cohesion, Popularity, and Openness to Others

Cohesion/ incohesion[1]	Distance from own group	Popularity/ unpopularity[2]	Distance of others from group	Openness/ closedness to others[3]	Distance from others
Ultra-Orthodox	3	Nonreligious	39	Religious	42
Druze	3	Ashkenazim	45	Ultra-Orthodox	48
Ethiopians	5	Traditional	48	Mizrahim	49
Arabs	7	Mizrahim	53	Traditional	50
Secular	9	Religious	57	Ashkenazim	54
Religious	12	Druze	62	Foreign workers	54
Russians	17	Russians	62	Ethiopians	56
Traditional	17	Arabs	70	Secular	57
Mizrahim	23	Ethiopians	71	Russians	67
Ashkenazim	23	Ultra-Orth.	75	Druze	68
Foreign workers	40	Foreign workers	83	Arabs	78
Mean	14	Mean	60	Mean	57

[1] Cognitive distance from own group measures the cohesion of the group.
[2] Cognitive distance of other groups vis-à-vis each group measures the popularity/unpopularity of the group in the eyes of other groups.
[3] Cognitive distance of the group vis-à-vis other groups measures the group's general openness or closedness toward them, i.e., orientations of inclusion/exclusion.
Source: Survey 3.

Ultra-Orthodox and the national religious, followed quite closely by the traditional and the nonreligious. We also find that Mizrahim and (to a lesser extent) Ashkenazim are quite open to others, as are Ethiopians and foreign workers. Among the Jewish groups, the least open are the Russians, who do not seem too eager to mix with others. Both non-Jewish minorities, the Arab and the Druze, share this attitude.

Finally, in regard to the attraction or exclusion that the groups exert on each other, the most popular groups are the nonreligious, the traditional, the Ashkenazim, the Mizrahim, and the religious. These attractions are not mutually exclusive, although each is unique in some way. Russians, Druze, Arabs, Ethiopians, the Ultra-Orthodox, and foreign workers generate weak attraction, irrespective of their own openness to others.

This general picture according to cohesion, openness to others, and popularity, shows that the nonreligious, the religious, the traditional, the Ashkenazim, and the Mizrahim are finally quite close to each other. The two last-mentioned are less cohesive than the others but all seem to be open and attractive to others. The Ultra-Orthodox and the Ethiopians, who are quite cohesive, join the foreign workers, who are less cohesive, to form a cluster that is less popular despite their own openness to others. The third cluster is made up of Druze, Arabs, and Russians, who are cohesive, less open to others than other groups, and not highly attractive.

In sum, this diversity of group profiles elicits a highly differentiated picture. Israel's multiculturalism, we see, is anything but coherent and symmetrical.

CENTER, PERIPHERY, AND COALITIONS

Reexamining our findings in Tables 10.1 and 10.2 and focusing exclusively on cognitive distances, we obtain the following characterizations:

a. **Ashkenazim** are close to the nonreligious category, to which most of them belong, and are relatively close to Mizrahim. They are particularly distant from Arabs, the Ultra-Orthodox, and foreign workers.

b. **Mizrahim** are relatively close to the nonreligious and to the traditional. They reciprocate the closeness that the Ashkenazim feel toward them and are aloof from the Ultra-Orthodox, Druze, Arabs, and foreign workers.

c. **Russians** are fairly close to the nonreligious and the Ashkenazim, more distant from the traditional and the Mizrahim, and very distant from Ethiopians, the Ultra-Orthodox, Druze, Arabs, and foreign workers.

d. **Ethiopians** feel close to the traditional and less so to the nonreligious, the religious, and Mizrahim. They are especially distant from Ashkenazim, the Ultra-Orthodox, Russians, Arabs, Druze, and foreign workers.

e. **The Ultra-Orthodox** are very close to the religious and less so to Ashkenazim, the traditional, and Mizrahim. They are slightly more distant from the nonreligious, more distant still from Russians and Ethiopians, and very distant from the non-Jewish groups.

f. **The religious** are close to the traditional, Mizrahim, Ashkenazim, and even the nonreligious; more distant from the Ultra-Orthodox, Russians, and Ethiopians; slightly farther from the Druze; and very distant from Arabs and foreign workers.

g. **The traditional** are close to Mizrahim and the nonreligious and less so to Ashkenazim and the religious. They feel more distant from Russians and Ethiopians and much more distant from the Ultra-Orthodox, Druze, Arabs, and foreign workers.

h. **The nonreligious** are close to the Ashkenazim; less so to Mizrahim and the traditional, more distant from Russians; even more distant from the religious, Ethiopians, Druze, Arabs, and foreign workers; and the most distant from the Ultra-Orthodox.

i. **Arabs** are quite distant from everyone but less so from Druze and somewhat less so from Mizrahim, the nonreligious, and Ashkenazim.

j. **Druze** are close only to the Arabs. All other groups are far away, although Mizrahim, Ashkenazim, the nonreligious, and the traditional are relatively less so.

k. **Foreign workers** are relatively close to Ashkenazim, less so to Mizrahim, and even less so to the nonreligious, the traditional, Mizrahim, and the religious. They feel very distant from Russians, Ethiopians, and the Ultra-Orthodox, and no less from Druze and Arabs.

Table 10.3. Symmetry/Asymmetry of Social Distance among Groups

Groups	Reciprocated closeness	Unreciprocated closeness	Reciprocated remoteness	Unreciprocated remoteness
Ashkenazim	Mizrahim (quite) Traditional	Nonreligious	Ethiopians Arabs Druze	Russians Ultra-Orthodox Religious Foreign workers
Mizrahim	Traditional	Russians (relative) Nonreligious	Ethiopians Arabs Druze	Ultra-Orthodox Religious Foreign workers
Russians	Nonreligious	None	Ethiopian Traditional Arabs Druze Foreign workers	Ultra-Orthodox Religious
Ethiopians	Religious	Traditional Nonreligious	Ultra-Orthodox	Arabs Druze Foreign workers
Ultra-Orthodox	None	Religious Traditional Nonreligious	Arabs Druze guest worker	
Religious	None	Traditional Nonreligious Arabs Druze		Foreign workers
Traditional	Nonreligious	Druze	Arabs	Foreign workers
Nonreligious	None	None	Arabs Druze	Foreign workers
Arabs	None	None	Foreign workers	Druze
Druze	None	None	Foreign workers	None

As shown above, the Ashkenazi category is composed overwhelmingly of nonreligious people and the Mizrahim category is similarly widely represented among the traditional. Thus, we may conclude that, in terms of perceptions of cognitive distance, the central core of Israeli society is made of nonreligious Ashkenazim and traditional Mizrahim. Moreover, each of these categories is relatively close to additional—

and different—groups. The religious, the Ultra-Orthodox, and Ethiopians see themselves as relatively close to the traditional, if not the Mizrahim; Russians feel relatively close to nonreligious Ashkenazim. Farther from the core are the non-Jewish groups, which are also quite isolated from each other.

It is in this context that Table 10.3 focuses on the issue of symmetry among groups. Taking into considerations only the most salient findings, it appears again that the feelings of some groups about others are weakly reciprocated. This is true for Ethiopians vis-à-vis the traditional and the nonreligious and of Russians vis-à-vis Ashkenazim. This shows that important groups practice exclusionism toward immigrants who wish to draw close to them. In a similar vein, the Ultra-Orthodox and the religious—the Ultra-Orthodox vis-à-vis the religious and both groups vis-à-vis the traditional and the nonreligious—seem to have unrequited open attitudes. The religious groups, it seems, do not find an attentive ear among other categories. Last but not least, Arabs, Druze, and foreign workers are genuine fringe groups. In a nutshell, Israeli multiculturalism means not only the assertion of cultural differences but also differential positions within the matrix of intergroup relations.

SOLIDARITY AND LANGUAGE

An additional and more material dimension of the configuration of multiculturalism concerns the extent to which groups constitute distinct cultural-linguistic entities and wish to retain their distinctiveness. We know with Bourdieu (1982) that this aspect of the social experience may be read as both a reflection and an articulation of collective identity (see also Adjemian, 1976). We investigated this aspect from two perspectives. The first focuses on the extent to which members of the groups insist on the importance of group solidarity; the second relates to their enthusiasm about the symbolic practices of group distinctiveness. In regard to the first issue, we asked about commitment; in regard to the second, we looked into language attitudes (see Edwards, 1988).

The strong correlation between the questions in Table 10.4 shows that the means of the weighted samples may serve as an index of solidarity. This index's values, moreover, correlated with cognitive distances among groups and yielded a significant positive correlation

(Pearson R = .17**), meaning that the more respondents report solidarity with their group regarding these specific issues, the more they tend to distinguish themselves as a group. We also found a correlation (weaker but still significant) between solidarity and cohesion: those who feel closer to their groups tend also to have stronger feelings of solidarity toward it.

From all these, it is clear that not all groups aspire equally to be solidaristic. The most determined in this respect are the Arabs, followed by the Ultra-Orthodox and the Russians. The least solidaristic groups are the nonreligious and the Ashkenazim. Religious, traditional, and Mizrahi respondents stand in between. Interestingly, this order overlaps widely, but not totally, with the findings about actual cohesion (Tables 10.1 and 10.2). The Ultra-Orthodox and Arab describe themselves as most cohesive and are also the most insistent in their expectations of members' collective commitment. The religious and the traditional fall into the middle range in both respects, and the Ashkenazim score low on both counts. In all these cases, our finding of differential crystallization of groups in Israel's multiculturalism is reconfirmed.

Incongruence between the two orders occurs mainly among the nonreligious, who belong to the upper category with respect to cohesion and to the lower category with respect to commitment. The meaning of this, in our opinion, is that the nonreligious find that they definitely constitute a very distinct group but are not motivated to crystallize as a particularistic entity. The nonreligious, the largest segment of Israeli society, seems to regard itself as representative of "Israeli Jewry" at large and takes exception to the very development

Table 10.4. Group Solidarity (Mean scores*)

All people should look after members of their own group first.

Nonrel	Trad	Rel	Ultra-O	Rus	Miz	Ash	Arabs	Samp[1]
28	35	33	48	44	34	29	61	37

Leaders should look first after members of their own constituency.

| 21 | 23 | 25 | 31 | 43 | 23 | 21 | 50 | 29 |

* On a scale from 0 = not at all to 100 = definitely. Foreign workers, Ethiopians, and druze were not asked these questions. Pearson r = .49**, Tau_b = .45**.
[1] Weighted sample, according to estimated proportions in general Israeli population.
Source: Survey 3.

of a society composed of distinct and autonomous communities. This contradiction between the awareness of a large and powerful population group of its *de facto* distinctiveness and its hesitancy about forming a solidaristic whole vis-à-vis others is in itself another major characteristic of Israeli multiculturalism.

The other two forms of incongruence are less extreme. The Russians take a middle-range stance on cohesion and find themselves at the higher level with respect to commitment. This seems to indicate that they have been less successful than they would like to be in mobilizing members to sustain their collective. The Mizrahim, who belong to the lower category of cohesion, fall into the middle range in commitment. Thus, their aspiration to retain their particularism and distinctiveness may be thought of as moderate. As earlier studies showed (Ben-Rafael, 1982; Ben-Rafael and Sharot, 1991), Mizrahim, especially those outside the low-income strata, are ambiguous about this concern.

The second issue that we considered in evaluating the firmness of the groups' convictions about their particularism was members' attitudes toward the symbolic practices represented by language. Here our inquiry overlooked Ethiopians, a small community, and foreign workers, who are divided into many small subsegments. We also refrained from presenting the language questions to Arabs and Druze, since an earlier study (Ben-Rafael, 1994) showed that these groups are widely bilingual, using Arabic (loaded with borrowings from Hebrew) in daily and cultural life among themselves and Hebrew in contacts with Jews. It is with these reservations in mind that Table 10.5 presents our data about the principal language (L1) and second language (L2) of Ashkenazi, Mizrahi, Russian, traditional, religious, Ultra-Orthodox, and nonreligious respondents.

Table 10.5 shows that large majorities of members of nearly all groups have adopted Hebrew as their first language, including within the family. The only exception consists of the Russians, who still widely use their original language in the family and in the community—as one might expect of recently arrived immigrants. The second important finding in the table is that about half the members of every group, again with the exception of the Russians, do not report using a second language with spouses. This gives unequivocal evidence of the spread of Hebrew as the language of Israelis in their most intimate circle—a matter of special interest in regard to the

Table 10.5. Retention and Use of Languages with Spouses (Percent)*

	Jewish groups by religiosity								Jewish groups by origin					
	Nonrel 499		Trad 337		Religious 99		Ultra-O 209		Russians 408		Mizrahim 429		Ashk 505	
N														
	L2	L1	L2	L1	L2	L1	L2	L1	L2	L1	L2	L1	L2	L1
Hebrew	5	87	6	90	7	84	10	83	21	3	4	92	7	83
English	26	2	14	1	15	5	19	3	1		17	1	23	2
Russian	2	3	4	1			1	1	2	75	1		4	4
Arabic	1		6		8		4				7	1		
Yiddish	2		3		2	1	9	7	5				4	
Spanish	2	1	2		1						1	1	2	1
French			4		2		2	2			4	1	1	1
Other										1				
No spouse	4	5	3	3	7	8	4	4	21	21	4	4	5	6
No L2	58		51		58		51		50		62		64	
Total	100	97	100	95	100	98	100	100	100	99	100	100	100	97

* First language = L1; second language = L2. Source: Survey 3.

Ultra-Orthodox, among whom Yiddish long prevailed (Ben-Rafael, 1994).

Significant use of a second language seems to be primarily a marker of Ashkenazim (and thus, to some extent, of the middle class); it applies only weakly to categories such as Mizrahim and the traditional (who are more often characterized by lower-class affiliation). Furthermore, among those who use a second language, English appears to hold the lead even among traditional, religious, and Ultra-Orthodox individuals. If we bear in mind that a negligible one percent of Israelis are native speakers of English (Ben-Rafael, 1994), this finding emphatically demonstrates the linguistic impact of globalization processes on Israeli society.

On the other hand, the findings also demonstrate the weakness of parochial languages among nearly all groups. Russians are a salient exception in this regard, and the Ultra-Orthodox are so to a much weaker extent—about 15 percent of the Ultra-Orthodox use Yiddish as L1 or L2. However, these data should be evaluated cautiously because our research asked respondents about their two principal languages only. Had we asked about a third language, we might have obtained a much wider spectrum of linguistic resources.

Table 10.6 elicits a congruent picture of languages used with children in the family. First, Hebrew again prevails as the first language, even among the Ultra-Orthodox. Only Russians, again, are wont in

Table 10.6. Retention and Use of Languages with Children (Percent)*

N	Jewish groups by religiosity								Jewish groups by origin					
	Nonrel 499		Trad 337		Religious 99		Ultra-O 209		Russians 408		Mizrahim 429		Ashk 505	
	L2	L1	L2	L1	L2	L1	L2	L1	L2	L1	L2	L1	L2	L1
a. Languages used with children														
Hebrew	4	74	3	84	2	80	6	85	29	6	1	80	5	77
English	9		7	1	9	1	11	1	1		5	1	11	
Russian	2	2	2				1		5	75			3	3
Arabic		1	3		7		2				4			
Yiddish					1	1	6	5	2				1	1
Spanish	2				1						1		2	
French		1	2				1				1			1
Other														
No children	19	22	11	14	12	17	4	8	5	17	16	19	14	17
No L2	61		70		67		67		57		69		61	
Total	97	100	98	99	97	99	97	99	99	98	97	100	94	99
b. Languages used for reading														
Hebrew	6	93	3	96	4	94	4	95	30	7	1	98	8	90
English	35	3	21	1	21	3	17	2	6		24	1	33	4
Russian	1	3	2	1			2		5	92			3	4
Arabic		1	1		2						1			
Yiddish						1	2	1					1	
Spanish	2												2	
French			2	1	2		1				2	1	1	1
Other					1									
No reading						1		1						
No L2	56		71		70		74		59		72		52	
Total	100	100	100	99	100	99	100	99	100	99	100	100	100	99

* First language = L1; second language = L2. Source: Survey 3.

large numbers to use Russian—though Hebrew is no longer negligible among them in this respect. More generally, English is again the most prevalent second language. As for languages used for reading, here too the predominance of Hebrew is overwhelming—again, with the exception of Russians. English ranks second once more except for the Russians, for whom it is preceded by Hebrew. Interestingly, however, the Ultra-Orthodox, Mizrahim, the traditional, and the religious exhibit low rates of use of a second language. They contrast with the pattern shown by Ashkenazim and the nonreligious, who make much more use of English.

Thus, as we know from the literature, the penetration of languages of global communication follows the line that separates the privileged from the underprivileged (Guy, 1989). In all, as Table 10.7 shows, Israel's multiculturalism appears to be characterized more by strong feelings of collective solidarity and commitment than by the groups' determination to adhere to their linguistic symbols. Even so, again the data should be interpreted cautiously because we asked respondents about their two principal languages only.

In brief, Russians show determination to remain loyal to their linguistic legacy, even though they do acquire Hebrew and use it in their dealings with other Israelis outside their home. The Ultra-Orthodox have adopted Hebrew, although a rather sizable minority mentions its use of Yiddish even when only the two principal languages are taken into account. Ashkenazim and the nonreligious demonstrate a linguistic profile in which English plays an important role and marks a boundary, so to speak—not of cultural heritages but of symbols of global orientations and status. This kind of linguistic marking shows that Ashkenazim and the nonreligious tend to form a privileged category more in terms of class or status than in terms of primordial attributes. Other groups, such as Mizrahim, the traditional, and the religious, are less easily circumscribed in their patterns of bilingualism—although we know from other sources

Table 10.7. Use of First and Second Languages among Jewish Respondents—Summary

	with spouses		with children		for reading	
N = 1415	L1	L2	L1	L2	L1	L2
Hebrew	73	8	66	8	79	9
English	2	17	0	7	2	25
Russian	14	2	13	2	16	2
Arabic	1	3	0	2	0	1
Yiddish	1	3	1	1	0	0
Spanish	1	2	0	1	0	1
French	1	2	0	1	1	1
Other		2	2		2	3
No spouse	7	7	—	—	—	—
No child	—	—	18	18	—	—
No L2	—	54	—	60	—	58
Total	100	100	100	100	100	100

Source: Survey 3.

(Ben-Rafael, 1994) that Mizrahim maintain characteristic linguistic markers in the form of a guttural accent and that traditional and, mainly, religious individuals like to mark their identity by inserting ready-made expressions of Biblical or Talmudic origin into their daily speech.

CONCLUSION

This chapter found that the constituent groups of Israeli society differ widely not only in respect to culture, religiosity, and national identity, but also in respect to their centrality within society as well as their social crystallization. We found differentiation in the distances of the groups from each other, the way they relate to each other, and the extent to which they are able to form coalitions with others. These groups are, indeed, characterized by very different degrees of internal cohesion and are thus also strongly differentiated by their potential ability to rally around collective claims.

Overall, Israeli society evinces a structure of concentric circles. At the core are groups that are relatively close to each other and that attract others—Ashkenazim, the nonreligious, the traditional, and Mizrahim. This shows, quite unexpectedly for some researchers, that a category such as the Mizrahim, often viewed as belonging to the margins of society, is actually positioned somewhere in the center. In contrast, the groups that are farthest from the core and, for this reason, may be described as the outermost periphery consist principally of non-Jews—Druze, Arabs, and foreign workers. Several additional groups—the religious, the Russians, and the Ethiopians—occupy the middle between core and periphery. The Ultra-Orthodox stand somewhere between this circle and the outermost one. In all, the varied positioning of groups reveals a diversified and nonpolarized multicultural setting. To reinforce this description, we note that the groups that seem the most central—the Ashkenazim, the Mizrahim, and the traditional—are not among the most cohesive and solidaristic, while more peripheral groups such as the Druze, the Arabs, and, of course, the Ultra-Orthodox, if not the religious and the Russian Jews, exhibit a solidarity that gives them political capacity.

Thus, while multiculturalism is definitely a characteristic of contemporary Israel, this society at large is still marked by the predominance of groups that are not ardently interested in presenting collective ethnocultural claims of their own. This configuration of multiculturalism is manifested in many respects, foremost linguistic activity. Most Jewish groups have adopted Hebrew as their first language, and the newly arrived, too, are well on their way to the same outcome. Moreover, non-Jews like Druze, Muslims, and Christian Arabs have also acquired Hebrew and use it on the job, in the market, in higher education, and so on. For them, Hebraization undeniably denotes "Israelization."

By the same token, we found varying degrees of particularistic linguistic marking among the most solidaristic groups, such as Russian Jews who continue to use Russian in the private and community domains, Ultra-Orthodox Jews who still adhere quite strongly to Yiddish, and, of course, druze and Arabs who retain Arabic as their first language.

The data that elicited these results also show that the groups that seem more "distinct" from others and more determined to remain so are also those that best illustrate the concept of "transnational diaspora." Foreign workers—be they Bolivians, Ghanaians, Filipinos, Thais, Romanians, or Turks—are by definition members of transnational diasporas because their status is temporary *ab initio*. Druze and Arabs in Israel make reference to collectives that maintain their major concentrations elsewhere: Israeli druze maintain strong ties with fellow ethnics in Lebanon and Syria; Muslim and Christian Arabs who define themselves as Palestinians link their collective identity with a diaspora—Lebanon, Syria, Iraq, Jordan—with which they retain strong relations, as well as with the center represented by the West Bank and the Gaza Strip. Among Jews, Russian Jews in Israel remain in close contact with their country of origin and with Russian Jews who emigrated to countries like Germany or America. The Ultra-Orthodox also illustrate this category of transnational diasporas due to their intense relations with counterparts in Antwerp, Paris, and New York. These transnational-diaspora links, which favor the retention of linguistic codes and cultural symbols, constitute power assets and encourage cohesion and solidarity, and it is in this wide context that the Israeli version of multiculturalism demonstrates that this dimension of social endeavor—and the power-building processes that it involves—may be concurrently very salient and moderate.

These considerations answer the research question that we posed at the beginning of our investigation. The purpose of this chapter was to determine the configuration of Israel's multiculturalism, i.e., the way the various collectives position themselves vis-à-vis each other and structure the multicultural space. We found that we may effectively describe this case of multiculturalism as a center-and-periphery setting where the closer a group is to the core the less it evinces a particularistic identity. Different concentric circles, positioned at different distances from the core, are populated by groups that are more strongly oriented toward particularism. The outermost circle consists of the most cohesive entities of all.

Furthermore, our research question also concerned itself with the possible formation of clusters. What we may conclude from our data is that Ashkenazim, Mizrahim, the nonreligious and the traditional, are effectively linked in a cluster of sorts. Within the more general space of clusters, individual groups feel closer to some and more distant from others, and their attraction to some of their counterparts is not necessarily reciprocated. To enunciate a governing principle in the multicultural order that we find here, we might say that ethnicity and religiosity act conjunctively but their importance increases as groups distance themselves from the core and venture deeper and deeper into the periphery.

CHAPTER ELEVEN

RULES OF MULTICULTURALISM

INTRODUCTION

The previous chapter elaborated on Israel's multiculturalism in view of the positioning of each constituent group vis-à-vis others. The focal question in this chapter is the extent to which the groups share attitudes that favor cooperation or tension and exclusion. It is these relations that outline what we call the "rules of multiculturalism."

Rapid social changes around the globe are inducing societies to accept and recognize cultural heterogeneity as a basic aspect of the social order. Israel, like many other contemporary societies, must also cope with internal discord pursuant to the conflicting values and interests that this situation brings about. Some of the attitudes that are currently emerging and acquiring legitimacy, however, not only differ from the mainstream but also tend to oppose and challenge, if not undermine, its dominance. It is in this context that this chapter probes the perceptions of Israel's social groups about the very fact that collectively they constitute an openly asserted multicultural reality. Are Israelis developing intellectual and ideological dispositions that lead them to regard themselves as being in harsh conflict with each other, or are they able to establish rules that allow them to share one setting without tearing each other apart? This question, we contend, is to pay special attention to the substantive character of multiculturalism in this case, namely, the issue of the relation to religion—not necessarily religiosity itself—embedded in the collective identities attached to both the dominant culture and major groups evolving in this setting.

This chapter summarizes a series of findings from our research that relate directly to this general issue. For each question, we present breakdowns of the major religiosity, ethnic, and national categories. For convenience, all responses are again re-expressed on a 0–100 scale in which, where possible and relevant, 100 represents the most favorable attitude toward multiculturalism and 0 represents the most negative. In the following tables regarding the ethnocultural groups, we made do in our statistical analyses with three groups—Mizrahim, Ashkenazim, and Russians—but did not include 3rd generation Israelis; regarding the religiosity cleavages, we did not include Russians. These measures were dictated by the absence of relevant items in the questionnaires that were used with these groups.

Table 11.1. The Presence of Different Cultures in Israel
Enriches the Country's Culture

a. By ethnicity	Mizrahim (429)	Ashkenazim (505)	Russians (408)	
Disagree	16	15	5	
So-so	17	12	6	
Agree	65	70	89	
No response	2	3	—	
Total	100	100	100	
Mean	72	75	79	
b. By religiosity	Ultra-Orth (50)	Religious (99)	Traditional (337)	Nonrelig (499)
Disagree	31	15	17	12
So-so	15	14	17	12
Agree	50	65	63	74
No response	4	6	3	2
Total	100	100	100	100
Mean	56	70	70	78
c. By national groups	Jews (1342)	Druze (150)	Arabs (300)	Fo. workers (50)
Disagree	13	20	26	35
So-so	13	9	8	18
Agree	72	61	55	39
No response	2	10	11	8
Total	100	100	100	100
Mean	74	67	55	52

Source: Survey 3.

Contradictory Approaches to Multiculturalism

A primary and major issue in the attitude of individuals and groups toward multiculturalism is the extent to which they regard the presence of different and distinctive particularisms as a source of enrichment or a pernicious burden. These questions reveal how respondents feel about Israel's contemporary multiculturalism.

Table 11.1 shows that a majority of Israelis in all sectors endorse cultural diversity as a national asset. However, they do not all endorse the principle to the same degree. The Russians, especially, are clearly more positive about this diversity than other groups; this is congruent with their strong commitment to their own original culture and language. Among religious groups, the Ultra-Orthodox seem to differ significantly from the others. Even though this group is the least supportive of cultural diversity, 50 percent of Ultra-Orthodox respondents accept the principle and only 31 percent do not. Finally, the breakdown by national identity indicates that non-Jewish groups tend to be more indifferent about the issue than the Jewish sectors. They probably feel that as non-Jews, their own particularisms are assured to be recognized by society in any case, and that, for them, the major cleavage of this setting is the one that separates them from Jews in general.

As for endorsing the principle of equality of all cultures, however, Table 11.2 points to reluctance among a majority in all groups. Insofar as "cultural development" is concerned, all groups agree widely that some cultures are "more developed" than others. Interestingly, the group most convinced of the reality of this distinction among cultures is the Ultra-Orthodox. This attitude seemingly reflects the strong conviction among the Ultra-Orthodox that their sector is a Jewish elite that cannot but view condescendingly the other cultures in society.

Be this as it may, it appears that while most Israelis recognize the contribution of cultural diversity to the national culture, this attitude is by no means embedded in an egalitarian perspective on the part of any ethnic, religious, or national group. Thus, Israel's multiculturalism contains an evident potential for tension. One may indeed ask, in this context, whether groups that profess a favorable attitude toward multiculturalism actually believe that their own models are to serve as references for other groups. In this respect, Table 11.3

shows that the various groups do wish, some more and some less, that others would be more like them. The only exceptions are Russian immigrants and foreign workers. The group that is most interested in having others resemble it is the Ultra-Orthodox, but only in regard to Jews and, especially, nonobservant Jews. The non-Jewish groups (Arabs, Druze, and foreign workers), in contrast, show little interest in the possibility of Jews' resembling them.

An additional issue investigated was whether all children should be taught a standard curriculum or whether each group's children should be educated in view of its particular legacy and culture. No other question can better test the essence of individuals' attitude toward multiculturalism and "how it should work."[1] Two questions in our surveys investigated attitudes toward curricular diversity or uniformity (Table 11.4). The first asked about the extent to which all schools (Ultra-Orthodox, religious, secular, etc.) should teach a standard syllabus; the second gauged the respondents' belief that every child should be entitled to learn his/her own language of origin (Russian, Yiddish, Amharic, Georgian, etc.) in school. Since the large majority of Arab children do attend schools that teach in Arabic, this question was not asked in the Arab sector.

Table 11.4 shows a general tendency among Jews to prefer a standard curriculum for all (67 percent). The attitude of all three ethnocultural categories seems quite moderate. Among Russians and Mizrahim, while one-fifth to one-third favor a totally homogeneous curriculum, a large majority advocates some degree of heterogenity, leaving only small minorities with a more extreme stance. Among the

---

[1] Notably, Israel's school setting is already divided into several systems. First, the state expresses its recognition of the national and cultural minority status of Arabs in Israel by maintaining separate Hebrew-speaking and Arabic-speaking school systems. In addition, there are schools affiliated with Ultra-Orthodox communities, many of which still teach in Yiddish. The Ultra-Orthodox system is prolonged by yeshivot (religious academies) for adolescents and young adults and kollels (colleges) for married men, some of whom devote their lives to religious study. The Mizrahi Ultra-Orthodox sector has duplicated this network, although its version is much less developed (the El ha-Ma'ayan system of schools and yeshivot). In a further differentiation, state (public) education is divided into a secular system and a national-religious system, both supervised by the Ministry of Education. Moreover, kibbutzim (collective settlements) and moshavim (cooperative settlements) have a network of schools that enjoy some degree of autonomy under the aegis of the Ministry of Education. Last but not least, a network of schools intended for children of Russian immigrants (Mofet) has been created in the 1990s.

Table 11.2. There is No Such Thing as a More- or a
Less-Developed Culture

a. By ethnicity	Mizrahim (429)	Ashkenazim (505)	Russians (408)
Disagree	50	54	72
So-so	18	14	8
Agree	31	28	18
No response	1	4	2
Total	100	100	100
Mean	43	37	32

b. By religiosity	Ultra-O (50)	Religious (99)	Traditional (337)	Nonrelig (499)
Disagree	67	48	50	50
So-so	10	17	17	15
Agree	17	30	30	32
No response	6	5	3	3
Total	100	100	100	100
Mean	27	42	41	42

c. By national groups	Jews (1342)	Druze (150)	Arabs (300)	For workers (50)
Disagree	55	61	64	51
So-so	14	7	6	12
Agree	28	25	23	37
No response	3	7	7	—
Total	100	100	100	100
Mean	38	38	37	48

Source: Survey 3.

religious categories, however, sharper differences emerge, with the
Ultra-Orthodox at one end, the nonreligious and the traditional at
the other, and the religious in the middle. Most Ultra-Orthodox
respondents want their children to take a curriculum that is unique
to them at least in half its contents. This attitude is shared by only
slightly more than one-third of the religious and by even smaller
proportions of the traditional and the nonreligious.

In sum, while multiculturalism is often viewed as of the utmost
importance, attitudes are much more reserved when it comes to education. Furthermore, quite a few individuals in all groups insist on
imparting particularistic heritages to the new generations. The most
extreme in this respect are the Ultra-Orthodox. With the exception

of this group, education is seen by a majority as an area in which
the conflictual potential of multiculturalism should be deflected.

Last but not least, one major marker of multiculturalism consists
of the multiplicity of linguistic resources and their use in speech and
communication situations, notwithstanding the concomitant and usually widespread use of official languages. This aspect was discussed
above in respect to individual cleavages, but here it looks into the
groups' understandings of the "game of multiculturalism." Thus, we
now asked our respondents to be more specific about their feelings
regarding the possibility of teaching their children their language of

Table 11.3. I Wish All Israelis were More Like Me in Behavior and Culture

a. By ethnicity	Mizrahim (429)	Ashkenazim (505)	Russians (408)	
Disagree	18	16	38	
So-so	18	17	15	
Agree	61	62	47	
No response	3	5	—	
Total	100	100	100	
Mean	33	30	46	
b. By religiosity	Ultra-O (50)	Religious (99)	Traditional (337)	Nonrelig (499)
Disagree	15	22	17	17
So-so	15	19	18	19
Agree	68	51	60	62
No response	2	8	5	2
Total	100	100	100	100
Mean	28	38	32	31
c. By national groups	Jews (1342)	Druze (150)	Arabs (300)	For workers (50)
Disagree	20	24	28	24
So-so	17	14	11	31
Agree	59	55	53	35
No response	4	7	8	10
Total	100	100	100	100
Mean	34	36	40	45

Source: Survey 3.

Table 11.4. All Pupils in Israel Should be Taught the Same Syllabus

a. By ethnicity	Mizrahim (429)	Ashkenazim (505)	Russians (408)
Not at all	4	2	5
Only partly	9	10	15
Half-and-half	19	19	16
Mostly	35	38	37
Completely	32	28	22
No response	1	3	5
Total	100	100	100
Mean	29	29	35

b. By religiosity	Ultra-O (50)	Religious (99)	Traditional (337)	Nonrelig (499)
Not at all	12	1	3	3
Only partly	21	10	7	10
Half-and-half	27	25	19	17
Mostly	25	40	34	39
Completely	13	21	35	30
No response	2	3	2	1
Total	100	100	100	100
Mean	48	32	27	29

Source: Survey 3.

origin in school (Table 11.5). The question focused on the extent to which groups envision a multicultural setting as one where each group not only uses its own language in the private sphere but also wants it to be its own principal language.

Again we find a sharp difference among ethnocultural groups—between the determinedly multiculturalist Russians and the less multiculturalist Mizrahim and Ashkenazim. Among the latter, and in accordance with what we saw in previous chapters, Mizrahim appear to be more multiculturalist than Ashkenazim and are somehow more willing than them to endorse the proposal that pupils learn their language of origin at school.

It is also noteworthy in this context that the various religiosity categories do not differ much from the prevailing norm among ethnocultural groups. In all groups, we find a general moderately positive attitude toward the possibility that pupils learn at school the language of origin of their parents and group. For their most part, the various groups do not endorse an extremist multicultural ideology.

Table 11.5. Every Child Should Learn His/Her Language of
Origin in School

a. By ethnicity	Mizrahim (429)	Ashkenazim (505)	Russians (408)
Disagree	34	43	11
So-so	14	14	6
Agree	51	41	82
No response	1	2	—
Total	100	100	100
Mean	42	49	76

b. By religiosity	Ultra-O (50)	Religious (99)	Traditional (337)	Nonrelig (499)
Disagree	33	40	39	37
So-so	14	17	11	15
Agree	50	39	48	46
No response	3	4	2	2
Total	100	100	100	100
Mean	54	50	44	45

Source: Survey 3.

RECIPROCAL PERCEPTIONS AND TOLERANCE

Pursuant to the inquiries reported above, we wanted to delve deeper into the respondents' reciprocal appreciations. We tackled this issue by asking the respondents how they understand other groups' contributions to society. These understandings, we assumed, should reveal how highly individuals respect members of other groups.

As shown by Table 11.6, the respondents do tend to be appreciative of other groups' contributions to society (average score = 72), although not every group is appreciated equally and is equally appreciative of the same groups. Generally speaking, the groups that tend to be the most appreciative of other groups are the nonreligious and the religious (76), while the least appreciative groups are the Druze, the Arabs, and the Russians. Conversely, the most appreciated groups are the Ashkenazim and the Mizrahim (88 and 87, respectively) and the least appreciated groups, in declining order, are the Ultra-Orthodox, the Arabs, and the Ethiopians.

Table 11.6 also shows that Ashkenazim and Mizrahim recognize each other's contributions and that the other Jewish groups firmly

Table 11.6. Appreciation of Groups' Contribution to Israeli Society* (Gr. means**)

Appreciated g	Ashk	Miz	Russ	Ultra	Relig	Trad	Nonr	Druz	Arab	Total
N	505	429	409	50	99	337	499	150	300	—
Ashkenazim	94	88	83	90	91	89	92	57	59	87
Mizrahim	93	90	72	90	92	90	91	56	59	88
Russians	81	69	—	64	78	69	80	51	53	72
Ultra-Orth	60	66	47	—	78	65	58	46	49	59
druze	74	73	57	46	67	72	78	—	60	71
Arabs	68	65	49	38	54	62	73	—	—	64
Ethiopians	73	70	38	66	73	74	63	52	53	64
Total***	75	72	58	66	76	74	76	52	55	72

* The contribution was indicated on a 5-point scale, from "The group has made no positive contribution" to "disagreement" with the same statement. The group means were converted to a 0–100 scale, with 0 denoting no contribution and 100 denoting a major contribution.
** The group means were converted to a 0–100 scale, with 0 denoting no contribution and 100 denoting a major contribution. We note separately the percent of respondents in the various groups who expressed agreement or strong agreement with the statement.
*** The total for the sample (Israel citizens) and the breakdown by groups do not include the respondents' assessment of the contributions of their own group.
Source: Survey 3.

acknowledge the contributions of both. The same is true for some groups with respect to the Russians, though several other groups (the Ultra-Orthodox, the traditional, and the Mizrahim) show less approbation in this respect.

Ultra-Orthodox are the least appreciated group. Russians, Druze and Muslim and Christian Arabs are the most critical but they are closely followed by the nonreligious and Ashkenazim. Even Mizrahim and the traditional were reluctant to rate the Ultra-Orthodox contribution favorably. Only the religious tend to praise the contribution of the Ultra-Orthodox. Furthermore, while the Ethiopians are among those whose contribution is not strongly recognized, the group that holds them in the lowest esteem is the Russians. This probably has to do with the Russians' reluctance to be lumped together with the Ethiopians as "new immigrants." Lastly, Arabs and Druze are not eager to lionize the contributions of any Jewish groups but receive moderate recognition from others, especially the Ultra-Orthodox, the religious, and the Russians. Thus, we find a consensus in regard to some categories only—confirming again that Israel's multiculturalism is wracked by endemic tensions.

Table 11.7. Attitudes toward Immigrants' Social Adjustment (Group Means*)

Ashk 505	Mizrahim 429	Russians 408	Ultra-O 50	Religious 99	Traditional 337	Nonrelig 499

1. Every immigrant should adjust to the Israeli culture.

36	33	59	44	35	30	37

2. The longer immigrants live in the country, the more they should adjust to Israeli culture.

32	26	—	37	28	24	32

Alpha Cronbach = .77; Russians > Ashk and Mizr; Ultra-O > relig, traditional, and nonreligious.

Ashk 505	Mizrahim 429	Russians 408	Ultra-O 209	Relig 99	Trad 337	Nonrel 499	Arabs 300	Druze 150

3. I would like Russian immigration to continue even if it means lowering standards of living.

65	50	69	59	59	54	61	21	21

4. I would like Ethiopian immigration to continue even if it means lowering standards of living.

62	59	39	56	72	60	60	20	21

Alpha Cronbach = .62; Ashkenazim > Mizrahim, Russians

* The group means were converted to a scale of 0–100, with 100 denoting a strong multiculturalism approach.
Source: Survey 3.

Table 11.7 focuses more specifically on the question of the attitudes toward immigrants and the demands that may be made of them in terms of adjustment to Israeli culture. This question was meant to reveal the extent that the attitudes of groups toward multiculturalism are coherently translated when it comes to particular cases, and especially to immigrants who find themselves in a vulnerable position. The findings are eloquent indeed. A strong consensus appears among Jewish groups—especially traditional, Mizrahi, and religious respondents—about the need for immigrants to adjust to prevailing models. In other words, multiculturalism does by no means signify a full recognition of groups' liberty of choices regarding behaviors and patterns of social insertion. On the other hand, Russians who are already one of Israel's largest group of origin, show a clear tendency to disregard such demands. This discrepancy indicates that tensions among groups—and not only between immigrants and nonimmigrants—are undeniable. At the same time, different findings show that respondents are pleased with the very fact of immigration and show willingness to sacrifice for the sake of its continuation. Importantly, however, some groups, such as the Mizrahim and the traditional, are less willing to sacrifice than others, and Arabs and Druze appear to be totally estranged from the subject.

When it comes to Ethiopian immigration, the willingness to sacrifice is weaker in some groups and stronger in others. Russians obviously have warmer feelings about Russian immigration but so do the Ultra-Orthodox and, to some extent, the Ashkenazim. Mizrahim, the religious, and the traditional are more welcoming to Ethiopians.

Another issue that pertains to the same discussion is the extent to which groups tolerate each other in respect to what is "different" about their behavior or claims—what may be called "reciprocal tolerance." Table 11.8 shows several claims that mark the daily lives—and tensions—of a multicultural setting and tests the respondents' attitudes toward them in accordance with group allegiance. Hence, when it comes to the deferral of military service for yeshiva

Table 11.8. Mutual Tolerance (Mean)

Ashk	Miz	Russians	Ultra-O	Rel	Trad	Nonrel	Arabs	Druze
505	429	408	50	99	337	499	300	150

1. Tolerance of exemption from military service for those who find it especially difficult*

19	23	24	57	32	21	17	37	31

2. Immodest advertising should be forbidden.*

27	30	26	71	50	33	21	—	—

3. Does it disturb you when people around you speak a language you do not understand?*

89	87	96	93	91	86	87	73	78

4. One should hope that there will be no ethnic parties in Israel.

41	49	51	72	50	51	37	37	37

* These questions were presented to half-samples only; the means were calculated from a five-step scale on which 1 represents the least multiculturalist attitude and 5 represents the most multiculturalist attitude.
Source: Survey 3.

students,[2] a claim that is dear to the Ultra-Orthodox, nearly all Jewish groups display very low tolerance except for the Ultra-Orthodox themselves and, to some extent, the religious, who empathize with them. It is for obvious reasons that non-Jewish groups do not blame Ultra-Orthodox for not serving in the military: Muslim and Christian Arabs are exempt from service for political reasons, whereas the druze wage intra-community polemics over the justification for serving in the Israeli military while belonging to the Arab world.

Moreover, the Ultra-Orthodox and, to a lesser degree, the religious and the Mizrahim are intolerant of immodest commercial advertising on streets and any public spot that has become a marker of secular consumption culture. On the other hand, respondents in any group are not disturbed about overhearing in public a language that they do not understand. Similarly, there is no condemnation of ethnic parties, signaling recognition of ethnocultural cleavages as legitimate political forces. Thus, while the very fact of multiculturalism receives wide support, various specific claims are much less tolerated. While multiculturalism as such is accepted, one cannot speak yet of an overall practical consensus about what is legitimate and what is not.

CENTRAL AUTHORITY

We wished also to know how strongly groups believe it necessary to have some central authority regulate the multicultural reality are ready to endorse the principle of autonomy for the various constituencies.

Table 11.9 considers the groups' attitudes toward the authority of the Knesset (the Israeli parliament). The main finding is that support for a strong central authority is not very firm (varying from 51 to 70). The Knesset is most strongly supported in regard to human rights (82). Then, in descending order, the respondents justify the authority of this central political body in respect to the national ideology, Zionism (65), the enforcement of religious Jewish law as an aspect of the social order (43), and convergence with constituencies'

---

[2] This deferral (which often becomes an exemption) is a major demand of Ultra-Orthodox parties in Israel. Although it is enshrined in law, it is always a hot topic in the public scene where Ultra-Orthodox parties oppose nonreligious parties.

leadership (36). Table 11.9 also shows that the Ultra-Orthodox and the religious favor the work of the Knesset mainly insofar as it pertains to religious legislation. This also shows, indirectly, that they view themselves as carriers of a special mission vis-à-vis society at large. This mission, it also turns out, is determinedly opposed by nonreligious Ashkenazim and Russians, while the traditional and Mizrahim stand somewhere in the middle. The Zionist principle that the State of Israel is a Jewish state does not evoke sharp opposition; one may speak of a mild consensus in this respect. Consensus is also there, and much stronger, with respect to human rights, which shows the liberal character of Israeli democracy. Last but not least, the groups are quite unanimous in their strong opposition to ethnic politics as a goal per se. More ethnic categories—Russians, Druze, Arabs, and, to some extent, the Ultra-Orthodox—are less opposed to ethnic politics, while other groups—Ashkenazim, Mizrahim, the traditional, and the religious—are more averse. Thus, while the politicization of multiculturalism is not endorsed, the opposition to it varies among groups.

It is in this context that our next inquiry concerns how the groups compare with each other in their identification with the national identity at large. In previous chapters, we discussed the relative importance of group identities. Now we wish to compare the groups from this angle by focusing on the setting as a whole.

Table 11.9. Attitudes about the Authority of the Knesset

The Knesset is entitled to promulgate laws provided they do not clash with . . .

	Ashk	Miz	Russ	Ultra	Relig	Trad	Nonrel	Arabs	Druze
N*	271	213	207	24	49	158	268	150	75
1. Jewish law	39	53	35	82	79	54	29	—	—
2. Human rights	84	86	85	81	85	83	86	66	71
3. Zionism	63	70	61	60	77	73	62	—	—
4. Your leader	26	37	45	45	37	34	26	57	45
Total	53	62	57	67	70	61	51	[62]	[58]

* This question was asked only to half of the samples. Cronbach: .73. Calculated on a 1–5 scale, where 1 is "no" and 5 is "strongly agree."
Source: Survey 3.

By measuring the frequency of the respondents' mention of "Israeli-ness" as their first or second identity (Table 11.10), we find that the nonreligious and the Ashkenazim are the "most Israeli" among the groups investigated. The traditional, the Mizrahim, and the religious are closely behind. A third circle is made of Russians, Druze, and Arabs. The "least Israeli" are the Ultra-Orthodox. Considering the issue on the basis of a more ambitious criterion, Israeliness as first choice, we find that only the nonreligious take this option by a (slight) majority, again followed at a distance by the Ashkenazim. The Mizrahim, the traditional, and the Russians form a second circle. Druze, Arabs, and the religious stand farther away. Again, the list is closed by the Ultra-Orthodox. In sum, Israeliness is evinced in three broad circles. The "most Israeli" are the nonreligious, the Ashkenazim, and, at a slight distance, the Mizrahim. Farther away are the traditional, the religious, and the Russians. The farthest cir-cle consists of non-Jewish minorities (Druze and Arabs) and the Ultra-Orthodox.

These differences by no means suggest that the groups at issue do not feel deeply anchored in society. This applies equally to the non-religious, the religious, Ashkenazim, Mizrahim, and the traditional. The Ultra-Orthodox and the Russians are somewhat distanced and the non-Jewish minorities are the farthest away. Thus, multiculturalism does not obviate feelings of social anchorage, although this is not manifested uniformly among the groups.

In a congruent finding, a large majority of members of all groups—with a slightly smaller majority among the Russians—would like their children to grow up and live in Israel. Hence, people seem unwilling to allow particularistic affiliation to attenuate their shared sense of social or national solidarity. Table 11.10 also shows that a large majority in all Jewish groups, with the slight exception of the Ultra-Orthodox, takes it personally when an Israeli is insulted anywhere. Finally, and most importantly, Table 11.10 indicates that the ethno-cultural landscape of Israel is divided into three circles in regard to the way Israelis define the relationship between their particularism and society at large:

(1) The nonreligious, the Ashkenazim, and the Russians emphasize "Israeliness" above all.
(2) The Ultra-Orthodox, the religious, the traditional, and the Mizrahim emphasize "Jewishness" first.

Table 11.10. Allegiances to the National Identity

	Ethnocultural categories				Religiosity categories[1]			National minorities	
	Ashk 304	Miz 261	Russ 397	Nonre 408	Rel 87	Ul-O 49	Trad 255	Druz 150	Arab 410
1. "Israeliness" as a component of identity									
First identity	44	29	21	52	13	4	24	17	15
Second identity	37	44	34	33	53	35	49	34	33
No mention	19	28	46	15	34	61	27	49	52
2. To what extent do you feel an integral part of Israeli society?									
Mean	82	80	52	81	85	73	81	70	53
"Positive"	79	78	41	80	80	69	76	58	29
3. Would you like your children to live in Israel?									
Mean	86	89	72	83	95	95	89	89	82
"Positive"	81	85	74	78	96	94	86	95	86
4. When something is done to insult Israel, do you feel insulted as well?									
Mean	77	80	76	75	78	75	82	57	42
"Positive"	72	76	81	69	77	59	77	47	29
5. What first identity would you like your children to profess in the future?									
Israeli	53	35	52	62	10	5	34	16	12
Jewish	34	53	34	25	78	92	53	—	—
Arab	—	—	—	—	—	—	—	22	61
druze	—	—	—	—	—	—	—	55	—
Palestinian	—	—	—	—	—	—	—	1	20

[1] Not including immigrants.
Source: Survey 3.

(3) The non-Jewish categories—Arabs and Druze—remain loyal to their own tokens first.

In other words, many groups identify primarily with a general, all-encompassing identity. The more secular choose Israeliness; the less secular opt for Jewishness. The non-Jewish groups remain loyal primarily to their particularistic identities. These differences represent different understandings of all-encompassing identities among Jews and different degrees of allegiances between Jews and non-Jews. They show that Israeli multiculturalism is grounded in basic differences of approaches toward the common endeavor that it represents.

CULTURAL ORIENTATIONS

Here we ask whether the various groups share common perspectives about the cultural orientations that they would like to see implemented or predominant in society. Do they give Jewish culture, Middle Eastern culture, or Western culture equal emphasis?

Table 11.11 and the tables that follow answer these questions. Table 11.11 points to a substantial difference among the Jewish categories concerning the importance of Jewishness to be asserted in the prevailing Israeli culture. The nonreligious, the Russians, and, at some distance, the Ashkenazim, advocate less emphasis on Jewishness than one finds today. The traditional and the Mizrahim want a somewhat more Jewish culture or, at least, a culture as Jewish as the prevailing one. The religious and the Ultra-Orthodox plainly advocate a more Jewish culture. Thus, Israelis are anything but monolithic in their attitude toward Israeli culture and Jewishness.

Turning to the groups' attitudes toward Middle Eastern culture (Table 11.12), the interesting question is whether or not Israeli Jews of all categories feel that the location of their country, in the heart

Table 11.11. Israeli Culture and Jewishness (Percent)[1]

Israeli culture should be

(N)	Mizrahim (261)	Ashkenazim (304)	Russians (397)
More religious	32	22	11
As it is	41	32	37
Less religious	24	40	49
No response	3	6	3
Total	100	100	100
Mean	54	43	36

(N)	Ultra-O (50)	Relig (99)	Tradit (337)	Nonrel (499)
More religious	89	66	34	9
As it is	7	28	43	36
Less religious	2	3	19	50
No response	2	3	4	5
Total	100	100	100	100
Mean	92	74	55	34

[1] Tau B = .61**.
Source: Survey 3.

of the Middle East, is a good reason to emphasize Middle Eastern values. This question takes on special importance in view of the large number of Jewish citizens who originate in North Africa and the Middle East. Do they believe that their legacies should have a stronger impact on the national culture? These questions are also of particular interest with respect to Arabs and Druze, whose language, cultural practices, and collective identities belong to the Middle Eastern environment. Table 11.12 shows that about half of the respondents, in nearly all groups, endorse the current state of affairs. The Russians do not share this attitude as more Russians than members of other groups deplore even the present emphasis on Middle Eastern symbols in Israeli society. Mizrahim, the traditional, and the religious are slightly more inclined than the nonreligious and the Ashkenazim to laud Middle Easternness as an element of Israeli culture. Furthermore, and unsurprisingly, Druze especially but also Arabs would like

Table 11.12. Israeli Culture and "Middle Easternness" (Percent)

Israeli culture should be

a. By ethnicity (N)	Mizrahim (261)	Ashkenazim (304)	Russians (397)
More Middle Eastern	25	11	13
As it is	55	49	28
Less Middle Eastern	14	30	53
No response	6	10	6
Total	100	100	100
Mean	54	42	34

b. By religiosity (N)	Ultra-O (49)	Religious (87)	Traditional (255)	Nonreligious (408)
More Middle Eastern	14	23	26	11
As it is	44	50	53	53
Less Middle Eastern	22	16	16	16
No response	20	11	5	8
Total	100	100	100	100
Mean	46	53	53	44

c. By national group (N)	Jews (1011)	Druze (150)	Arabs (408)
More Middle Eastern	17	67	36
As it is	47	31	46
Less Middle Eastern	28	13	18
No response	8	8	10
Total	100	100	100
Mean	45	67	60

Source: Survey 3.

a stronger Middle Eastern orientation in society—Druze apparently being relatively more attached than Arabs to their particularism.

Having found that "Middle Easternness" is a feeble option in Israel—with the major exception of Druze and Arabs—we now ask about "Westernness." Do the groups resent Westernization in Israel or would they like their society to be even more Western than it is? Table 11.13 shows that Russians, the nonreligious, and Ashkenazim firmly support Westernization; Mizrahim and the traditional are inclined to take a more balanced approach; the religious and, above all, the Ultra-Orthodox are staunchly opposed. Unsurprisingly, a substantial cohort of Druze and Arabs, who hold their own culture in high esteem—one-fourth and one-third, respectively—are reluctant to embrace Westernization.

Table 11.13. Israeli Culture and Westernization (Percent)

Israeli culture should be

a. By ethnicity (N)	Mizrahim (261)	Ashkenazim (304)	Russians (397)
More Western	25	39	79
As it is	54	37	14
Less Western	15	14	3
No response	6	10	4
Total	100	100	100
Mean	54	61	82

b. By religiosity (N)	Ultra-O (49)	Religious (87)	Traditional (255)	Nonrelig (408)
More Western	17	20	25	41
As it is	42	44	54	42
Less Western	23	32	16	9
No response	18	4	5	8
Total	100	100	100	100
Mean	46	46	54	64

c. By national group (N)	Jews (1011)	Druze (150)	Arabs (410)
More Western	41	36	21
As it is	40	37	39
Less Western	13	27	34
No response	6	2	6
Total	100	100	100
Mean	62	54	44

Source: Survey 3.

Finally, Table 11.14 shows that Israel is divided—but not polarized—in its views about the desired sociopolitical order. This question, which we did not ask the non-Jewish groups, again elicits three circles. The Ultra-Orthodox and the religious clearly favor a Jewish state, possibly because for them Israel is legitimized primarily by its primordial religious identity. Mizrahim and the traditional take a middle-of-the-road stance; these groups share strong feelings for heritages and religiosity but also express more sensitivity than the Ultra-Orthodox and the religious for the importance of democracy. The third circle is tenanted by the most secular groups—the nonreligious, the Russians, and the Ashkenazim—which clearly favor a democratic state above all. One can easily imagine a fourth circle composed of Druze and Arabs, who pledge no allegiance whatsoever to Jewishness and, as minorities, are interested mainly in a state that will safeguard their freedom.

We may simplify this differentiation by looking at the findings from a different perspective, i.e., reordering the groups according to the extent to which they endorse the statement that Jewishness and democracy are equally important. We then find a continuum with two opposite extremes. At one end, the Ultra-Orthodox are now alone in withholding support of democracy on the grounds of the crucial importance that they accord to Jewishness. At the other pole are the Russians, who overwhelmingly favor democracy as the leading principle. Between them are the religious, who join traditional,

Table 11.14. Would You Prefer Israel to be a Jewish State or a Democratic State? (Percent)

a. By ethnicity	Ashkenazi	Mizrahi	Russian	Total
A Jewish state	20	32	19	24
A democratic state	50	37	62	47
Both	30	31	18	28
N (Cramer's V = 0.16**)	505	429	408	1342

b. By religiosity	Ultra	Religious	Trad	Nonrel	Total
A Jewish state	86	58	32	9	25
A democratic state	3	10	33	63	45
Both	11	29	34	28	29
N (Cramer's V = 0.38**)	49	99	337	499	984

Source: Survey 3.

Mizrahi, Ashkenazi, and nonreligious respondents in affirming the equal-value contention, with about one-third of respondents in each group.

CONCLUSION

In sum, there is a general consensus in Israel that favors multiculturalism, but this by no means signifies that the diverse groups have internalized the principle of equality of cultures. Many respondents in all groups evince nonegalitarian perspectives when they ponder their society's many cultural variants. This, of course, places in doubt the extent to which agreed "rules of the game" effectively exist among them.

One widely accepted rule surfaces in the fact that majorities in all groups do not expect "other Israelis" to reach out to their own culture. Another widely accepted rule, which emerges in the attitude toward education, is the relative moderation of the groups' attitudes toward the implementation and crystallization of multiculturalism, i.e., most groups do not want their children to receive a blatantly particularistic education. These moderate perspectives, however, do not gainsay the existence of tensions.

Thus, the data make it quite clear that the groups and categories have not developed consistent, let alone homogeneous, conceptions about "rules of multiculturalism." A group that stakes out a clearly multicultural position in regard to one dimension may adopt the opposite position in respect to another dimension. In one of many examples, Russians are much more prone than other groups to state that the existence of other cultures enriches Israeli culture but are the least inclined to agree that all cultures are of equal value. Many of the inconsistencies stem from the complex nature of the concept and the fact that the common basis among groups in Israel, where such a basis exists, is neither shared equally nor interpreted identically by all.

These findings do not indicate that diverse groups cannot share nuanced attitudes and perceptions of each other. Some groups, we have seen, recognize each other's contributions. Other groups are less appreciated, and the contributions of still other groups are questioned by some and asserted by others. Finally, some groups—especially, but not only, those that are not Jewish—tend to be marginalized in this respect.

As for the attitude toward immigration, Jewish groups favor it strongly; after all, Israel is a country of immigrants. However, there is tension over the requirements that the absorbing setting is expected to meet vis-à-vis immigrants. All Jewish groups show—albeit unevenly—willingness to continue receiving immigrants and to accept the necessary sacrifices, but the level of enthusiasm varies from group to group and in accordance with the immigrant group in question. On the other hand, the preoccupation with immigration does not speak to non-Jewish groups.

Thus, the rules of multiculturalism in Israel do not always imply tolerance. In fact, the threshold of tolerance is low when certain groups that are unpopular present specific claims; it is higher in contexts of ethical exigencies and manifestations of multilingualism. Moreover, Israelis at large accept today that ethnocultural constituencies form political parties to represent them whenever they have a cause to defend. Various groups, however, oppose ethnic politics as a goal per se. Overall, too, there is a strong consensus that backs the authority of the center on the grounds of both the Zionist national ideology and human rights. We add here that this simultaneous highlighting of two perspectives cannot but entail frictions and dilemmas.

Furthermore, it is in accordance with our basic premise regarding the link of religion and nationalism that the various groups are also concerned about religiosity as a focus of national identity. Some strongly favor the use of religious texts as focal points of reference in legislation. Others resist the demands of the more religion-oriented, and still others occupy the middle ground. In this complex context, Israelis' identification with their national identity is also differentiated among constituencies. The "most Israeli" circle clearly distinguishes itself from the "most Jewish" one and, again, there is a third circle in between. These circles are exclusively Jewish; understandably, the non-Jewish minorities here occupy a fourth, outermost, circle.

These conclusions relate directly to the question of collective identity and the cultural orientations which it commands. Here we may again speak of four clusters of forces:

1. A cluster that does not emphasize Jewishness, does not insist on a Middle Eastern orientation, and strongly favors Westernization.
2. A cluster that gives stronger emphasis to Jewishness and the Middle Eastern orientation but does not disparage Westernization.

3. A cluster that gives Jewishness a much stronger emphasis, treats the Middle Eastern orientation with little enthusiasm, and takes exception to Westernization.
4. A cluster that spurns the Jewish orientation altogether, favors the Middle Eastern orientation strongly, and affirms Westernization cautiously.

In other words, the allegiance to Jewishness—with all the links that bind it to historical-religious legacies—does constitute here a major parameter—with several different possible values—of the formulas of collective identity carried by constituencies. This aspect intervenes together with nationalism *per se* and modernity (in its Western version) in the formation of cultural orientations and identity preferences.

All in all, we are led by the findings discussed in these pages to the conclusion that multiculturalism in Israel denotes multidirectional pressures and aspirations, as well as divergent perspectives about the culture that this setting should adopt. It implies ongoing debates about the essentials of the social order, even though society is characterized not by bipolar opposition around a single dramatic issue but by a diversity of forces that confront each other from different perspectives.

In brief, while non-Jewish minorities are clearly peripheral, Jewish groups switch positions and circles amidst the shifting issues, finding new protagonists and allies each time. However, for many, multiculturalism and differential positions and statuses do not thwart feelings of social anchorage and belongingness. Despite multiculturalism, many groups align themselves primarily with a general, all-encompassing identity; only the non-Jewish groups entrust their first loyalty to their own tokens. This multiculturalism, we contend, is a reality that has gained legitimacy through the labor of politics. However, it is definitely not enshrined in a coherent ideology that commands a broad consensus.

The rules that come out in this discussion preclude the extremes of sweeping consensus. Instead, they bespeak an interweaving of tension and consent. It is at this point that our discussion of the rules of Israel's multiculturalism leads us to the polity.

CHAPTER TWELVE

IDENTITY AND NATIONAL POLITICS

THE POLITICAL DIMENSION

As shown in Chapters 10 and 11, the question of how society influences sociocultural groups is transcended by the inverse question: "How do sociocultural groups influence society?" This question is primarily political. In a democracy indeed, nearly any group that is willing to mobilize its membership may have the opportunity to gain access to the polity, even when it is met with the disapproval of the elite or large segments of the population (Barth, 1969). Such a group may attain influence if circumstances allow it to exploit the rivalries that unavoidably characterize a democratic scene. Its eventual success in amassing power may then inspire others to political action and force society to legitimize the multicultural game, even if the dominant culture is basically hostile to it. In turn, the social order, pressured by different groups from a variety of directions, becomes increasingly fragmented (Rex, 1996).

Globalization is a factor in this picture as it induces flows of immigrants from non-Western to Western countries and engenders new diasporas. In these general circumstances, as already emphasized, the relative cultural uniformization promoted by Western influence around the globe (Bauman, 1998) is countered by a new cultural diversity expanding throughout the West itself following the multiplication of transnational diasporas (Castles, 2000). The proliferation of collective identities, moreover, evokes new approaches to citizenship, handing contemporary societies a major challenge (Schnapper, 1994b).

Such developments question the accountability of the state. Held (2000) believes that contemporary circumstances are causing a reconfiguration of political power and the emergence of new forms of governance. McMichael (2000) notes that people and governments no longer control key decisions that shape their lives. Castells (1996) speaks of a contemporary crisis of legitimacy caused by pressures exerted by groups on behalf of the multiculturalization of society—what Calhoun (1994) calls "identity politics." It is to the question of

how aptly Israel illustrates this problématique that our study now
turns.

Israel is a modern setting that resembles any Western society in
many of its features—economic structures and development, liberal
democratic system, and widely secular political culture. Israel also
verges on Western European modernity in its tradition of ideological controversies about the role of the state in shaping the social
order and the sharpness of the public debate over progress and
equality. As a nation of immigrants, Israel approximates at the same
time the models of modernity prevailing in the New World. In some
respects, however, Israel is unique, especially in the trajectory of its
march toward multiculturalism.

The most important formative factor in contemporary Israel, one
that directly concerns the role of the state in society, is probably the
protracted conflict with the Arab world in general and with the
Palestinians in particular. We mention the conflict here because it
has much to do with the role of the state in Israeli society. Apart
from the implications of this situation for matters such as the status
of the military in society, the importance of the arms industry, and
the high profile of national solidarity in emergency periods, it also
explains the preeminence of security-related issues in the polity and
in the debates among rival parties and coalitions. This domain of
issues definitely overshadows any other item on the public agenda
so severely as to have become the only factor in Israel's predominant right/left political cleavage. Indeed, the term "Right" in Israel
means, more than anything else, a hawkish, hard-line attitude toward
the Palestinians, whereas "Left" is associated with dovish or compromising positions. It is in this context that this chapter asks about
the extent and the forms of articulation of multiculturalism in the
polity, notwithstanding and concurrent with the preeminence of the
right/left cleavage.

The Politics of Multiculturalism

No fewer than 40 percent of members of the Knesset (MKs) who
were voted into office in the 2003 general elections were elected—
directly or indirectly, explicitly or implicitly—on ethnic, religious, or
national-minority tickets. The vying parties included Russian parties
such as Yisrael Beitenu (in coalition with two rightist factions in the

framework of the National Union) and Yisrael Ba-aliya (which united with the Likud shortly after the elections); the National Religious Party, which aspires to represent the settlers and competes, in this respect, with the National Union; the Ashkenazi Ultra-Orthodox United Torah Judaism party, the Mizrahi Ultra-Orthodox Shas, and three Arab parties. Additionally, more than a dozen MKs on the list of the Likud (the national-liberal right-of-center party), five or six Labor MKs (left-of-center), several members of Meretz (left) and Shinui (center) were chosen by their party institutions due to their representative appeal to specific constituencies (Table 12.1).

A thumbnail count of MKs who affiliate with religious, ethnic, or national communities is fifty to fifty-five out of the 120 members of the house (Table 12.1). This shows that one need not overstate the issue to describe multiculturalism as a strong component of the contemporary Israeli political scene. The parties themselves fall into three categories:

1. national parties that cut across ethnic or religious categories;
2. national parties vigorously supported by some groups rather than by others;
3. parties supported by a significant part of a given ethnocultural or religious constituency.

The general assessments of the ethnocultural, religiosity or national composition of parties' supports listed in Table 12.2 are based on information culled from election returns as published in newspapers. The first category in the table—national parties that draw support from nearly all strata and communities, although not evenly—includes Israel's leading parties: the Likud, gains support from all strata but more from Mizrahim and, relatedly, from the traditional; the Labor fits into the same model but is supported more by the nonreligious and the Ashkenazim, with some support from Arabs and Druze.

The second category is made up of national parties that are supported mainly by specific strata and communities. The National Union (far right), which attracts support from a wide range of groups but mainly from settlers, belongs in this group. Meretz, on the left, is composed mainly of the nonreligious and attracts almost no support from the religious and the traditional. It gets its support from middle-class Ashkenazim as well as Arabs and Druze who find its dovish platform alluring. Shinui fits into the same mold, although it

Table 12.1. The 2003 Knesset

Parties	Number of MKs	Parties	Number of MKs
Far Right		Left of center	
National Union[1]	7	Labor+Meimad[5]	19
National Religious	6	One Nation	3
Right		Left	
Shas[2]	11	Meretz	6
United Torah[3]	5	Far Left	
Right of center		Hadash[6]	3
Likud[4]	40	Balad[7]	3
Center		Ra'am[8]	2
Shinui	15	Total	120

[1] A coalition of the settlers' Moledet and Tekuma and the rightist-Russian Yisrael Beitenu.
[2] Ultra-Orthodox Mizrahim.
[3] Ultra-Orthodox Ashkenazim.
[4] Including two MKs of the Russian Yisrael Ba-aliya party,
[5] Meimad is made up of national religious who do not identify with the rightist orientation of the National Religious Party.
[6] A Communist party comprising an Arab majority and a small number of Jews.
[7] Dominated by a pro-Syrian politician.
[8] A coalition of various Arab groups.

is closer to the center than Meretz. It repels the religious due to its strong anticlericalist stance and deters non-Jews because it is reluctant to appear too dovish.

The third category consists of parties that address, and obtain most of their support from, specific ethnocultural, religious, or national communities. United Torah Judaism is the party of the Ashkenazi Ultra-Orthodox, most of whom vote for it. The National Religious party is very closely associated with the settlers. Meimad (allied with Labor) is a moderate national religious faction. Shas, as we have seen, has an Ultra-Orthodox Mizrahi leadership but targets the traditional Mizrahi population. Its appeal is strongest among the stratum of low-income Mizrahim, where it competes mainly with the Likud. Yisrael Ba-aliya, a right-of-center party, targets Russian immigrants in direct competition with Yisrael Beitenu, another Russian party that is farther to the right. The Arab parties are differentiated by ideological allegiances: the Communist Hadash party; the nationalist pro-PLO Ra'am and the pro-Syrian Balad.

Table 12.2. Israeli Parties and Constituencies

Parties	Constituencies
National parties that attract support across community lines:	
Likud (right of center)	Support across all strata but more in Mizrahim and traditional lower-middle-class and lower-class
Labor (left of center)	Support from the nonreligious, Ashkenazim, and some traditional circles; also some support among Arabs and Druze
National parties that attract special support from specific groups:	
Moledet (far right)[1]	Gathers support mainly from settlers.
Meretz (left)	Nonreligious middle-class Ashkenazim; Arabs and Druze
Shinui (center)	Nonreligious middle-class Ashkenazim; some Russians
One Nation (left of center)	Trade unionists, supported mainly by Mizrahim
Parties claiming to represent specific communities:	
United Torah Judaism (right of center)	Ultra-Orthodox Ashkenazim
National Religious Party (right)	National religious individuals with a strong following among settlers
Meimad (left of center)	National religious people
Shas (right of center)	Ultra-Orthodox and traditional Mizrahim
Yisrael Ba'aliya (right of center)	Russians
Yisrael Beitenu (rightist)[1]	Russians
Hadash (left)	Mostly Arabs, a few Jews
Balad (left)	Arabs
Ra'am (left)	Arabs

[1] Moledet, Tekuma, and Yisrael Beitenu form the National Union.
[2] Merged with Labor.
[3] Merged with Likud.

Some groups may tend to react to parties that call for their special support but others are not sensitive to such calls. The nonreligious lend their support to nonethnic parties and Ashkenazim—besides the Ultra-Orthodox—tend to do the same. At the opposite pole, Ashkenazi Ultra-Orthodox, Arabs, and, to some extent, Russians clearly prefer parties speaking on their behalf. In between are the traditional and the Mizrahim, who spread their allegiances widely though many support a communitarian party, Shas, insofar as they do not support the Likud. Last but not least, the settlers show strong allegiance to the National Religious Party and to the National Union.

Thus, communitarianism in the Israeli polity varies in strength among different groups. Interestingly enough, it is weakest among the strongest components of the setting—middle-class Ashkenazim and Mizrahim—and strongest among those on the fringes: the Ultra-Orthodox, Arabs, Russians, lower-class Mizrahim, and even settlers. Hence, communitarianism is a marker of the less powerful parties, though the cohesion of their constituencies augments the impact that they may have and together they represent a large part of the political community. In this respect, however, it is worth noting that they by no means represent a coordinated coalition.

Some of the forces described here, by the very nature of their interests, may indeed have more or less maneuvering room. Arab parties are unavoidably bound to the left, and to it only, because their political interests dictated by their empathy for the Palestinian cause lie with the more dovish cluster. The National Religious Party and the National Union, in turn, are ideologically bound to the settlers and the far right. Things are slightly different for Shas, United Torah Judaism, and Yisrael Ba-aliya. Despite their natural tendency to prefer the right to the left, they may contemplate different possibilities of coalition due to their attachment to very specific demands.

All in all, communitarianism has become an important—though by no means the most important—element in the polity because the forces that play this card have managed to take advantage of, and gain from, the competition between mainstream elites of Likud and Labor (see for an early assessment: Peres and Shemer, 1984). Exploiting the openness of the democratic game, they have been able to impose multiculturalism and to downplay the imperative nature of the melting-pot ideology that guided the original Zionist enterprise. It is an interplay of forces in which transnational diasporas fully participate. For instance, the fact that Arab MKs communicate regularly with Palestinian Authority leaders contributes to the attention they receive from Jewish politicians. Ultra-Orthodox MKs present themselves as speakers on behalf of Ultra-Orthodox Jewry worldwide. The fact that Russian Jewish public figures are in touch with Jews in Russia— even the Russian government itself—is an asset on which they build their own status in Israeli politics.

All this is bound to the question of the interplay of multiculturalism with the issue that dominates Israel's polity, the conflict with Arabs and Palestinians, that generates the centrality of the right/left cleavage. Additional inquiries confirm and illustrate this assessment.

PARTICULARISMS IN NATIONAL POLITICS

Table 12.3 investigates the nexus of particularistic cleavages and national politics. Here nonimmigrants seem to be the least united: one-third lean to the right, one-third tend to the left, one-fourth rest in the center, and slightly more than one-tenth are undecided. Russians are more right-oriented but more than 40 percent are undecided. Arabs tend massively to the left, although they, too, express hesitancy. This rudimentary ethnocultural differentiation suffices to point to very different political attitudes.

Table 12.4 itemizes the orientations of nonimmigrants other than "undecided." The table shows that Ashkenazim, the nonreligious, high-income individuals, and more educated people lean to the left and that Mizrahim, the religious, the traditional, and lower-income and less educated respondents tilt to the right. Among categories, the religious and the Ultra-Orthodox are the most determined (Table 12.4).

It is clear, then, that the right/left cleavage corresponds strongly to multiculturalism cleavages in Israeli society—as confirmed by political research (Shamir and Arian, 1999). The Arabs occupy the leftmost pole, followed by nonimmigrants who are mostly Ashkenazim,

Table 12.3. Political Orientations of Ethnocultural Categories (Percent)

Orientations	Arabs (N = 300)	Russians (N = 408)	Nonimmigrants (N = 1003)
Right	6	15	23
Center-Right	2	14	10
Center	15	19	23
Center-Left	7	6	13
Left	31	6	18
Undecided	39	41	13
Total	100	100	100

Source: Survey 3.

Table 12.4. Nonimmigrants' Political Attitudes (Percent)

		Right	Center	Left	Total	(N)
Ethnicity	Ashkenazim	29	26	45	100	438
	Mizrahim	48	26	26	100	383
	Russians	47	31	22	100	245
	Arabs	4	25	71	100	180
	Total	38	26	36	100	821
Religiosity	Ultra-Orthodox	86	11	3	100	36
(Jews only)	Religious	68	21	11	100	85
	Traditional	52	31	17	100	287
	Nonreligious	20	25	55	100	464
	Total	38	26	36	100	872
Income—Jews	Lower	41	25	33	100	427
	Higher	34	27	39	100	277
	Total	38	26	36	100	704
Education—Jews	Secondary	48	25	27	100	404
	Higher	29	26	44	100	464
	Total	38	26	36	100	868

Source: Survey 3.

nonreligious, and members of the middle and upper classes. One cannot really say who occupies the center, but moving to the right, again we find clear tendencies of different groups—Russians, Mizrahim, the traditional, and lower-class individuals. Farther to the right are the religious (including, principally, the settlers) and the Ultra-Orthodox. This indicates that different political orientations are embedded in different cultures and, as a whole, add up to a rather clear division between right and left—even though the differences are largely functions of the relative weight of different orientations among the groups, and not of widely consensual monolithic orientations—except for Arabs.

Table 12.5 points to an additional variable that influences the political orientations of sociocultural groups: the geosocial distinction between center and periphery. In the Israeli case, we know that sociocultural communities are less salient in metropolitan ("central") areas, where Ashkenazim and members of the middle class, are more preponderant, than in peripheral towns, where Mizrahim and lower-class elements prevail. Hence, Mizrahim who live in central areas are less rightist and more similar to their Ashkenazi neighbors, while

Table 12.5. Ethnicity, Center/Periphery, and Political Orientations (Percent)

Ethnicity	Orientations	Periphery N = 322	Center N = 493	Total N = 815
Ashkenazim	Right	34	26	29
(N = 438)	Center	27	27	26
	Left	44	46	45
	Total	100 (N = 155)	100 (N = 279)	100 (N = 434)
Mizrahim	Right	57	41	48
(N = 383)	Center	17	33	26
	Left	26	26	26
	Total	100 (N = 167)	100 (N = 214)	100 (N = 381)
Total	Right	46	33	38
(N = 821)	Center	20	30	26
	Left	34	37	36
	Total	100	100	100

Source: Survey 3.

Ashkenazim in peripheral areas, who are often less wealthy than other Ashkenazim, are closer to lower-class Mizrahim.

This internal variability of political positions also pertains to Russians of European origin versus Russians of Asian origin (Table 12.6). Yet, in this group we find contrary tendencies to those that characterize the nonimmigrants. Even though European Russians, as a group, are better educated and more affluent than Asian-origin Russians, and even though they are in Israel longer, they appear to support the right more vigorously. In this, Russians break the rule that applies to the socioeconomic and class divisions among Ashkenazim and Mizrahim in regard to allegiances to right and left.

Table 12.7 reconfirms that politics effectively creates opposed ethnocultural, religiosity, and national blocs, especially at the extremes. However, this polarization is bound exclusively to political camps per se. When we examine specific groups, we find no polarization between holders of antagonistic political orientations. Neither Ashkenazim nor Mizrahim, for instance, evince an overwhelming sense of estrangement from the camp that accounts for a minority in their group, although Mizrahim tend to be more open to the left than Ashkenazim are to the right. On the whole, it is the religiosity divide, not the ethnocultural intra-Jewish divide, that generates the clearest sociopolitical antagonism. Indeed, the nonreligious stand in stark contrast to the religious and the Ultra-Orthodox in this respect. It is only thanks to the traditional that the acuity of the picture is somewhat toned down.

THE ACUITY OF POLITICAL ANTAGONISMS

To what extent do respondents perceive the Right/Left conflict as a matter of far-reaching significance for all players? This issue is crucial in the context described above, and we investigated it by asking bluntly, "Do you think prolonged rule by the Right/by the Left endangers Israel's existence as a democratic state?" This question, we thought, would reveal how deeply the intercamp antagonisms run. Table 12.8 shows a tendency on both Right and Left to demonize the other camp. About half of supporters of the Right consider prolonged rule by the left a menace to Israel's democracy and about 40 percent of supporters of the Left feel this way about lengthy Right rule. Thus, the tendency to reciprocal demonization is not the province of marginal voices only, although a rather large proportion of respondents disagree with these dramatic perspectives. Interestingly, when

Table 12.6. Political Positions among Russians

		Right	Center	Left	Waver	N	Total
Origin	European	30	20	13	37	337	100
	Asian	21	15	9	55	67	100
	Total	29	19	12	40	404	100
Immigration	1989–1992	40	18	15	26	201	100
(year)	1993–1996	18	22	11	48	122	100
	1997–2000	15	18	6	61	85	100
	Total	28	19	12	40	408	100
Education	Secondary	25	20	11	45	188	100
	Higher	32	18	13	36	216	100
	No answer		50		50	4	100
	Total	28	19	12	40	408	100
Religiosity	Religious	43	43	14		7	100
	Traditional	28	19	9	44	96	100
	Nonreligious	31	19	13	37	269	100
	Antireligious	4	12	16	68	25	100
	No answer	14	43	14	29	7	100
	Total	28	19	12	40	407	100

Source: Survey 3.

Table 12.7. Political Positions and Images of Social Distance

	Left (265)		Center (142)		Right (269)	
Perceptions of distances	From Right	From Left	From Right	From Left	From Right	From Left
Feels like one of them	7	83	26	23	80	11
Neither close nor distant	23	11	47	54	11	23
Feels distant	69	3	23	19	6	62

	Mizrahim (317)		Ashkenazim (382)	
Perceptions of distance	From Right	From Left	From Right	From Left
Feels like one of them	54	31	27	47
Neither close nor distant	22	27	26	24
Feels distant	19	37	43	24
Misc.	5	5	4	5
Total	100	100	100	100

	Ultra-O (47)		Religious (74)		Tradit (236)		Nonrelig (397)	
Perceptions of distance	From R	From L	From R	From L	From R	From L	From R	From L
Feels like one of them	63	11	66	23	51	51	23	53
Neither close nor distant	23	19	20	31	24	24	25	23
Feels distant	10	67	9	42	20	20	46	18

Source: Survey 3.

seen from the viewpoint of ethnocultural categories, attitudes in general are neither drastic nor extreme; a majority refrains from demonizing the other camp or at least hesitates to do so. It is when it comes to the religious cleavage that demonization is more evident.

The schism is especially appositive in attitudes toward the left of the Ultra-Orthodox and, to some extent, of the religious. Here is the soil where the seeds of extremist ferment in Israeli politics seem to lie. We cannot refrain, at this point, from associating these findings with the fact that all extremist manifestations of Jewish political violence in recent decades—the Jewish underground of the mid-1980s, Baruch Goldstein's suicide bombing amidst Palestinians in Hebron on February 25, 1994, and the assassination of Prime Minister Yitzhak Rabin on November 4, 1995—all originated in the extreme fringe of the national religious camp. However, we also know—although

Table 12.8. Prolonged Right/Left Rule Endangers Israel's Existence as a
Democratic State (Percent)

1. Perceptions by political cleavages

	Left (265)		Center (142)		Right (142)	
Attitudes	Right	Left	Right	Left	Right	Left
Agree	44	5	14	14	5	52
Maybe	15	8	16	16	5	13
Disagree	39	85	66	66	86	30

2. Perceptions by political cleavages

	Ashkenazim (382)		Mizrahim (317)	
Attitudes	Left	Right	Left	Right
Agree	20	26	33	14
Maybe	11	15	12	9
Disagree	63	54	51	73

3. Perceptions by religious cleavages

	Nonrelig (397)		Tradit (236)		Religious (74)		Ultra-O (48)	
Attitudes	Right	Left	Right	Left	Right	Left	Right	Left
Agree	29	15	15	31	4	40	5	75
Maybe	15	10	10	12	5	18	10	11
Disagree	51	70	70	52	89	39	76	10

Source: Survey 3.

the kind of violence we are about to mention is not comparable to
the former examples—that Ultra-Orthodox youngsters frequently
attend violent demonstrations as part of their struggle in Jerusalem
against traffic that transgresses Sabbath observance.

Against this background, the question that arises concerns the
extent that respondents resent politics as involving tension and sharp
divides. The answers vary. Table 12.9 shows that about one-third
of the respondents do consider the right/left cleavage a flashpoint
of tension. A closer examination of the same findings, from the particularistic perspective, elicits a similar picture: only minorities in the
different groups see this cleavage as of overwhelming significance.
When it comes to the religiosity divide, however, things are again
different. The Ultra-Orthodox and, to a lesser degree, the national
religious appear as the fiercest opponents of the left. This again

Table 12.9. Politics as a Focus of Tension in Daily Life (Percent)

1. Politics as an acute focus of tension, by political orientation

	Right (269)	Center (142)	Left (265)
Agree	36	25	32
Maybe	38	46	44
Disagree	25	28	22

2. Politics as an acute focus of tension, by ethnocultural groups

	Nonimmigrants (749)	Mizrahim (317)	Ashkenazim (382)
Agree	32	37	29
Maybe	42	39	43
Disagree	25	24	26

3. Politics as an acute focus of tension, by religiosity

	Ultra-Orthodox (N = 48)	Religious (N = 74)	Traditional (N = 236)	Nonreligious (N = 397)
Agree	42	31	28	46
Maybe	37	43	43	27
Disagree	20	25	27	21

Source: Survey 3.

Table 12.10. Politics as a Focus of Social Tension

Relations	Right voters (269)		Center voters (142)		Left voters (265)	
	Friends	Relatives	Friends	Relatives	Friends	Relatives
I have . . .	—	—	78	61	81	44
I have . . .	68	46	76	70	—	—

Source: Survey 3.

confirms that religiosity is the divide that generates the greatest tension among Jews.

In this context, we also wanted to know whether the right/left cleavage is socially disruptive. Thus, we asked, "Do you have relatives and friends who belong to the other political camp?" Table 12.10 shows that right and left do not correspond closely to distinctly separate social networks. Table 12.10 strengthens these conclusions further by showing that in this respect, too, the right/left cleavage is by no means a cause of social breakdown. People have friends and relative in all categories—including people who occupy the center and constitute a particularly weak cohesive constituency.

CONFLICTUAL MULTICULTURALISM

Thus, we have seen that the right/left cleavage is an important divide in its own right, i.e., one that cannot be reduced to other social schisms. Ethnocultural, religious, class, and other divisions participate unevenly in the opposing political camps but, with few exceptions, cross the intercamp boundaries in a major way. Some overlap exists between right and left and given sociocultural divisions, but in a nutshell, the political cleavage meets only weakly the definition of a close, exclusive, and clear-cut social division.

The major axis of the Israeli polity runs from left-of-center to right-of-center. On this axis, parties are differentiated by their dovish or hawkish attitudes toward the Israeli-Palestinian conflict. This axis tends partly to overlap—in a very flexible manner for most of the groups—the axes of Israel's ethnocultural, religious, and national divides. This scheme evinces a tendency toward dissociation within the very core of Israel's multiculturalism, i.e., between the nonreligious and the Ashkenazim, on the one hand, and the Mizrahim and the traditional, on the other hand. The nonreligious, many Ashkenazim (especially in the middle class), and Mizrahim (again, largely in the middle class) lean to the left-of-center Labor or the leftist Meretz; (lower-class) Mizrahim, Ashkenazim, and traditional elements lean to the right-of-center Likud. In a second circle, farther to the Left, one finds the Arabs, a large majority of whom support nationalist Arab parties; on the other side, closer to the right, one finds the Shas constituency, sustained by traditional and lower-class Mizrahim, which competes with the Likud, the Russians of Yisrael Ba-aliya, and the Ultra-Orthodox of United Torah Judaism. Still farther to the right, we encounter the national religious (especially the settlers) of the National Religious party and the National Union, and the nationalist Russian Jews of Yisrael Beitenu. In other words, the fundamental division of the polity starts from the core of society that provides the two major rival national forces, Likud and Labor, with their power base. It is the division within the core that sets in motion the large coalitions that oppose each other in the polity and that, through their confrontations, give expression to Israel's multiculturalism. This core is riven in a way that leads all political actors to a right/left divide—notwithstanding, and concomitant with, the fact that it is the relative closeness of its components to each other that structures the society as a whole. This kind of divide does not emanate from extremes that mobilize groups in their proximity and point them in the direction of the core. Instead, it originates in the core itself, whence opponents mobilize groups in their proximity and reach down to the extremes. This feature, we believe, means that this divide, however comprehensive, falls short of representing a genuine rift that splits society to its depths.

However, a transcendent feature of this reality at the present time is the subordination of many issues—including claims that relate to ethnocultural groups—to security and economic challenges. This point should be reemphasized whenever multiculturalism in Israel's polity is discussed. In regard to these challenges, the concepts of right and left carry meanings that are independent of other criteria. This subordination of many issues to an overriding one probably mitigates the power of the claims related to them by relegating them to a frame of reference defined as "secondary." Which, however, does not make them inherently less crucial for the social order.

Here lies our answer to the research question that guided our investigation in this phase of our work. The model of multiculturalism that we have encountered entertains forms of intergroup coalitions *and* undeniable frictions and conflicts. Overall, however, the extents of both divergence and convergence are limited by the interests of most groups in more fundamental issues that concern all and with respect to which some groups are naturally bound to a given side of the right-left cleavage while the positions of others are less—if at all—predetermined by intrinsic orientations.

We may also say that we find here what we have called in previous pages a form of "conflictual multiculturalism" for still additional reasons which are more directly related to the link of Jewish nationalism to religion. We firstly mean that several cleavages represent here claims vis-à-vis the social order that concern not just their specific interests but also their overall respective perspectives on society. What is more, these actors conflict with each other over what each of them feels is "best for the whole."

Hence, the Ultra-Orthodox, the National Religious, and Shas all convey views of the Israeli society which aspire to perform basic alterations of its development: the Ultra-Orthodox want to impose constitutional arrangements that would tighten the bound of this society of religious commands; the national-religious forces want to bring about the implementation of policies that would set the entire society at the service of a quasi-messianic vision; and Shas wants the state to commit itself to a particular legacy as the principal reservoir of national symbols. In other words, every one of these cleavages requests to major changes in the social order that relates and reinterpret the openly stated link of Zionism with Judaism.

Moreover, while the Russians pressurize the social order in an opposite direction—they want the downgrading of the religious principle as a constitutional principle—Ethiopians want a reinterpretation of the overall collective identity that legitimizes their own historical-religious parcours. Last but not least, directly in opposition to the link between nationalism and religious legacies in the Jewish dominant culture, Arabs and Druze want to assert their right to exit the margins they are confined. Not to speak of the foreign workers who would like to see their qualities as non-Jews and non-Israelis withdraw from the discussion of their status in society.

In final analysis, we thus see that the link to religion of Jewish nationalism not only accounts for many divergences among perspectives in the polity, but is also embedded in the numberless confrontations among actors taking place on their road to influence the social order. It is, again, against this background that Israel's national scene is one of permanent polemics and harsh debates where "nothing is taken for granted." In this sense as well, to be sure, Israel definitely illustrates a form of "conflictual multiculturalism."

The link *per se* of religion and nationalism is here quite evident regarding some groups—especially the national-religious, on the one hand, and the Arabs, on the other—but less evident regarding other groups—Russians or the nonreligious. Even more evident and fundamental, actually, is the fact that at the very root of the left/right cleavage in Israel lies Israel's conflict with its Arab-Palestinian environment and that this conflict is strongly entrenched in both sides' dominant cultures which express allegiance to forms of nationalism where religion plays a major part.

It is these compound forms of nationalism—Zionism that allies Jewish nationalism and Judaism, and Arab nationalism that refers strongly to Islam—that explain, in the view of commentators (Gorny,

1987; Lewis, 2003) the severity of Israel's conflict with its environment and the difficulties of finding compromises which would respect the interests and dignity of all parties involved. The substantial discussion of this issue is beyond the scope of these pages and it is by no means the intention here to assert the impossibility to bring this conflict to an honorable compromising modus vivendi. What may be suggested is that as long as such a compromise has not been worked out, the link of religion to nationalism in both camps has contributed to the antagonism, ever since its first phase and up to the present day.

SECTION VI

HORIZONS AND UNCERTAINTIES

CHAPTER THIRTEEN

CLEAVAGES TRANSFORMED

THE THEORETICAL SCHEME

In conclusion of the study presented above, we now want, in this chapter and the following, to sum up, and elaborate on the general significance of, our answers to the research questions formulated at the onset (Chapter Two), which guided us all along these pages. Israel is but one example of a contemporary society in which a variety of sociocultural groups coexist amidst innumerable tensions. This pluralism is manifested in different syndromes and represents forces of social transformation. Our research aspired to capture current developments of these syndromes and the ways they give shape to multiculturalism—an instance of multiculturalism that may be seen as emblematic due to its numerous facets and manifestations.

We started our theoretical discussion by focusing on the notion of collective identity as implying commitment to a group, perceptions of it as culturally, historically, or socially singular, and the positioning of the group vis-à-vis "others." This collective identity involves, beyond the structures and interests in which it may take shape, dilemmas that different versions of the identity confront in different ways. Furthermore, while the tenets of such a collective identity affect the extent to which they represent a potential for social mobilization, i.e. a focus of identification, this latter aspect is also a function of additional factors. We emphasized, in this respect, not only the extent to which these tenets are, as such, rooted in strong definitions of primordial ties but also the circumstances of place and time that also widely determine how far a group identity may be appealing to members. We contended that the attitude of the dominant culture toward groups and their social evolving in society also do much to account for this aspect. Moreover, we insisted that the contemporary phenomenon of transnational diaspora, as an aspect of globalization, makes as well, wherever relevant, a contribution to the development of groups' identification in their target societies.

Beyond the study of individual cleavages and the development that each of them experiences in front of a specific dominant culture and through interactions with other cleavages, there is the dimension of the evolution—eventually the transformation—of the setting as a whole, as determined by the drives of the various forces in presence. This dimension is especially crucial in a democratic regime where the access to the polity of grass-roots claims of any kind is feebly safeguarded by *a priori* normative bans and have often good chances to become issues in the competition for support of rival political leaderships.

All in all, the relations that develop between cleavages and the dominant culture determine the ways multiculturalism crystallizes. In a dichotomous manner, we distinguished between "liberal" and "conflictual" multiculturalisms according to the extent that the development of the cleavages vis-à-vis the dominant cultural relations comes up to the institutionalization of areas of autonomy for the various constituencies or, on the contrary, is reflected in competition over the definition of all-societal arrangements.

It was also our assumption that whether multiculturalism evolves in one direction or another depends, among other factors, on the substantive contents of the collective identities in presence. We firstly emphasized here the importance of whether or not the all-societal collective identity—another word for nationalism in today's societies—carried by the dominant culture reflects a committed link with the society's past culture and religious traditions. In some present-day societies, indeed, dominant cultures do still share veneration for the historical-cultural legacies of the dominant groups, while in others such legacies are discarded and relegated to the margins of the cultural endeavor. Hence, in some societies of settlers, dominant cultures tend to revolve around myths relating to settings' entrance in the modern era.

Another question which arises is whether the various groups that confront the dominant culture represent entities that, in view of their insertion in society, meld their own collective identity with the identity represented by the dominant culture. This is the case, most plausibly, where groups which settled in the society did not share any special allegiance to their target society prior to their settlement, and have here to be accepted by, and accommodate to, their new environment. In other cases, however, where such *a priori* allegiances account—in part at least—for the very settlement of groups in the specific society—such as Jewish immigrants in Israel, aussiedlers from

Ukraine or Russia in Germany or Algerian Pieds-Noirs in France—
they possibly carry their own versions of the all-societal identity.
They may also feel uneasy with the all-societal versions of the national
identity carried by the dominant culture and constitute a factor of
conflictual multiculturalism. This, we still have to add, should be
particularly plausible when it is applied, on the side of both the dominant culture and the groups, to versions of the collective identity
that share links to religious traditions, values, symbols, or beliefs
endowing emotional gravity to the divergences.

In brief, it is our contention that all other factors being kept equal—
including political configurations—the institutionalization of liberal
multiculturalism is more likely in the first type of cases, and conflictual
multiculturalism in the second—mainly where a religious dimension
is involved. Other factors are never equal and circumstances may
bring protagonists in a conflictual multicultural situation to find
arrangements that open the door to liberal multiculturalism, and, vice
versa, given developments destabilize a form of liberal multiculturalism and precipitate it to a conflictual form of multiculturalism.

By focusing on precise research questions, we applied the scheme
sketched in studying the cleavages that characterize early twenty-
first-century Israel and the multiculturalism that they give shape to.
In this chapter we discuss our principal findings concerning individual cleavages, and in the next one we consider the contours of
the multicultural setting as a whole before drawing out the major
theoretical significance which these analyses might comprise.

Israel's Cleavages

Israel's long-dominant culture, the one that absorbed successive waves
of immigrants, was shaped by Eastern European Jewish nationalists
in 1890–1925. This quasi-Jacobinian culture sought to impose sweeping uniformization of the society on the ground of a newly created
national culture and identity. Like the original Jacobinian model,
however, it enacted social differentiation of its own by referring to
a specific social category (the pioneers and their offspring) as an ideal
for all. Just the same, this dominant culture underwent transformation
over time as the original pioneer ethos gradually dissolved and
Westernization gained in influence, while mass immigration and
regional wars amplified the importance of practical and pragmatic

outlooks. These developments left room for ever-stronger emphases on meritocracy, individualism, and material success. These new emphases, however, did not obviate the basic allegiance to the founding nationalism that draws its major symbols, metaphors and narratives from old religious legacies. It is against this background that the permanent confrontation with the Jewish state's environment and links to the Jewish diaspora have remained powerful mobilizing forces. Over time and in the footsteps of changing circumstances, old cleavages have taken on new forms and cleavages unknown in the past have emerged.

Challenges to the Singularity of the Collective

Jewishness *per se* is an important constituent in the collective identity of a large majority of Israeli Jews. Although the Jewishness at issue may not be religious in form, the intimate and timeless nexus of Jewishness and Judaism may allow religious people, who are a minority, to feel that they represent a form of Jewishness that is "more Jewish" than other forms and to be convinced that they have an edge over the nonreligious in this respect. While the nonreligious may feel that Judaism is pluralistic and do not necessarily—in fact, do not at all—mind that Jews may be religious in one way or another, religious people—the Orthodox in particular—can hardly consider nonreligious Jews to be as "good Jews" as they are. From this viewpoint, tension if not conflict is endemic to contemporary Judaism.

From a cross-generational perspective, however, we observe a trend—albeit a rather weak one—of voluntary disengagement from religiosity throughout the population. Moreover, the images of conflict are not wholly symmetrical. Both the Ashkenazi Ultra-Orthodox and the national religious have demanding attitudes toward less religious Jews but their conflictual images of this relationship are less tense than the nonreligious' visions of their demandingness. The religious are convinced that they are acting in the best interests of the nonreligious, who by no means reciprocate. The main factor that mitigates these tensions is the presence of a large category of "traditional" Jews who, while not declaring themselves religious in the full sense of the term, hold some religious norms dear. Furthermore, the religious camp does not present a unified front: the national religious and the Ultra-Orthodox cannot be confused as each group emphasizes different issues—the territorial question for the former, the supremacy of rabbinical law for the latter. An additional factor, ecological self-segregation, mitigates and amplifies the tensions concurrently. National religious activists tend to concentrate in settlers' colonies in the West Bank and the Gaza Strip; the Ultra-Orthodox concentrate in given urban neighborhoods. This ecological distinctiveness mitigates conflictual contacts but provides each community with a basis of power and mobilization. In this context of multiple tensions, not only do the nonreligious, who are largely a middle-class group, feel threatened by the different kinds of religious, but typically enough, one also finds, in all categories of religiosity, many individuals who are convinced that their people are deprived.

Ultra-Orthodox, especially, proclaim that they are discriminated against and they are reluctant to open themselves up to the nonreligious—which the nonreligious reciprocate. The traditional and the national religious adopt a somewhat similar attitude toward the Ultra-Orthodox, even though the latter feel a relative affinity for them—which they do not vis-à-vis the nonreligious.

Our findings illuminate here two paradoxes. First, the Ultra-Orthodox, who display numerous salient markers and tend to live in neighborhoods of their own, are often thought of as forming self-segregative enclaves. We rather found that Ultra-Orthodox are characterized by orientations that are moving them toward other components of Israeli Jewish society. The exclusion that exists actually emanates from non-Ultra-Orthodox segments of the society—the nonreligious, in particular—and is aimed at the Ultra-Orthodox. The second paradox is that while the Ultra-Orthodox are open to other segments of the population, they are strongly endogamous when it comes to the core of community life, marriage. In regard to this pinnacle of socializing, they prove to be highly self-segregative. Their attitude contrasts with the open-mindedness, albeit unequal, that characterizes relations between traditional, religious, and nonreligious individuals. Thus, Ultra-Orthodox aspire to be open to society in order to gain influence but are staunchly unwilling to allow their community boundaries to be destroyed from the inside. This shows how difficult it is for Ultra-Orthodox to pursue their twofold ambition of leadership over Jews in general and retention of their own distinctiveness as the bearers of holy symbols and values.

This discrepancy does much to account for Ultra-Orthodox's identification with their cause. Confronting a dominant culture that is quite unreceptive to their orientations, they still aspire to remain an enlisted collective, and on behalf of this cause, wish to strengthen their relation to the rest of society. In this confrontation, as shown by our findings, Ultra-Orthodox have accepted *de facto* the existence of Israel as a state of the Jews, have learned modern Hebrew, and use the language among themselves. Today, the Ultra-Orthodox are definitely willing to be a constituent of Israeli society. If up to now they agreed to enter governmental coalitions by sustaining them from the outside—a pattern that safeguarded at the same time their aspiration to disengage from what the government symbolizes and the wish to play a role in the definition of policies (not to speak of the fostering of their specific interests), in recent years, they give signs of a readiness—if not a velleity—to directly participate in governments.

All in all we may summarize as follows our answers to our relevant research questions:

1. Israel's Ultra-Orthodox converge with Israeli culture, plausibly more than Ultra-Orthodox abroad toward local cultures.
2. They resent but little alienation from Israeli society, at least regarding some segments (the national religious and the traditional).
3. They feel a sense of vacillation and lack of self-assertiveness vis-à-vis their environment in various respects.
4. They maintain numerous signifiers as a protection of singularity, indicating the efforts they make here to retain their identification with their ambitious collective goals.
5. Ultra-Orthodox seem to be losing some of their cohesion over the years and their community can no longer be described as an enclave.
6. They remain weakly attractive to others, and even awaken resentment by some groups (the nonreligious Jews, Russians, Ethiopians).

Relations between the national religious and the nonreligious are also tense, but this cleavage derives primarily from the political scene, where the former constitute, in large part, an ultra-"hawkish" faction opposed to the "dovish" left-of-center. This conflict, however, is essentially political and ideological; it has no serious effect on the configuration of social relations. As far as religiosity-bound social relations are concerned, the national religious belong to the centrist sectors and mitigate, rather than aggravate, the tensions that place the nonreligious and the Ultra-Orthodox at loggerheads.

Furthermore, our findings in respect to this cleavage give some insight into the more specific sector of the settlers in the post-Oslo era. By legitimizing the establishment of a Palestinian state in the West Bank and the Gaza Strip, Oslo inflicted a painful ideological defeat on the Greater Israel camp those who, led by Gush Emunim and its successors, favor the annexation of the territories in order to form an expanded Israeli state. Contrary to expectations, however, this defeat has not weakened the grip of leaders over the settler population to the advantage of "nonideological" settlers who moved to the territories for practical reasons such as inexpensive housing or the appeal of a rural environment. One might have expected these "instrumental" settlers to take the lead of this sector from a perspective that emphasizes realistic options (including possibilities of compensation in return for moving out from their houses following an eventual Israeli withdrawal from the areas). In actuality, while the settlers have effectively been in a deep crisis ever since Oslo, the instrumental among them have been lining up behind the positions of the ideological settlers, who more than ever offer uncompromising responses to Palestinian claims. These responses, which express settlers' struggle in apocalyptic terms meet an establishment hesitant to lead them in a head-on confrontation. The settler population, a colonizing population that has moved onto disputed territory, bases its actions, indeed, on religious convictions that are not alien to the sources of the dominant culture itself, i.e., the notion of the Land of Israel as conveyed by the Jewish tradition and, although in non-messianic terms, by secular Zionism. The themes that settlers can broach may even create embarrassment among their foes. This position, although by no means a "secret weapon" against Israeli governments willingness to negotiate with the Palestinians, explains—at least partly—why Israel's rulers are reluctant to take harsh action against settlers even when they transgress legality.[1]

Nevertheless, the settlers cannot but redefine their exigencies in the wake of the peace process. They now speak of conceding a minimal portion of land to the Palestinians within the framework of

---

[1] The transgressions at issue include the establishment of illegal settlements and violent resistance to efforts to dismantle them. In both cases, the police and the army usually show special restraint and understanding.

a peace agreement with them—implicitly recognizing the ineluctabi-
lity of a Palestinian state. This may seem completely irrelevant at a
time when most Israeli Jews have formed a consensus about the need
to establish a Palestinian state. However, in spite of its restricted
scope, this concession signals an ideological transition—by no means
irreversible, however—from uncompromising totalism to the legitimization of instrumental considerations when discussing the fate of
parts of Biblical Eretz Yisrael.

The following summarizes the findings of Chapter 4 and their
contribution to the answering of our research questions:

1. The national religious experience two basic options: Zionism-*and*-
   religion and Zionism-*accounted-for-by*-religion.
2. The settlers cement their distinctiveness from the rest of the population and the strength of their collective identification by locating themselves in a particular geographical space.
3. The irredentism of the settlers should not always be taken at face
   value, even though they do formulate their calling in most extreme
   terms.
4. A fringe of this segment reflects a most extremist stand.
5. On the other hand, profound processes among the younger
   generation take place in a postmodern-religiosity vein.

Jewish Ethnic Divides

Our research on Jewish ethnic cleavages considered, successively,
relations between Mizrahim and Ashkenazim and between them and
from Soviet Union and Ethiopian immigrants. Mizrahim, we have
shown, belong both here and to the category of religiosity divides,
though, all in all, their anchor in the ethnocultural landscape is
stronger than in the religiosity divide. Even Ultra-Orthodox Mizrahim,
who are the major force that aspires to speak on behalf of this group
and most often do it on the ground of religious claims, term their
identity in reference to a particular legacy, "Sephardic" Judaism.

Hence, we found that large majorities on both sides of the Mizrahi–
Ashkenazi cleavage define themselves primarily in terms of broad
collectives (Israeli/Jewish). Mizrahim, among whom the traditional
and the religious are preponderant, are more prone than Ashkenazim
to pledge allegiance to Jewishness first and Israeliness second, while
Ashkenazim, who are more often nonreligious, tend to rank Israeliness

first and Jewishness second. However, the differences are larger in the first generation than in the second, at which point Mizrahim converge toward the Ashkenazi pattern in a move toward "de-ethnicization" and dissociation from tradition.

Importantly, our findings also show that socially mobile Mizrahim move toward Ashkenazim in many respects and that, albeit to a lesser extent, this is also true of nonmobile Mizrahim. Mizrahim, as noted, originally tended to interpret their immigration to Israel in terms of "the dawn of Redemption" promised by the Bible, and it is in this sense that many resented the secular character of the social and political setting that absorbed them. Today, three generations later, Mizrahim have widely assimilated modern secular principles and most often view their legacies as deserving of respect but not strict obedience. It is from this perspective that most Mizrahim vote for nonethnic and even nonreligious parties, are not reluctant to marry nonobservant spouses, and engage in family planning—in contradiction to religious ethics. However, some young Mizrahim are still attracted to the rabbinical world and many more—especially but not only in lower-class communities—treat rabbinical figures with respect, participate in ethnic festivals, and, at times of community tension, feel solidarity with their origin group. In other words, the new formulations of the Mizrahi collective identity are definitely not in total rupture with past orientations as shown by the following sentences which sketch out the answers of our findings to the pertinent research questions.

1. The Ashkenazi–Mizrahi cleavage is characterized by relatively narrow cognitive and social distances between the categories.
2. Substantial differences do remain in voting and political behavior.
3. Former taboos against ethnic parties have lost their inhibitive power, allowing Shas to emerge.
4. The ethnicity illustrated by Mizrahim centers on positive orientations toward heritages.
5. Ethnic allegiances are losing ground in socially mobile milieus.
6. Shas's emergence among traditional Mizrahim is bound to persisting cultural codes.
7. These codes are strong enough to bring youngsters to yeshivas but not enough to withstand the fact that many Mizrahi young people increasingly place "Israeliness" before "Jewishness."

8. This development is the context of the emergence a Mizrahi Ultra-Orthodoxy.
9. The strengthening of nonmobile Mizrahim as a disputed constituency for all parties and as a basis for the emergence of an important ethno-religious party has widened the space of social opportunities available to mobile Mizrahim, many of whom seceded from their community.

Russian immigrants are a different population. For them, Jewishness means primarily an awareness of belonging to a historical-cultural collective that lacks precise references to a given legacy. Thus, while many immigrants already regard Israeliness as an important component of their identity, the primary identification of the majority lies with a Jewishness that is hyphenated with Russianness. These immigrants have developed a sense of solidarity with their new society but many do not feel yet that they are an integral part of it. This does not enjoin them from expecting and wanting their children to link their future with Israel. Coupled with this identification with Israel, however, is a varying degree of alienation. Russian immigrants feel most estranged from the Ultra-Orthodox but much less so from nonreligious Ashkenazim, even though the latter do not reciprocate enthusiastically. Russians respond to their relative solitude by emphasizing their remaining a component of the Russian-Jewish transnational diaspora. In a nutshell, they are motivated by willingness to integrate into society, learn its language, and reach out to some of its constituents, but they frown on the idea of abandoning their cultural and linguistic particularism, and their transnational relations with their original homeland and other Russian-speaking diasporas.

At the same time, findings show that the collective identity of Russian Jews in Israel is undergoing a metamorphosis. The Russian Jews' notion of Jewishness now denotes adherence to symbols and values acquired and learned in Israel, and it is this new concept that the immigrants tend to hyphenate with Russianness. Israeliness plays a role in this complex identity-building by referring to current new life and experiences. The principal findings that we may draw from our study are phrased in the following:

1. Russian Jews in Israel undergo "ethnicization" as their "Israelization" is progressing.

2. Circumstances allow them opportunities to develop community endeavors quite freely.
3. As a potentially mobile group, they seem to become Israel's first secular middle-class ethnic group of (mostly) European origin.
4. Their collective identity now blends Jewishness expressed in commitment more than in contents, Russianness referring to cultural and linguistic resources and Israeliness reflecting the acquisition of Hebrew and full citizenship.
5. A major hardship for them is the feeling of distance and an incapacity to recognize themselves in the definitions and symbols offered by the dominant culture as a basis of sociocultural insertion.
6. This distance from the dominant culture is a source of weakness, when things come to shaping changes in the definition of the all-national identity.

Still a very different entity, Ethiopian Jews construe their immigration to Israel as related to their *ab initio* allegiance to *their* Jewishness. They are aware that given groups—especially the Ultra-Orthodox—have reservations about their collective identity but they do not hesitate to repay this hostility in kind. In response to Ultra-Orthodox claims, Ethiopian Jews insist that in Israel they belong to the traditional public and are open to the adoption of many symbols that they encounter here and that appear to them as consensual markers of traditionalism—such as Hebrew, which was unknown in the "old country," and men's skullcaps. Even so, Ethiopians perceive themselves as quite isolated, although they feel close to traditional Mizrahim.

All these are related to the transformation of Ethiopian Jews' collective identity, which is now willing to adopt new markers, to subordinate particularism to the national personality, and to establish a new relationship with the social and cultural environment—a picture that is sketched out in the following:

1. The data do not indicate that the racial question *per se* is a major issue for the time being or this group is reduced to an enclave condition.
2. The specific particularism of the Ethiopian Jews has been an impediment to communication with other groups but it is still the ground of their acceptance into society.

3. They situate themselves in the large traditional category, close to Mizrahim.
4. The issue of their religious recognition—in view of their special rites and customs—pressurizes them to adapt to Judaism as it widely prevails in this country.
5. They resent these exigencies and articulate claims of their own—such as the demand for bringing over their relatives of the Falash-mura which they see as a part of their transnational diaspora.

"Otherness" as a Divide

The third facet of the broader national identity, the attitude toward "others," involves the divide that distinguishes between Jews and non-Jews. Muslim and Christian Arabs constitute here the principal category for Israeli Jews and this attitude is reciprocated. Israeli Arabs contemplate with frustration the fact that they are surrounded by sovereign Arab states while they themselves are the only Arab population, from the Atlantic Ocean to the Persian Gulf, that is a subordinate national minority. That the people whom they consider a reference group for their national identity, the Palestinians, have been confronting Israel for decades further aggravates this reality. Thus, many choose "Arab" and "Palestinian," and not their civic identity, "Israeli," as their first collective identity. Moreover, ever since autumn of 2000, the sense of crisis among Arabs in Israel has deepened. Fewer individuals than ever are now willing to identify themselves as "Israeli Arabs" and many Jews have responded by developing hostile feelings toward them. Even today, however, the psychological aloofness from Jews does not prevent Arabs from meeting and socializing with Jews. Both sides are still convinced that encounters are necessary as a way to reestablish understanding and that coexistence remains a common interest. In sum, Arabs in Israel are an example of a minority that strongly differs from the majority in its identity but converges toward it no less emphatically in culture and modes of behavior. This cultural convergence should, in turn, have some effect on the collective identity by helping to create the notion of "Israeli-Arabness" or "Israeli-Palestinianness" that denotes a difference—at least where the singularity of the collective is concerned—from other kinds of Arab or Palestinian identities.

Druze are another national minority in Israel. According to their religious faith and collective memory, they see themselves as a group that should not be confused with the rest of the Arab population. Druze in Israel also fully recognize Israel as a Jewish state. Yet, they feel quite close to Muslim and Christian Arabs and less so to Jews. Druze use Arabic as their primary language but a large majority are fluent in Hebrew. On the other hand, they are solidaristic and firmly attached to their own longstanding traditions and have maintained their particularism as a Middle Eastern transnational diaspora. Though, while retaining the essentials of their legacy, Druze are acquiring new cultural traits that encourage them to converge toward Israeli Jews and diverge from their counterparts in other Middle Eastern countries. Moreover, they also regard Jews as fellow citizens within the framework of the Israeli state.

Another cleavage concerns the "non-Jewish non-Israeli" category that we examined in this study by the example of Filipino foreign workers. Having spent several years in Israel, these people no longer feel completely strange despite their marginal status. Many even contemplate settling in Israel for good. They feel closer to Israeli Jews than to the non-Jewish minorities but they also belong to the broader heterogeneous category of "guest workers." The Filipinos remain a solidaristic group that aspires to safeguard its culture. By maintaining allegiance to their culture, they cement their self-respect and project a self-image that demands respect from others. Their behavior in this matter also sets the stage for the establishment of transnational-diaspora settings.

The following sums up here our principal conclusions regarding non-Jews in Israeli society:

1. Israeli Palestinians are internally divided between their Palestinian collective identity and Israeli citizenship, but their ultimate inclination is to be a part of the country, even if Palestinians establish their own state and Israel retains a Jewish majority.
2. Druze see themselves as a singular entity, though they see themselves as Arabs. At the same time, they formally side up with the Jews politically, and do not wish to be confused with other Arabs.
3. Druze and Muslim and Christian Arabs have been undergoing modernization under the influence of their Israeli environment, but retain their respective particularisms. These particularisms are fueled by the dominant culture's own emphasis on a national collective identity that reduces them to the rank of national minorities.

4. An easing of the present-day difficult circumstances should provide the minorities with better possibilities to diminish the cost—in terms of civil rights and privileges—of nonmembership in the mainstream of society.
5. Regarding foreign workers, Filipinos look for ways to insert themselves into the social reality though they also wish to remain loyal to themselves.
6. Filipinos contribute new forms to the country's multiculturalism while they themselves undergo changes of lifestyles.
7. Filipinos do not tend to join the non-Jewish components of this society but rather to settle on the margins of the Jewish population.

Identification Compared

Another dimension that we have investigated is collective identification which, as we elaborated in the above, is a function not only of the tenets of the identity but also of circumstances like the inclusionism versus exclusionism of the dominant culture and the group's location on the society's stratificational map.

Our data confirm, on the basis of the Arab and Druze examples that the combination of relegation of a group to an underprivileged location and confrontation with an exclusionist dominant culture contributes to the crystallization of a conflictual collective. Additionally, among both Arabs and Druze, mobile elements remain a part of the community and contribute to the transformation and mobilization of their groups. These dynamics do much to explain both groups' tendency to generate high levels of self-identification. These developments are amplified by the fact that both groups hold religious convictions and face a dominant culture that relates to a different faith. Thus, structural conditions and identity tenets combine to produce conflictual situations, even though groups and individuals converge toward the cultural models prevailing in mainstream society.

Among Jews, major differences in collective identification are marked not by religion but by religiosity. The secular dominant culture asserts an allegiance to the Jewish people that cannot be defined without reference to religion. In front of it, the Ultra-Orthodox, partly concentrated in underprivileged socioeconomic strata, are convinced that they constitute a kind of "vanguard" to the "Jewish people." The national religious, too, constitute a militant group even though they generally belong to the middle class, and are not subjected to exclusionist treatment by the dominant culture. The settler segment of the national religious is clearly positioned among those whose identification with the collective identity is of tremendous importance. They often spice their personal revolution with mystic if not messianic overtones, relating their "mission" to the unfolding of the "destiny of the 'Nation.'" Hence, here too, religiosity is a major underlying element in the power of collective identification.

When it comes to Mizrahim, one can no longer speak of "religiosity" as a general rule (except for those who affiliate with the Shas party) but of an allegiance to religious traditions. Indeed, Mizrahim are a majority in the tradition-oriented category and a majority of Mizrahim belong to the tradition-oriented category. Collective identification is less predictable among Mizrahim than among Ultra-Orthodox and the national religious. Although it is particularly evident among those who are still characterized by low-class condition, it has not totally vanished among the large subclass of mobile Mizrahim, even when they insert themselves into the nonethnic middle class and, thereby, embrace the inclusionist attitude of the dominant culture. However, these mobile elements, who have seceded from their communities of origin, are also more exposed to the influence of their new milieu and often show a tendency to de-ethnicization. Thus, a subtle interaction is taking place between structural aspects and tenets of the collective identity. In this interaction, class situations influence the collective identification of Mizrahim even though this identification, which is to some extent a function of class realities, takes on the form of religious traditionalism rather than class identity.

Ethiopians follow the Mizrahim on this gradient. They have embraced traditionalism and are severely confined to low-class communities. The contemporary dominant culture abets their "difference" by being much less eager than in the past to impose cultural uniformization on Jewish society and by being more tolerant of pluralism. Yet, many Ethiopians are also willing to melt into general society. It is this kind of profile that explains the clashing tendencies that this group evinces. Thus, it is still too early, two decades or so since their immigration from Ethiopia, to speak of a clear mode of development. What is already clear is that it is through their allegiance to given religious traditions that they still mark their particular presence today.

For Russians and non-observant Ashkenazim, the religious principle has ceased to play a role in their internal endeavor. Like
Mizrahim, Ethiopians, and Arabs, many Russians find themselves in
lower social strata. Unlike them, however, the Russians' human capital abets hopes of rapid social advancement. Again, as with Ethiopians,
the dominant culture is no longer hostile to manifestations of particularism among immigrant communities, which responds to the
group's expectations to retain its original culture and to continue
using its language in the private and community spheres. Many
Russians are plainly eager to assimilate into Israel's nonethnic middle class, but others are definitely more retentionist. The Russians
are probably the only example in present-day Israel of a secular
"symbolic" ethnicity that benefits from participation in transnational-
diaspora networks. No one, however, should bet on the Russian Jews'
ability to continue shoring up the dike of retentionism as social insertion progresses and the mobility of many Russians creates close relations between them and non-Russian Jews.

In any case, quite a few Russians will be attracted to the nonobservant middle class, which is mostly Ashkenazi but also includes
many individuals of Mizrahi or mixed Ashkenazi-Mizrahi extraction.
This social category, as we have seen, is aloof not only from the
religious principle but also from ethnic identification. Furthermore,
this stratum—a privileged one in terms of its class positioning—is
the standard-bearer of the dominant culture and is defined by its
members more as a socioeconomic category or at most as a status
group than as an ethnic entity. Individuals in this category tend to
see their ethnocultural nature more as an "identifier" than as an
identity or a focal point of identification.

Summing up, our comparison shows that the groups' identification
ranges from strong to weak. This means that not every group pressures the dominant culture with the same resolve. In this respect,
we may divide the major groups into three categories. The most
demanding—i.e., those whose identification is the strongest—are
Arabs, Druze, Ultra-Orthodox, and the national religious. The middle category includes low-class Mizrahim, Russians, and Ethiopians.
The least demanding category is comprised of the secular middle
class, tenanted by many Ashkenazim and no few Mizrahim.

When one examines this categorization closely, one gets the impression that the principle of transnational diaspora is quite important
in some of the cleavages at issue, especially when combined with

the Israel-Palestinian conflict. Arabs in Israel, for instance, belong to a transnational diaspora and their allegiance to it exacerbates relations with the Jewish majority as long as the conflict lasts. Ultra-Orthodox also belong to a transnational diaspora, the world of Ultra-Orthodox Judaism; this strengthens their power to present the Israeli establishment with demands. The model of transnational diaspora, however, is best exemplified by the Russian Jews. For them, as for the Ultra-Orthodox, transnational-diaspora networks seem to be essential in social insertion strategies at the group level. The upshot of these examples is that the proliferation of social cleavages is combining with new forms of interconnectedness with the rest of the world. Globalization itself is present in the heterogeneization of society. To be accurate, however, we should note that the globalization/heterogeneization nexus has existed since the dawn of Zionism and remains evident today in the definition of the Israeli state as Jewish. By defining itself as such, Israel proclaims its solidarity with the dispersed groups that comprise the "Jewish people." In fact, it is this definition that accounts for the unwillingness of Jews in Israel to accept any program for an agreement with the Arab-Palestinian environment that would force Israel to sever relations with the world Jewry. In this sense, Israel's own dominant culture defines the large majority of the population as constituent of a transnational diaspora and gives globalization a major role in the shaping of this society and the formulation of its challenges.

THE END OF HEGEMONY

By viewing Israeli society as an entity that, like its components, implies a collective identity—what we termed "dominant culture"—we classified its cleavages in terms of the facets of this identity that they challenge most particularly. The investigation of Israel's cleavages has then shown the contours of confrontations leading to the possibility of answering to what extent the dominant culture still retains its dominance and, in turn, its hegemony.

Our analyses have, actually, shown that one is not entitled at this point to speak of the "end" of the dominant culture. This culture, indeed, still represents the focus of reference that all other forms of collective identity turn to in order to define their stand vis-à-vis the society in which they participate. In this sense we cannot but confirm that the Israeli society is still marked by a given dominant culture which allies Jewish nationhood, modernity, and cultural impacts of this society's experience as a society of immigrants at war (Ben-Rafael, 1982; Ben-Rafael and Sharot, 1991; Ben-Rafael, 1994).

We saw, however, that this dominant culture is not "what it was" anymore—at least in one crucial respect, from the point of view of the topic of these pages, namely, the recognition of pluralism and the acceptance of the existence of a variety of sociocultural groups as permanent actors in the dynamic development of the setting. In other words, the democratic political reality has imposed, from bottom up, the multiculturalization of the Israeli society (Mautner, Sagui, and Shamir, 1998). The importance of this development for the dominant culture resides, of course, in the fact that it is has now to coexist, openly interact and compete with alternate understandings of the social order. In this, the dominant culture has lost its hegemony and every truth that it enounces can now be questioned and discussed.

Our data have, indeed, shown the numerous appeals formulated against the assessments of the dominant culture and, in several cases, we learned from the attitudes of respondents the exigencies of new emphases, nay, even drastic innovations. Groups of most divergent perspectives stand up with claims that make unrealistic any assertion about the hegemony of the dominant culture. The meanings of these circumstances for the society as a whole pertains to the next chapter's discussion of Israel's model of multiculturalism.

CHAPTER FOURTEEN

MULTICULTURALISM AND THE PURSUIT OF MEANINGS

TENSIONS AND DILEMMAS

Our era is definitely marked by pluralism and multiculturalism. Nearly every contemporary society includes a variety of sociocultural groups, experiences innumerable intercommunity tensions, and in one way or another rewards this diversity with recognition and institutionalization. The march toward multiculturalism was not foreseen at the dawn of the modern era. At that time, when nation-states were founded, it was more often assumed that citizens' primary—if not exclusive—identity and identification would reside with the national collective. It was also thought that the predominance of modern meritocratic-individualistic orientations within societies would abet the dissolution of ethnocultural allegiances. Our study, in the wake of many others, shows not only that pluralism can sustain itself in modernity and may be expressed in a wide variety of syndromes but also that it encourages further societal transformation. Especially in democracy, sociocultural groups become political actors and imprint themselves in the social order, often inducing the surfacing of multiculturalist ideologies that endow multiculturalism with positive values and moral meanings. Concepts of multiculturalism, in turn, lay down "proper rules" for the regulation of relations among groups and between them and the core of society.

In a democracy indeed, determined groups may find access to the public scene on behalf of their claims—even when the dominant culture discourages this—and are often able to set up parties or lobbies that participate in the daily shaping and reshaping of the social order. Thus, the question of how society influences sociocultural groups is twinned with the no-less-crucial question of how sociocultural groups influence society. It is from this perspective that another issue inevitably arises: what keeps sociocultural groups together as constituents of a society whose dominant culture is waning and losing much of its influence?

It is also arguable, however, that in this process each group forges its singularity—within the setting and as a political actor—by selecting and devising its symbols not only by drawing them from its own original legacies but also through contacts with, and exposure to the influence of, the dominant culture. Furthermore, the legitimization of players' actions in and on the society unavoidably passes through a process of recognition and acceptance of rules and symbols that pertain to the dominant culture. In this process, actors are given the "right" to act as a part of the setting—an entitlement that they could not receive as "aliens." By adopting given rules and symbols that pertain to society at large while articulating symbols that are specifically its own, each group actually creates (or "invents") an interculture of sorts. Such an interculture carries the trademarks of its enterprise as a form of culture invention that indicates both attributes of the group: belongingness to, and singularity within, society. When one considers such processes holistically and applies them to the entire array of sociocultural groups in one society, one may assume that, however crucially they may differ from each other and from the dominant culture, these groups will eventually have many features in common. Not every group will share the same features or share them evenly, of course, but the dissemination of the features among the groups will make it possible to speak of a "family resemblance" in the Wittgensteinian sense (Wittgenstein, 1961).

By invoking this notion, one may also expect a dominant culture to continue to be viewed as such even as multiculturalization ensues, as that culture gradually loses its hegemony and becomes fully identified with one specific constituency only, i.e. the former elites and their hinterland. When groups concurrently retain particularistic symbols and adopt new codes, the dominant culture still serves as an ingredient in the cultural transformation that these groups experience. This transformation, however, is not necessarily even and uniform among the various groups: multiculturalism is a dynamic and changing constellation of unequal participants.

The Constellation of Israel's Multiculturalism

Our research found that the Israeli setting is best described in terms of a "core" composed of specific groups that coexist at varying distances and often refer to each other asymmetrically. Thus, the picture that we elicited portrays several groups as more marginal than the others. Figure 14.1 provides a heuristic illustration.

This picture tends to describe a rather open nonpolarized multi-cultural setting that is far from symmetrical and coherent. It is made of groups that are interconnected in very different ways. The periphery is best depicted as fragmented and the core, too, is by no means homogeneous. Some groups do not feel friendly toward other groups and some groups' friendly feelings are not necessarily reciprocated. Indeed, multiculturalism means here the assertion not only of cultural differences but also of differential status.

As theoretically elaborated by sociolinguists (Fasold, 1987), some groups in Israel are vigorously bilingual even though their language of origin is now influenced by the legitimate language. Another group, the Russians, adopts Hebrew as its first language but continues to use its previous first language as a community and family vernacular. Still others may retain only a few words and expressions from their previous first language or express their identity by retaining an accent. Concurrently, a worldwide communication language, English is diffused among all strata but is particularly used by the privileged as a marker of their status. This indicates how powerfully globalization penetrates this society along unequal lines, highlighting the inequalities and granting them new meanings. In brief, a globalization that represents uniformization at the global level may fuel sociocultural heterogeneity and inequality when it penetrates an individual society like Israel.

In brief, we may outline as follows the principal lines of Israel's multiculturalism:

1. One finds here a center-and-periphery setting, the closer a group is to the core the less it evinces a particularistic identity.
2. The outermost circle is tenanted by the more cohesive entities.
3. A space of clusters forms where Ashkenazim and Mizrahim, and the nonreligious and the traditional, are effectively linked in a cluster of sorts.
4. Within this space, individual groups feel closer to some and more distant from others, and their attraction to some of their counterparts is not necessarily reciprocated.
5. Ethnicity and religiosity act conjunctively but their importance increases as groups distance themselves from the core into the periphery.
6. The political dimension of multiculturalism witnesses forms of coalitions *and* conflicts—though the interests of most groups are

submitted to fundamental issues with respect to which some groups are naturally bound; whether to the right or the left.

7. One may speak of a form of conflictual multiculturalism where "nothing is taken for granted," several cleavages represent claims vis-à-vis the social order that concern not just their specific interests but also involve their overall respective perspectives on society.

Figure 14.1 presents the constellation construed by the various groups which effectively stand at unequal distance from each other. This picture illustrates, in a heuristic manner, where each group stands vis-à-vis others, and where the groups relatively close to the dominant culture occupy a more central place than others.

Another question of concern to us was how people perceive the very working of multiculturalism. Here we found that people endorse the principle of the plurality of cultures but differentiate among cultures in terms of prestige. Many individuals in the groups that we studied do not believe that people should retain their singular cultural features at all costs: overall, the groups do not accept excessive cultural diversity *ab initio*. On the other hand, many judge their own culture to be a proper object of reference for others. This again shows how fraught multiculturalism is with tension, rivalry, and conflict. Multiculturalism leaves room for mutual appreciation, though

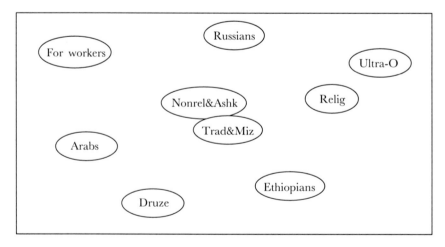

Figure 14.1. A Heuristic Picture of Israel's Multicultural Setting

not in every case: people definitely scorn some groups more than others.

The general landscape that we discover in a society like Israel's may appear less chaotic up close than at first glance. All cleavages fit into a rather stable political configuration along what we have called the right–left continuum. Some groups stand at the extreme left, others lean to the center, and still others associate with the right and even with the far right. Yet, blatant polarization is not evident; instead, the differences among groups seem to involve varying influences and interests. Everything else being equal, the Israeli polity is characterized by Arabs on the left and settlers on the right, most less ethnic-oriented on the left, the left-of-center or the center, and many Jewish sociocultural constituencies on the right-of-center.

Generally speaking, the Israeli case confirms that multiculturalism means societal transformation. The crux of this transformation is the dethroning of the long-dominant culture in favor of a diversity that is hierarchical and tainted by disputes. The dominant culture does continue to deserve the adjective "dominant" but this is mainly because all other variants refer to it as a source of symbols, rules, and perspectives at the same time as a focal point of conflict.

However, now that the society has become multicultural, this dominance is no longer synonymous with hegemony.

A REALITY IMPOSED FROM BOTTOM UP

Our analyses of the Israeli case definitely confirm Touraine's assertion that multiculturalism is a reality imposed from "bottom up"— from the periphery—and not "top-down"—from the center or society's elites (Touraine, 1997; 1992). It represents the realization of a leading principle that endorses and legitimizes demands for recognition of individuals and groups who assert themselves as being "different." Multiculturalism alleges that culture and community are not homogeneous throughout society and that they undergo changes—despite all forces, such as nationalism, that seek to impose uniformity.

Israel, as we have shown, is a good example of this process. Israeli society is defined by a dominant culture that has a strong primordialist twist and has long concerned itself with the cultural uniformization of the nation. This configuration, however, is quite different from other models discussed in the literature. Hence, American

society, says Heideking, is a case of a liberal, democratic, and mer-
cantile nation marked by sharp tensions between the desire for "republican harmony" and the legitimization of diverging group interests
(Heideking, 2002). As an immigrant society that could never fulfill
the wish to become a homogeneous nation-state, the U.S. witnessed
the emergence of a civil religion rooted in Puritan utopian beliefs
that, in this context, offered an alternative to European-type cultural
homogeneity (see also Ackerman, 1991; Arieli, 1992).

The Israeli case is different. Here it was the political reality that
eventually gave particularisms a chance and overcame the unifying
ideal of early Zionism. In 1977, when the Labor Party was unseated
after decades of uninterrupted rule, the attitude of the state toward
multiculturalism underwent a drastic shift. Since then, sociocultural
constituencies began amassing power in the polity as the targets of
competing leaderships and parties. The new rules of the game acted
first to the benefit of the Mizrahi public, resulting in the emergence
of Shas. The Russians were the next to gain as their turn came in
the 1990s. Both sectors joined forces with the Arab and Ultra-
Orthodox parties to lend Israel's polity a strong communitarian
coloration that it has not forfeited ever since. When the settlers
crystallized as a significant factor, they, too, joined the new constellation
of power. The power of these forces create—from the bottom up—
a new political reality in which multiculturalism is imposed and deter-
mines new rules. One of these rules concerns the standard-bearer of
the dominant culture, the predominantly Ashkenazi middle class. This
category, which has long seen itself as representative of "Israeliness"
at large, has become, unwillingly to be sure, merely one constituency
among others, at least in the eyes of others (Ochana, 1998).

This, however, is not to deny that the very groups that make up
a multiculturalist setting may also—and in fact unavoidably—allow
their cultural-linguistic personalities to erode under the influence of
modernity, universalistic perspectives, and aspects pertaining to the
identity of the dominant culture (Milroy, 1989; Dorian, 1981; Haugen,
1989). Even groups that retain if not strengthen their particularistic
personalities on the basis of firmly rooted primordial allegiances cannot but experience some degree of acculturation and gradually become
"less different" from the strata that embody the predominant values
and norms. Be this as it may, these circumstances—which apply to
Israel's sociocultural groups, as we have seen—do not thwart the

evolution of multicultural politics in which a proliferation of actors debate, often virulently, the rules that should govern their coexistence and cooperation.

New Meanings of the State

An important upshot of these developments, transcending the description of our findings, is that this multicultural reality actually represents a drastic redefinition of the state–nation relationship. Ever since this issue surfaced in past centuries, different societies have responded to it differently. German thinkers such as Herder, Mommsen, and Schlegel stress that in Germany the nation itself is perceived in primordial terms and is given primacy over communities and individuals (Schnapper, 1991). Back in 1932, Max Hildebert Boehm asserted that the core of each individual's personality is the *Volk* (people). Notwithstanding the appalling Nazi abuse of the "Volk concept," this approach was echoed by historians Othmar Spann in 1967 and Theodor Veiter in 1970 (Schnapper, 1991). From this perspective, the state embodies the collective personality of the nation and is endowed with the function of leadership. The same attitude may be found in France in the anti-revolutionary tradition illustrated by Joseph de Maistre in the late eighteenth century, who spoke of France as the "elder daughter of the Church." This attitude, however, was resisted by the intellectual tradition that flowed from the Revolution, which posits a voluntaristic concept of nation grounded in a liberal-universalistic notion of civism (see also Dumont, 1983). This perspective also defines the state as the leader of the nation but legitimizes its authority by positing that the state embodies universalistic values that everyone can endorse provided that they accept the identity and values that the nation personifies. It is this approach that consolidated the modern dominant culture of France, which thus far has asked immigrants to fully assimilate into society.

As a matter of course, both models of dominant culture, the French and the German, have undergone far-reaching changes. Both societies have had to confront particularisms and, ultimately, to legitimize them in some ways. France has coped with the particularisms of Corsica, North African immigrants, and even regional groups like the Bretons; Germany has dealt with Turkish and Moroccan immigrants firmly determined to retain particularistic symbols. Amidst these challenges, however, the state's leading role over society has weakened in both countries, taking on more flexibiliy.

Thus, both France and Germany have drawn closer to the American model of minimalistic statehood, as sketched by Glazer and Moynihan (1974). In the multiculturalist model, the state is not expected to preside over a melting pot and treats religious groupings with respect, even when they intervene in national politics.

By legitimizing diverse groups' particular cultures as permanent aspects of the social order, the recognition of pluralism inevitably leads to social fragmentation and blurs what the society stands for. Conversely, however, groups that are viewed as legitimate actors in polity and, therefore, participants in political life also become components *of* society and are urged to assume wider responsibility that may draw them into a more intimate relationship with the dominant culture (Orans, 1971; Olzak, 1983; Ben-Rafael, 1994). This development engenders new concepts of civism that carry weaker cultural and ideological significance, thereby eroding the concept of the nation-state (Castles, 2000).

The Israeli case confirms this dialectic development: sociocultural groups that are deeply influenced and molded by their experience in society also do much to give society its shape. Israel endeavors the transformation of a nation-state that was created on the basis of an exceptionally ambitious program. Seminal Zionism not only aspired to create a state that would allow a nation to crystallize but also urged a population dispersed throughout the world to gather on a given territory, to adopt a common language, and to abandon previous norms and customs in favor of a new culture. The dominant culture that expressed these ambitions emphasized the role of the state, under the leadership of the Zionist Labor Movement, as the focal core entitled to present a highly heterogeneous population with explicit common challenges. The Labor model broke down because the rightist opposition, after years of exertions, developed the ability to challenge incumbents by putting together a coalition of under-privileged elements. The unseating, as noted above, came in 1977 when the Likud rose to power due largely to the support of Mizrahim and religious elements. To enlist this support, the right-wing Likud boldly endorsed the legitimacy of pluralism and sociocultural claims. The new forces, in turn, transformed the political arena by making multiculturalism an obvious reality. In 2002, the rise of Shinui, a radically secular party that demonstratively linked itself with the middle class, further strengthened the rootedness of particularisms in national politics.

The apparent lesson is that once sociocultural groups manage to access the political arena and become actors in it, they render some roles of the state obsolete and impose new ones. Indeed, the new reality has partially eroded the old myths of the establishment of Israel.[1] In their place, new respect is shown for symbols pertaining to the legacy or endeavors of groups that for years were viewed "from the top" as "marginal." The state itself is still considered a crucial arena for debate in view of the need to work out a viable *modus vivendi*, but the power behind the actors lies not only with the state but also with the constituencies themselves. In sum, Israel exemplifies a case in which the state has surrendered some of its potency to new power centers.

Experiencing Multiculturalism

If so, the crucial question concerns the practice of multiculturalism after a dominant culture has lost its hegemony. Multiculturalism means not only the prior legitimization of diverse interests and values and the end of an integrative approach but also the rejection of the pluralistic solution, which assumes that the dominant culture will retain control over separate and distinct communities. Of special interest here is Louis Dumont's contention that recognized differences may coexist without equality if they are understood as the implementation of a central principle of the social order (Dumont, 1977; 1983). On the other hand, following Giddens (1980; 1987), a sociocultural community may also be defined, partly, in terms of differential access to forms of self-actualization and empowerment. Thus viewed, multiculturalism also signifies the production of difference, exclusion, marginalization, and conflict. This, we said, is the gist of conflictual multiculturalism—a notion, we have seen, that widely applies to the Israeli reality.

Furthermore, in a vein that recalls Smith's perspective (Smith, 1998), Israel, like many other modern states, is above all a form of

---

[1] The kibbutz movement is a case in point. Once a pillar of the social order and a protagonist in the depiction of this society's "pioneer epic," the kibbutzim today are merely one "sector" among many others.

CHAPTER FOURTEEN

nation-state that is intrinsically a focal point of primordialism that implies a historical memory and a sense of affective belonging if not of mission. In such a case, multiculturalism undoubtedly goes against the national project by endorsing the coexistence of sociocultural groups as a permanent reality that restricts the significance and exclusiveness of the national identity and what it aspires to represent. When some groups act on this basis to hyphenate their Israeli self-definition with "Ultra-Orthodox," "Russian-Jewish" or the like, they give rise to a "postnational" identity of sorts, just as the formation of the European Union allows one to depict French, German, or British Europeanness as a new "postnational" identity (Habermas, 1981).

The Israeli case may, however, shed light on different possible meanings of this process. We have seen how strong the primordial attachment to the national identity—Israeli Jewishness—is for some groups, which construct their own primordialism in reference to this fundamental token. This applies to secular Ashkenazim who view themselves as primarily "Israeli Jewish" and hardly evince any other criterion of primordialism; it also applies to the Shas constituency, which is building its own primordialism within, and as a form of, this Israeli Jewishness. It applies less to the Ultra-Orthodox, who portray themselves as the sole bearers of "authentic" Jewishness and the national religious, who assert that only they can correctly interpret Israeli Jewishness. Russian Jews, in contrast, tend to distinguish between Israeliness and Jewishness and profess the latter in conjunction with Russianness. Israeliness itself is problematic for Arabs, who tend to express it as an instrumental reality while asserting their own autonomous primordialism—Arabness or Palestinianness. Thus, the link between the national identity and the sociocultural token constitutes a genuine dilemma that different groups (and milieus within groups) tackle in diverse ways. For Israel, the nature of this dilemma is the topic of endless debates that have become permanent features of Israeli social endeavor in this era of multiculturalism.

DIVERSITIES IN FAMILY RESEMBLANCE

The diversity of sociocultural groups that assert their distinctiveness vis-à-vis the "rest" of society is manifested not only in different references to the same broader national identity but also in constant contact and communication with each other in the various arenas of social life. This very co-presence questions the "something" that allows them to relate to each other, if such a "something" exists at all. Our research on the Israeli setting has led us to view this "something" as best captured by Wittgenstein's concept of "family resemblance" (Wittgenstein, 1961). Wittgenstein, as noted in our introductory chapter, uses this term to denote the similarity that one encounters among *language games*, which, notwithstanding their semantic and structural differences, belong to the same linguistic system. He likens their similarity to a family resemblance because, like relatives, they share features and modes of behavior that are unevenly distributed among elements but still create a sense a familiarity throughout the group. This kind of family resemblance, like the literal kind, by no means excludes tensions and conflicts. It is in the family setting, in fact, that the sharpest conflicts of all may break out. They may destabilize the entire group due to the very fact of the closeness of the members and the emotional capital they must invest in order to fight each other. We apply the concept of family resemblance to sociocultural groups in multiculturalism because their coexistence in one setting necessitates interaction and reciprocal influences among groups and, primarily, between each group and the dominant culture. This interaction cannot but cause the groups to be "touched" by the symbols and myths of society at large and of the other actors on the arena. Thus, each group, in its own way, develops some resemblance to the cultural or symbolic aspects of the dominant culture and of other groups' cultures. This is how the diverse groups become familiar to each other. This feeling neither denotes equal degrees of closeness nor excludes antagonisms and fragmentation. It must not even bring about the recognition of a common supreme authority. However, it signals the group's acknowledgment of lines of resemblance.

In the Israeli case, these processes are well reflected in the domain of language. We know the importance of the revival of Hebrew as the cement of modern Israel and the symbol of the Jews' "return" to their ancestral land. All groups of Jewish immigrants—some with more enthusiasm than others—adopted the language, underwent linguistic transformation, and contributed—mostly willingly—to the development of a new local original literature and culture. However, different groups invested Hebrew with very different connotations. Some, mainly the nonreligious Ashkenazim, stopped using their original languages from the first generation and their sons and daughters became Hebrew speakers as if Hebrew had been their mother tongue, i.e., using a mainstream accent that sounded "authentically Israeli." In other groups—Mizrahim, generally speaking—the switch to Hebrew was also complete but accents that trace to specific origins were retained. The Ultra-Orthodox adopted Hebrew belatedly and continued to use Yiddish, albeit amidst rampant codeswitching with Hebrew. It is among Russian Jews that the diasporic language seems to have remained the most vital, even though their Russian provides many occasions for borrowing from Hebrew. The latter has been definitely acquired and is now used as the main language in the public domain. For Arabs and druze, Hebrew remains a second language. Arabic is prevalent in their communities, both in private and in public—even though it is packed with Hebrew borrowings. Concurrently, languages of global communication, especially English, are penetrating society and have become markers of privileged strata.

All these remind us of what has already been elaborated with respect to other situations (Gumperz, 1967; Haarmann, 1986) but the generalized use of Hebrew means that the groups, however diverse they are, refer to a common set of symbols that justifies the notion of an "Israeli" collective and makes meaningful intergroup communication possible. In return, however, Hebrew is developing and changing under the simultaneous influence of the numerous language contacts that it is experiencing and the imprinting of group markers in Hebrew itself. This development of Hebrew and of its relations with other codes provides the best indication of all about what is happening to Israel's dominant culture in this era of multiculturalism. Indeed, the outcome is that Hebrew is not the only language that one hears in the street; other codes have gained *droit de cité*. Moreover, Hebrew itself is spoken differently by diverse milieus. Nevertheless, Israel is a Hebrew-speaking society and each culture that exists in the country has been deeply and irremediably influenced by the dominant culture through its very confrontation with it—even though the influence has acted in the other direction as well.

It is in this light that the observer may appreciate the factors that hold sociocultural groups *together* as constituents of one society. Although different in important ways, the various sociocultural groups actually develop a "family resemblance." Even when the dominant culture loses its hegemony and becomes the culture of one constituency alone, it is still a major *ingredient* in the intercultures that groups elaborate by means of their social insertion—a process in which efforts to maintain allegiance to legacies coincide with efforts to acquire, and adapt to, new codes and symbols. This is the kind of adhesive that seemingly restrain those who share a setting but hardly keep from dividing it.

THE RELIGION PRINCIPLE

Our analyses of Israel's multiculturalism also lead to evince the importance of the religion principle—we include in this category differences of religion and modes of religiosity, including explicit nonreligiosity. This principle is rooted in the formation of major national and particular collective identities and offers the ground for confrontations. This is important both in the tensions that oppose individual sociocultural groups with the dominant culture and in the configuration of Israeli multiculturalism as a whole.

At all points in our discussion, we have, indeed, encountered the religion principle in a variety of forms. We have seen how alienating is the fact of belonging to religions different from the one that is unequivocally bound to the definition of the prevailing national identity. Within the population that refers to this religion-linked national identity, religiosity is then a parameter of further differentiation, not only according to degrees—from Ultra-Orthodoxy to nonreligiosity—but also to manners and emphases—from total dedication to the religious law to empathy for traditions and down to velleities to assert nonobservance. All these represent a diversity of partially divergent and partially convergent projects which may find in the notion of multiple modernities a relevant frame of interpretation when applied to one setting.

It is in this perspective, actually, that one may read this study which started from the conviction that religion may remain crucially important in the formation of social groups and nations. A possibility, as already mentioned in the earlier pages, that it has long been anything but obvious.

An idea that is very popular in contemporary sociology is that nations represent "invented traditions" that are "socially constructed." The concept of invented tradition refers to sets of practices and rituals that inculcate values and norms intended to imply continuity with the past (Hobsbawm and Ranger, 1983). From this perspective, the nation-state, with its demarcated territory and standardized national language, is an eminently modern phenomenon, and flags, languages, and histories are produced by social engineering. In a similar vein, Anderson (1991) asserts that the nation is nothing but an "imagined" community. It derives its emotional resonance from the fact that, in the modern era, it has replaced kinship and religion as the main locus of individuals' loyalty and willingness to make self-sacrifice.

This position—as already discussed in Chapter 1—has come under fierce attack in recent years (see Stille, 2003, for a review). No few contemporary scholars now define religion as a founding element in nationalism (Marx, 2003; Colley, 1992). This thesis, these scholars contend, helps us understand the emergence and development of many a national movement. Nationalism and religion, we now know, are often natural allies. The ineradicable nexus of religion and peoplehood or nationhood in Judaism supports this thesis. As our analysis shows, this link was the very source of Zionism even though most Zionists were nonreligious. The revolution enacted by secular Zionism in Judaism, following Katz's analysis (Katz, 1960), was but a reinterpretation of traditional perspectives in the light of new ideas. By no means was it a divorce from Judaism.

In this respect, our study actually shows that what one may say about the Jewish nationalism conveyed by Israel's dominant culture also applies to sociocultural groups. Indeed, by contemplating Israel's patchwork of cleavages from this perspective, we see that awareness of collective identity combines with identification to form a gradient on which religion, religiosity, and religious traditions play a major role in both the formation of national minorities and differentiation among Jewish categories. Arabs and Druze distinguish themselves from Jews by national identities, but this distinction is sustained by references to religious faiths to which collectives and individuals are committed.

Moving on to intra-Jewish divisions, where religiosity replaces religion as the differentiating factor, we see the impact of the religiosity factor for the Ultra-Orthodox and the national religious, the undoubted protagonists in the most active cleavages on the Jewish scene. It is on behalf of their divergent interpretations of the Jewish faith that these groups justify their political ambitions and endeavors and attack the nonreligious. As they prosecute their struggle, they find allies or, at least, sympathizers among Mizrahim who—notwithstanding the influence of Shas—are not overly eager to define themselves simply as "religious" and often prefer the concept of "traditional" to characterize their loyalty to their traditions. Ethiopians who struggle to assert their Jewish identity also affirm their devotion to the religious values of their legacies. Thus, all these groups and categories tend to define themselves in relation to, and to assert their identification with, some form of the religiosity principle. Even foreign workers, the only category that is neither Jewish nor Israeli, often tend to build communities and coalesce as a specific sector by establishing churches affiliated with the denominations that best express continuity with their homelands.

The only Jewish categories that cannot be linked to the religious principle—although they are characterized along religious lines relative to non-Jews—are the Russians and the nonreligious. Indeed, the Russians are probably the best—if not the only—example in Israel of a group that primarily identifies itself in terms of cultural and linguistic traits irrespective of religiosity or legacies. This aspect, it may be proposed, accounts to a large extent for the fact that Russian Jews feebly relate to other Jewish groups in Israel, notwithstanding their common origin with a large and powerful segment of this society, namely, the offspring of the founders.

The nonreligious, as we noted, are experiencing a situation in which a blurring formulation of collective identity is coupling itself with decreasing identification with this identity in favor of self-images that stress class and status attributes on the one hand, and the national—Jewish-Israeli—identity, on the other. Hence, in this case, the loss of relevance of the religious principle is concomitant with the acquisition of a Jewish-Israeli culture that draws from the same sources as religion but that tries to delineate a difference between a secular Israeli Judaism and the Jewish religion, even though it is still tied to a same reservoir of symbols. In other words, unlike Russians, the nonreligious do have a synagogue . . . which they do not attend.

A Kind of Conflictual Multiculturalism

Multiculturalism, to be sure, is a difficult notion to elaborate. It indicates a condition that by definition assumes innumerable possibilities. Its specific contours in any particular society at any given moment widely depend, at least, on the groups in presence, which vary from place to place; on the configuration of power that characterizes their relations, which are anything but necessarily stable; and on the rules of access to polity that vary from one democracy to another.

To facilitate our discussion, we distinguished liberal and conflictual multiculturalisms according to the extent that collective actors aspire but to establish some area of autonomy within the setting warranting a community endeavor at their convenience, or aspire to achieve influence over the center and the social order on behalf of their convictions and beliefs. This distinction dichotomizes the space of multiculturalisms but it does not preclude considering the wide variety of *sui generic* possibilities that may be found in either category according to circumstances. Moreover, as already noted in earlier pages, a type 1 multiculturalism may evolve into a type 2 when events aggravate relations between groups or between some of them and the dominant culture, or vice-versa, when protagonists succeed to find ways to institutionalize satisfactory compromises.

Israel, as we have seen, definitely responds to the conflictual-multiculturalism type. However, within this wide category, this society illustrates more specifically a case where an allegiance to traditional symbols imprinted with religion and religiosity is linked to the formulation of the national identity as conveyed, primarily but not only, by a secular dominant culture. This basic feature is an axis of confrontations between this dominant culture and major sociocultural groups: for some, confrontations refer to the religion invoked itself; for other—and less isolated—ones, they concern the very understanding of the religion-nationalism link; for still other groups, they concern the very fact of the link and its consequences.

What is obvious in this kind of multiculturalism is that particular tensions and conflicts that, in other societies, play a central role in the polity, are here clearly compartmentalized to specific areas without strong inference in the national political life. We think here of class conflicts which are very important on the scene of labor relations but of secondary impact when it comes to national politics. Socialist, social-democrat, and class-conflict rhetoric is mainly articulated by middle-class individuals and parties, and left-versus-right polemics refer exclusively to attitudes vis-à-vis Israel's goals in its conflict with its environment.

On the other hand, the major conflicts that do take place here, beside the right-left quarrel, involve cleavages that illustrate, in one way or another, the link of religion and nationhood. It is around questions relating to this area of problems that revolve a good part of the principal debates in the polity. What is more, one of the principal factors in the central Right-versus-Left quarrel is directly connected with the conflict that opposes one religious-ideological force—the settlers—with other groups and the center itself driven, as it is, by overall pragmatic considerations. This importance of the link of religion to nationhood accounts for the fact that even at the highest hours of secular Zionism, religion has always been recognized as a national institution—through the Rabbinical hierarchy in charge of all matters involving personal status. In the same context it was also (and still is) allowed to express the pluralism of Judaism by a dualism of rabbis (Ashkenazi and Sephardic) at all levels of the hierarchy.

This element that figures, under varying formulations, in the national identity substantiates the latter's primordialism in the eyes of all. It is a factor of all-societal solidarity. Yet, at the same time it defines the multiculturalism illustrated by Israel as conflictual as it involves constant rivalries over emphases by divergent versions of that national identity. In brief, and reminding again the Wittgensteinian metaphor, it is spoken of a form of conflictual multiculturalism which conveys quarrels typical of an extended family torn by opposed passions and emotional investments.

All in all, this perspective at multiculturalism looks on contemporary reality as a reflection of both allegiances to historical-cultural symbols, values and traditions and present-day prevailing influences stemming from major foci of societal development—modernity, nationalism, globalization—as well as conjectural circumstances. This perspective focuses on sociocultural groups in a dialectic frame of analysis: how these groups are transformed by society—without necessarily disappearing as distinct entities—and how they, in turn, transform the society—without necessarily diluting its identity.

Here lies the difficulty to answer our fundamental, theoretical, and practical question: Is Israel One? Our discussions of Israel's diverse cleavages as well as of the setting that they make up together, lead us to answer this question both positively and negatively. No, Israel is not one, as the version of national identity conveyed by the dominant culture is at the center of bitter polemics because it communicates partial exclusion for groups of different national and religious allegiances, and challenges others which keep, with vigor, to different versions of the same identity. This indicates the acuity of rifts threatening the societal solidarity. On the other hand, we can also say in spite of all this: Yes, Israel is one, because this multiculturalism is articulated by one major issue—the relation of nationalism and religion. This issue situates every single cleavage of the numerous ones that this setting fosters, in a specific relation with both the dominant culture and other cleavages. In other words, it is spoken of as a system of cleavages; a system that is open and evolves according to both internal dynamics and external influences, but where all entities are primarily turned toward what they obtain and sacrifice as parts of this society. Behind the specific interests and goals that are particular to each group, all of them are concerned by the prospects in the polity of the specific approaches which they carry, regarding the very same issue. In sum, that Israel is one can by no means be denied, but this statement cannot be endorsed as a definitve assessment; it is a challenge for all those involved.

BIBLIOGRAPHY

Abercrombie, N., and Turner, B.S. (1983) "The dominant ideology thesis" in Giddens, A., and Held, D. (eds.) *Classes, Power and Conflict: Classical and Contemporary Debates*, London: Macmillan.

Abramov, S.Z. (1976) *Perpetual Dilemma—Jewish Religion in a Jewish State*, London: Associate University Press.

Abrams, D., and Hogg, M.A. (1990) "An Introduction to the Social Identity Approach" in Abrams, D., and Hogg, M.A. (eds.) *Social Identity Theory: Constructive and Critical Advances*, New York: Harvester Wheatsheaf.

Abu Nimr, M. (1993) *Conflict Resolution Between Arabs and Jews In Israel: A Study of Six Intervention Programs*. S. L: S. N.

Ackerman, B. (1991) *We The People*. Cambridge, Mass.: Harvard University Press.

Adjemian, C. (1976) "On the nature of interlanguage systems," *Language Learning* 26: 297–320.

Adler, S. (ed.) (1999) *Immigrant Absorption* (1998) Jerusalem: Ministry of Immigrant Absorption.

Agassi, J. (1990) *Religion and Nation: Toward an Israeli National Identity*, Tel-Aviv: Papyrus. (Hebrew)

Agassi, J., Buber-Agassi, I., and Brant, M. (1991) *Who is a Jew?* Tel-Aviv: Kivunim. (Hebrew)

Albrow, M. (1996) *The Global Age. State and Society Beyond Modernity*. Cambridge: Polity Press.

Al-Hadj, Majid (1993) "The changing strategies of mobilization among the Arabs in Israel" in Ben-Zadok (ed.) *Local Communities and the Israeli Polity*, New York: State University of New York Press.

Almog, O. (1997) *The Sabra—A Profile*. Tel-Aviv: Am Oved. (Hebrew)

Alphere, Y. (1994) *Settlements and Borders*. Tel-Aviv: Jaffee Center for Strategic Studies Press. (Hebrew)

Amara, M. (1997) *Political Violence among Arabs in Israel*, Guivat Chaviva: Institute for Peace Research. (Hebrew)

Anderson, B. (1991) *Imagined Communities: Reflections on the Origins and Spread of Nationalism*, London: Verso.

Anderson, P. (1984) "Modernity and Revolution," *New Left Review* 144(2): 96–113.

Appadurai, A. (1990) "Disjuncture and Difference in the Global Cultural Economy", in Featherstone, M. (ed.) *Global Culture: Nationalism, Globalization and Modernity*. London: Sage.

—— (1996) *Modernity at Large. Cultural Dimensions of Globalization*. Minneapolis: University of Minnesota Press.

Appelbaum, L., and Newman, D. (1990) "From monopoly to pluralism," *Tichnun Svivati* 44–45: 35–49. (Hebrew)

Appiah, K.A. (1995) "African Identities" in Nicholson, L., and Seidman, S. (eds.) *Social Postmodernism: Beyond Identity Politics*, Cambridge: Cambridge University Press.

Aptekman, D. (1993) "Jewish emigration from the USSR, 1990–1992: Trends and Motivations," *Jews and Jewish Topics in the Soviet Union and Eastern Europe* 1 (20): 15–33.

Aran, G. (1987) *From Religious Zionism to Zionist Religion*, doctoral dissertation, Hebrew University, Jerusalem. (Hebrew)

Arieli, J. (1986) "Modern times and the problem of secularisation," in Gafni, J., and Motskin, J. (eds.) *Clergy and Monarchy: Religion and State relations in Israel and Among the Nations*, Jerusalem: Shazar Institut. (Hebrew)

Arieli, Y. (1992) "American Civilization as an Archetype of Modern Civilization" in Arieli, Y., *History and Politics*. Tel-Aviv: Am Oved. (Hebrew)

Arnason, J.P. (2002) "The multiplication of modernity" in Ben-Rafael, E. and Sternberg, Y. (eds.) *Identity, Culture and Globalization*, Leiden and Boston: Brill.

—— (2003) *Civilizations in Dispute: Historical Questions and Theoretical Traditions*, Leiden and Boston: Brill.

Avineri S. (1981) *The Making of Modern Zionism: The Intellectual Origins of the Jewish State*, NY: Basic Books.

Bachi, R. (1956) "A Statistical analysis of the revival of Hebrew in Israel," *Scripta Hierosolymitana* 3: 179–247.

Bacon, G.C. (1996) *The Politics of Tradition: Agudat Yisrael in Poland, 1916–1939*, Jerusalem: Magnes Press.

Banton, M. (1994) "The actor's model of ethnic relations," *Ethnic and Racial Studies*, 17(1): 98–104.

Bar-On, D., and Sela, A. (1991) "The vicious circle: From immigration to reality and the relation to the Holocaust among young Israelis," *Psichologia*, b/5: 126–138.

Barth, F. (1969) "Introduction" in Barth, F. (ed.) *Ethnic Groups and Boundaries*, Boston: Little Brown.

—— (1997) "How is the self conceptualized? Variations among cultures" in Neisser, U., and Jopling, D.A. (eds.) *The Conceptual Self in Context: Culture, Experience, Self-Understanding*, Cambridge: Cambridge University Press.

Bartram, D. (1998) "Foreign Workers in Israel: History and Theory Conditions," *International Migration Review*, 32: 302–325.

Bar-Zuri, R. (1999) "Foreign Workers in Israel: Attitudes and Policy Implications" in Nathanson, R. (ed.) *The New World of Work in an Era of Economic Change*, Tel-Aviv: Friedrich Ebert Foundation.

Baubock, R. (1994) *Transnational Citizenship*, UK: Edward Elgar.

—— (1998) "The Crossing and Blurring of Boundaries in International Migration: Challenges for Social and Political Theory" in Baubock, R., and Rundell, (eds.) *Blurred Boundaries: Migration, Ethnicity, Citzenship*, Aldershot (UK): Ashgate.

Bauman, Z. (1996) "From Pilgrim to tourist—or a short history of identity" in Hall, S., and Du Gay, P. (eds.) *Questions of Cultural Identity*, London: Sage.

—— (1998) "Parvenu and pariah: hereos and victims of modernity" in Good, J., and Velody, I. (eds.) *The Politics of Modernity*, Cambridge: Cambridge University Press.

Beck, U. (2000) *What is Globalization?*, Cambridge: Polity Press.

Beebe, L.M., and Giles, H. (1984) "Speech-Accommodation Theories: A Discussion in Terms of Second-Language Acquisition," *International Journal of the Sociology of Language* 46: 5–32.

Bellah, R.N. (1967) "Civil Religion in America," *Daedalus* 96: 1–21.

Ben Amos, A., and Beit El, A. (1996) "Rituals, education and history: The Shoa commemoration in Israeli schools" in Ektes, A., and Paldakhay, R. (eds.) *Education and History*, Jerusalem: Shazar Centre. (Hebrew)

Ben-Chaim, L. (2003) *Higher Education and Religiosity—The Case of Israel*, doctoral dissertation, Tel-Aviv University, Tel-Aviv.

Ben-Eliezer, U. (1998) *The Making of Israeli Militarism*, Bloomington: Indiana University Press.

Benoist, J.-M. (1977) "Facettes de l'identité" in Levi-Strauss, C. (ed.) *L'Identité*, Paris: Quadrige PUF.

Ben-Porat, A. (1989) *Divided We Stand*, Westport, CT: Greenwood.

—— (2001) "Inequality in Israeli Society" in Yaar, E., and Shavit, Z. (eds.) *Tendencies in Israeli Societies*, Tel-Aviv: The Open University. (Hebrew)

Ben-Rafael, E. (1982) *The Emergence of Ethnicity: Cultural Groups and Social Conflict in Israel*, Westport, Conn.: Greenwood Press.

—— (1994) *Language Identity and Social Division: The Case of Israel*, Oxford: Oxford University Press/Clarendon.

—— (2002a) "Ethnicity, Sociology of," *International Encyclopedia of the Social and Behavioral Sciences*, London: Elsevier, Vol. 7: 4838–42.

—— (2002b) *Jewish Identities: 50 Intellectuals Answer Ben-Gurion*, Leiden and Boston: Brill.

Ben-Rafael, E., and Brosh, H. (1995) "Jews and Arabs in Israel: The cultural convergence of divergent identities" in Nettler, R. (ed.) *Mediæval and Modern Perspectives on Muslim-Jewish Relations*, London: Harwood Academic Publications.

Ben-Rafael, E., and Leon, N. (2005) "Middle-Eastern Ultra-Orthodoxy" in Cohen, U., Ben-Rafael, E., Bareli, A., and Yaar, E. (eds.) *Israel as Modern Society*, Beer Sheva: Ben-Gurion Center and the Ben-Gurion University of the Negev Press.

Ben-Rafael, E., and Sharot, S. (1991) *Ethnicity, Religion and Class in Israeli Society*. Cambridge: Cambridge Univesity Press.

Ben-Rafael, E., Olshtain, E., and Geijst, I. (1997) "The socio-linguistic insertion of Russian Jews in Israel," in Lewin-Epstein, N., et al. (eds.), *Russian Jews on Three Continents*. London: Frank Cass.

Blau, P.M., and Duncan, O.D. (1967) *The American Occupational Structure*, New York: John Wiley and Sons.

Bourdieu, P. (1982) *Ce que parler veut dire*, Paris: Fayard.

Bowen, J.R. (1993) *Modernizing Muslims Through Discourse*. Princeton, N.J.: Princeton University Press.

Brubaker, W.R. (1989) *Immigration and the Politics of Citizenship in Europe and North America*, London: University Press of America.

—— (1992) *Citizenship and Nationhood in France and Germany*, Cambridge, Mass.: Harvard University Press.

Brym, R.J. (1997) "Jewish Immigration from the Former U.S.S.R.: Who? Why? How Many?" in Lewin-Epshtein N., Roi, Y., and Ritterband, P. (eds.) *Russian Jews on Three Continents*. London: Frank Cass.

Buber, M. (1973) *On Zion: The History of an Idea*, Bath, UK: East and West Library.

Burgess, M.E. (1978) "The Resurgence of Ethnicity: Myth or Reality," *Ethnic and Racial Studies* 1: 265–285.

Calhoun, C. (1993) "Nationalism and Ethnicity," *Annual Review of Sociology* 19: 211–239.

—— (1994) "Social theory and the politics of identity," in Calhoun, C. (ed.) *Social Theory and the Politics of Identity*, Oxford: Blackwell.

—— (1997) *Nationalism*. Buckingham: Open University Press.

Champion, F., and Hervieu-Léger, D. (eds.) (1990) *De l'émotion en religion. Renouveaux et traditions*. Paris: Centurion.

Chaney, E. (1981) "Migrant workers and national boundaries: The basis of rights and protections" in Brown, P., and Shue, H. (eds.) *Boundaries: National Autonomy and its Limits*, New Jersey: Rowman and Littlefield.

Castells, M. (1996) *The Information Age, Volume 2: The Power of Identity*. Oxford: Blackwell.

Castles, S. (2000) *Citizenship and Migration: Globalization and the Politics of Belonging*, Houndmills: Macmillan Press.

Castoriadis, C. (1997) *World in Fragments: Writings in Politics, Society, Psychoanalysis and the Imagination*. Stanford: Stanford University Press.

Chermesh, R. *A State Within a State: Industrial Relations in Israel, 1965–1987*, Westport: Greenwood Press.

Chomsky, W. (1957) *Hebrew, The Eternal Language*, Philadelphia: Jewish Publication Society of America.

Cohen P.S. (1983) "Ethnicity, class and political alignment in Israel," *Jewish Journal of Sociology* 25: 119–130.

Cohen, A., and Zusser, B. (1998) "Between consensus and the break of consensus—

Changes in religion-state relations" in Mautner, M., Sagui, A., and Shamir, R. (eds.) *Multiculturalism in a Democratic and Jewish State*, Tel-Aviv: Ramot. (Hebrew)

Cohen, R. (ed.) (1996) *The Sociology of Migration*. Cheltenham, UK: E. Elgar.

Cohen, R., and Layton-Henry, Z. (eds.) (1997) *The Politics of Migration*, Cheltenham, UK: E. Elgar.

Colley, L. (1992) *Britons: Forging the Nation, 1707–1837*, New Haven: Yale University Press.

Connor, W. (1994) *Ethnonationalism: The Quest for Understanding*, Princeton, N.J.: Princeton University Press.

Daalder, H. (1971) "On Building Consociational Nations: The Case of the Netherlands and Switzerland," *International Social Science Journal* 23: 355–370.

Dahrendorf, R. (1959) *Class and Class Conflict in Industrial Society*. London: Routledge.

Damian, N., and Rosenbaum-Tamari, Y. (1993) "Attitudes of the Israeli public toward immigration" in *Soviet Jewry in Transition* 178–183. (Hebrew)

Dawidowicz, L.S. (1981) *The Holocaust and the Historians*, Cambridge, Mass.: Harvard University Press.

De Levita, D.J. (1965) *The Concept of Identity*, New York: Basic Books.

Denzin, N.K. (1991) *Images of Postmodern Society: Social Theory and Contemporary Cinema*. London: Sage.

Deshen, S. (1999) "The religiosity of North African and Middle-Eastern Jews" in Haaz, H. (ed.) *Leisure Culture in Israel—1998, Panim* 10: 107–139. (Hebrew)

Donitsa-Schmidt, S. (1999) *Language Maintenance or Shift—Determinants of Language Choice among Soviet Immigrants in Israel*, doctoral dissertation, University of Toronto: Ontario Institute for Studies in Education.

Don-Yehiya, E. (1991) "Solidarity and Autonomy in Israel-Diaspora Relations" in Don-Yehiya, E. (ed.) *Israel and Diaspora Jewry: Ideological and Political Perspectives, Comparative Jewish Politics*, vol. 3: 9–27.

—— (1993) "The book and the sword: the nationalist yeshivot and political radicalism in Israel" in Marty, M.E., and Appleby, R.S. (eds.), *Accounting for Fundamentalisms: The Dynamic Character of Movements*, Chicago and London: University of Chicago Press.

Dorian, N. (ed.) (1989) *Investigating Obsolescence: Studies in Language Contraction and Death*. Cambridge: Cambridge University Press.

Doubnow, S. (1970) *Nationalism and History*, New York: Atheneum.

—— (1976) *History of the Jews in Russia and Poland*. Philadelphia: Jewish Publication Society of America.

Dumont, L. (1977) *Homo hierarchicus—Le systeme des castes et ses implications*, Paris: Gallimard.

—— (1983) *Essai sur l'individualisme*, Paris: Le Seuil.

Early, G. (ed.) (1994) *Lure and Loathing: Essays on Race, Identity and the Ambivalence of Assimilation*, New York: Penguin Books.

Edwards J. (1988) *Language, Society and Identity*. Oxford: Blackwell.

Eisenstadt, S.N. (1966) *Modernization: Protest and Change*. Englewood Cliffs, N.J.: Prentice Hall.

—— (1992) *Jewish Civilization: The Jewish Historical Experience in a Comparative Perspective*, Albany: State University of New York Press.

—— (1999) *Fundamentalism, Sectarianism and Revolution: The Jacobin Dimension of Modernity*. Cambridge: Cambridge University Press.

—— (2000) "Multiple Modernities," *Daedalus* 129(1): 1–29.

—— (2001) "The Vision of Modern and Contemporary Society" in Ben-Rafael, E., and Sternberg, Y. (eds.) *Identity, Culture and Globalization*, Boston: Brill.

—— (2003) *Comparative Civilizations & Multiple Modernities*, 2 volumes. Leiden and Boston: Brill.

Elias, N. (1998) "Civilization, Culture and Identity" in Rundell, J., and Mennell,

S. (eds.), *Classical Readings in Culture and Civilization.* London: Routledge and Kegan Paul.

Ellenson, D. (1989) *Tradition in Transition: Orthodoxy, Halakhah, and the Boundaries of Modern Jewish Identity*, Lanham, Md.: University Press of America.

Elon, A. (1971) *The Israeli Founders and Sons.* New York: Holt Rinehart and Winston.

Employment Office, 10/2000, *2000 Statistic*, Jerusalem: Ministry of Labor.

Encyclopedia Judaica (2002) Jerusalem: Judaica Multimedia, CS-ROM edition.

Eriksen, T.H. (1993) *Ethnicity and Nationalism*, London: Pluto Press.

Evron, B. (1995) *Jewish State or Israeli Nation*, Bloomington: Indiana University Press.

Fackenheim, E. (1992) *Judaïsme au présent*, Paris: Albin Michel.

Farago, U. (1989) "The Jewish identity of Israeli youth, 1965–1985," *Hahadut Zmanenu: Contemporary Jewry*, 5: 259–285.

Fasold, R. (1987) *The Sociolinguistics of Society*, Oxford: Blackwell.

Featherstone, M. (1995) *Undoing Culture: Globalization, Postmodernism and Identity*, London: Sage.

Feige, M. (1999) "Yesha is here, territories are there: Scientific practices and space constitution in Israel," *Teoria Ubikoret 14*: 111–131. (Hebrew)

Friedman, J. (1994) *Cultural Identity and Global Process.* London: Sage.

Friedman, M. (1986) "Haredim confront the modern city," *Studies in Contemporary Jewry* 2: 74–96.

—— (1990) "Jewish zealots: Conservative versus innovative," in Sivan, E., and Friedman, M. (eds.) *Religious Radicalism and Politics in the Middle East*, Albany: State University of New York Press.

Friedman, R. (2004) *The New Holy Revolt*, Tel-Aviv: Tel-Aviv University, Department of Sociology.

Friesel, E. (1994) "The Holocaust as a factor in contemporary Jewish consciousness" in Webber, J. (ed.), *Jewish Identities in the New Europe*, Oxford: Littman Library.

Fröbel, F., Heinrichs, J., and Kreye, O. (2000) "The New International Division of Labor in the World Economy" in Timmons Roberts, J., and Hite, A. (eds.) *From Modernization to Globalization: Perspectives on Development and Social Change*, Oxford: Blackwell.

Furet, F. (1995) *Le passé d'une illusion: Essai sur l'idée communiste au XXe siècle.* Paris: Clamann-Levy.

Furstenberg, R. (1995) "Israeli culture," *American Jewish Yearbook*, 1995: 448–465.

Ganam, A., and Ginat, Y. (1995) "The Arab minority of Israel—1967–1991," *Ha-Mizrakh He-Khadash*, 11(7): 246–250. (Hebrew)

Gans, H.J. (1979) "Symbolic Ethnicity: The Future of Ethnic Group and Cultures in America," *Ethnic and Racial Studies* 2: 1–20.

Geertz, C. (1963) "The Integrative Revolution" in Geertz, C. (ed.) *Old Societies and New States*, New York: Free Press.

—— (1973) *The Interpretation of Cultures*, New York: Basic Books.

Gellner, E. (1983) *Nations and Nationalism*, Ithaca, New York: Cornell University Press.

—— (1994) *Encounters with Nationalism.* Oxford: Blackwell.

Giddens, A. (1980) *The Class Structure of the Advanced Societies*, London: Hutchinson.

—— (1987) "Structuralism, post-structuralism and the production of culture" in Giddens, A., and Turner, J. (eds.) *Social Theory Today*, Oxford: Blackwell.

—— (1991) *Modernity and Self-Identity.* Cambridge: Polity Press.

Gilad, N. (forthcoming) *The story of Yesha*, doctoral dissertation, Tel-Aviv: Tel-Aviv University.

Gittelman, Z. (1994) "Soviet-Jewish Identity in a Period of Transition" in *Soviet Jewry in Transition* 16: 148–154.

—— (2003) "The meanings of Jewishness in Russia and Ukraine" in Ben-Rafael, E., Gorny, Y. and Ro'I, Y. (eds.) *Contemporary Jewries: Convergence and Divergence*, Leiden and Boston: Brill.

Glazer, N., and Moynihan, P. (1974) *Beyond the Melting Pot*, Cambridge, Mass.: MIT Press.

Glinert, L. (1990) "The historiography of Hebrew and the Negation of the Golah," SOAS Language Revival Conference, London, 7–8 June.

Gold, S.G. (1995) "Soviet Jews in the United States," *Soviet Jewry in Transition* 17: 70–85.

Goldberg, G. (1993) "Gush Emunim new settlements in the West Bank: From social movement to regional interest group," in Ben Zadok, E. (ed.) *Local Communities in Israeli Polity*, New York: State University of New York Press.

Goldberg, G., and Ben-Zadok, A. (1983). "Regionalism and a territorial cleavage in the making: Jewish settlement in the territories," *Medina, Mimshal Ve-Yechasim Benleumiim*, 21: 69–94. (Hebrew)

Gorny, Y. (1987) *Zionism and the Arabs, 1882–1948: A Study of Ideology*, Oxford: Clarendon.

Gorny, J. (1990) *The quest for a national identity*, Tel-Aviv: Am Oved. (Hebrew)

—— (1998) *Between Auschwitz and Jerusalem*, Tel-Aviv: Am Oved. (Hebrew)

Goulborne, H. (1991) *Ethnicity and Nationalism in Post Industrial Britain*, Cambridge: Cambridge University Press.

Grillo, R.D. (1989) *Dominant Languages: Language and Hierarchy in Britain and in France*, Cambridge: Cambridge University Press.

Groman, Sh. (1999) "The Map of the New Russian-Jewish Exodus," *ICPA-2. Information Bulletin of 2nd International Conference on Personal Absorption of Jewish Immigrants (Repatriates) from the Former USSR*, No. 1 (2 November). (Russian)

Guarnizo, L.E., and Smith, M.G. (1998) "The Locations of Transnationalism" in Smith, M.P., and Guarnizo, L.E. (eds.) *Transnationalism from Below*, New Brunswick: Transaction.

Gudkov, L. (2000) "The Attitude Toward the Jews in Russia, on the Basis of Data from Sociological Studies in 1990–1998," *Soviet Jewry in Transition* 19: 231–249.

Guibernau, M. (1996) *Nationalisms: The Nation-State and Nationalism in the Twentieth Century*, Cambridge: Polity Press.

Gumperz, J.J. (1967) "Linguistic Markers of Bilingual Communication," *Journal of Social Issues* 23: 137–153.

Guy, G.R. (1989) "Language and social class" in Newmeyer, F.J. (ed.) *Linguistics: The Cambridge Survey IV: Language: The Socio-cultural Context*, Cambridge: Cambridge University Press.

Haarmann, H. (1986) *Language in Ethnicity—A View of Basic Ecological Relations*, Berlin: Mouton de Gruyter.

Habermas, J. (1981) "Modernity versus Postmodernity," *New German Critique* 22 (Winter): 3–14.

Halevy, H. (1981) *Social Distance among Ethnic Groups in Israel*, Haifa: Department of Sociology. (Hebrew)

Hall, S. (1994) "The question of cultural identity" in *The Polity Reader in Cultural Theory*, Cambridge: Polity Press.

—— (1996) "New Ethnicities" in Morley, D., and Chen, K.H. (eds.) *Stuart Hall: Critical Dialogues in Cultural Studies*, London: Routledge.

—— (2000) "The Question of Cultural Identity" in Nash, K. (ed.) *Readings in Contemporary Political Sociology*, Oxford: Blackwell.

Hannerz, U. (1996) *Transnational Connections. Culture, People, Places*, London: Routledge.

Harvey, D. (1989) *The Condition of Postmodernity*. Oxford: Blackwell.

—— (2000) "Capitalism: The Factory of Fragmentation" in Timmons Roberts, J., and Hite, A. (eds.) *From Modernization to Globalization: Perspectives on Development and Social Change*. Oxford: Blackwell.

Haugen, E. (1989) "The rise and fall of an immigrant language—Norwegian in America" in Dorian, N. (ed.) *Investigating Obsolescence: Studies in Language Contradiction and Death*, Cambridge: Cambridge University Press.

Heideking, J. (2002) "The discourse on modernity in the United States" in Ben-Rafael, E., and Sternberg, Y. (eds.) *op. cit.*

Held, D. (2000) "Regulating Globalization? The Reinvention of Politics," *International Sociology* 15(2): 394–408.

Herman, S.J. (1988) *Jewish Identity: A Social Psychological Perspective*, New Brunswick: Transaction.

Hervieu-Léger, D. (1998) "The transmission and formation of socioreligious identities in modernity," *International Sociology* 13(2): 213–228.

Hirschfeld, P. (2000) *Oslo: A Formula for Peace, From Negotiations to Implementation*. Tel-Aviv: Am Oved. (Hebrew)

Hobsbawm, E., and Ranger, T. (1983) *The Invention of Tradition*, Cambridge: Cambridge University Press.

Hofman, J.E., and Fisherman, H. (1972) "Language shift and language maintenance in Israel" in Fishman, J.A. (ed.) *Advances in the Sociology of Language* 2, The Hague: Mouton.

Hollinger, D.A. (1995) *Post-ethnic America: Beyond Multiculturalism*, New York: Basic Books.

Horowitz Donald (1985) *Ethnic Group and Conflict*, Berkeley: University of California Press.

Horowitz, N. (1996) "The national ultra-Orthodox: New figures in Israeli politics," *Mifneh* 14: 25–30. (Hebrew)

Horowitz, Sh. (1990) "The 'Kehilati' (communal) model: A new component in the settlement array," *Tichnun Svivati 44–45*: 25–34. (Hebrew)

Horowitz, T. (1989) *The Soviet Man in an Open Society*, Lantham: University Press of America.

Horowitz, T., and Leshem, E. (1998) "Soviet immigrants in Israel's cultural space" in Sikron, M., and Leshem, E. (eds.) *A Portrait of the Immigration*, Jerusalem: Magness. (Hebrew)

Hutchinson, J., and Smith, A.D. (eds.) (1996) *Ethnicity*, Oxford and New York: Oxford University Press.

ICBS (Israel Central Bureau of Statistics) (1988; 1989; 1999) *Statistical Abstract of Israel*. Jerusalem.

Inglehart, R. (1997) *Modernization and Postmodernization*, Princeton: Princeton University Press.

Jacobson, D. (1996) *Rights Across Borders: Immigration and the Decline of Citizenship*, Baltimore, Md.: Johns Hopkins University Press.

Jenkins, B., and Sofos, S. (eds.) (1996) "Introduction" in *Nation and Identity in Contemporary Europe*, London: Routledge.

Kagansky, M. (1999) Paper presented at the 2nd International Conference on Personal Absorption of Jewish Immigrants (Repatriates) from the Former USSR, 2 November.

Katriel, T. (1986) *Talking Straight: Dugri Speech in Israeli Sabra Culture*, Cambridge: Cambridge University Press.

Katz, E. (1997) "Behavioral and Phenomenological Jewishness" in Liebman, C.S. and Katz, E. (eds.) *The Jewishness of Israelis*, New York: State University of New York Press.

Katz, J. (1960) *Between Jews and Gentiles*. Jerusalem: Bialik Institute. (Hebrew)

Kemp, A., Rajman, R., Resnik, J., and Schammah, G.S. (2000) "Contesting the limits of political participation: Latinos and black African migrant workers in Israel," *Ethnic and Racial Studies* 23(1): 94–119.

Khanin, V. (2003) "Russian Jews in Israel," paper presented at the *New Israeli Elites Seminar*, Tel-Aviv University.

Kimmerling, B. (2001) *The Invention and Decline of Israeliness: State, Society and the Military*, Berkeley: University of California Press.

——— (2004) *Immigrants, Settlers, Natives: The Israeli State and Society between Cultural Pluralism and Cultural Wars*, Tel-Aviv: Am Oved. (Hebrew)

Kincheloe, J.L., and Steinberg, Sh.R. (1997) *Changing Multiculturalism*. Buckingham and Philadelphia: Open University Press.

Kraemer, R., Zizenwine, D., Levy-Keren, M., and Schers, D. (1995) "Study of Jewish Adolescent Russian Immigrants in Israel: Language and Identity," *International Journal of the Sociology of Language* 116: 153–159.

Krausz, E., and Tulea, G. (eds.) (1998) *Jewish Survival: The Identity Problem at the Close of the Twentieth Century*, New Brunswick and London: Transaction.

Kuper, L. (1965) *An African Bourgeoisie: Race, Class and Politics in South Africa*, New Haven, Conn.: Yale University Press.

Kupovetsky, M. (2000) "Jews of the Former Soviet Union: Population and Geographical Dispersion" in Dymerskaya-Tsigelman, L. (ed.), *Soviet Jewry in Transition*. 4(19): 134. (Hebrew)

Lal, B.B. (1983) "Perspectives on Ethnicity: Old Wine in New Bottles," *Ethnic and Racial Studies* 6: 154–173.

Landau, J.M. (1969) *The Arabs in Israel: A Political Study*, London: Oxford University Press.

—— (1993) *The Arab Minority in Israel, 1967–1991: Political Aspects*, Oxford: Clarendon Press.

Lerer, M. (1996) "There is nothing more permanent than a temporary worker," *Industries*, 257: 17–18.

Leshem, E. (1993) "The Israeli population and its attitude toward immigrants of the 1990s," *Bitakhon Sotsiali*, 40: 54–73.

Leshem, A., and Sicron, N. (1998) "Processes of Absorption of Immigrants from the Former Soviet Union, 1990–1995: Main Findings" in Sicron, M., and Leshem, A. (eds.) *A Portrait of Immigration*, Jerusalem: Magnes.

Levy, Sh. (1996) *Values and Jewishness of Israeli Youth*, Jerusalem: Guttman Institute.

Levy, Sh., and Guttman, L. (1976) "Zionism and Jewishness of Israelis," *Forum*, 1(24): 39–50.

Levy, Sh., Levinsohn, H., and Katz, E. (1997) "Beliefs, Observances and Social Interaction among Israeli Jews: The Guttman Institute Report" in Liebman, C.S., and Katz, E. (eds.) *op. cit.*

Lewin, K. (1948) *Resolving Social Conflicts: Selected Papers on Group Dynamics*, New York: Harper.

Lewin-Epstein, N., Menahem, G., and Barham, R. (1993) "Immigration yes, immigrants as well? Attitudes of Tel-Aviv/Jaffa inhabitants toward the absorption of immigrants" in Nahmias, D., and Menahem, G. (eds.) *Tel-Aviv/Jaffa Research: Social Processes and Public Policy*, Tel-Aviv: Tel-Aviv University. (Hebrew)

Lewinson, H. (1995) *Jews and Arabs in Israel: Common Values and Mutual Images*, Jerusalem: Sikui. (Hebrew)

Lewis, B. (2003) *What Went Wrong?: The Clash between Islam and Modernity in the Middle East*. New York: Perennial.

Liciczia, S. (forthcoming) *Russian Jews in Israel*, doctoral dissertation, Tel-Aviv University.

Liebkind, K. (1989) "Conceptual approaches to ethnic identity" in Liebkind, K. (ed.) *New Identities in Europe*, Aldershot, UK: Gower.

Liebman, C. (2003) "Unraveling the ethnic package" in Ben-Rafael, E., Gorny, Y., and Ro'I, Y. (eds.) *Contemporary Jewries: Convergence and Divergence*, Leiden and Boston: Brill.

Liebman, C.S. (1997a) "Religion and Modernity: The Special Case of Israel" in Liebman, C.S., and Katz, E. (eds.) *The Jewishness of Israelis*, New York: State University of New York Press.

—— (1997b) "Cultural Conflict in Israeli Society" in Liebman, C.S., and Katz, E. (eds.) *op. cit.*

—— (1992) "Jewish fundamentalism and the Israeli polity", in Marty, M.E., and

Appleby, S. (eds.) *Fundamentalism Comprehended*. Chicago and London: University of Chicago.

Liebman, C.S., and Don-Yehiya, E. (1984) *Religion and Politics in Israel*, Bloomington: Indiana University Press.

Lipschitz, H., and Noam, G. (1996) *The Insertion of Ethiopian Immigrants in Universities and Colleges*, Jerusalem: Joint and Brookdale Institute. (Hebrew)

Lipset, S.M. (1967) *The First New Nation*, New York: Anchor Books.

Lissak, M. (1995) "Immigrants from the FSU between separation and insertion" in Kop, Y. (ed.) *Allocation of Resources for Social Services, 1994–1995*, Jerusalem: Center for Social Policy in Israel. (Hebrew)

—— (1996) "'Critical' sociology and 'establishment' sociology in the Israeli academic community: Ideological struggles or academic discourse," *Israel Studies* 1: 247–294.

Luhmann, N. (1990) "The Paradox of System Differentiation and the Evolution of Society" in Alexander, J., and Colomy, P. (eds.) *Differentiation Theory and Social Change*, New York: Columbia University Press.

Manlin, J., Vaughan, C., and Ensel, W.M. (1981) "Social resources and occupational status attainment," *Social Forces*, 59(4): 00–00.

Markowitz, F. (1993) *A Community in Spite of Itself: Soviet Jewish Emigres in New York*, Washington: Smithonian Institution Press.

Martiniello, M. (1994) "Citizenship of the European Union: A Critical View" in Baubock, R. (ed.) *From Aliens to Citizens: Redefining the Status of Immigrants in Europe*, Avebury: Aldershot.

Marx, A.W. (2003) *Faith in Nation: Exclusionary Origins of Nationalism*, Oxford: University Press.

Mautner, M., Sagui, A., and Shamir, R. (eds.) (1998) *Multiculturalism in a Democratic and Jewish State*, Tel-Aviv: Ramot. (Hebrew)

McMichael, P. (2000) "Globalization: Myths and Realities" in Timmons Roberts, J., and Hite, A. (eds.) *op. cit.*

Meyer, H.D. (2000) "Taste formation in pluralistic societies: The role of rhetorics and institutions," *International Sociology*, 15(1): 33–56.

Meyer, J.W. (2000) "Globalization: Sources and Effects on National States and Societies," *International Sociology* 15(2): 233–248.

Meyer, John W., Boli, J., Thomas, G., and Raminez, F. (1997) "World Society and the Nation-State," *American Journal of Sociology* 103: 144–181.

Miller, M.J. (1989) "Political participation and representation of noncitizens" in Brubaker, W.R. (ed.) *op. cit.*

Milroy, L. (1989) *Language and Social Networks*. Oxford: Blackwell.

Mittleman, A.L. (1996) *The Politics of Torah: The Jewish Political Tradition and the Founding of Agudat Israel*, Albany: State University of New York Press.

Morris, B. (1987) *The Birth of the Palestinian Refugee Problem, 1947–1949*, Cambridge: Cambridge University Press.

Naim, G., Benita, A., and Wolfson, M. (1997) *Neighbors Integrate: The Relations between Ethiopian Immigrants and their Neighbors*, Jerusalem: Joint and Brookdale Institute. (Hebrew)

Nakhleh, K. (1975) "Cultural determinants of collective identity—The case of the Arabs in Israel," *New Outlook*, 18(7): 31–40.

Niznick, M. (2003) "The dilemma of Russian-born adolescents in Israel" in Ben-Rafael, E., et al. (eds) *Contemporary Jewries: Convergence and Divergence*, Leiden: Brill, 235–254.

Nudelman, R. (1997) "In Search of Ourselves," *Soviet Jewry in Transition* 18: 19–40.

Ochana, D. (1998) *The Last Israelis*, Tel-Aviv: Ha-kibboutz Ha-meoukhad. (Hebrew)

Olzak, S. (1983) "Contemporary Ethnic Mobilization," *Annual Review of Sociology* 9: 355–74.

Ong, A. (1996) "Cultural citizenship and subject-making: Immigrants negotiate racial and cultural boundaries in the United States," *Current Anthropology*, 37(5): 737–762.

Orans, M. (1971) "Caste and Race Conflict in Cross-Cultural Perspective" in Orleans, P., and Russell, W.E. (eds.) *Race, Change and Urban Society*, Beverly Hills: Sage.

Oron, A. (1993) *The Jewish Israeli Identity*, Tel-Aviv: Sifryat Hapoalim. (Hebrew)

Orr, A. (1994) *Israel: Politics, Myths and Identity Crises*, London: Pluto Press.

Otzki-Lezer, S., and Ganem, A. (1995) *Between Peace and Equality: Arabs in Israel at Mid-term of the Labor-Meretz Government*, Givat Haviva: Givat Haviva Center for Peace.

Parkin, F. (1974) "Strategies of social closure in class formation" in Parkin, F. (ed.) *The Social Analysis of Class Structure*, London: Tavistock.

—— (1979) *Marxism and Class Theory: A Bourgeois Critique*, New York: Columbia University Press.

Parsons, T. (1975) "Some Theoretical Considerations on the Nature and Trends of Change of Ethnicity" in Glazer, N., and Moynihan, D.P. (eds.) *Ethnicity: Theory and Experience*, Cambridge, Mass: Harvard University Press, 53–83.

Peres, Y. (1986) *Ethnic relations in Israel*, Tel-Aviv: Sifryat Hapoalim (2d edition). (Hebrew)

Peres, Y., and S. Shemer (1984) "The ethnic factor in the elections for the 10th Knesset," *Megamot* 28: 316–331.

Peri, Y. (1998) *Military-Society Relations in Crisis*. Paper presented to the 29th Conference of the Israel Sociological Association, Haifa, February. (Hebrew)

Raday, F., and Bunk, E. (1993) *Integration of Russian Immigrants into the Israeli Labour Market*, Jerusalem: Hebrew University Sacher Institute for Legislative Research and Comparative Law. (Hebrew)

Rajman, R., and Kemp, A. (2002) "State and nonstate actors: A multilayered analysis of labor migration policy" in Korn, D. (ed.) *Public Policy in Israel*, Lexington, Ky.: Lexington Books.

Ram, U. (1995) *The Changing Agenda of Israeli Sociology: Theory, Ideology and Identity*, Albany: State University of New York.

Ravitzky, A. (1993) *Messianism, Zionism and Jewish religious radicalism*, Tel-Aviv: Am Oved. (Hebrew)

Rekhess, E. (ed.) (1996) *Arab Politics in Israel at a Crossroads*, Tel-Aviv: Dayan Center for Middle Eastern Studies, Tel-Aviv University.

Rex, J. (1996) *Ethnic Minorities in the Modern Nation State*, Warwick, UK: Centre for Research in Ethnic Relations.

Ritterband, P. (1997) "Jewish Identity among Russian Immigrants in the US" in Lewin-Epshtein, N., Roi, Y., and Ritterband, P. (eds.) *Russian Jews on Three Continents*, London: Frank Cass.

Robertson, R. (1992) *Globalization: Social Theory and Global Culture*, London: Sage.

Robinson, R.V., and Kelley, J. (1979) "Classes conceived by Marx and Dahrendorf," *ASR*, 44(1): 38–58.

Romaine, S. (1989) *Bilingualism*, Oxford: Blackwell.

Rosenbaum-Tamari, J., and Demiam, N. (1996) *Five Years of Initial Absorption of Immigrants from the Former USSR (1990–1995): Report No. 9*, Jerusalem: Israel Ministry of Immigrant Absorption.

Rosenfeld, H. (1978) "The class situation of the Arab national minority in Israel," *Comparative Studies in Society and History*, 20: 374–407.

Rothenberg, V. (2000) "Self-Identity of Jews from the Former Soviet Union in Israel," *Soviet Jewry in Transition* 19: 213–220.

Rouhana, N. (1997) *Palestinian Citizens in an Ethnic Jewish State: Identities in Conflict*, New Haven and London: Yale University Press.

Rubin, B. (1995) *Assimilation and its Discontents*. New York: Times Books/Random House.

Rubinstein, A. (1977) *Lihiot am khofchi (To Be a Free People)*, Tel-Aviv: Schockan.
—— (1980) *From Herzl to Gush Emunim*, Jerusalem: Shokan.
—— (1997) *From Herzl to Rabin and Later: 100 Years of Zionism*, Tel-Aviv: Shockan. (Hebrew)
Sahlins, P. (1989) *Boundaries: The Making of France and Spain in the Pyrenees*, Berkeley: University of California Press.
Sankoff, D. (1980) "Language use in multilingual societies: Some alternate approaches" in Sankoff, D. (ed.) *The Social Life of Language*, Philadelphia: University of Pennsylvania Press.
—— (1989) "Sociolinguistics and syntactic variation" in Newmeyer, F.J. (ed.) *Linguistics: The Cambridge Survey IV—Language: The Socio-Cultural Context*, Cambridge: Cambridge University Press.
Schama, S. (1989) *Citizens, Civic Values*, New York: Knopf.
Schatzki, T.R. (1996) *Social Practices: A Wittgensteinian Approach to Human Activity and the Social*, Cambridge: Cambridge University Press.
Schnapper, D. (1991) *La France de l'intégration*, Paris: Gallimard.
—— (1994) *La communauté des citoyens: Sur l'idée moderne de nation*, Paris: NRF-Gallimard.
—— (1994a) "The debate on immigration and the crisis of national identity" in Baldwin-Edwards, M., and Schain, M. (eds.) *The Politics of Immigration in Western Europe*, Essex: Frank Cass.
Segal, Ch. (1987) *Dear Brothers*. Jerusalem: Keter. (Hebrew)
Semyonov M., and Lewin-Epstein N. (1987) *Hewers of Wood and Drawers of Water*. Ithaca, N.Y.: Cornell Institute of Labor Studies.
Semyonov, M., et al. (forthcoming) *The Impact of the Income of Migrant Workers in the Philippinian Society*, The Hague: NIRP-Nuffic.
Shabtai, M. (2001) "To Live with a Threatened Identity: Life Experience with Skin Color Difference among Ethiopian Youngsters and Adults," *Megamot*, 41(1–2): 97–112. (Hebrew)
Shafer B.C. (1972) *Faces of Nationalism: New Realities and Old Myths*, New York: Harcourt Brace Jovanovich Inc.
Shafir, G. (1984) "Changing nationalism and Israel's 'open frontier' on the West Bank," *Theory and Society*, 13(6): 803–827.
Shalev, M. (1992) *Labour and the Political Economy in Israel*, Oxford: Oxford University Press.
—— (1996) "Time for theory: Critical notes on Lissak and Sternhell," *Israel Studies* 2:
Shamir, M., and Arian, A. (1999) "Collective Identity and Electoral Competition in Israel," *American Political Science Review* 93(2): 265.
Shapira, Y. (1996) *A Society Jailed by Politicians*, Tel-Aviv: Sifryat Hapoalim. (Hebrew)
Sheleg, Y. (2000) *The New Religious Jews*, Jerusalem: Keter. (Hebrew)
Shils, E. (1956) *The Torment of Secrecy*, London: Heinemann.
Shokeid, M. (1985) "Cultural ethnicity in Israel: The case of Middle Eastern Jews' religiosity" *AJS Review* 9: 247–271.
Sikron, M. (1990) "Human Capital of Immigration and Processes of Immigrants' Occupational Integration" in Sikron, M., and Leshem, E. (eds.), *A Portrait of Immigration*, Jerusalem: Magnes.
Silberstein, L.J. (1996) "Cultural Criticism, Ideology and the Interpretation of Zionism: Toward a Post-Zionist Discourse" in Kepnes, S. (ed.) *Interpreting Judaism in a Postmodern Age*, New York: New York University Press.
Slutsky, B. (1999) "Evreiskoye Schast'ye," *Vesty-Okna* (Tel Aviv), 11 November. (Russian)
Smith, A.D. (1981) *The Ethnic Revival*, Cambridge: Cambridge University Press.
—— (1987) *The Ethnic Origins of Nations*, Oxford: Blackwell.
—— (1991) *National Identity*. Reno, Nev.: University of Nevada Press.
—— (1998) *Nationalism and Modernism: A Critical Survey of Recent Theories of Nations and Nationalism*. London: Routledge.

Smith, B. (1994) *Classifying the Universe: The Ancient Indian Varna System and the Origins of Caste*, New York: Oxford University Press.

Smooha, S. (1972) *Israel Pluralism and Conflict*, London: Routledge and Kegan P.

—— (1976) "Arabs and Jews in Israel Minority-Majority Relations," *Megamot 22(4)*: 397–424. (Hebrew)

—— (1992) *Arabs and Jews in Israel: Conflicting and Shared Attitudes in a Divided Society*, Boulder, Colo.: Westview.

Solodkina, M. (1995) "Non-Material Factors and Their Effect on Immigrant Absorption," *Soviet Jewry in Transition* 17: 166–175.

Soysal, Y. (1994) *Limits of Citizenship*. Chicago: University of Chicago Press.

—— (2000) "Citizenship and Identity: Living in Diasporas in Post-war Europe," *Ethnic and Racial Studies* 23(1): 1–15.

Spolsky, B., and Shohamy, E. (1999) *The Languages of Israel: Policy, Ideology and Practice*. Clevedon: Multilingual Matters.

Sprinzak, E. (1989) "The emergence of the Israeli radical right," *Comparative Politics*, 21(2): 171–192.

—— (1998) "Extremism and violence in Israel: The crisis of messianic politics," *Annals of the American Academy of Political and Social Sciences* 555: 114–126.

Stille, A. (2003) "Historians Trace an Unholy Alliance: Religion and Nationalism," *NY Times*: New York.

Tamir, Y. (1993) *Liberal Nationalism*. Princeton, N.J.: Princeton University Press.

Taylor, C. (1994) "The Politics of Recognition" in Taylor, C., et al., *Multiculturalism. Examining the Politics of Recognition*. Princeton, N.J.: Princeton University Press.

—— (1994a) *Multiculturalism*, Princeton, N.J.: Princeton University Press.

—— (1998) *Les sources du moi*, Montreal: Boréal.

Touraine, A. (1992) *Critique de la modernité*, Paris: Fayard.

——. (1997) *Pourrons-nous vivre ensemble?* Paris: Le Seuil.

Treiman, K.J. (1977) *Occupational Prestige in Comaprative Perspective*, NYU, London: Academic Press.

Troen, I.S., and Bade, K.J. (eds.) (1991) *Returning Home: Immigration and Absorption into their Homelands of Germans and Jews from the Former Soviet Union*, Beer Sheva: Humphrey Institute for Social Ecology, Ben-Gurion University of the Negev.

Tsfati, Y. (1999) "The ethnic devil in Israel: In the bottle and on small fire," *Megamot*, 1: 1–30. (Hebrew)

Turner, B.S. (1991) *Religion and Social Theory*. London: Sage.

Vujacica, V. (online 2002) "Nationalism, Sociology of," *International Encyclopedia of the Social & Behavioral Sciences*.

Walzer, M. (1981) "The distribution of membership" in Brown, P., and Shue, H. (eds.) *Boundaries: National Autonomy and its Limits*, N.J.: Rowman and Littlefield.

Weber, M. (1958) "The Social Psychology of the World Religions" in Gerth, H.H., and Mills, C.W. (eds.) *From Max Weber: Essays in Sociology*, New York: Oxford University Press.

Weber, M. (1978) "Ethnic groups" in Roth, G., and Wittrich, C. (eds.) *Economy and Society*, Vol. 1, Berkeley and Los Angeles: University of California Press.

Weil, Sh. (1997) *Ethiopian High School Graduates of the Educational System in Israel, 1987–1989: Past, Present and Future*, Jerusalem: School of Education, Hebrew University.

Weinberg, Y. (2002) "Letter to Ben-Gurion" in Ben-Rafael, E., *Jewish Identities: Fifty Intellectuals Answer Ben-Gurion*, Leiden and Boston: Brill.

Weingrod, A. (1990) *The Saint of Beersheba*, Albany: State University of New York Press.

Wiener, M. (1996) "Determinants of immigrant integration: An international comparative analysis" in Carmon, N. (ed.) *Immigration and Integration in Post-Industrial Societies: Theoretical Analysis and Policy Related Research*, London: Macmillan Press.

Willett, C. (1998) "Introduction" in Willett, C. (ed.), *Theorizing Multiculturalism: A Guide to the Current Debate*, Oxford: Blackwell.

Withold de Wenden, C. (1994) "Changes in the Franco-Maghrebian association movement" in Rex, J., and Drury, B. (eds.) *Ethnic Mobilization in a Multicultural Europe*, Avebury, UK: Aldershot.

Wittgenstein, L. (1961) *Tractatus logico-philosophicus*, suivi de *Investigations philosophiques*, Paris: Gallimard.

Wittrock, B. (2002) "Rethinking Modernity" in Ben-Rafael, E., and Sternberg, Y. (eds.) *Identity, Culture and Globalization*, Leiden and Boston: Brill.

Wolfsfeld, G. (1997) "Competing frames of the Oslo Accords: A chance for peace or a national disaster?" in Wolfsfeld, G. (ed.) *Media and Political Conflict: News from the Middle East*. Cambridge: Cambridge University Press.

Wright, E.O. (1985) *Classes*, London: Verson.

Yaar, E., and Herman, T. (2001–2004) *Monthly Peace Index*, Tel-Aviv: Steinmetz Center, Tel-Aviv University.

Yaar, E., and Shavit, Z. (eds.) (2001) *Tendencies in the Israeli Society*, Tel-Aviv: Open University. (Hebrew)

Yalma, Sh. (1980) *The Way to Jerusalem*, Tel-Aviv: Reshafim. (Hebrew)

Yaniv, M. (1998) *Collective Identity and Personal and Collective Image and the Link to the Jewish-Arab Divide*, Ramat-Gan: Khamul. (Hebrew)

Yanovitzky, Y. (1996) *The attitudes of the Jewish settlers in the West Bank and Gaza towards law and democracy in Israel, 1980–1994*. Haifa: M.A. thesis in the Department of Sociology and Anthropology. (Hebrew).

Yuchtman-Yaar, E. and Peres, Y. (1998) *Between Consent and Dissent: Democracy and Peace in the Israeli Mind*. New York: Rowman and Littlefeld.

Zilberg, N. (1998) "The Russian-Jewish Intelligentsia in Israel: Quests for New Models of Integration," *Soviet Jewry in Transition* 19: 196–212.

Zilberg, N., and Leshem, A. (1999) "Imaginary Community and Real Community: The Russian-Language Press and the Resumption of Community Life among Former Soviet Immigrants in Israel," *Society and Welfare* 19: 9–37.

INDEX

Abercrombie, N., 9–10
absorption, 131, 154–156. *See also*
  assimilation
acculturation, 13–16, 133–134,
  288–289. *See also* assimilation
Acre, 167
Addis Ababa, 152, 153
Adler, S., 133
advertisements, 78–79, 143–144, 234
African-Americans, 4, 23, 163
Africans, 159, 163, 191
Agudat Yisrael, 84n7, 125
Alef (journal), 35n2
Am Yisrael (People Israel), 61, 108, 124
Amana (organization), 93
Amharic vernacular, 152
Anderson, B., 296
antisemitism, 129–131
Appadurai, A., 16
appreciation, reciprocal, 230–234,
  242–243, 286–287. *See also* social
  distance
Arab-Islamic world, 38, 246, 281
Arab nationalist party, 168
Arab/Palestinian conflict, 251
Arab parties, 168, 247–248, 250, 258
Arabic vernacular, 181, 220, 294
Arabs, 36, 159, 167, 178. *See also*
  Israeli Arabs; Palestinians
Arafat, 96
Arian, A., 251
army. *See* military service
Ashkenazi-Mizrahi cleavage, 40–42,
  47–48, 123–124, 272–274
Ashkenazi Ultra-Orthodox. *See also*
  Ashkenazim; Ultra-Orthodox
  about, 39, 61–64
  concept of *eda*, 110
  Jewish identity of, 268
  and Mizrahim, 125–126
  and political spectrum, 51
  research questions, 52
  socioeconomic standing of, 48
Ashkenazim. *See also* Ashkenazi
  Ultra-Orthodox
  Ashkenazi-Mizrahi cleavage, 40–42,
    47–48, 123–124, 272–274
  bilingualism, 215–218

and central authority, 235
class reality of, 117
cognitive distance of, 210–213
cohesion, openness, and popularity,
  207–210, 214
collective identity of, 70
concept of *eda*, 110
as core group of Israeli society, 219,
  288
education of, 115–117, 229
elections, 120–121
and Ethiopian Jews, 158, 161, 162
ethnicity of, 113–117, 123–124
generation effect, 113, 115
identification of, 113–117, 123, 280
on intermarriage, 117–118
and Israeli Arabs, 173
Israeliness of, 113–117, 272–273,
  288
Jewish identity of, 136, 238,
  241–242, 272–273, 292
Middle Eastern culture, 238–240
and Mizrahi Ultra-Orthodox, 272
and Mizrahim, 47–48, 110–111,
  118–119, 123–124, 272
national identity of, 236–237
political allegiances of, 247, 249,
  251–253, 258
reciprocal appreciation, 230–234
religiosity of, 65–66, 115
and Russian Jews, 136, 138–140,
  280
solidarity among, 214
Western culture, 240
assimilation. *See also* absorption;
  acculturation
  defined, 13–16
  of Israeli Arabs, 183
  of Jews in Russia, 130
  of Mizrahim, 109–110
  of Russian Jews, 132, 133, 147

Balad (political party), 248
Belgium, 23
belligerence, 32, 36–38, 267
Ben-Chaim, L., 85
Ben-Rafael, Eliezer, 113, 124, 144,
  215, 218–219

Beta Israel (the House of Israel), 151–155
biculturalism, 18–19
bilingualism, 144, 213, 215–220, 285, 293–294. *See also* languages
Birobidjan (Siberia), 129
birth rate, 84
Black Hebrews, 163
Black Panthers movement, 118–119
Boehm, Max Hildebert, 289
Bourdieu, P., 205
Britain, 23, 43
Bund, 28

Cairo, 179
Calhoun, C., 245
caliph (al-Sekim), 179
Canaanite ideology, 34–35
Canada, 18, 23
capitalism, 204
caste, 27–28
Castells, M., 245
Castoriadis, C., 204
center-and-periphery setting, 219–221, 285
Center for Assistance and Information for the Foreign Community, 190
central authority, 234–235, 243. *See also* Knesset
Central Europe, 125
Centre of Young Hebrews, 35n2
Chosen People, 27, 30, 152. *See also* Jewish people
Christian Arabs. *See* Arabs; Israeli Arabs; Palestinians
Christianity, 147, 151
cinema, Jewish, 100–101
citizenship
  defined, 187
  approaches to, 245
  and foreign workers, 191, 194, 196, 198
class
  conflicts within, 44–49, 298
  and identity, 279
  reality of, 11–12, 14–15, 33, 117
  stratification of, 12, 45, 47
cleavages
  about, 53–54, 265–266
  Ashkenazi-Mizrahi cleavage, 40–42, 47–48, 123–124, 272–274
  ethnic cleavage, 47–49
  ethnocultural cleavage, 203
  Jewish/Arab cleavage, 47–49

left/right cleavage. *See* left/right cleavage
multiculturalism cleavage, 251–252
national religious cleavage, 98
religious cleavage, 38–40, 64–67, 253–258, 296
social cleavage, 3, 40–42
sociocultural cleavage, 3, 4, 12
socioeconomic cleavage, 44–49, 298
Yesha settlers as, 102–103
clothing, traditional, 7
clusters, formation of, 221, 243–244, 285
coalitions, 250, 259, 285–286, 288
Cochin Jews, 163
coexistence, 16, 284–287
cognitive distance, 210–214, 273, 285
cohesion, internal, 207–210, 214
collective boundaries, 13–16
collective identification. *See* identification
collective identity. *See also* dominant culture; identification
  defined, 6–9, 265
  of Ashkenazim, 70
  assimilation and acculturation, 14
  and cultural orientations, 243–244
  of Druze, 180, 276–277
  of Ethiopian Jews, 157, 162, 260, 275–276
  and ethnicity, 69–70
  facets of, 7–8
  group solidarity and bilingualism, 213
  historical-cultural legacies, 266
  of Israeli Arabs, 170–172, 182–183, 276, 277
  and Jewish identity, 236, 238, 243–244, 268
  of Mizrahim, 70, 123–124, 136
  and multiculturalism, 24
  of nonreligious Jews, 70–71, 297
  religion principle, 296
  religiosity, 80–81
  of religious Jews, 70–71, 297
  residency desires, 66–68
  of Russian Jews, 135–138, 146, 274–275
  of traditional Jews, 70–71
  of Ultra-Orthodox, 61–62, 70–71, 82–84
  of Yesha settlers, 96–98
Colley, L., 21
commitment, 7–8

Communist party, 168
communitarism, 250, 259, 285–286, 288
conflict. *See also* cleavages; conflictual multiculturalism; tension
   with Arab-Islamic world, 246
   in multiculturalism, 205, 225, 244, 259, 285–286
   and religiosity, 72–73, 82, 253–254
conflictual multiculturalism. *See also* multiculturalism rules
   about, 23, 291
   Israel's constellation, 286
   versus liberal multiculturalism, 266, 267, 298
   religion/nationalism link, 147–148, 259–261, 298–299
   and social order, 259–260
conversion, 151, 153–155, 199
cooperation, 223
crisis of self-legitimacy, 100
cultural codes. *See* values
cultural diversity. *See also* others
   asset or burden, 225
   Filipinos on, 194
   as result of immigration, 245
   Russian Jews, 225, 242
   sociocultural groups, 286–287, 292–293
cultural orientations, 238–240, 243–244. *See also* Middle Eastern culture; Western culture
curriculum, 226–229. *See also* education
customs and rites, 152, 163–164, 295
   See also invented traditions

Dahrendorf, R., 204
Declaration of Independence, 38, 167
Degel Hatora, 84n7
Demiam, N., 144
democracy
   foreign workers, 188
   Jewish state, 42–43, 241–242
   multiculturalism, 204, 282–283
   non-Jewish majority, 42–43
   sociocultural groups, 245
   transformation of, 266
   Ultra-Orthodox, 76–77
demonstrations
   by Ethiopian Jews, 153
   during the intifada, 175
   by Mizrahim, 119
   by Ultra-Orthodox youth, 256
   by Yesha settlers, 97

denizenship, 187
diaspora, 18, 28–29, 108–109. See also *mizug galuyot*; transnational diaspora
Diaspora Jewry, 32–33, 90, 205
discrimination
   against Israeli Arabs, 169, 178
   against Mizrahim, 119
   and religiosity, 73
   against Ultra-Orthodox, 82, 269–270
diversity, cultural. *See* cultural diversity
dominant culture. *See also* collective identity
   defined, 9–11, 52
   and cleavages, 265–266
   and collective boundaries, 13–16
   hegemony of, 281–282, 284, 287, 294
   and identification, 280
   immigration, 266–267
   multiculturalism, 5–6, 204, 283–284
   primordialism, 22
   religion/nationalism link, 41–42, 147–148
   religious forces within, 39–40
   and Russian Jews, 275
   tolerance within, 146–147
   and Ultra-Orthodox, 62
Donitsa-Schmidt, S., 144–145
Dorian, N., 13
Druze. *See also* others
   about, 42–43
   Arabic vernacular, 181
   bilingualism, 215, 220, 294
   cognitive distance of, 211–213
   cohesion, openness, and popularity, 207–210
   collective identity of, 180, 276–277
   and Ethiopian Jews, 159, 161
   history of, 178–179
   identification of, 278, 280
   and Israeli Arabs, 178–180
   Israeliness of, 180–181, 276–277
   Middle Eastern culture, 238–240
   military service, 179, 234
   as minority in Israel, 185, 276–278
   between modernization and particularism, 184–185, 277
   multiculturalism, 182
   national identity of, 236–237
   on the periphery of Israeli society, 219
   political allegiances of, 247
   population of, 178
   reciprocal appreciation, 230–234

religion as differentiating factor, 296
religion/nationalism link, 260
research questions, 54
social distance of, 179–180
transnational diaspora, 184–185, 220
Western culture, 240
Dumont, Louis, 28, 291

Eastern Europe, 125, 267
economic challenges, 259
eda concepts, 110
education
  Ashkenazim, 115–117, 229
  Ethiopian Jews, 154–155
  Israeli Arabs, 169, 226n1
  Mizrahim, 115–117
  preferences for, 226–229, 242
  Russian Jews, 131, 226n1
  Ultra-Orthodox, 85, 226n1
Eldad ha-Dani, 153
elections, 62–63, 111–112, 120–121
Elohei/Torat Yisrael (God/Teaching of
  Israel), 28, 61, 108, 124
emancipation, 125
England, 23, 43
English vernacular, 33–34, 50–51,
  216–218, 285, 294
Enlightenment, 28
equality of cultures, 225–226, 242,
  286–287
Eretz Yisrael (Land of Israel)
  concept of, 28–30
  as Mizrahi principle, 108, 124
  and national religious, 88
  and Palestinian state, 272
  as Promised Land, 89, 92
  and religious Jews, 90
  as Ultra-Orthodox principle, 61
  Yesha settler's notion of, 97, 100,
    271
Ethiopia, 151–152
Ethiopian Jews
  attitude toward "others", 157–159,
    161–162
  Beta Israel in Ethiopia, 151–152
  bilingualism, 215
  as Chosen People, 152
  cognitive distance of, 211–213
  cohesion, openness, and popularity,
    207–210
  collective identity of, 157, 162, 260,
    275–276
  conversion to Christianity, 151
  between core and periphery of
    Israeli society, 219

customs and rites of, 152, 163–164
demonstrations by, 153
education and absorption, 154–156
ethnicity of, 156–157, 161
as ethnocultural cleavage, 203
identification of, 156–157, 162, 279,
  280
immigration to Israel, 152–154
Israeliness of, 155, 157, 161
Jewish identity of, 156–157, 159,
  162
military service, 154
and Mizrahim, 158, 161–162,
  275–276
population of, 154
and racism, 162–163, 275
reciprocal appreciation, 161,
  230–234
and religiosity factor, 297
research questions, 53
and Russian Jews, 154, 158–159
as social cleavage, 40–41
social distance of, 157–159
social mobility of, 162
and Ultra-Orthodox, 157, 159,
  161–162, 275
ethnic cleavage, 47–49. *See also*
  Ashkenazi-Mizrahi cleavage
ethnic politics, 235, 243
ethnicity
  of Ashkenazim, 113–117, 123–124
  and collective identity, 69–70
  of Druze, 180, 237
  of Ethiopian Jews, 156–157, 161
  of Filipino workers, 194, 197, 277
  of Israeli Arabs, 170–172, 182–183,
    237
  in Israeli multiculturalism, 285
  of Mizrahi Ultra-Orthodox, 107–108
  of Mizrahim, 113–117, 124, 272–273
  and religiosity, 69–70, 115
  of Russian Jews, 135–138, 144–147,
    148, 274–275, 280
  of sociocultural groups, 3–4
  of Ultra-Orthodox, 69–70
ethnocultural cleavage, 203
ethnocultural identification, 132–133,
  159–161
Europe, 125, 167
European Union, 292
evolution, 266. *See also* transformation
Evron, Boaz, 35
exclusionism, 15, 223
exile, 18, 28–29, 108–109. See also
  mizug galuyot; transnational diaspora

exogamy, 117–118. *See also* marriage
extremism, 93, 103, 255–256

Faitlovitch, Jacob, 151
Falashas. *See* Beta Israel; Ethiopian
  Jews
Falashmura, 154–155, 276
family resemblance, 24–25, 284,
  292–294, 299
Fatimid dynasty of Egypt, 179
Feige, M., 94
feminist movement, 101
festivals, 101
Filipino workers
  about, 43, 189
  attitudes toward Israel, 277
  citizenship, 191, 194, 196, 198
  on cultural diversity, 194
  ethnicity of, 194, 197, 277
  identification of, 197
  influence on society, 198
  as minorities, 198–199
  social distance of, 191–196, 278
  transnational diaspora, 197–198
foreign workers. *See also* Filipino
  workers; others
  about, 43
  bilingualism, 215–216
  citizenship, 191, 194, 196, 198
  class stratification, 45
  cognitive distance of, 211–213
  cohesion, openness, and popularity,
    207–210
  and Ethiopian Jews, 159, 162
  history of, 188–189
  illegal versus legal, 189
  and Jewish state, 189–190, 199
  labor migration, 187
  Latin American, 190
  particularism and community
    activities, 190–191
  on the periphery of Israeli society,
    219
  religion as differentiating factor, 297
  research questions, 54
  Romanian, 43, 189
  self-help organizations, 188, 190–191
  social distance of, 194
  social status improved, 260
  Thai, 43, 189
  transnational diaspora, 220
  West African, 163
former Soviet Union (FSU), 129–131,
  142–143
France, 43, 289–290

French Revolution, 289
Friedman, Jonathan, 17
Friedman, R., 100–103
Fröbel, F., 17
Furet, F., 204

galut, 18, 28–29, 108–109. See also
  mizug galuyot; transnational diaspora
Gaza strip, 89–92, 96, 183–184, 271
  See also Yesha
Gellner, E., 20
generation effect
  ethnicity of Ashkenazim and
    Mizrahim, 113, 115, 273
  religiosity, 65–66, 70, 72, 81
  and Russian Jews, 145, 149–150
  and Yesha's youth, 103
geographical-origin identities, 9
geosocial distinctions, 252–253, 269,
  272
German Jews, 145
Germany, 130, 289–290
Giddens, A., 291
Gilad, Noga, 96, 103
Gini index, 44
Glazer, N., 290
globalization
  defined, 16–17
  bilingualism, 285
  immigration, 17, 245
  multiculturalism, 205
  transnational diaspora, 281
God/Teaching of Israel (*Elohei/Torat
  Yisrael*), 28, 61, 108, 124
Goldstein, Baruch, 255
Gondar, 152, 153
Goren, Shlomo, 153
Great Britain, 43
Greater Israel discourse, 87, 93–96.
  See also Yesha
Green Line, 42n4, 91, 95
guest workers. *See* foreign workers
Guez vernacular, 152, 163–164
Gush Emunim, 92–93, 93–94, 271

Ha-behira ha-Democratit
  (political party), 141
Ha Histadrut Ha-Khadasha
  (New Federation), 46. *See also*
  Histadrut
Habermas, Jürgen, 292
Hadash (political party), 248
Haifa, 167
Halevy, H., 118
Hardal, 84–85, 99

Haredim. *See* Ashkenazi
 Ultra-Orthodox
Harvey, D., 205
Haugen, E., 13
Health Insurance for Children of
 Foreign Workers Law, 190
Hebrew vernacular
 Biblical Hebrew, 61
 bilingualism, 215–218, 220
 Druze and, 181
 versus English, 33–34
 in Ethiopia, 152
 linguistic development of, 50,
  293–294
 Mizrahim and, 111
 national religious and, 90
 reinvention of, 31–32
 Russian Jews and, 132, 144–145,
  285
 Ultra-Orthodox and, 63, 216, 218
hegemony of dominant culture,
 281–282, 284, 287, 291–292
Heideking, J., 288
Held, D., 245
Herder, Johann Gottfried, 289
Hermann, T., 95, 183
heterogeneization, 281
hevra le-mofet (exemplary society), 30
Histadrut, 46, 48–49
Hobsbawm, E., 20
Holocaust, 30, 145
homogenizing dominant culture, 10–11
Horowitz, N., 85
human rights, 182, 189–190, 235

identification. *See also* collective identity
 about, 9–13, 265
 of Ashkenazim, 113–117, 123, 280
 versus collective boundaries, 14
 of Druze, 278, 280
 of Ethiopian Jews, 156–157, 162,
  279, 280
 ethnocultural identification, 132–133,
  159–161
 of Filipinos, 197
 of Israeli Arabs, 183, 278, 280
 of Mizrahim, 113–117, 123,
  279–280
 of national religious, 278–280
 of nonreligious Jews, 68–69, 297
 and religion principles, 296
 of religious Jews, 68–69
 of Russian Jews, 129, 132–133,
  146–147, 274, 280

 of sociocultural groups, 11–13,
  278–281
 of traditional Jews, 68–69
 of Ultra-Orthodox, 68–69, 83–84,
  278–280
identity. *See* collective identity
identity space, 8–9
immigration. *See also* Ethiopian Jews;
 Filipino workers; foreign workers;
 Russian Jews
 attitudes toward, 140, 144, 232–233,
  243
 and dominant culture, 266–267
 and globalization, 17, 245
 Jews versus non-Jews, 205
 pioneers, 31–32, 110n1, 149, 267
 time factor in, 136–137, 140
 to Western societies, 17–18
Imperial Russia, 129
Independence War, 167
inequality, 44–45, 111
interculture, creation of, 284
intermarriage, 117–118. *See also*
 marriage
internal cohesion, 207–210, 214
intifada (1987), 189
intifada (2000)
 fence construction, 95
 Jewish-Arab relations, 169, 173–175,
  175–178, 182, 276
 peace agreement, 99
 security challenges since, 98
 self-legitimacy crisis, 100
invented traditions, 295. *See also*
 customs and rites
Israeli Arabs. *See also* Arabs; others;
 Palestinians
 about, 42–43
 Arab nationalist party, 168
 bilingualism, 215, 220, 294
 cognitive distance of, 211–213
 cohesion, openness, and popularity,
  207–210
 collective identity of, 170–172,
  182–183, 276, 277
 communitarism, 288
 discrimination against, 169, 178
 and Druze, 178–180
 education of, 169, 226n1
 ethnicity of, 170–172, 182–183, 237
 history of, 167–169
 hostility towards, 36
 identification of, 183, 278, 280
 and Israeli polity, 287

Israeliness of, 170–172, 180–181, 236–237, 276, 277, 292
Israelization versus Palestinization, 169, 172, 182–183
Jewish-Arab relations, 169, 173–175, 175–178, 182, 276
Middle Eastern culture, 238–240
military service, 179, 234
as minority in Israel, 169, 182, 183, 185, 276, 277–278
peace agreement, 168–169
on the periphery of Israeli society, 219
political allegiances of, 247, 249, 251–252, 258
political leadership, 168
population of, 167, 169
reciprocal appreciation, 174–175, 230–234
religion/nationalism link, 185
religion principle, 296
research questions, 53–54
social distance of, 173–175, 176–180, 191, 194
social mobility of, 183
solidarity among, 214
transnational diaspora, 183–184, 220, 250, 281
Western culture, 240
Israeli culture, 31–32, 32–34, 238–240. See also cultural orientations
Israeli government, 95, 99. See also Knesset
Israeli Jews. See also Ashkenazi Ultra-Orthodox; Ashkenazim; Ethiopian Jews; Mizrahi Ultra-Orthodox; Mizrahim; nonimmigrants; nonreligious Jews; religious Jews (Orthodox); Russian Jews; traditional Jews; Ultra-Orthodox
Jewish-Arab relations, 169, 173–175, 175–178, 182, 276
social distance of, 180–181, 191
Israeli-Palestinian conflict, 93–94, 121, 258, 260. See also Jewish/Arab cleavage; Jewish-Arab relations
Israeli Palestinians. See Israeli Arabs
Israeli parliament. See Knesset
Israeli pioneers, 31–32, 110n1, 149, 267
Israeli youth. See youth
Israeliness. See also national identity
Ashkenazim, 113–117, 272–273, 288

Druze, 180–181, 276–277
Ethiopian Jews, 155, 157, 161
Israeli Arabs, 170–172, 180–181, 236–237, 276, 277, 292
Mizrahim, 113–117, 125, 236–237, 272–273
Russian Jews, 135–138, 144–147, 236, 274, 292
sociocultural groups in comparison, 235–237, 292
Israelization of Israeli Arabs, 169, 172, 182–183

Jacobinian model, 267
Jaffa, 167
Jesus, 147
Jewish/Arab cleavage, 47–49. See also Israeli-Palestinian conflict
Jewish-Arab relations, 169, 173–175, 175–178, 182, 276. See also Israeli-Palestinian conflict
Jewish cinema, 100–101
Jewish extremism, 93, 103, 255–256
Jewish identity
of Ashkenazi Ultra-Orthodox, 268
of Ashkenazim, 136, 238, 241–242, 272–273, 292
and caste syndrome, 28
and collective identity, 236, 238, 243–244, 268
of Ethiopian Jews, 156–157, 159, 162
Israeli society, 38
of Mizrahim, 125, 238, 241–242, 272–273, 292
versus religiosity, 71–72
of religious Jews, 72, 238, 241–242, 268
research questions, 147
of Russian Jews, 135–138, 146, 238, 274–275, 292
of traditional Jews, 71–72, 241–242, 268
of Ultra-Orthodox, 71–72, 238, 241–242, 268–269, 292
and Zionism, 31
Jewish nationalism, 29–30, 40, 260–261. See also nationalism; Zionism
Jewish people, 27–28, 31, 281. See also Chosen People
Jewish state
and democracy, 42–43, 241–242
endorsement of, 235

and foreign workers, 189–190, 199
  Israel recognized as, 175, 179
Jewishness. *See* Jewish identity
Jews, nonreligious. *See* nonreligious
  Jews
Jews, religious. *See* religious Jews
  (Orthodox)
Judaism, 27–30, 39–40, 88–90,
  260–261
Judea, 90–92. *See also* Yesha
Judeo-Arabic vernacular, 111

Kaleb, King of Ethiopia, 151
Katz, E., 80
Katz, J., 296
kibbutz galuyot (ingathering of the exiles),
  30. See also *mizug galuyot*
kibbutzim, 226n1, 291n1
Kincheloe, J.L., 205
Knesset, 121, 140, 234–235, 246–248,
  250. *See also* Israeli government
Kolekh Forum, 101
kollels (colleges), 226n1
Kook, Abraham I., 92n2
Kook, Zvi Yehuda, 92
Kraemer, R., 144

labor disputes, 45, 48
labor migration. *See* foreign workers
Labor Party
  axis of Israeli polity, 258
  communitarism, 250
  and Histadrut, 49
  identification of supporters, 247
  role in left/right cleavage, 51,
    258–259
  unseated by Likud, 288, 290
Lake Tana (Ethiopia), 151–152
Land of Israel. See *Eretz Yisrael*
  (Land of Israel)
languages. *See also* bilingualism
  Amharic, 152
  Arabic, 181, 220, 294
  Biblical Hebrew, 61
  English, 33–34, 50–51, 216–218,
    285, 294
  Guez, 152, 163–164
  Hebrew. *See* Hebrew
  Judeo-Arabic, 111
  language of origin, 226, 228–229
  Russian, 131–132, 216–218, 220,
    294
  Yiddish, 31, 61–63, 216, 218, 220,
    294

Latin American workers, 190
Law of Return, 131, 153, 155
left, political, 93, 173, 246, 254–258.
  See also left/right cleavage; political
  parties; right, political
left/right cleavage
  and Ashkenazi-Mizrahi cleavage, 123
  and Israeli-Palestinian conflict, 258,
    260
  as major cleavage in Israeli society,
    256, 287
  multiculturalism, 251–252
  nonreligious and national religious,
    270
  primordialism, 51–52
  religion/nationalism link, 298–299
  as risk to democracy, 254–256
  role of Labor and Likud, 51,
    258–259
  security challenges, 37
  social boundaries, 257–258
  and sociocultural groups, 251–252
legislation, religious, 235
leisure and recreation, 101–102
Leon, N., 124
Leshem, A., 134
Levy, Sh., 80
liberal multiculturalism, 22–23,
  266, 267, 298. *See also* conflictual
  multiculturalism; multiculturalism
  rules
Liebman, C., 34
Likud Party
  axis of Israeli polity, 258
  communitarism, 250
  identification of supporters, 247
  opposition to Labor Party, 290
  role in left/right cleavage, 51,
    258–259
location. *See* geosocial distinction
Luhmann, Niklas, 16

Maale School of Television, Film, and
  the Arts, 100–101
Mapai (political party), 168
margizenship, 187–188
marriage, 73, 117–118, 269. *See also*
  intermarriage
Martiniello, M., 187–188
McMichael, P., 245
Meimad Party, 90, 248
members of the Knesset (MKs), 121,
  140, 246–247, 250. *See also* Knesset
Menelik II, Negus of Ethiopia, 151

Menelik (son of King Solomon), 151
Meretz (political party), 51, 247–248, 258
Mesila, 190
methodology, 55–58
Meyer, H.D., 4, 204–205
Meyer, J.W., 16
Middle Eastern culture, 238–240, 243–244
military service
    Druze and Israeli Arabs, 179, 234
    Ethiopian Jews, 154
    as gateway to society, 36–37
    Israeli youth, 36
    Ultra-Orthodox, 77–78, 233–234
Milroy, L., 13
minimalistic statehood, 290
Ministry of Education, 190, 226n1
Ministry of Labor and Social Affairs, 189
minorities
    Africans as, 163
    Druze as, 185, 276–278
    Filipinos as, 198–199
    human rights, 182
    Israeli Arabs as, 169, 182–183, 185, 276–278
    non-Jewish groups as, 244
mitnahalim, 92
Mizrahi-Ashkenazi cleavage, 40–42, 47–48, 123–124, 272–274
Mizrahi Democratic Rainbow, 119
Mizrahi Ultra-Orthodox. See also Mizrahim; Shas Mizrahi movement
    about, 107–108, 124–127, 274
    and Ashkenazim, 272
    ethnicity of, 107–108
    Israeli Jewishness, 292
    religion/nationalism link, 203
Mizrahim. See also Mizrahi Ultra-Orthodox; Shas Mizrahi movement
    advertisements, 234
    Ashkenazi-Mizrahi cleavage, 40–42, 47–48, 123–124, 272–274
    and Ashkenazi Ultra-Orthodox, 125–126
    and Ashkenazim, 47–48, 110–111, 118–119, 123–124, 272
    assimilation of, 109–110
    bilingualism, 215–219, 294
    and central authority, 235
    class reality of, 117
    cognitive distance of, 210–213

cohesion, openness, and popularity, 207–210
    collective identity of, 70, 123–124, 136
    communitarism, 288
    demonstrations by, 119
    discrimination against, 119
    education of, 115–117
    education preferences, 226, 229
    elections, 111–112, 120–121
    and Ethiopian Jews, 158, 161–162, 275–276
    ethnicity of, 113–117, 124, 272–273
    generation effect, 113, 115, 273
    identification of, 113–117, 123, 279, 280
    inequality and particularism, 111
    on intermarriage, 117–118
    Israeliness of, 113–117, 125, 236–237, 272–273
    Jewish identity of, 125, 238, 241–242, 272–273, 292
    Middle Eastern culture, 238–240
    political allegiances of, 247–248, 250–253, 258
    political behavior, 120–121
    political leadership, 111–112, 126
    reciprocal appreciation, 230–234
    religiosity of, 65–66, 115, 125, 296
    research questions, 53
    and Russian Jews, 136, 138–140
    as Shas Mizrahi supporters, 121–123
    as social cleavage, 40–41
    social distance of, 173–174
    social mobility of, 108–109, 126–127, 273–274
    solidarity among, 214–215
    values of, 124–126
    Western culture, 240
    youth, 125, 273
mizug galuyot (fusion of exiles), 30, 109, 111, 133
MKs (members of Knesset), 121, 140, 246–247, 250. See also Knesset
modern societies, 5, 32–34, 206, 283
Moetset Gedolei ha-Torah (Council of Torah Sages), 64
Mommsen, Theodor, 289
Moscow, 142–143
moshavim, 226n1
Moynihan, P., 290
multiculturalism. See also conflictual multiculturalism; multiculturalism rules

bilingualism, 215–220
from "bottom up", 287–289
as center-and-periphery setting,
    219–221
as cleavage, 251–252
versus coexistence, 16, 284–287
cognitive distance, 210–213
cohesion, openness, and popularity,
    207–210
collective identity, 24
concept of, 203–205, 297–298
conflict, 205, 225, 244, 259,
    285–286
democracy, 204, 282–283
dominant culture, 5–6, 204, 283–284
and Druze, 182
education preferences, 226–228
equality and cultural diversity,
    225–226
and Ethiopian Jews, 162
ethnicity, 285
family resemblance, 284, 294, 299
and Filipinos, 198
formation of clusters, 221
globalization and transnational
    diaspora, 205–206
group solidarity, 213–215
Israel's specific case, 284–287
language of origin, 226, 228–229
liberal multiculturalism, 22–23,
    266–267, 298
loss of hegemony, 291–292
multiple modernities, 5, 206
nation-states, 289–291
particularism, 5–6
pluralism, 4
politics of, 19–20
religion/nationalism link, 20–23,
    147, 298
religion principle, 295–297
research questions, 54–55, 207
Russian immigration, 145
and sociocultural groups, 19–20,
    203–204, 282
and United States, 287–288
multiculturalism rules. See also conflict;
    tension
about, 223–224
central authority, 234–235
cooperation versus tension, 223
cultural diversity and equality of
    cultures, 225, 242
cultural orientations, 238–240,
    243–244

language of origin and curriculum,
    226–229
national identity, 235–237
reciprocal appreciation, 230–234,
    242–243, 286–287
sociopolitical order, 241–242
multiple-modernities theory, 5, 206
Muslim Arabs. See Arabs; Israeli Arabs;
    Palestinians

Naim, G., 154
nation-building, 20–21
nation-states, 289–290, 295–296.
    See also states
national identity. See also Israeliness
    primordialism, 292
    religiosity, 243
    residency desires, 68–69, 137, 236
    rules of multiculturalism, 235–237
national politics. See politics, national
national religious. See also Yesha
    about, 39, 87–91
    as cleavage, 98
    and Eretz Yisrael, 88
    extremism originating from, 255
    feminist movement of, 101
    identification of, 278–280
    Jewish identity of, 268–269
    leisure and recreation of youth,
        101–102
    military service, 78
    national politics, 51
    and nonreligious Jews, 103, 269–272
    religion/nationalism link, 203
    religious cleavage, 256–257, 296
    research questions, 52–53
    social order, 259–260
    and Ultra-Orthodox, 87–89
    Zionism, 88–90
National Religious Party, 98, 247–248,
    250, 258
National Union (political party), 247,
    250, 258
nationalism. See also Zionism
    defined, 20–22
    historical-cultural legacies, 266
    and Jewish identity, 244
    Jewish nationalism, 29–30, 40,
        260–261
    and multiculturalism, 147–148
    and religion, 296
    Zionism versus Arab, 260–261
nationalism/religion link.
    See religion/nationalism link

nations. *See* nation-states; states
Naturei Karta (Guardians of the City), 64
Nazareth, 167
Nekuda (journal), 58, 96
New Age festivals, 101
New Federation (Ha Histadrut Ha-Khadasha), 46. *See also* Histadrut
NGOs (Non-Government Organizations), 182, 189–190, 235
Niznick, M., 144
nonimmigrants
  and Ethiopian Jews, 154
  political allegiances of, 251–252
  and Russian Jews, 134, 136–140
nonreligious Jews
  bilingualism, 215–218, 293–294
  and central authority, 235
  cognitive distance of, 211–213
  cohesion, openness, and popularity, 207–210
  collective identity of, 70–71, 297
  as core group of Israeli society, 219
  education preferences, 227
  ethnicity of, 69–70, 115
  identification of, 68–69, 297
  Israeli culture perceived by, 76–80
  Jewish identity of, 71–72, 238, 268
  Middle Eastern culture, 238–240
  national identity of, 68–69, 236–237
  and national religious, 269–272
  political allegiances of, 247, 249, 251–252, 258
  reciprocal appreciation, 230–234
  and religion principle, 297
  religiosity of, 64–67, 71–72, 268–269
  and religious cleavage, 253–254
  social distance of, 173
  and sociopolitical order, 241–242
  solidarity among, 214–215
  and Ultra-Orthodox, 72–76, 80–82
  Western culture, 240
Nudelman, R., 134, 135

obligations, 10
observance, 64–65, 147–148. *See also* religiosity
Operation Joshua, 153
Operation Moses, 153
Operation Solomon, 153
origin, 66–69. *See also* generation effect
Orthodox. *See* religious Jews (Orthodox)
Oslo agreement. *See also* peace agreement

about, 94
  concerns of Israeli Arabs, 168
  self-legitimacy crisis, 100
  and settlers, 96, 99, 271
others
  Arabs, Druze and foreign workers as, 42–43
  collective boundaries, 14
  and Ethiopian Jews, 157–158, 161–162
  as facet in collective identity, 8
  as facet in dominant culture, 10
  and national religious, 88
  openness toward, 207–210, 276–278
  and Yesha, 97

Palestine Liberation Organization (PLO), 168
Palestinian Authority, 95–96
Palestinian-Israeli conflict, 93–94, 121, 258, 260. *See also* Jewish/Arab cleavage; Jewish-Arab relations
Palestinian state, 175, 272
Palestinian uprising. *See* intifada
Palestinians. *See also* Arabs; Israeli Arabs
  commuting to Israel, 45, 188–189
  Independence War, 167
  Israel in conflict with, 246
  and Israeli Arabs, 276
  Six-Day War, 168
  as viewed by Ethiopian Jews, 161
  as viewed by Yesha, 97
Palestinization of Israeli Arabs, 169. *See also* Israelization of Israeli Arabs
Parkin, F., 12
particularism
  asset or burden, 225
  of Ethiopian Jews, 276
  of Mizrahim, 111
  and multiculturalism, 5–6
  in national politics, 251–254
parties, political. *See* political parties
peace agreements
  and Israeli Arabs, 168–169
  Israel's hesitancy toward, 281
  Oslo agreement, 94, 96, 99–100, 168, 271
  and settlers, 99, 103, 271–272
Peace Index, 95
periphery and center, 219–221, 285
"personality" of society, 20, 22
Philippines, 197–198

pioneers, 31–32, 110n1, 149, 267
PLO (Palestinian Liberation
  Organization), 168
pluralism, 4, 145, 283, 290
pluralistic dominant culture, 10–11
political allegiances, 247–253, 258
political behavior, 84, 120–121,
  141–142, 148. *See also* elections
political leadership
  Israeli Arabs, 168
  Mizrahim, 111–112, 126
  Russian Jews, 140–141
  Ultra-Orthodox, 62–63
political order, 24. *See also* coalitions;
  conflict; tension
political parties
  Balad, 248
  Ha-behira ha-Democratit, 141
  Hadash, 248
  Labor. *See* Labor Party
  Likud, 51, 247, 250, 258–259, 290
  Mapai, 168
  Meimad, 90, 248
  Meretz, 51, 247–248, 258
  National Religious Party, 98,
    247–248, 250, 258
  National Union, 247, 250, 258
  Ra'am, 248
  United Torah Judaism, 247–248,
    250, 258
  Yahad, 51
  Yisrael Ba'aliya, 141, 247–248, 250,
    258
  Yisrael Beiteinu, 141, 246–248, 258
politics, national, 51, 246–251,
  251–254. *See also* Knesset; left/right
  cleavage
polity, major axis of, 19, 258, 287
popularity of groups, 207–210
population
  of Druze, 178
  of Ethiopian Jews, 154
  of Israeli Arabs, 167, 169
postmodern religiosity, 102, 272
postnational identity, 292. *See also*
  national identity
power relations, 72–73
President of Israel, 63–64, 112
primordialism, 20–22, 24, 51–52,
  292
Promised Land, 89, 92. See also
  Eretz Yisrael (Land of Israel)

Québec, 18

Ra'am (political party), 248
rabbinical hierarchy, 125, 299
Rabin, Yitzhak, 93, 255
racism, 162–163, 275
Ranger, T., 20
Ratosh, Yonathan, 32–33
reciprocal appreciation, 161, 174–175,
  230–234, 242–243, 286–287. *See also*
  social distance; tolerance, reciprocal
recreation and leisure, 101–102
Reform Judaism, 28
religion, 21–22, 38–40, 64–68,
  295–297, 298. *See also* religiosity
religion/nationalism link
  about, 21–22, 43
  conflictual multiculturalism, 147–148,
    259–261, 298–299
  dominant culture, 41–42, 147–148
  and ethnoreligious groups, 203
  and Filipinos, 198–199
  Israeli Arabs and Druze, 185, 260
  as major dilemma in Israeli society,
    299–300
  multiculturalism, 20–23, 147, 298
  and Russian Jews, 148–149
religion principle, 295–297. *See also*
  religion
religiosity. *See also* religion
  of Ashkenazim, 65–66, 115
  collective identity, 80–81
  conflict, 72–73, 82, 253–254
  conflictual multiculturalism, 298
  as differentiating factor between
    groups, 268–269, 296–297
  ethnicity, 69–70, 223–224
  generation effect, 65–66, 70, 72, 81
  identification among Jews, 278–279
  versus Jewish identity, 71–72
  of Mizrahim, 65–66, 115, 125, 296
  multiculturalism, 285
  national identity, 243
  of nonreligious Jews, 64–67, 71–72,
    268–269
  and origin, 66–69
  postmodern, 102, 272
  power relations, 72–73
  religion principle, 295–297
  religious traditionalism, 279, 296
  of Russian Jews, 147–150, 280
  varying degrees of, 64–67, 80
religiosity divide. *See* religious cleavage
religious cleavage, 38–40, 64–67,
  253–258, 296. *See also* settlers;
  Ultra-Orthodox; Yesha

religious identity, 9. *See also* collective identity
religious Jews (Orthodox)
  advertisements, 234
  bilingualism, 215–217
  cognitive distance of, 211–213
  cohesion, openness, and popularity, 207–210
  collective identity of, 70–71, 297
  between core and periphery of Israeli society, 219
  education preferences, 227
  ethnicity of, 69–70, 115
  Jewish identity of, 72, 238, 241–242, 268
  Middle Eastern culture, 238–240
  national identity of, 68–69, 236–237
  national religious as, 87–88
  perception of Israeli culture, 76–80
  political allegiances of, 247–248, 251–252
  reciprocal appreciation, 230–234
  religiosity of, 64–67
  and religious cleavage, 253–254
  social distance of, 72–76, 173
  solidarity among, 214
  Western culture, 240
religious legislation, 235
religious traditionalism, 279, 296
research projects, 55–58
research questions, 52–54, 207, 223
retentionism, 15, 62, 147
right/left cleavage. *See* left/right cleavage
right, political, 173, 246, 254–258. *See also* left, political; left/right cleavage; political parties
riots in Wadi Salib, 118
rites and customs, 152, 163–164, 295. *See also* invented traditions
Romanian workers, 43, 189
Rosenbaum-Tamari, J., 144
rules of multiculturalism. *See* multiculturalism rules
Russia, 129–131, 142–143
Russian identity, 135, 137, 146, 274
Russian Jews
  absorption of, 131
  acculturation of, 133–134
  and Ashkenazim, 280
  assimilation of, 132–133, 147
  bilingualism, 144, 215–218, 220, 285, 294
  and central authority, 235
  class differentiation, 48
  cognitive distance of, 211–213
  cohesion, openness, and popularity, 207–210
  collective identity of, 135–138, 146, 274–275
  communitarism, 288
  between core and periphery of Israeli society, 219
  cultural diversity, 225, 242
  education of, 131, 226n1
  education preferences, 226, 229
  equality of cultures, 226, 242
  and Ethiopian Jews, 154, 158–159
  ethnicity of, 135–138, 144–148, 274–275, 280
  generation effect, 145, 149–150
  identification of, 129, 132–133, 146–147, 274, 280
  immigration, 130–131, 140, 144, 232–233
  Israeliness of, 135–138, 144–147, 236, 274, 292
  Jewish identity of, 135–138, 146, 238, 274–275, 292
  Middle Eastern culture, 238–240
  and Mizrahim, 136, 138–140
  of non-Ashkenazi origin, 146, 253
  and nonimmigrants, 134, 136–140
  observance of Christianity, 147
  as pioneers, 149
  political allegiances of, 248–249, 251–253, 258
  political behavior, 141–142, 148
  reciprocal appreciation, 230–234
  religion/nationalism link, 148–149, 203
  religion principle, 297
  religiosity of, 147–150, 280
  research questions, 53
  in Russia, 129–130
  as social cleavage, 40–41
  social distance of, 138–140, 173
  social mobility, 145–146, 275
  social order, 260
  solidarity among, 214–215
  transnational diaspora, 133, 142–143, 220, 250, 274, 281
  Western culture, 240
Russian vernacular
  bilingualism, 216–218, 220, 294
  in Israeli culture, 132
  in Soviet Empire, 131
Russianness. *See* Russian identity

Saadia Gaon, 27
sabra (nativist), 33
Sahlins, P., 21
Samaria, 90–91, 96. *See also* Yesha
Sankoff, D., 10
Schlegel, August Wilhelm von, 289
school systems. *See* education
sect, Druze as, 179
security challenges, 37, 98, 246, 259
self-legitimacy, 100
self-segregation, 73, 269–270
Sephardim, 41n3, 110, 143
settlements, 90–92, 93–94. *See also*
    Yesha
settlers. *See also* Yesha
    as cleavage, 102–103
    collective identity of, 96–98
    geosocial distinctions, 272
    identification of, 279
    instrumental versus ideological, 91,
        102, 271
    Israeli government, 99
    Israeli polity, 287
    left/right cleavage, 299
    peace agreement, 99, 103, 271–272
    political allegiances of, 247, 250
    political power of, 288
    post-Oslo era, 271
    social distance of, 173
Shafer, B.C., 21
Shamir, M., 251
Sharot, S., 113, 215
Shas Mizrahi movement
    about, 39, 41
    communitarism, 250
    demonstrations by, 119
    history of, 107–108, 111–112,
        124–127
    MKs, 121, 247
    and Russian Jews, 145
    social order, 259–260
    supporters of, 121–123, 248, 273
Sheba, Queen of, 151
Shinui (political party), 247–248, 290
Shoa, 30, 145
Siberia, 129
Six-Day War
    aftermath of, 188
    Green Line, 42n4
    and Israeli Arabs, 168
    Jewish-Arab relations, 175, 182
    and national religious, 89
    settlements after, 91–92
Smith, A.D., 22, 291

social cleavage, 3, 40–42
social distance. *See also* appreciation,
    reciprocal; tolerance, reciprocal
    of Ashkenazim and Mizrahim,
        117–120, 273
    of Druze, 179–180
    of Ethiopian Jews, 157–159
    of Filipinos, 191–196, 278
    of Israeli Arabs, 173–181, 191, 194
    of Mizrahim, 173–174
    and religiosity, 73
    of religious Jews, 72–76, 173
    of Russian Jews, 138–140, 173
    of sociocultural groups, 207–208
    of traditional Jews, 173
social insertion, 294–295
social mobility
    about, 12–13
    assimilation and acculturation, 15
    of Ethiopian Jews, 162
    of Israeli Arabs, 183
    military service, 37
    of Mizrahim, 108–109, 126–127,
        273–274
    of Russian Jews, 145–146, 275
social order, 259–260
socialism, 6
sociocultural cleavage, 3–4, 12. *See also*
    Ashkenazi-Mizrahi cleavage;
    Ethiopian Jews; Russian Jews
sociocultural groups. *See also specific*
    groups
    acculturation, 288–289
    class reality, 11–12, 14–15
    clusters, formation of, 285
    cognitive distance of, 210–214, 285
    collective boundaries, 13–16
    cultural diversity, 286–287, 292–293
    education preferences, 226–229, 242
    equality of cultures, 225–226
    ethnicity of, 3–4
    family resemblance, 24–26, 293
    identification of, 11–13, 278–281
    influence on society, 19–20, 245,
        283–284, 290–291, 299
    Israeliness in comparison, 235–237,
        292
    left/right cleavage, 251–252
    particularism and multiculturalism,
        19–20, 203–204
    primordialism, 22
    religiosity of, 65
    social distance of, 207–208
    transformation of, 284

socioeconomic cleavage, 44–49, 298
sociopolitical order, 241–242
solidarity, 213–215, 218
Soviet Union, 129–131
Soysal, Y., 205
Spann, Othmar, 289
states, 245, 289–291. *See also*
   nation-states
statistical analysis, 57
Steinberg, Sh.R., 205
stratification, 12, 45, 47
strikes, 45
suicide bombings, 255
symbols, 6–7, 8, 10. *See also* values

Tami Steinmetz Center for Peace
   Studies, 95
Taylor, C., 204–205
Tel Aviv Municipality, 190
television, 143–144
tension. *See also* conflict
   acceptance of immigrants, 232–233
   versus cooperation, 223
   within multiculturalism, 225, 244
   reciprocal appreciation, 231
Territorialism, 28
terrorism, 95. *See also* Jewish extremism
Thai workers, 43, 189
The Way to Jerusalem (Yalma), 163
tiqun ʿolam (repairing the world), 102
tolerance, reciprocal, 233–234, 243.
   See also appreciation, reciprocal;
   social distance
Tourraine, A., 24, 25, 204, 287
traditional Jews
   bilingualism, 215–217
   and central authority, 235
   cognitive distance of, 211–213
   cohesion, openness, and popularity,
      207–210
   collective identity of, 70–71
   conflicts within Israeli society,
      72–76
   as core group of Israeli society,
      219
   education preferences, 227
   ethnicity of, 69–70, 115
   identification of, 68–69
   and immigrants, 232–233
   Israeliness of, 236–237
   Jewish identity of, 71–72, 241–242,
      268
   Middle Eastern culture, 238–240
   Mizrahi Ultra-Orthodox as, 107–108

perception of Israeli culture, 76–80
political allegiances of, 247,
   250–252, 258
religious cleavage, 64–67, 253–254
social distance of, 173
solidarity among, 214
Western culture, 240
traditionalism, religious, 279, 296
traditions, invented, 295
transformation, 266–267, 284, 287
transnational diaspora
   defined, 17–18
   dominant culture, 280–281
   of Druze, 184–185, 220
   of Filipinos, 197–198
   of foreign workers, 220
   immigration, 245
   of Israeli Arabs, 183–184, 220, 250,
      281
   MKs, 250
   multiculturalism, 24, 205–206
   of Russian Jews, 133, 142–143, 220,
      250, 274, 281
   of Sephardim, 143
   of Ultra-Orthodox, 63, 83–84, 143,
      220, 250, 281
Tsfati, Y., 118
Turner, B.S., 9–10

Ultra-Orthodox. *See also* Ashkenazi
   Ultra-Orthodox; Mizrahi
   Ultra-Orthodox; Shas Mizrahi
   movement
   advertisements, 78–79, 234
   and central authority, 235
   cognitive distance of, 211–213
   cohesion, openness, and popularity,
      207–210
   collective identity of, 61–62, 70–71,
      82–84
   conflict with nonreligious Jews,
      72–76, 80–82, 203
   between core and periphery of
      Israeli society, 219
   cultural diversity, 225
   and democracy, 76–77
   demonstrations by youth, 256
   discrimination against, 82, 269–270
   education of, 85, 226n1
   education preferences, 227
   elections, 62–63
   equality of cultures, 225–226
   and Ethiopian Jews, 157, 159,
      161–162, 275

ethnicity of, 69–70
Hebrew usage, 63, 216, 218
identification of, 68–69, 83–84,
  278–280
Israeliness of, 236–237, 292
Jewish identity of, 71–72, 238,
  241–242, 268–269, 292
marriage, 269
military service, 77–78, 233–234
and national religious, 87–89
perception of Israeli culture, 76–80
political allegiances of, 249,
  251–252, 258
political behavior, 84
political leadership, 62–63
reciprocal appreciation, 230–234
religion principle, 296
religiosity of, 64–67
religious cleavage, 253–254, 256–257
retentionism of, 62
social distance of, 173
social order, 259–260
solidarity among, 214
transnational diaspora, 63, 83–84,
  143, 220, 250, 281
as underprivileged, 48
Western culture, 240
Yiddish, 61–62, 63, 216, 218, 220,
  294
youth of, 99, 256
United Kingdom, 23, 43
United States, 18, 130, 159, 287–288.
  See also African-Americans
United Torah Judaism (political party),
  247, 248, 250, 258
uprising. See intifada

values. See also symbols
  of Ethiopian Jews, 159–161
  as facet in collective identity, 8
  as facet in dominant culture, 10
  historical-cultural legacies, 266
  in invented traditions, 295
  of Mizrahi communities, 124–126
  in multiculturalism, 4–5
Veiter, Theodor, 289
Volk concept, 289. See also states
Vujacica, V., 20

Wadi Salib riots, 118
wars
  impact on Israel, 32, 36–38, 267
  Independence War, 167
  Six-Day War. See Six-Day War

Weber, Max, 3
Weil, Sh., 154
West Africa, 163
West Bank, 89–91, 183–184, 271.
  See also Yesha
Western culture
  and collective identity, 243–244
  cultural orientations, 238, 240
  Ethiopian Jew's appreciation of, 159
  influence on Israel, 76, 245, 267
Western societies, 17–18, 205, 246
Wittgenstein, Friedrich Carl, Freiherr
  von, 24, 284, 293
women, 36, 85, 101, 154
World Congress of Russian-Speaking
  Jews, 143
World Jewry. See Diaspora Jewry

Yaar, E., 95, 183
Yahad (political party), 51
Yalma, Shmuel, 163
Yesha. See also settlers
  collective identity, 96–98
  demonstrations by, 97
  Gaza strip, 89–92, 96, 183–184,
    271
  ideological versus economic motifs,
    91, 102, 271
  individual feelings in, 96–98
  Jewish extremism in, 93
  Kolekh Forum, 101
  as major cleavage, 102–103
  notion of Eretz Yisrael, 97, 100
  Oslo agreements, 94
  postmodern religiosity, 102, 272
  role of Gush Emunim, 92–93
  self-legitimacy crisis, 100
  terrorism against, 95
  Ultra-Orthodox youth, 99
  as viewed by Israeli society, 99–100
  West Bank, 89–91, 183–184, 271
Yesha Council, 92
Yeshivat Mercaz Harav, 92n2
yeshivot (religious academies), 92n2,
  111, 125, 226n1
Yiddish vernacular
  reinvention of Hebrew, 31
  and Ultra-Orthodox, 61–63, 216,
    218, 220, 294
Yisrael Ba-aliya (political party)
  axis of Israeli polity, 258
  communitarism, 250
  as independent Russian party, 141
  political spectrum, 247, 248

Yisrael Beiteinu (political party), 141,
    246–247, 248, 258
Yossef, Ovadia, 112, 152–153
youth
    collective identification of, 34
    extremism of, 103
    military service, 36
    Mizrahim, 125, 273
    national religious, 101–102
    Ultra-Orthodox, 99, 256
    Yesha settlers, 100, 272

Zilberg, N., 134
Zionism. *See also* nationalism
    defined, 27–30
    anti-Zionism, 34–35, 129–130
    contemporary dilemmas, 34

creation of a new Israeli culture,
    31–32
Jewish identity, 31
Jewish nationalism and Judaism,
    260–261
and national religious, 88–90
political program of, 290
post-Zionism, 35
and religion, 40, 296
role during Russian immigration,
    145
and Ultra-Orthodox, 62–64
Zionism *accounted for* by religion,
    89–90, 91, 102, 272
Zionism *and* religion, 89–90, 102,
    272
Zionist Labor Movement, 290